THE FIDDLEHEAD MOMENT

The Fiddlehead Moment

Pioneering an Alternative Canadian
Modernism in New Brunswick

TONY TREMBLAY

McGill-Queen's University Press
Montreal & Kingston • London • Chicago

ISBN 978-0-7735-5907-3 (cloth)
ISBN 978-0-7735-5908-0 (paper)
ISBN 978-0-2280-0054-9 (ePDF)
ISBN 978-0-2280-0055-6 (ePUB)

Legal deposit fourth quarter 2019
Bibliothèque nationale du Québec

Printed in Canada on acid-free paper that is 100% ancient forest free
(100% post-consumer recycled), processed chlorine free.

This book has been published with the help of a grant from the Canadian Federation for the Humanities and Social Sciences, through the
Awards to Scholarly Publications Program, using funds provided by
the Social Sciences and Humanities Research Council of Canada.

We acknowledge the support of the Canada Council for the Arts.

Nous remercions le Conseil des arts du Canada de son soutien.

Library and Archives Canada Cataloguing in Publication

Title: The Fiddlehead moment : pioneering an alternative Canadian
    modernism in New Brunswick / Tony Tremblay.
Names: Tremblay, M. Anthony (Michael Anthony), author.
Description: Includes bibliographical references and index.
Identifiers: Canadiana (print) 20190161078 | Canadiana (ebook)
    20190161124 | ISBN 9780773559080 (paper) | ISBN 9780773559073
    (cloth) | ISBN 9780228000549 (ePDF) | ISBN 9780228000556 (ePUB)
Subjects: LCSH: Modernism (Literature)—New Brunswick. |
    LCSH: Canadian literature—New Brunswick—History and criticism.
Classification: LCC PS8131.N3 T74 2019 | DDC c810.9/97151—dc23

This book was typeset by True to Type in 10.5/13 Sabon

For Ellen

Contents

Illustrations

Preface

Some years later Frank Baird, '96, wrote to the [University] *Monthly* from the Old Country[,] "I was permitted to hear a lecture on 'The Literature of Canada.' Fully three-fourths of the lecturer's time was spent in talking of graduates of the U.N.B. ... Afterwards I was asked, 'Is it true that it is impossible to go to that college and *not* write poetry?'"[1]

> Fusing earth and rain
> Unfolding scroll of green
> Symbol of the sun
> You are the brain of harmony
>
> Tender fingers stretch
> And midget leaves unfold
> Subtle dream of Truth
> You are a many-fingered thought.[2]

In Canada today, New Brunswick is thought of in consequential terms: that is, as both recipient and construct of wealth transfers. As exemplar of the social eugenics of distributed federalism, it is frequently denigrated by a rising tide of neo-liberal sentiment that looks askance at its apparent inability to get ahead on its own. No less an authority than former New Brunswick premier Frank McKenna has popularized that view, stating frequently that New Brunswickers "have to decide if we're going to sit around [waiting] for someone else to look after us [i.e., Alberta] or are we going to take responsibility for looking after our own future."[3] McKenna's point is clear, if poorly derived: federal handouts have weakened the provincial resolve to the extent that residents lack ambition and goals. So denigrated, New Brunswick becomes conduit to the more pastoral lands of Nova Scotia and Prince Edward Island, the province a patchwork of "small communities with their disused schools and abandoned halls" where there are "more people in the graveyard[s] than in the village[s]."[4] New Brunswick, in short, has been reduced to obituary and footnote, its deficiencies foremost in the local and national imagination.

How soon a nation forgets that New Brunswick was once in the Canadian literary vanguard. The first novel published in Canada by a native-born Canadian was written in the province, Julia Catherine Beckwith Hart's *St. Ursula's Convent* (1824), "which initiated the important task of fostering Canada's 'native genius in its humblest beginnings.'"[5] A generation later, a national literature was cultivated on New Brunswick soil in the work of the Fredericton school of the Confederation poets. Charles G.D. Roberts, the "Father of Canadian literature," and Bliss Carman, the country's unofficial poet laureate, were especially influential. Roberts's animal stories were widely imitated and his poetic evocations of place provided early glimpses into the psychic conditions of citizenship that Northrop Frye and Margaret Atwood would popularize generations later. Carman's precocious, if tentative, modernism was similarly lauded by poets such as Ezra Pound and Wallace Stevens, opening doors to the more daring mythopoeia of the McGill school of Canadian modernists. By the middle of the twentieth century, the *Fiddlehead* started publishing – it is now one of the country's longest-surviving literary magazines – and a generation later Antonine Maillet became the first non-European winner of the prestigious Prix Goncourt. Today, New Brunswick authors Herménégilde Chiasson, David Adams Richards, and France Daigle, all Governor General's Literary Award winners, are among the most unique stylists in the country.

The province's contributions to the critical records of Canada and the Commonwealth are equally outstanding. Consider, first, George Parkin's influence on a young Winston Churchill at Harrow, his lecture on imperial federation later fortifying Churchill's wartime resolve.[6] Consider, as well, that in 1904 New Brunswick's Chester Martin was the first recipient of a Rhodes scholarship, not just for Canada but for the whole of North America. Martin would go on to write some of the most influential post-Confederation historical studies of Canada, including *Empire and Commonwealth* (1929) and *Foun-*

dations of Canadian Nationhood (1955), books that established an identity narrative that all subsequent critics had to address. Finally, in the literary realm, consider the stewardship of the groundbreaking *Literary History of Canada*. Two of its five original editors – A.G. Bailey and Desmond Pacey – were based in New Brunswick, and a third, Northrop Frye, spent his formative years in the province. In addition, a number of contributors to that seminal collection had New Brunswick roots. David Galloway, author of the opening chapter, was a member of the English Department of the University of New Brunswick (UNB), as was Fred Cogswell, who wrote four of the twenty-five chapters in the book's second edition. When broadened to include the expatriates H. Pearson Gundy and Alec Lucas, both of whom taught in the province, New Brunswick scholars accounted for more than 25 per cent of the authors who contributed to the country's most authoritative literary history. And, while that percentage was partly attributable to the unusual concentration of Canadianists on the east coast in mid-century, it is nevertheless significant for revealing the extent to which scholars from or associated with New Brunswick were at the forefront of formalizing the critical practice of Canadian literature.

Yet, despite the fact that New Brunswick writers and critics were influential in determining literary directions in the country – one need only think of Roberts's influence on Archibald Lampman, A.G. Bailey's tutelage of a young John Sutherland, and Desmond Pacey's and Malcolm Ross's shaping of the Canadian literary canon, to name just a few more examples – the study of that influence, or of the incubation of a New Brunswick aesthetic, has been absent. While select authors have received attention, no critical study has ever been undertaken of how a New Brunswick aesthetic took shape in the province and how it complemented other movements elsewhere in the country. Miriam Waddington's editorial work on John Sutherland reveals the consequences of that lack, her comment that "there's no explaining a person like John ... he seemed to come from nowhere"[7] suggesting the necessity of initial spadework (for Sutherland's modernist roots were in New Brunswick). This book embarks on that spadework by examining the New Brunswick modernist aesthetic that coalesced in the middle decades of the twentieth century under the direction of A.G. Bailey, Desmond Pacey, and Fred Cogswell.

In doing so it will illuminate a corner of Canada that is currently defined more by lack than by the important and constructive roles its citizens played in pioneering a form of literary modernism that was markedly different from the urban modernism in Montreal and Toronto that we know so much about from central Canadian critics. Part renovation, part rescue, part reminder, the book aims to reintroduce a province that is less consequential now, and certainly less understood, than it was a century ago.

Though the book begins by situating New Brunswick in the decades before Confederation (1867), the more focused temporal scope of the treatment starts in the late 1920s when A.G. Bailey begins his intellectual apprenticeship at the University of Toronto and, a few years later, his practical training at the New Brunswick Museum in Saint John. From the 1930s, the book follows the work of Bailey, Pacey, and Cogswell as they construct multiple critical means to reimagine Canada as a federation of disparate regions, thus putting into motion a more pluralist view of nationhood that accommodates their localist avant-garde.

The spatial scope of the book radiates outward from Saint John and Fredericton, which are the primary foci, to the contiguous regions of the Maritimes and the rest of Canada. I use the term *contiguous* to signal not only how an aesthetic movement coalesced in New Brunswick, but also how it moved beyond the province to touch other parts of the country. Bailey, Pacey, and Cogswell were not isolated in Fredericton. They corresponded extensively with provincial and regional writers, and with influential national figures such as Lorne Pierce, Roy Daniells, Carl F. Klinck, A.J.M. Smith, Alan Crawley, Louis Dudek, Dorothy Livesay, and Michael Gnarowski, each of whom was engaged in similar modernist renewal elsewhere in the country.

The book, then, examines early- and mid-twentieth-century New Brunswick as a cultural and intellectual space. As importantly, it reveals how a group of Fredericton modernists navigated the often-intransigent utilitarianisms of that space to imagine New Brunswick as something more than dependent and marginal, the perennial poor cousin of Canadian federalism. Because of the absence of histories, critical biographies, and other knowledge resources in New Brunswick – the province still does not have a scholarly history that extends past 1867 – I devote time to examining the ancestries, apprenticeships, and social milieu of my three principal subjects, thus providing a context for understanding how they emerged and why they undertook the work they did in the province. As a result, the book is partly an intellectual history of mid-century New Brunswick, one that I hope will contribute to reversing the paucity of knowledge resources that have made it difficult for New Brunswickers to understand themselves as a people. As the book will illustrate, the problem of that lack of understanding is a serious one, for when people don't know themselves, they are defined by and must settle for what others say about them.

The book's first chapter situates New Brunswick in larger configurations of imperial power, tying its literary and social status to the vicissitudes of British mercantilism, Confederation, and a post-Confederation Laurentian logic that defined the nation in the early decades of the twentieth century. Cast and characterized as "supplicant" in the post-Confederation narrative, New Brunswick becomes a useful foil to justify economic investment in more prosperous regions of the country. Federal finance minister Jim Flaherty's 2009 description of Ontario's auto industry as key to the nation's economy, therefore deserving a large taxpayer bailout, is one example. When he made that comment, New Brunswickers remembered that only months earlier he had used the spectre of chronic subsidy to declare that there must be "no 'corporate welfare' for closing mills" in the Atlantic region.[8] The same logic is being used today to justify the federal government's purchase of Kinder Morgan's Trans Mountain pipeline, though not a word about "the national interest" was spoken when Ottawa cancelled the Energy East pipeline expansion to New Brunswick just a few months earlier. The opening of this book examines those contradictions for what they say about distributive federalism, how they position New Brunswick within the larger federation, and how a discourse of anti-modern backwardness precipitated the emergence of the Fiddlehead school.

Chapter 2 examines A.G. Bailey's dual role in resuscitating the authority of a nineteenth-century New Brunswick while also bringing a rehabilitative modernism to the province in the twentieth. Bailey's revolutionary poetics and administrative influence at the University of New Brunswick were instrumental in building a critical mass of intellectuals who kept New Brunswick's interests at the forefront. Using Beaverbrook's substantial resources, Bailey, a contemporary of Robert Finch and Earle Birney at the University of Toronto, built the UNB library; he founded the Bliss Carman Society, forerunner to the *Fiddlehead*; he mentored John Sutherland, Desmond Pacey, Fred Cogswell, Elizabeth Brewster, and a number of other Canadian

poets and cultural workers; and, as dean of arts, he formalized programs of cultural literacy and graduate study that shaped creative
expression and arts policy in the province for decades to come. As significantly, his pioneering ethnomethodology opened the province to
its Indigenous and Acadian histories, introducing an ethics of the
"acted-upon" that anticipated the post-colonial turn a generation
later. His influence on Canadian history and literature not only challenged the centralized view of the nation but also brought renewed
cultural authority to New Brunswick.

Chapter 3 takes a similar approach to introducing a figure who
worked from New Brunswick to alter radically the national landscape
of his field. Recruited by Bailey in 1944 to bring a broader national
perspective to UNB's small but growing English Department, Pacey
applied his Cambridge methodologies to creating a canon of Canadian texts and a critical apparatus to understand them. If Bailey was the
intellect behind the Fiddlehead school, Pacey was the engine room.
By 1952, he had published *Creative Writing in Canada*, the first book
on Canadian writing to employ the New Critical method of close textual analysis, thus both professionalizing literary criticism and removing from it the biases of class, empire, and gentlemanly opinion. A few
years later, he would publish influential anthologies of Canadian literature and another important critical book, *Ten Canadian Poets*. What
Pacey brought to the Fiddlehead school was the conviction that New
Brunswick wasn't second rate, and that a whole generation of Canadian literary scholars could be trained in the province. He directed his
graduate students to studies of Bliss Carman, Charles G.D. Roberts,
E.J. Pratt, Thomas Raddall, and other eastern Canadians, not only
beginning the practice of regional studies in Canada but also com-
municating the explicit message that a national literature in a federation as balkanized as Canada's was impossible, thus turning critical
attention to regional and local response.

Chapter 4 focuses on Pacey's ablest student, Fred Cogswell, a New
Brunswick farm boy who was as indefatigable as his teacher. A student
of Bailey and a member of the Bliss Carman Society, Cogswell was
groomed by his mentors to take on the editorship of the *Fiddlehead*,
assuming control in 1953. In his inaugural issue as editor, he asked UNB
president A.W. Trueman to break the news that the Bliss Carman Society was extending its reach and audience, opening the *Fiddlehead* "to
poets anywhere in the English-speaking world."[9] Cogswell, then, used
the occasion to enunciate an editorial policy of eclecticism that he

believed would provide the best modelling and therefore the surest training for local writers. When challenged by well-known Canadian poets Dorothy Livesay and Al Purdy to make the magazine more responsive to Canadian talent, Cogswell responded that "the best chance for Canadian writers is to produce work that can compete with English and American."[10] If New Brunswick writers were to succeed, thought Cogswell, they must do so against an international standard – and without the safety nets of nativism or provincialism. It was a radical idea for its time, but no more so than Cogswell's support of Acadian writers, which was manifest in a program of translation that was one of the earliest in the country. Working toward Bailey's vision of a self-reliant and self-aware New Brunswick, Cogswell mapped strategies for language parity in the province, lending to the process the province's formidable academic resources and articulating for the country one of the first fully theorized models of bicultural awareness.

The concluding chapter summarizes how the efforts of Fiddlehead modernists countered what, in mid-century, was a growing and troubling centralizing tendency in the country, at least culturally. To ensure that new monies and cultural infrastructure – both emerging in a post-war, post-Massey/Lévesque-Commission era – were evenly distributed, Bailey, Pacey, and Cogswell adapted continental modernism to their own unique social setting, thereby positioning New Brunswick to take full advantage of change. Together they built academic and cultural programs, shared and steered students toward particular emphases, and worked from the margins of an uneven federalism to expand the idea of the country. Their work to hybridize urban modernism so that it could be both cosmopolitan and local was an early example of a Canadian post-colonialism, a struggle for self-definition undertaken by smaller parts of the federation as a method of differentiation from centralizing and homogenizing pressures. The example was later exported to Acadian cultural workers who used similar strategies to forge their own cultural and historical identities. What becomes clear in reflecting on their work is that the absence of the Fiddlehead school from historical and critical records is not so much an oversight as an exclusion that maintains two dominant narratives of Canada: that social and literary renovation are urban and central phenomena, and that New Brunswick, as the perennial supplicant, cannot possibly have had the agency to contribute to how modernism was shaped in the country. Seeing those narratives clearly against the exception of the Fiddlehead school is to understand both how literary invention functions in Canada and, more profoundly, how Canada has narrated itself into existence.

Since much of this book's authority derives from archival sources, I would first like to thank the many archivists and librarians who assisted me as I was doing my work. At the top of the list is the staff at Archives and Special Collections at the University of New Brunswick's Harriet Irving Library. Francesca Holyoke, Patricia Belier, Patsy Hale, and Patti Auld Johnson were always gracious and patient in helping me and my students navigate the Bailey, Pacey, Cogswell, *Fiddlehead*, Hathaway, and other collections at UNB. That UNB has the richest archival resource in the world to accommodate work of the kind that I did should also be noted, as much to remind current administrators of its incalculable value as to invite other scholars to come to New Brunswick to do their Canadian and Atlantic Canadian research. I am also grateful to the archivists at the University of British Columbia (UBC) (Roy Daniells Fonds); the University of Calgary (Alden Nowlan Fonds); the Victoria University Library [University of Toronto] (Northrop Frye Fonds); the Thomas Fisher Rare Book Library [University of Toronto] (Malcolm Ross, Robert Finch, and A.J.M. Smith Papers); Rare Books and Special Collections [McGill University] (Hugh MacLennan Papers); and Library and Archives Canada (Desmond Pacey, Elizabeth Brewster, and Louis Dudek Fonds). For permission to use those materials I am grateful to Francesca Holyoke (UNB), Erwin Wodarczak (UBC), Lisa J. Sherlock (Victoria/Toronto), and Richard Virr (McGill). I am also thankful for the cooperation and permissions extended to me by the executors of my three principal subjects, specifically G.S. d'A. Bailey, literary executor for A.G. Bailey; Peter Pacey, literary executor for Desmond Pacey; and Kathleen Forsythe, literary executor for the Estate of Fred Cogswell.

I was able to travel to those libraries and archives with the support of the Social Sciences and Humanities Research Council of Canada (SSHRC) – with funding from the Canada Research Chairs Secretariat and a Standard Research Grant – and St Thomas University. I benefited as well from student research assistantship funding from Employment and Social Development Canada (Canada Summer Jobs Program), SSHRC (Canada Research Chairs Secretariat and Editing Modernism in Canada [Strategic Knowledge Clusters], Dean Irvine), and St Thomas University. My undergraduate and graduate student research assistants were exceptional, and each now continues to work or study in the fields of literature, history, or publishing. Those students are Tammy Armstrong, Cynthia Bouzanne, Alexandra Cogswell, Charlie Fiset, Monica Furness, James W. Johnson, Gene Kondusky, Koral LaVorgna, and Peter Mersereau.

I would like to acknowledge, as well, the support of the Research Office at my university (Michael Dawson, Danielle Connell, Gayle MacDonald, and Josephine Adda) and the encouragement of colleagues along the way, especially those who roam the same scholarly paths. At the risk of omission, I acknowledge in particular John Ball, Michael Boudreau, Margaret Conrad, Barry Craig, David Creelman, Gwen Davies, David Frank, Bob Gibbs, Michael Higgins, Tom Hodd, Dean Irvine, Marie-Linda Lord, Susan Montague, Chantal Richard, Cynthia Sugars, Peter Toner, Demetres Tryphonopoulos, Christl Verduyn, Doug Vipond, Don Wright, Herb Wyile, and the anonymous readers of this book. Each provided crucial support at important moments. In many ways, this book encompasses the spirit of Bob Gibbs, one of only two members of the early Fiddlehead group still living. Bob's lifelong commitment to New Brunswick and to his students and colleagues has been a shining example to those of us who have followed, and so I am especially pleased to be able to thank him publicly for decades of cultural work.

Final thanks, as always, go to my wife, Ellen, whose wisdom, radiance, understanding, and care continue to make everything possible. This book is for her.

THE FIDDLEHEAD MOMENT

New Brunswick as Colony, Province, and Supplicant

For few and lonely are the sentinel cities of the north
And rivers and woods lie between.
Far, few, and lonely ...

Space surrounds us, flows around us, drowns us.
Even when we meet each other space flows between.
Our eyes glaze with distance.
Vast tracks of Arctic ice enclose our adjectives.
Cold space.
Our spirits are sheer columns of ice like frozen fountains
Dashed against by the wind.

Drown it out. Drown out the wind.
Turn on the radio.
Listen to boogie-woogie or a baseball game.
Listen to the news.
Pretend we belong to a civilization, even a dying one.
Pretend. Pretend.
But there are the woods and the rivers and the wind
    blowing.
There is the sea. Space. The wind blowing.[1]

This book examines a group of writers and cultural workers who have never enjoyed the status of a school or movement yet whose concentration of social interests, locale, and literary objectives were so consonant that they did coalesce into a definable movement in post-Second World War Canada. Desmond Pacey called them the "Fiddlehead

School,"[2] the name a tribute to the literary magazine that provided the occasion for their early association.

The principals of that group were Alfred G. Bailey, Desmond Pacey, and Fred Cogswell, all men in an era when the professoriate was almost solely male and literature's aim of moral uplift the domain of gentlemen scholars. Each taught at the University of New Brunswick during the middle decades of the twentieth century; each consciously embraced modernism as a means of both literary and social reform; each cultivated communities of students and like-minded artists to advance the cause of New Brunswick's cultural interests; and each worked from Bailey's original vision to adapt continental modernism – the modernism of the republican Ezra Pound and the royalist T.S. Eliot – to Canada's margins, particularly New Brunswick. In doing so, they employed strategies very different from those of Canada's urban modernists, about whom we know considerably more. In the view of Atlantic Canadian critic Terry Whalen, their hybridization of the continental and local became a unique Maritime form of "cosmopolitan regionalism" that counterbalanced the more acerbic "technical" modernism of A.J.M. Smith and his first-generation modernist confrères, F.R. Scott, Robert Finch, Leo Kennedy, and A.M. Klein.[3]

The modernism of the Fiddlehead school thus contributed to the more local, left-leaning, and activist literary deployments that characterized what Brian Trehearne has called second-generation modernism in Canada.[4] Yet, while Trehearne credits the *First Statement* and *Preview* groups of Montreal modernists (John Sutherland, P.K. Page, Louis Dudek, and Irving Layton) with the development of second-generation modernism in Canada – insisting that "the subsequent growth of Canadian poetry into a number of vital styles may be traced more or less directly to those [groups'] choices"[5] – the non-Laurentian sites of modernism, including New Brunswick's Fiddlehead school, are never mentioned. It is as if they never existed, the implication of which is that a rapidly maturing mid-century Canadian literary modernism was urban, central, and dominated by a handful of Montreal editors, poets, and academics.

The primary aim of this book is to correct that oversight, therefore providing a missing piece to our understanding of Canadian literary modernism in the twentieth century. From 1930 to 1965, the Fiddlehead school of New Brunswick modernists contributed substantially not only to the development of Atlantic Canadian literature but also to cognate national movements in many parts of the country.

DE-CANONIZING CANADIAN MODERNISM

To date, Bailey, Pacey, and Cogswell have received a fraction of the attention their contributions deserve. Not only are they ignored in studies of pan-Canadian modernism such as Trehearne's *Montreal Forties* and Glenn Willmott's *Unreal Country*,[6] but their influence (significant though it was) is not mentioned in treatments of the cultural workers whose careers they both intersected and influenced.[7] Perhaps the most egregious omission, however, is in Louis Dudek and Michael Gnarowski's *Making of Modern Poetry in Canada* (1967) – "egregious" because of Dudek's earlier mention of the Fiddlehead group in the essay "The Role of Little Magazines in Canada"[8] and the extensive albeit at times testy association among Pacey, Dudek, Cogswell, and Gnarowski. (Ken Norris, Dudek's doctoral student in the mid- to late 1970s, makes a similar omission in *The Little Magazine in Canada, 1925–80: Its Role in the Development of Modernism and Post-Modernism in Canadian Poetry*.) Though Dudek would credit the Fredericton group with autonomous "freedom of thought,"[9] he, Gnarowski, and Norris never extended to the Fiddlehead writers the status accorded to the Smith/Scott, Dudek/Souster schools of modernism.[10] E.D. Blodgett does a better job in *Five Part Invention*, saying a few useful things about Pacey, though John Metcalf's essays about the Fredericton poets in *Kicking Against the Pricks* and *An Aesthetic Underground* delight mostly in revealing disparaging details about Pacey, Cogswell, and Robert Gibbs, another Fiddlehead modernist. What Metcalf proffers beyond the pretense of literary gossip is the conclusion that "Nova Scotia and New Brunswick are drunken and violent societies,"[11] an insight that falls far short of what he might have shared about the New Brunswick literary landscape when he was writer-in-residence at UNB in 1972.

These are not the only oversights, however. Bailey, Pacey, and Cogswell are also omitted in treatments of Atlantic Canadian literature. As individuals, they are mentioned fewer than ten times in total across *Under Eastern Eyes*, *Setting in the East*, *Writing the Everyday*, and *Surf's Up!*[12] And in the two most comprehensive books about New Brunswick literature in English – *Arts in New Brunswick* (1967) and *A Literary and Linguistic History of New Brunswick* (1985) – they are relegated to scattered sentences and footnotes. In no scholarly study to date have they been grouped as a school or movement, despite being recognized as such by William Patterson,[13] Elizabeth Brewster,[14] Malcolm Ross,[15] Esther Clark Wright,[16] Hilmur Saffell,[17] Robert Gibbs,[18] and Tom Marshall[19] – and by Pacey[20] and Cogswell[21] themselves.

If we fast-forward to the present, the critical landscape, along with the scholarship that feeds canonical memory, is unchanged. Not only is the province in the rear-view mirror in recent anthologies that purport to represent the nation – *A New Anthology of Canadian Literature in English* is one instance[22] – but it is barely visible in Dean Irvine's comprehensive survey of little magazines in Canada.[23] Despite the pivotal role the *Fiddlehead* played in Canadian modernism, as well as A.G. Bailey's mentorship of John Sutherland and Louis Dudek in the methodological apparatus of cultural change,[24] the Fredericton group's material contributions warrant less than half a paragraph in Irvine's twenty-seven-page examination.[25]

This is not a quarrel with Irvine's fine essay, but rather the identification of a gap, and thus an opportunity, in the field. History is fickle in the absence of criticism, which, by its very nature, situates and preserves. Irvine illustrates this exactly in observing that "[Louis] Dudek's unrivalled role as editor and historian of the 'little magazine' in Canada has shaped the ways in which generations of readers and critics have understood the formation of Canadian modernism at mid-century."[26] The "literary-historical narrative" that developed, Irvine suggests, implicating figures like Trehearne in his observation, exhibited the kind of bias that championed one group of modernists to the exclusion of others and thus, if not denigrating the work of the New Brunswick modernists, certainly pushing that work to the periphery.

This book enters the Canadian discussion at that point, partaking of both a redress of bias and of contemporary critical efforts to expand the understanding of variant and overlooked modernisms. In American and British modernist studies, that effort has been manifest in works such as John Carey's *Intellectuals and the Masses* (1992), Peter Nicholls's *Modernisms* (1995), and Delia Caparoso Konzett's *Ethnic Modernisms* (2002), studies that challenge the urban and Eurocentric paradigms of canonical modernism. In Canada, Leon Surette's *Birth of Modernism* (1993), Irvine's *Editing Modernity: Women and Little-Magazine Cultures in Canada* (2008), and work by Ian McKay, Candida Rifkind, and Lynda Jessup[27] have all sought, similarly, to deepen our understanding of the complexities of modernism around issues of gender, locus, social allowance, and persuasion. In eastern Canada, the work of Danielle Fuller[28] and Herb Wyile[29] has followed that lead. In the process, our understandings of modernism are being dismantled and reconstituted. And, more fundamentally, literature is being reinterpreted as a wider social operation that both indexes and repels an ever-shifting authority that is unevenly distributed through society. That now-classic view, first articulated in cultural theorist Raymond Williams's *Marxism and Literature* (1977), argues that cultural forms like literature are constitutive social processes rather than simple extensions of artistic will or ideology, a perspective that compels critics to look much more deliberately at what was socially constitutive and privileged at any given time.

Finding the seeds of that approach in the work of New Brunswick critics Desmond Pacey and Malcolm Ross, theorist Barbara Godard applies Williams's work to Canada, asserting that "much of the historical 'scholarly labour remains to be done' in order to position Canadian literature not just in space, but in time."[30] Building on that suggestion, Imre Szeman employs Régis Debray's critical work on materialism to invite a new kind of criticism in Canada that examines "the structures that form the conditions of [the] possibility of literature and culture in any given moment,"[31] an appeal that democratizes literary criticism by removing the bias of dominance that Irvine identified above and legitimizing the study of cognate cultural forms, be those contiguous or distant forces. Godard's and Szeman's work has been especially useful to Canadian critics for encouraging a re-examination of movements like literary modernism as distributive, decoupled phenomena – that is, as phenomena removed from the urban authority and opinion to which previous critics tied them.

This study of the Fiddlehead school of modernism occupies exactly the temporal field of socio-cultural inquiry that Godard and Szeman invite – and thereby engages in the important dialectical operation of recovery in asserting a presence hitherto blacked out by the "volatile, subjective ... and illogical transformation" of culture at the hands of the canonizing desires of well-positioned writers and critics.[32] In addition, the book's secondary aims are equally important: they are to contribute to the knowledge base of New Brunswick historiography, thus participating in the current identity project being undertaken in the province; and, more generally, to contest the still dominant opinion that, in terms of modernism, the national and international supersede the local in matters of artistic production and innovation (a view most famously expressed by Pound, who regarded provincialism, however defined, as the enemy[33]). Quite to the contrary, the example of the Fiddlehead school illustrates how cultural production is more usefully thought of as an amalgam, or, as Wallace Stegner writes, "a pyramid to which each of us brings a stone."[34] In the work of Gerald Friesen[35] and Aritha van Herk,[36] that understanding of cultural production has led to rewriting the history of the Canadian west by way of reimagining the nation as a constellation of interdependent subjectivities and localisms. In following that line, my own study will show that the local does indeed matter in larger social formations and that local producers, even in hinterlands like New Brunswick, influence the arc of movements in the country as a whole. That New Brunswick occupies the periphery of the nation, in other words, no longer matters, nor should it.

NEW BRUNSWICK'S HUMAN GEOGRAPHY

Part of the reason that it did matter – that the province's status as "supplicant" determined its treatment at the centre[37] – was because no countervailing narrative emerged from New Brunswick to contest the dominant presumptions of uniformity and lack. The reason for the absence of that countervailing narrative is attributable to the province's many divisions and contradictions, and to the fact that no provincial writer, filmmaker, or critic has been able to capture those divisions with any symbolic import. That it would even be necessary to do so in a province of such small population and land mass is perhaps the first assumption that should be dispelled. And Bailey did just that, observing in an early work of criticism that, despite its size, the tiny province of New Brunswick "experienced an adverse set of circumstances that were peculiarly its own": specifically, "it was difficult for a sense of provincial identity, or a common purpose, to emerge in a land of which the different parts were so isolated from one another, and among a people who had been so uprooted as were the Loyalist exiles."[38]

Bailey's two observations were valid in mid-century and remain so today. New Brunswick was, and remains, divided, with distinct ethnicities, political loyalties, linguistic variants, and narratives of settlement and grievance spread across the province. Accordingly, the deepest grammars of New Brunswick are still its rivers and mountain ranges, which demarcate and preserve those differences. The northeastern parts of the province are home to post-Expulsion villages of Acadians who fled to the protection of distant woods after the British aggressions of *Le Grand Dérangement* of 1755–62. These Acadians have little in common with the Brayon republicans who occupy the northwestern part of the province one hundred miles away. Though often incorrectly assumed to be Acadian, Madawaska County francophones have ancestral ties to Quebec, share social affinities with the people of the bordering American state of Maine, but claim neither Québécois nor American identity. Rather, they identify as *les Brayons*, fly their own flag in the declared capital of Edmundston, and consider themselves a republic within the political boundaries of New Brunswick. (Technically, the founding of the République du Madawaska during the Aroostook War [1838–39] was negated when the Webster-Ashburton Treaty [1842] split the Madawaska territory into American and Canadian parts, establishing the current border between the two countries.)

Similar variations in language, historical affiliation, and identity politics are present in the Acadian populations of southeastern New Brunswick, their uniqueness characterized by a language and imaginative heritage extracted from the fifteenth-century France of François Rabelais. What these three distinct groups of French-speaking New Brunswickers have in common is a historical enmity to the English – not an antipathy, necessarily, but a distrust of the province's anglophone elites that has been hardened by years of poor treatment and substandard service. One need look no further than the Maritime literary record to find evidence of that mistreatment and subjugation, Lucy Maud Montgomery's famously tart Marilla claiming that "those stupid, half-grown little French boys" are the only help available to Protestant farmers, "and as soon as you do get one broke into your ways and taught something he's up and off to the lobster canneries or the States."[39] Alden Nowlan's Kevin O'Brien reiterates that Anglo-Protestant view in *The Wanton Troopers*, echoing his grandmother's belief that "the French were a heathenish and perverse people."[40] Because that attitude was also state- and church-sanctioned, noted provincial MLA Phillippe Guerette in a 1964 speech, it was widely interpreted in Acadian society as genocidal: "My rights are encroached upon," Guerette said. "I can address you in French, but the British North America Act does not recognize that I have the right to speak this language."[41] It was exactly that indignity that would fuel the Acadian cultural renaissance of the 1970s.

To illustrate the attitude of the English to Acadian aspirations, political historian Arthur T. Doyle cites the comment of a well-known Methodist minister that "Acadian society was 'a half-way house between the Indians and the white people'"[42] – the comment recalling Loyalist leader Edward Winslow's summation of the Acadians as a "slovenly race" that was "wanting in industry."[43] Following Winslow, New Brunswick authorities felt that widespread illiteracy made the French and Indigenous populations too innocuous to cause any prob-lems, which was partly true. More consequential to provincial citi-zenship, however, was their isolation. Not surprisingly, their learned response to dominance, paralleling that of most subordinate popula-tions that are "geographically clustered,"[44] was to retreat into family and community, erecting barriers against outside incursion. Historian Graeme Wynn captures the extent of that isolation in recalling Lieu-tenant-Colonel Joseph Gubbins's forays into Acadian territory when he was part of the New Brunswick Militia in 1813. Gubbins, writes Wynn, "described a coast so little known 'even at the seat of govern-ment' that he was unable to obtain 'certain intelligence' as to the exis-tence of roads in the direction that he wished to travel. Arriving at Grand Digue, near Shediac, by boat, he was met by 'a numerous assembly of the ladys of the neighbourhood, who were in the full dress of the Norman mode as it was perhaps a century before.' Sever-al days later Gubbins received the impression that the Acadians of Escuminac 'were in utter ignorance of what was going on in the world ... [and] had not even heard of Bonaparte or of the war with France.'"[45]

Upon consideration, even that degree of isolation is not surprising, for it reflected an instinct for self-preservation, not the narcissism or cowardice that is sometimes described. In her fictional history of the Acadian peoples of southeastern New Brunswick, Antonine Maillet makes that point clearly: "The only survivors in the Massacre of the Holy Innocents were the Innocents who knew enough to hold their tongues" – and who, returning after Expulsion, "came home by the back door, and on tiptoe."[46] Such has been the schooled isolation of New Brunswick's French populations in scattered pockets of settle-ment on the eastern and northern peripheries of the province. Each has learned not to poke the English bear. Maillet's likening of their ken to that of the fox – careful, stubborn, and sly[47] – is thus the most accurate representation of the largest linguistic minority in a province of legislated linguistic plurality. The contradiction is one of many in the province.

The English profile in New Brunswick is no less disjointed or shaped by histories of insularity and grievance, much of that import-ed from countries of origin. Enmities, many class-generated, have informed the interactions of anglophone immigrant groups in the province. And whereas clashes between the Irish and Loyalists are the

best-known instances of conflict – Benjamin Marston, an early Loyalist sheriff, famously denouncing the Irish as "a drunken and illiter-
ate lot"[48] – the Scots also had a New World history of difficult relations with the First Nations and settler groups they encountered. In
the Miramichi area of central New Brunswick, whole families of Scots
under William Davidson and John Cort fled to the St John River
(Maugerville) to escape theft and fires perpetuated by the Mi'kmaq
upon whose lands they were encroaching. And even the Loyalists,
with whom the Scots were generally allied, never allowed them to for-
get their secondary status in society. New Brunswick historian W.S.
MacNutt relays the story of the Scots of Saint John, for example, who,
having "contributed to the building of Trinity Church, discovered
that, because it was filled to overflowing every Sunday, their accents
brought them invitations to go elsewhere."[49] Resentments continued
to fester when the Loyalists began demanding top dollar from the
Scots for choice land on fertile "intervals," land that had been given as
"free grant" to the Loyalists shortly after 1783. Over time, Scottish settlement fixed itself in English enclaves in northern and central New
Brunswick, mostly in locales where the Scots were free to pursue
enterprise unencumbered.[50]

Similar relocations to peripheral locales occurred with the large
influx of New England Planters into New Brunswick, their arrival
slightly predating that of the Loyalists and their Protestant Congrega-
tionalism finding little accommodation under what was soon the dominance of the Church of England. The experience of the Baptists and
New Lights under preacher Henry Alline was comparable, resulting in
an entrenchment of evangelical Christianity in the non-populous Carleton County of western New Brunswick, far from the more liberal
Anglican and Catholic enclaves of Fredericton and Saint John. There,
safely ensconced, the revivalists were removed from the "adepts in
wickedness" that the undisciplined Loyalists were considered to be.[51]

What the sum of these demographic histories illustrate is that, writ
large, the Loyalist, English, Anglican, royalist dominance that took
root in New Brunswick in the mid-1780s pushed linguistic, religious,
ethnic, and other variances to the province's peripheries, in effect creating a patchwork of human geographies that had remarkably few
points of intersection. Even in a province as small as New Brunswick,
there was enough room for whole communities to go into exile within provincial borders, that exile creating the conditions for "irreconcilable contradictions among nationalities."[52] Bailey was correct about

that, but he erred in confining the experience of exile to the Loyalists. Theirs was not a monopoly on deracination; rather, forced deracination was central to the experience of each of New Brunswick's larger populations, beginning with the Mi'kmaq and Maliseet nations that were displaced by New World settlement. It would be much more accurate to observe that exile was the province's common condition: the Acadians were displaced by British imperialism; the Scots by land clearances, restrictions, and the Act of Union between Scotland and England; the Planters by religious intolerance; the Loyalists by American secession; the Irish by famine; and the Indigenous populations by the consequences of those disruptions. Facing strife, each group sought and found refuge in a New Brunswick where a major cause of exile (British imperialism) had reasserted itself, pushing all but the Loyalists toward marginal, in some cases subordinate, existence. Sally Armstrong's historical novel about New Brunswick is useful on that point: "it's the Loyalists who are all taking the posts in this [new] province," and thereby determining its future.[53] The consequence for Armstrong's characters and for the actual para-social geography of the province is that New Brunswick is a territory of the vanquished, where Indigenous and immigrant communities have had to be aggressively insular to ensure the survival of their values, affiliations, and character. Is it any wonder that Joseph Gubbins encountered such anachronism among the Acadians or that Alden Nowlan would write to Baron St-Castin: "Take heart, monsieur, four-fifths of this province / is still much as you left it: forest, swamp and barren. / Even now, after three hundred years, your enemies / fear ambush, huddle by coasts and rivers, / the dark woods at their backs"?[54]

Today, the deep divisions that developed around histories of insularity are still determinative in social, economic, and political culture. The provincial election of 25 September 2018 illustrated that continued fragmentation on the electoral map. Thrust into the first minority government since the 1920s, the incumbent Liberals, backed widely by francophones, quickly lost a confidence vote in the House, unable to secure the backing of the urban-dominated Greens and the anglophone-dominated People's Alliance. The result was a call to the Conservative Party to form a government; that party has only one francophone MLA, is widely believed to be anti-French, and enjoys almost no voter support in the northern, western, or eastern parts of the province. The result makes plain the provincial reality: New Brunswick is deeply fractured between north and south, rural and urban, industrial and bureaucratic, labour and wealth, French and English, Catholic and Protestant. Bifurcation and the suspicions it spawns has become the provincial ethos, making it very difficult to achieve consensus across counties, class, demography, language, and other divides.

Fuelling this, as the 2018 election also made clear, are political operatives who use difference to advantage, often flaming tribal instincts for partisan ends. That tendency has pitted district against district and village against village for years in a perceived zero-sum game of scarcity politics. Historically, for instance, party members from both sides of the Miramichi River were famously vigilant in ensuring that political favours accrued by the Protestant town of Newcastle and the Catholic town of Chatham were roughly equal,[55] and the same keen eye for self-interest was demonstrated by citizens in the northern New Brunswick towns of Campbellton, Dalhousie, and Bathurst. One final example will suffice. In the 1980s, thanks to bipartisan initiatives to develop transportation infrastructure in northern New Brunswick that would serve the region's dominant forestry, pulp, and mining industries, the small northern village of Charlo received sizeable provincial and federal subsidies to upgrade its airport. Those subsidies funded an 1,800-metre runway expansion, a tripling of passenger terminal and industrial warehousing capacity, state-of-the-art navigational technologies, and enhanced training for bilingual Nav Can personnel in the latest air-traffic protocols. The investment was not arbitrary. Because of its central location between the identified regional growth poles of Campbellton and Belledune, its flat topography, and its fog-free site (a natural feature of air circulation caused by tidal replenishment), Charlo was deemed by provincial planners to be the ideal location for the north's regional airport. It was not only in the middle of the east-west corridor of the province's north, but it was also in the middle of a north-south corridor that extended from Bathurst to Quebec's Gaspé peninsula, where New Brunswick industries had important markets and landholdings. And, while the bipartisan logic of that choice held for a time, supporting the growth of an industrial sector that depended on the airport for the movement of people and goods, the idea of Charlo as a northern air-transportation hub became increasingly challenged by its closest neighbours. As provincial governments changed so did the logic of their decisions, a vocal group in Bathurst convincing Fredericton and Ottawa that the larger centre of Bathurst should be the new air-transportation hub of the north – and this despite its airport having a considerably shorter runway, poorer field infrastructure, an inadequate terminal, and older navigational technologies. Regardless of the presence of a fully equipped, ultra-modern airport less than 100 kilometres to the north, the Bathurst airport authority, spurred by outspoken local MP Yvon Godin (NDP) and equally tenacious MLA Brian Kenny (Liberal), got to work to find $60 million to build a duplicate facility. The result was a heated war of words that pitted one area of northern New Brunswick against another, ultimately serving neither's interest. Today, the Charlo airport is almost deserted and the Bathurst group continues to lobby for what it sees as logical. Because representatives of the Bathurst airport group were competing for scarce resources, their political representatives saw advantage in fanning the flames of grievance and mistrust.[56] These lessons have been poorly learned in New Brunswick, for the same thing is happening among French and English hardliners in the province today as both attempt to interpret recent election results in their favour: specifically, as a need for the province's francophones to retrench (the French "constitutional" argument) or as a need to unwind the costly bureaucratic duplications involved in maintaining official bilingualism (the English "common sense" view).[57]

To some extent, this warring and dysfunctional factionalism can be forgiven, for New Brunswick's socio-political landscape, observed political scientist P.J. Fitzpatrick, has been deliberately shaped to these kinds of parochial ends, thus neutering any possibility that isolated populations might coalesce to challenge the dominant authorities in the southern cities. The strategy has been a master construction, argues Fitzpatrick, "sustained by gerrymandering, patronage, and constituencies with hereditary political loyalties kept intact by ancient ethnic and religious antagonisms."[58] To illustrate, he offers the example of "a British Protestant New Brunswicker of United Empire Loyalist stock" for whom "the idea of voting Liberal might well be unthinkable, an act of cultural treachery equivalent to conversion to Roman Catholicism."[59] The consequence for New Brunswick today is a political system in which distrust and cynicism abound, and with that a hardening of the otherwise healthy republicanism of New Brunswickers. Author Wayne Curtis captures that spirit in a memory of his father, who "would work himself into a frenzy about the government," observing that "the only difference between a Conservative and a Liberal was that a Conservative prayed in public and drank in private, whereas a Liberal drank in public and prayed in private."[60]

Curtis's observations beg an important question that keeps surfacing in New Brunswick: namely, if the province, as settled and constructed as a field of competing electorates, is even governable across the diversity of its isolated and disconnected interests. That it has been very difficult to do so has given rise to an unusually paternalistic system of governance in which elected officials have tended to infantilize New Brunswickers, all the while acting, they claim, in the province's best interests. The practice, evident in the 2009 backroom deal to sell NB Power to Hydro-Québec, has stunted participatory democracy and furthered the sense of alienation from government that citizens feel. But, in that incident, paternalism went too far. Disgusted citizens took to the streets in record numbers, not just protesting their non-involvement in a decision directly affecting them, but voting Shawn Graham's Liberals out of office after only one term, the first time that had happened in New Brunswick in a century.

The incident was significant for revealing one of the rare points of consensus that citizens share: the vague sense of a coercive determinism that has robbed the province of its proper place in the nation. And, while most New Brunswick citizens do not express that feeling in macro-economic terms, they certainly do so in micro, focusing their animus on the industrial behemoth that is New Brunswick's Irving Empire. (The deal with Hydro-Québec, it was later revealed, fixed one rate for residential consumption and a considerably lower rate for corporate use, thus not only giving the Irving industries the lower power rates they had long been demanding but requiring that residential customers in the province subsidize those lower rates.) The Irving corporation's dominance across all facets of the provincial landscape (energy, forestry, media, labour, and governance) has, then, become a modern surrogate for "Loyalist," symbolizing the English, Protestant, urban, and wealth hegemony of southern New Brunswick. Citizens feel cowed in its presence. They speak begrudgingly of the concessions the Empire has won from successive governments on taxation, utilities, and resource allocations, and they blame the Empire's various monopolies for creating feudal conditions under which New Brunswick's growth toward self-reliance has been stunted. Even a provincial government as vibrant and populist as Louis Robichaud's Liberals of the 1960s was no match for the Empire, observed Russell Hunt and Robert Campbell, the clear lesson being that "[it] would be a long time before a government laid its future on the line by trying to tax

the English businessman [K.C. Irving] to pay for social development among the dispossessed."[61]

That ordinary citizens cannot express this view to the media – Irving owns all the daily and all but a few of the English weeklies in the
province – further frustrates, recreating the conditions for aggression
and isolation that earlier, less mobile generations faced. A brief snap-
shot of the current iteration of this circumstance will illustrate the
parallels between past and present, the occasion a CBC story that the
province of New Brunswick was announcing its long-awaited
Forestry Plan, one that would free up more crown land for major
industrial harvesters, of which J.D. Irving (JDI) Ltd is king.[62] Though
the story was not about the Irvings, the CBC online audience in New
Brunswick, without exception, assumed that it was, an assumption
confirmed a day later when Jim Irving, co-CEO of JDI, announced the
investment of $513 million in mill refurbishments in the province.
Said Mr Irving with rare unguarded finality: "The province did its
part with the new forestry strategy," a statement that clearly twinned
the government's Forestry Plan and JDI 's commercial interests.[63]
Online comments from readers a day before, however, made JDI's
announcement moot and the government's complicity in Irving's
affairs a poorly kept secret. One person commented: "New Brunswick
– Owned and operated by the Irving family. If they want something,
they most likely will get it. Lower taxes, lower cost of raw materials,
you name it. New Brunswickers have paid for it." Another reader
wrote: "WOW! We now have Industry controlling the decisions around
shale gas development, forest development, and provincial government policies. Irving being the most influential. Did not the finance
minister work for Irving? Sorry, I guess the entire Tory government is
currently working for Irving." Yet another reader opined: "[Minister
of Finance] Higgs worked for the Irvings how many years? Not sure
myself if he ever left!!"[64] If popular endorsement is the barometer of
social truth, then one reader's summation of the affair spoke for the
majority. "Fredmom" simply wrote, "New Brunswick = the Irving
plantation," a sentiment that seemed to capture the public mood.[65]
Only a few days later at a conference convened at the Université de
Moncton, Charles Thériault, a private woodlot owner and documentary filmmaker in the province, spoke about the same collusion
between the Irvings and the government in New Brunswick. Observed journalist Damien Dauphin,

Charles Thériault n'hésite pas à déclarer que la famille Irving est parvenue à prendre le contrôle de la machine législative au Nouveau-Brunswick. Une famille que peu s'aventurent à critiquer, car elle donne des emplois. Maniant l'art de la métaphore, il compare la situation au Syndrome de Stockholm, quand une personne kidnappée en vient à penser que son ravisseur lui veut du bien.

[Charles Thériault does not hesitate to declare that the Irving family has managed to take control of the legislative machinery in New Brunswick. A family that few venture to criticize because it provides employment. Wielding the art of metaphor, he compares the situation to the Stockholm Syndrome, in which a kidnapped person comes to believe that his abductor wishes him well.[66]]

Beyond the generalizing histrionics of these comments – and the fact that almost everyone who commented assumed that the government's plan was a ruse concocted to serve the Irving interests – the effect of their frequency reveals another of the contradictions that characterize the province's condition. On the one hand, the Irving Empire controls the dominant print media, resulting in a diminished capacity to speak and thus to reach across divisions to build networks of similarly disenfranchised or engaged groups. On the other hand, the digital platforms of new media have unleashed a kind of speech that is not necessarily representative of the views of average citizens. And so, once again, the response of many New Brunswickers has been to withdraw, some citizens retreating in fear of reprisal (the Irving Empire is genuinely feared), others intimidated by the enormity of the task, and still others put off by the absolutes demanded by both sides. What remains is that in New Brunswick, one of the smallest provinces in the nation, the spaces between people and districts continue to be more distant than anywhere in the country.

CREATING SUPPLICATION UNDER FEDERALISM

Intersecting these patterns of settlement and balkanization in New Brunswick was the larger phenomenon of federalism, which became a powerful narrative in the province's sense of itself and of how it was perceived by others. And, though interpreting the fortunes of the province against the history of political and economic federalism is a complex and contentious area of provincial debate,[67] some attention must be paid to that concern because more than half of New Brunswick's history has been integrative – that is, tied to the history of Canada.

The place to begin, however, is with pre-Confederation history, for in the Maritime provinces cultural memory continues to glory in myths of a pre-Confederation Golden Age of self-reliance and regional self-determination. The reason, simply, is because each of British North America's colonies had a long and distinct history before the idea of a united or "federated" Canada was conceived – and before "the post-Confederation gloom" descended.[68] For New Brunswick, the event that contributed most directly to laying a foundation for a golden age was the New World's involvement in the Napoleonic Wars of 1792–1815. With its Loyalist ethos and seaboard trading economy dictating its affiliations, New Brunswick became entangled in Anglo-French struggles in a way that was both inevitable and fortuitous, the lucky result, wrote historian W.S. MacNutt, of "imperial paternalism and imperial needs."[69]

Two war-related events in particular were crucial. The first was U.S. president Thomas Jefferson's 1807 Embargo Act, which, in an attempt to answer Britain and France's interference in American trade (and avoid entry into the European conflict), banned all foreign export trade from U.S. ports and restricted imports from the warring European nations. The new law, aimed at showcasing American neutrality in the Anglo-French war, had drastic consequences for the United States, effectively shutting down New England's maritime economy.[70] New Brunswick and Nova Scotia were the immediate beneficiaries, made even more so when the British, heavily reliant on American goods, opened ports in both Maritime colonies to American ships. Under the terms of the swift but decisive Free Ports Act (1807), Saint John became one of many ports in the region to experience exponential growth as a go-between for British and American trade. For a time, even out-migration reversed course as American merchants and sailors flowed into southern New Brunswick to do business. The result was an unusual degree of buoyancy in the still new colony and an abundance of capital to invest in ships, ports, warehousing, and other trade infrastructure, all of which would be needed to support the other event that advantaged New Brunswick at the time.

That event also trickled down from the Anglo-French war and was attributable to both Jefferson's Embargo Act and to Napoleon's decision in 1806 to impose a continental blockade that affected the movement of timber westward across Europe. In the first instance, the Embargo Act halted the flow of timber from New England to Britain, a trade that had always favoured northern New England harvesters over New Brunswick's because of the province's sparse development north of Fredericton. Desiring for New Brunswick "the development of an agricultural society from which a rigid social structure would emerge," the founding Loyalists, says MacNutt, "discouraged the unsettled habits and uncertain ventures that were attendant upon life in the backwoods."[71] The Embargo, however, changed that, bringing the wider development of the colony's interior into the public conversation.

Napoleon's Berlin Decree of 1806 and Milan Decree of 1807 were even more influential. Both pieces of legislation outlawed the trade of British goods in European countries allied with the French. To embed their effect geopolitically, both decrees imposed a continental blockade that cut off Britain from its mostly Baltic wood supply, a serious blow (especially in wartime) to the country's timber-dependent Royal Navy.[72] With its wood trade from New England and eastern Europe blocked, its domestic supply dwindling and becoming prohibitively expensive, and the Industrial Revolution demanding vast stores of wood for factory and other constructions, Britain looked across the Atlantic to its colonies for timber inventory. "More than any other of the British provinces New Brunswick was able to take advantage of this rich opportunity," wrote MacNutt.[73] The opportunity opened the New Brunswick interior to wood harvesting and fundamentally changed the social economy from one of agriculture and the gentleman farmer to one of forestry and the itinerant (sometimes unruly) labourer. "Between 1805 and 1809," reports Graeme Wynn, "British North America wood exports increased tenfold, and then doubled again within the next decade."[74] Hundreds of ships were built in New Brunswick ports in the first few decades of the century, millions upon millions of board feet of lumber, masts, and square-timbers were loaded on those ships and sent across the Atlantic to Britain, and thousands of immigrants boarded those ships in British ports for the return trip, lured by promises of high wages and plentiful, arable land. Logging operations, mills, shipyards, sustaining industries, and towns sprang up overnight, and New Brunswick, Britain's pre-eminent "timber colony,"[75] had its first economic boom, a prosperity that would continue to expand during the War of 1812. The colony's vast forests and river systems made that prosperity possible. By 1845, roughly nine thousand men were employed in upward of six hundred mills. It was an upturn that would last for three generations, providing the capital that would make leisure, and therefore culture, possible. When New Brunswickers think of good times, they invariably remember this pre-Confederation period. Rightly or wrongly, 1867 is the date after which fortunes change, the fault line, argues Phillip Buckner, which marks both end and beginning.[76]

Why those fortunes changed continues to be a subject of vigorous debate, a debate shaped by the exceptional work of a group of New Brunswick historians brought to the University of New Brunswick by A.G. Bailey. The group warrants mention not only to highlight Bailey's essential role in provincial historiography but also because its work has been unrivalled in the influence it has had on the later scholarship of the province's political economists, social scientists, and literary critics.

The question those historians sought to answer is *what happened?* Why did provincial fortunes wane after such a long period of prosperity and why did those fortunes never rebound? To put the matter more provocatively, why, asked economic historian David Alexander, did the region as a whole descend so rapidly after being in recent possession of "one of the world's foremost shipbuilding industries, the third- or fourth-largest merchant marine, financial institutions which were the core of many of the present Canadian giants, and an industrial structure growing as fast as that of central Canada"?[77] There were recessions, of course, but recessions and global retractions are not isolated to regions or provinces; they affect world markets uniformly. Why, then, did the Laurentian corridor of southern Quebec and Ontario survive those recessions when the Maritimes did not? That question, more than any other, has become both a Maritime and New Brunswick preoccupation.

Some common ground was found in mid-century in Harold Adams Innis's view that reversing fortunes in the Maritime region were a result of inflexibilities borne of an innate conservatism, specifically with regard to the reluctance to move from an old maritime economy of wood, wind, and sail to a new post-Confederation, continental economy of industry and rail.[78] That "staples" view of geographic determinism was later challenged and has now been replaced by the opinion that a number of structural factors, not subjective or commodities weaknesses, worked against the region's success. Foremost among those were what contemporary Marxists would call processes of planned, albeit uneven, development.

In "The National Policy and the Industrialization of the Maritimes, 1880–1910," a seminal essay first published in 1972, UNB historian T.W. Acheson shifted attention to the macro-economic effects of the National Policy, the program of economic mercantilism introduced by John A. Macdonald's Conservative government in 1879 that implemented a tariff regime on imports to protect the country's fledgling manufacturing sector. Macdonald's coincident plan of railway construction – the latter (transportation) serving the former (manufacturing) – would literally wrench Canada's trade profile 90 degrees: from a north-south seaboard economy, which favoured Maritime enterprise, to an east-west continental economy that favoured the Canadas. Macdonald's rationale for such a sweeping policy was foremost political: to build structures that would advantage Canadian manufacturing while also attempting to reduce trade reliance on the United States, thereby creating a unified nation that was independent of the Americans.[79] In a post-Reciprocity era (free trade with the United States ended in 1866), the Americans had imposed their own set of high tariffs, making Macdonald's ploy appear as reasonable as it was responsive.

In the Maritime business community, the National Policy, reports Acheson, was initially embraced in that spirit, "as a new mercantilism which would reestablish that stability which the region had enjoyed under the old British order."[80] And it did work for a time, resulting in rapid expansion of a number of manufacturing enterprises.[81] Likewise, as first proposed, the policy in New Brunswick – promoted, it must be said, by its principal architect, New Brunswick native son Leonard Tilley – was considered favourably as a means of diversifying an economy heavily reliant on lumbering and the manufacture of wooden ships, both in decline and hit hard by the recession of the early 1880s. Since "forty-five of the fifty savings banks in the Dominion were located in the Maritimes,"[82] there was abundant reason to believe that the capital needed to fund this new east-west manufacturing economy would be readily available to eastern Canadians.

Problems soon revealed themselves, however, and the original logic of Confederation – that "the federation will persist only so long as it succeeds in sensitively defining useful and mutually attractive purposes"[83] – soon started to fray. To begin with, manufacturing was a nascent sector in the Maritimes; where it flourished, it served or complemented the more dominant timber and shipping sectors. Manufacturing unrelated to those sectors consisted of small, commodity-producing enterprises, most making supplies for domestic use. Creating the conditions for a robust manufacturing economy, then, while successful for a short time, did not advantage the larger sectors upon which the Maritime economy was based. At best, the National Policy in the region, and certainly New Brunswick, supported tertiary industries like mop factories, hardly the formula for sustained growth. Moreover, the more deeply embedded plan to re-route the trade corridor from vertical to horizontal (from Atlantic to overland) *did* affect New Brunswick's primary sectors, accelerating their decline. In effect, what the National Policy did was constrain the region's maritime economy while at the same time boosting the already-strong manufacturing sector of southern Ontario and Quebec – a sector doubly privileged by its proximity to "the apex of the U.S. industrial triangle."[84] Tilting the playing field against Maritime interests in that way moved the fulcrum of commerce definitively to the centre, and, not surprisingly, the manufacturing profile of the lower provinces changed dramatically in a post-National Policy Canada. "Relative to Canada," asserts political economist Donald Savoie, "the Maritimes accounted for 14 per cent of goods produced in 1880, only 9 per cent in 1911, and 5 per cent in 1939."[85] At exactly the period in history when the British lumber market faltered and the steel hull made the wooden ship obsolete, the Maritime economy was ill-suited to the national government's formula for industrial development. Central Canada's economy, on the other hand, benefited considerably, a fact that would bear directly on a narrative of the country that was slowly taking shape.

Compounding the imbalance of manufacturing were freight-rate changes in the transportation sector. Built as a Maritime condition of entry into Confederation, the fledgling Intercolonial Railway (ICR) offered low and flexible freight rates as a means of cultivating Maritime industry. In doing so, writes historian Ernest Forbes, "the interests of transportation and national policy neatly coalesced. At a time when the traditional Maritime economy ... was in eclipse ... the railway offered manufacturing industries access to new markets in Central and later in Western Canada."[86] Distance from centralized markets was compensated for – "rates for up to 100 miles were approximately 20 per cent lower than on Central Canadian lines; but for over 400 miles they were more than 30 per cent lower, and for 700 miles more than 50 per cent lower"[87] – and a level playing field, at least in the first decades of the ICR, was achieved. The arrangement was protectionist only if considered myopically. From the Maritime perspective, such an arrangement was a condition of Confederation and recognition of the fact that patterns of commerce and trade had been radically altered. With trade corridors now running east to west, Maritime entrepreneurs were dependent on the railway to export their goods to the large central Canadian market. But they had to do so at a distance, which required adjusted costs. Recognizing that spatial reality (the disadvantage of distance) with lower rates was not protectionist, but equalizing.

Others didn't see it that way, and despite the economic development it spawned, the ICR's freight-rate subsidy to the Maritime provinces was short-lived. Montreal merchants were a leading cause. Canada had become a nation whose most powerful businessmen, now based in central Canada's largest industrial cities, were deeply invested in maintaining their advantages. As a result, the Maritime-sensitive ICR policy was viewed as unfairly subsidizing one area of the country over another, "a prospect which the business community of Montreal and environs could hardly be expected to view with equanimity."[88] It didn't matter that the National Policy already advantaged Montreal and environs; political manoeuvring ensured that Montreal's dominance would continue to win out, even if that city's business elite had to employ hardnosed tactics to block another group's subsidies to protect its own. What was a level playing field, then, tilted against Maritime interests again, with a rising chorus of complaints from central Canadian manufacturers leading, in 1912, "to the abolition of the East-West differential," the dismantling of the New Brunswick headquarters of the ICR (it was moved to Toronto), and rate increases on many of the region's leading export commodities to match the rates of Ontario and Quebec.[89] Those rates would become crippling, rising "between 140 and 216 per cent" between 1916 and 1920.[90] The effect in the Maritimes was almost immediate: "In the years between 1920 and 1926," comments John Reid, "some 42 percent of the manufacturing jobs in the region simply disappeared."[91] If the National Policy was strike one, indifference to the economic disadvantages of distance was strike two. By the start of the 1920s, two things had become clear: that rational arguments to level the playing field didn't work and that out-migration had depopulated the Maritimes to the point where political representation was no longer sufficient to leverage protest.[92] Simply put, for a New Brunswick industry, "geography would defeat any attempt to compete at parity with a central Canadian enterprise."[93] If subsidizing transportation to centralized markets was off the table, in other words, the chair manufactured in a New Brunswick furniture factory had to be built for 25 per cent less than the same chair in Quebec to make up for the 25 per cent transportation costs to get that New Brunswick chair to the Quebec market.

A major consequence of this planned, asymmetrical development – which was, in reality, nothing less than a program of structural impoverishment – was a wresting of control. Maritimers no longer felt they controlled their own destiny. Colonials under an earlier British administration, they were at least self-reliant colonials, moving freely in a large Atlantic world "that reached from Boston to the Bay of Chaleur" to Britain and its colonies. Said literary historian Malcolm Ross: "It was a region of the mind that over-arched all the political fences and fusses. As one born and bred in the region, I never thought it strange that I was as much at home in Scituate [Mass.] or Skowhegan [Maine] as in Chamcook, Shediac or Nashwaaksis [New Brunswick]. And not at home at all in such foreign towns as ... Toronto, Ont."[94] Under the policies of Confederation, Ross and his fellow New Brunswickers were still colonials, defined and controlled by distant Ottawa and Toronto rather than by distant Whitehall, but colonials who had been considerably reduced: their mobility was now limited, their world had shrunk, and they had few socio-economic options beyond those of planned dependency. With the consolidation of major industries in central Canada and the movement of capital following shortly thereafter – "as late as 1900 there had been 13 banks in the Maritimes, but by 1910 only three were left"[95] – the region had literally been remade into a dependent state, marginalized and increasingly defined by its unequal relations with the centre. No less an authority than Stanley Saunders, the economist who undertook the first detailed study of the region's Confederation economy for the Rowell-Sirois Royal Commission on Dominion-Provincial Relations (1937–40), reached the following conclusion about the post-Confederation economy: that it "was not merely an inequality between industries but also an inequality between regions."[96]

Saunders was not exaggerating. As a result of the National Policy, freight-rate increases, capital consolidation outside the region, and what historian David Frank describes as the colossal ineptitude of absentee managers of major Maritime businesses,[97] the eastern provinces had been refashioned into a supply depot, a locus where human resources, raw materials, and money flowed west. In real and symbolic terms, the citizens who remained in this space became neocolonials, branch-plant subjects who took their orders from a ruling class at the centre. As David Alexander observed, the effect of this bread-crumb subsistence would soon become the stuff of national comedy: "the efforts to generate development which will actually confer benefits to residents com[ing] down to a decision by the [federal] Department of Regional Economic Expansion [DREE] whether Moncton or Corner Brook would provide the best location for a hockey-stick plant."[98] A local New Brunswick wit followed suit by naming his dog "DREE," the joke parodying the trickle-down largesse of the national government.[99]

Today, moving beyond Saunders and Alexander, Marxist cultural geography provides a fuller, more sophisticated understanding of this pattern of development. The construction of unequal relations is part of what Henri Lefebvre has called "the production of space," that production reflecting capitalism's need "to extend [its] reach to space in its entirety: to the *land* ... to the *underground* resources ... and lastly to what might be called the *above-ground* sphere."[100] To control and remake spatial economies so they are brought in line with dominant forms of capitalism is the goal, one that begins when the political class takes steps "to subjugate [territory] into complete insignificance."[101] From there, continues economic geographer Neil Smith, spatial relations are calibrated to deliver use-value, one avenue to which is centralization. Without that centralization, spatial isolation can never be overcome, and distant regions never integrated into capitalism's central authority.[102] As the process develops, "it becomes necessary for the bourgeoisie to extend its control to cover not just the exchange process but also the production process. This in order to ensure the continual supply of commodities for exchange."[103] Uneven development and the unequal spatial relations it manifests, then, are not natural or normal or evolutionary – and certainly not reflective of early stages of development – but are structural outcomes that deliver particular and important benefits to ruling authorities. The essential thing to understand, writes Smith, is "that uneven development is the hallmark of the geography of capitalism": "it is not a question of what capitalism does to geography but rather of what geography can do for capitalism."[104]

Under new adjunct status, New Brunswick and the other Maritime provinces thus acquired an important but undignified role. In an earlier Atlantic economy their major centres had been waypoints and departure sites – far stations, admittedly, in a colonial economy but destinations nevertheless beyond which it was not necessary to venture or imagine. Saint John and Halifax were complete in themselves, harbours where voyages ceased and settlement took root. Each became two of the most vibrant cities in the New World. In the new Confederation economy, that status and the narratives attached to it changed. With the balance of economic and political power shifted to the centre, New Brunswick and the lower provinces now formed a periphery – and that periphery, by definition, was no longer complete in itself. The railway was material proof of that: far from bringing the Maritime periphery *into* the centre of the country, the railway accentuated its distance *from* the centre, a condition that became more acute as early railways lost money and had to amalgamate. The change was subtle but significant, the problem seen as not Canada's but the Maritimes'. The region was just too far from the new centre of the country, the railway not a link but an ever more frayed umbilical cord.

That peripheral status, however, as Smith suggests above, had an important ideological function. With its autonomy and self-reliance changed to dependency in a Confederation economy, the region became not just supplicant but functional supplicant, a marker of essential difference from the centre. And the more different it could be made to appear – the more unable or unwilling to match the Laurentian corridor's efficiencies and successes – the more essential, natural, and benevolent did Confederation's model of distributive federalism seem. Embedded in Confederation's Laurentian logic, then, was a fundamental political and economic utility. That utility reinforced regional dependency to justify central bureaucracy and control, while at the same time signalling central and western Canada's fitness as more robust loci for investment and development. On that point, New Brunswick political economist Donald Savoie's work has been especially valuable. In his many books, he has argued passionately that coercive utility – the pursuit of uneven development to justify control and underscore vitality – has always determined which areas of the country succeed and which do not. Almost every move by Queen's Park or Ottawa, he suggests, serves that logic, whether the construction of the St Lawrence Seaway, the drafting of the Canada-U.S. Auto Pact, or the creation of supposedly "national" crown corporations. Savoie writes: "In 1964 only 7 percent of the automobiles built in Canada were sold in the United States, but the proportion jumped to 60 percent by 1968. The pact created thousands of jobs in Ontario but all it did for the Maritimes was to make the purchase of a car more expensive. [Consider also] the thirty-two crown corporations created to assist the war effort in the early 1940s. They would later provide the basis for Canada's [post-Second World War] manufacturing sector. Not a single crown corporation was established in the Maritimes – all were set up in central Canada."[105]

Savoie's examples are compelling. Had the eastern provinces regained their economic footing after Confederation, there would be little need for a united Canada, its distances and costs of equalization too great to justify continuance. Canada would have returned to a more natural state of entropic balkanization. In a state of chronic economic depression, however, a state in which a marginalized east had grown dependent on the narcotic of wealth adjustments, distributive federalism was easily naturalized as an essential corrective – a corrective, moreover, that could justify drawing uneven wealth to the centre as long as the centre had to subsidize the margins. Central Canada, in other words, needed an impoverished eastern flank, and needed it to be dependent. With chronic underachievement so essential in the capitalist dialectic between the centre and the east, so emerged narratives of backwardness and underdevelopment, and so were New Brunswick and the other Maritime provinces cast in a new national drama. It is to the region's assigned role in that new drama that I now turn, for the work of the New Brunswick literary modernists directly addressed that narrative.

MYTHOLOGIZING THE SUPPLICANT

That Confederation changed the Maritime narrative is perhaps not surprising. Nor is it surprising that simultaneous albeit differently intentioned post-Confederation narratives were forming right across the country. A particularly sinister narrative touched Canada's First Peoples. This is not to suggest that conditions and consequences were in any way similar among the groups that were determined by narrative, but only that the operation of mythmaking was paramount in a nascent Canada: narratives formed that buried historical and structural processes of wilful incursion while foregrounding the social stagnation and personal deficit that resulted. Canadian public intellectual John Ralston Saul attributes the orchestration of that mythmaking to what he terms "Victorianism," the authority and expression of which was vital in the imaginations of early settlers. For Saul, Victorianism reproduced itself in narratives that celebrated uniformity and megalomaniacal self-replication, whether in patterns of settlement, policies of assimilation, or the languages of administrative control. The objective, he states, was to demarcate an Indigenous periphery against which a European centre could be contrasted: "Historians such as Francis Parkman, François-Xavier Garneau and Abbé Groulx, along with the poet and Indian Affairs official Duncan Campbell Scott ... provided the supporting intellectual arguments ... Their message – stated or implied – was that if this [Indigenous] race was disappearing, it followed that to mix with them was to dilute pure blood."[106] Nineteenth-century science was used to support that ideological position, the evidence of the Indigenous peoples' poor immunity to European disease taken as proof that they were weak and thus in need of management and care. Stories of infirmity followed that underlined difference and the need for segregation. Lord Dalhousie's description of the Maritime Mi'kmaq as "little better than outcasts of society" captured exactly the Victorian attitude that Saul describes.[107] As in all mythmaking, amnesia was vital, and so the Victorian narratives of Canada's First Peoples focused on broken, colonized subjects rather than on the historical conditions that changed social structures and speeded population decline.

Other narratives emerged to orient and educate the larger Canadian imagination, those reflecting a wide swath of intentions, some malevolent, some borne of the naive acceptance of received opinion, and most, as Daniel Francis points out in *National Dreams*, "express[ing] something that we wanted to believe about ourselves."[108] In all cases, ideology as decontextualized truth – a misreading of social effect for historical cause – positioned citizens to believe that the stories they were hearing were as natural and true as they were unmediated.

The Maritime region of Canada was not immune to those generalized processes of myth and narrative. Perhaps surprisingly, though, much of what became understood as "the Maritime condition" came from Maritime sources, the literary ethos of the pre- and post-Confederation periods a fertile ground where stories of the broken eastern subject were incubated as national narrative. One need only consider the dominant regional themes of lethargy, betrayal, exile, and loss to understand the point. In colonial Nova Scotia, for example, early-nineteenth-century satirists Thomas McCulloch and Thomas Chandler Haliburton made much of the bluenosers' lack of initiative, attributing attitudes of leisure and communitarianism to a penchant for Loyalist entitlement – that entitlement satirized by William Cobbett as creating a gentry of "captains and colonels without soldiers[,] and squires without shoes or stockings."[109] McCulloch's best-known protagonist, the lame and thoroughly Calvinist Mephibosheth Stepsure, describes this attitude among his neighbours, who, when encountering "bad land, hard luck, and poor returns ... are obliged to spend much of their time in mutual visits, for the purpose of unburdening their minds, condoling, and keeping each other in heart."[110] What they refuse to do, opines Stepsure, is the hard work that will reverse their poor fortunes. Haliburton's Yankee peddler, Sam Slick, is even more direct in describing the features of Maritime entitlement: "They do nothin' in these parts but eat, drink, smoke, sleep, ride about, lounge at taverns, make speeches at temperance meetin's, and talk about 'House of Assembly.' If a man don't hoe his corn and don't get a crop, he says it is all owin' to the bank; and if he runs into debt and is sued, why, he says the lawyers are a curse to the country. They are a most idle set of folks, I tell you."[111]

For Haliburton, especially, Nova Scotians are little more than "colony frog[s]" softened by privilege, dependent by nature, and rife with expectations of unearned riches.[112] When fortunes turned negative in the region it would be this already-mythologized lack of gumption, and not any structural cause, that was blamed.

As the eastern colonies edged closer to Confederation, this sense of Maritime entitlement begins to change, as evidenced in the dominant narrative of French New Brunswick and Nova Scotia. By that time (more than a generation after McCulloch and Haliburton), Henry Wadsworth Longfellow's *Evangeline: A Tale of Acadie* (1847) had taken a powerful hold on the imagination, so powerful, in fact, that translators had made it a favourite project, taking great liberties with the story in the process. The most popular version of the poem was produced by Pamphile Le May in 1867. A member of the Quebec literary circle of François-Xavier Garneau, Antoine Gérin-Lajoie, and Joseph-Charles Taché, Le May found a wide and appreciative audience in storytelling. With great skill, he retold the history of *les voyageurs Québécois* as *contes fables*, or moral lessons, adding editorial spice to his creative interpretations of Quebec heritage.[113] His translation of Longfellow's poem was similarly liberal, as much fabrication as translation of an original text. As Acadian literary critics Denis Bourque and Denise Merkle illustrate, Le May's *Evangeline* is more politically provocative, its Loyalist characters more uncompromising and brutal, and its Acadian victims more outcast and despondent than Longfellow ever intended.[114] The result is a tale of deep visceral pathos that turns the vicissitudes of Acadian history to heightened pain – and by extension seeds the myth of a strong but defeated people who are made to suffer mercilessly under occupation. That the region's French clergy enthusiastically endorsed Le May's translation furthered its effect, the tale's presentation of a people under occupation paralleling not only that of the Catholic minority under Protestant dominion but also the suffering of the reverent in a wicked world. Always legitimized at the pulpit, pain, after Le May, assumed new symbolic resonance for a large minority of the region's French population, its meaning "commensurate with the decline of the age of sail and of the Maritime region after Confederation."[115]

Less emotionally amplified but evoking the same feelings of loss and despair was the work of the New Brunswick school of the Confederation poets, among whom Charles G.D. Roberts and Bliss Carman were the best known. Both were lauded in the region (and country) for pioneering a geo-emotive sensibility of place in the early years of post-Confederation nationalism – and both perfected that sensibility in elegiac tones of emotional suffering and torpor, tones that expressed the ache of exile over what had been lost or changed. Carman's "The Ships of Saint John" provides an example of that elegiac tone, its register of loss and sorrow palpable, especially in combination with an understanding of the passing of Maritime fortunes:

Where are the ships I used to know,
    That came to port on the Fundy tide
half a century ago,
    In beauty and stately pride?

                    ...

The creatures of a passing race,
    The dark spruce forests made them strong,
The sea's lore gave them magic grace,
    The great winds taught them song.

                    ...

The fog still hangs on the long tide-rips,
    The gulls go wavering to and fro,
But where are all the beautiful ships
    I knew so long ago?[116]

Even better known than Carman's elegy for a lost culture of sail was Roberts's requiem for his beloved Tantramar. "The Tantramar Revisited" (1886), the most important poem to come out of New Brunswick in the nineteenth century, employs epic structures and hexametric form (the same form that Longfellow used in *Evangeline*) to leaven the joy and sorrow of return. Despite the powerful reminiscences that his return evokes – sun-drenched summers and orchards, green hills, wind-blown marshes, and boyhood dreams – the poem's speaker finally turns his back on the beloved home of his youth, fearing that change has made it unrecognizable. The final lines of the poem are an anthem for a *fin-de-siècle* Maritime condition:

Yet will I stay my steps and not go down to the marsh-land, –
Muse and recall far off, rather remember than see, –
Lest on too close sight I miss the darling illusion,
Spy at their task even here the hands of chance and change.[117]

The poem achieves its deepest emotional effect with the words "even here," their inference signalling a new narrative for the region. No longer at the centre of the North Atlantic colonial experiment, Roberts's New Brunswick is now positioned deliberately on the periphery of an unfamiliar space. "Even here," the narrative intimates, all that was willed to withstand the ravages of modernity and change is now lost. The province and region are escheated, literally orphaned, their fate in others' hands. It is hardly coincidence, then, that the complementary narrative of a wilful, though vulnerable, orphan girl would appear at exactly this time of Maritime history with Montgomery's *Anne of Green Gables* (1908), the story of an unwanted child who must forge new relationships in an initially cold household and among peer rivals in an unfamiliar social setting. As first experienced, Anne Shirley's new circumstance is grim indeed: "The whitewashed walls were so painfully bare and staring that she thought they must ache over their own bareness. The floor was bare, too, except for a round braided mat in the middle such as Anne had never seen before ... The whole apartment was of a rigidity not to be described in words, but which sent a shiver to the very marrow of Anne's bones."[118]

Anne's challenges were the region's own: both literally had to remake themselves amidst inhospitable conditions and their own psychological despair. As literary critic David Creelman would observe many years later, the narrative that formed around those experiences imagined a future far less bright than the past, "a culture of memory unleavened by dream."[119] The Loyalist ideal of a segregated, self-sufficient utopia was dead, said Maritime storytellers, the region not only suddenly liminal but its citizens under new absentee management.

If the leading literary speakers of the region planted the seeds for this new narrative in the generations before and around Confederation, other pieces of collateral evidence speeded their growth. The formation of the first Duncan Commission into the Maritime coal industry in 1925 provides a good example of that other kind of evidence – and a fitting precedent for the many other federal and provincial commissions that were formed in the 1920s and 1930s to study the Maritime region's place in the post-Confederation economy. The list alone is impressive: the Royal Commission on Maritime Claims (1926), the Royal Commission Investigating the Fisheries of the Maritime Provinces (1928), the Royal Commission Respecting the Coal Mines of Nova Scotia (1932), the Nova Scotia Royal Commission Provincial Economic Inquiry (1934), the Royal Commission on Financial Arrangements between the Dominion and the Maritime Provinces (1935), and the Rowell-Sirois Royal Commission on Dominion-Provincial Relations (1937–40). Though each commission was specific to an industry, sector, or set of relationships, the frequency of their appearance, when mapped onto the dispositions that McCulloch and Haliburton had popularized, seemed to point to an irrefutable truth about the absence of self-determination in the region. Moreover, that most of those commissions were borne of Maritime grievance and an increasing tendency toward mobilization against the federation – the agitation of the Maritime Rights Movement of the 1920s was often cited[120] – suggested an unhealthy sectoral pathology in a country founded on the principals of "peace, order, and good government."[121] It did not matter that the grievances may have been legitimate – that "the [national] policies which ultimately turn regional diseconomies into positive advantages" were lacking;[122] rather, what mattered was what appeared on the surface. In the eyes of outsiders, concluded T.W. Acheson, the evidence was clear: "The Maritimes had become a 'problem' of interest primarily to social scientists whose function was to prescribe an appropriate cure for the ailing patient."[123]

When contrasted with the compelling evidence of expansion in the Canadian west – and the narratives emerging around a buoyant pioneer optimism (a largely constructed immigrant optimism that, at least on western Canadian soil, was ahistorical) – the Maritimes must indeed have seemed shorn of dynamism. To embellish its difference from that lack of vibrancy, the prairie narrative overflowed with agency and physicality, with pioneers taking matters into their own hands and turning inhospitable space into productive land. Dust, drudgery, and self-doubt, the narratives shouted, were beside the point, as Frederick Philip Grove's main character in *Settlers of the Marsh* (1925) made clear. For Niels Lindstedt and Grove's other western pioneers, work was to be welcomed, for the prairie "seemed to have been created to rouse man's energies to fullest exertion."[124] Furthermore, said the narratives, the space that hard work opened to settlement and prosperity was without the restrictions of the older societies from which settlers had come. It was a clean slate that had none of the peerage, class, and other social orders of staid nations – in other words, none of the entitlement baggage the Loyalists brought to the Maritimes. As Niels experiences it, "none of the heath country of his native Blekinge [Sweden] ... none of the pretty juniper trees; none of the sea with its rocky islands. These poplar trees seemed wilder, less spared by an ancient civilisation that had learned to appreciate them. They invited the axe, the explorer."[125] Without pretext or excuse, the west was therefore a place that enabled forward progress by removing the constraints of the past. As such, it was a landscape in possession "of a fundamental human right: the right of every human being to determine his own course of action."[126]

In contrast, the economic, literary, and political records of the east told a different story: that region seemed a place where contraction had become endemic and where citizens (like Roberts and Carman) were especially fond of wallowing in halcyon days – so fond, in fact, that the past seemed to hold Maritimers in its spell, immobilizing them in the same way that Roberts's observer is immobilized at the end of "The Tantramar Revisited." An assessment of the regional character of easterners in *Maclean's Magazine* in 1926 followed those assumptions to the letter, concluding that "the Maritime provinces were like a housewife who having married for money which failed to materialize 'neglected her housework, went down to the seashore ... watched the ships go by and pouted.'"[127] The region became of interest, then, says Forbes (anticipating later Marxists), "only as a foil against which to demonstrate the vitality of the frontier approach;

simple logic suggested that, if the frontier encouraged progressive, egalitarian and democratic attitudes, then that part of the country furthest removed from the frontier stage must be conservative, socially stratified and unprogressive."[128]

In such an overdetermined narrative environment, central Canadian historian Frank Underhill's oft-quoted remark that "[a]s for the Maritimes, nothing, of course, ever happens down there"[129] could easily be believed: easily, that is, but for the backstory of the structural changes imposed by Confederation. Nevertheless, these kinds of remarks were believed and did coalesce to form powerful national stories of Maritime melancholy and malaise, as journalist Jeffrey Simpson made clear in 2001. For Simpson, whose national stature would normally presuppose a fairly sophisticated understanding of Canadian history, the new myths hold powerful sway. "Atlantic Canada," he writes, "has a bit of an image problem. It's been down, economically speaking, for so long that people in the rest of Canada think of the region as nothing more than four provinces full of friendly people looking for handouts. You know the image. Unemployment insurance. Seasonal workers. Make-work projects. Regional development agencies. Pork-barrel politics. Equalization."[130]

But Simpson is not alone. Even the country's leading politicians continue to embrace the old myths for their functional use value. For example, as noted in the Preface, when federal finance minister Jim Flaherty described the Ontario auto industry in 2009 as a key economic driver for the nation, and hence deserving of a large taxpayer bailout, he also said that there must be "no 'corporate welfare'" for failing New Brunswick paper mills.[131] That apparent contradiction disappears when considered in light of the narrative of one region's weakness legitimizing another's strength.

Citing what he calls "the privation of history," myth theorist Roland Barthes observes that the "miraculous evaporation of history is ... common to most bourgeois myths" because, at the centre of each, "irresponsibility of man" is paramount.[132] In other words, myths operate by replacing the agency of human meddling and intention with the fallacy of natural cause. By stripping conditions of their history and human footprint, myth is therefore free to "invent itself ceaselessly. It takes hold of everything, all aspects of law, of morality, of aesthetics, of diplomacy, of household equipment, [and] of Literature."[133] Moreover, adds Barthes, "in passing from history to nature, myth acts economically: it abolishes the complexity of human acts, it gives them the simplicity of essences, it does away with all dialectics, with any going back beyond what is immediately visible, it organizes a world which is without contradictions because it is without depth, a world wide open and wallowing in the evident, it establishes a blissful clarity: things appear to mean something by themselves."[134]

And so the myths persist, fed by internal and external agents and often defying the logic of evidence. To understand the resilience of mythology, adds Terry Eagleton, "is to understand the complex, indirect relations between those [myths] and the ideological worlds they inhabit."[135] It doesn't matter that they are true or false; what matters is that they circulate – and that they become the scripts (indeed, says Jacques Lacan, the very consciousness) through which citizens interpret their country. Myths embed stereotypes so assuredly because they are perceived to be non-ideological, "to work with poor, incomplete images, where the meaning is already relieved of its fat."[136] Take, for example, Canada's two most recognizable regional protest movements of the inter-war period. In the first instance, the 1919 Winnipeg General Strike and Social Gospel evangelism merge loosely against a backdrop of western dynamism to form the positivist Canadian myth of prairie radicalism,[137] the same radicalism that informed the country's political narrative under former prime minister Stephen Harper's Reform regime. In the second instance, the 1919–27 Maritime Rights Movement, though contributing far more substantively to the evolving definition of distributive federalism, is interpreted against a backdrop of eastern malaise and grievance to be little more than whining.[138] In both instances, the meaning of what remains is indeed already relieved of its fat: and consequentially, William "Bible Bill" Aberhart, the Alberta populist, is accorded the status of Canadian maverick while Nova Scotia's Joseph Howe, a far more significant figure in Canadian history, is remembered primarily for opposing Confederation. It is not the evidence of history that has created these myths, but the myths themselves that created the historical consciousness of Canadians, to restate what Marx and Engels said in *The German Ideology* (1845–46).

As the first decades of the twentieth century progressed, and the eastern provinces became more and more peripheral to economic and other expansions, the stories circulating about all facets of the region began to show the influence of that new consciousness. A final example will suffice, the story's altering of the reputations of New Brunswick's Confederation poets having a profound and ultimately positive effect on a young Alfred G. Bailey, the figure around whom literary modernism in New Brunswick would become galvanized. The story is of literary excellence, a story that was particularly important to the educated classes of the Maritime provinces because it concerned an aspect of their society about which they could rightly be proud. In the decade before and after 1900, New Brunswick had been given the distinction of being the literary capital of Canada. Not only were its poets the most visible of the writers of that generation, but they had also captured the attention of American and British readers, an achievement that has always been of singular importance to Canadians. Ezra Pound's view that "among contemporary North American poets Bliss Carman was 'about the only one of the lot that wouldn't improve by drowning'"[139] was typical of the acclaim bestowed on the New Brunswick poets.

When the first waves of a nationalist criticism emerged after Confederation, scholarly consensus stood behind that view. In 1913 Thomas Guthrie Marquis's "English-Canadian Literature," one of the first sustained treatments of a Canadian "voice," minced no words in describing Charles G.D. Roberts as "without an equal in Canadian literature as a writer of mellifluous prose."[140] So exact were his "sea, sky, [and] landscape[s]" that Marquis compared his evocations of the new Dominion to Thomas Hardy's evocations of Wessex and Egdon Heath. Marquis lavished similar praise on Roberts's poetry, calling it "verse of a high order, carefully done, showing scholarship and with something of the atmosphere of Shelley, Keats and Tennyson."[141] Perhaps most praiseworthy for a "colonial" poet was the fact that "there was nothing provincial about it" – that, taken as a whole, "the poems were, indeed, almost flawless."[142] Critic James Cappon had made similar comments in an earlier study of Roberts (1905), a study that was the first in Canada to examine a writer in his native Canadian milieu. Cappon called Roberts "the most distinguished of our Canadian poets,"[143] comparing the quality of his verse to that of Wordsworth.[144] Citing Roberts's *Songs of the Common Day* (1893) as exemplar of "a true Canadian atmosphere,"[145] Cappon described the authentic Canadian poet as one "who manages to get the right materials of Canadian life into his song in such a way that all the world may feel what it is that gives Canada character and significance among nations."[146] For Cappon, Roberts was the first Canadian poet to meet that aesthetic threshold.

National critics were equally enthusiastic about Bliss Carman's work, Marquis adopting Arthur J. Stringer's opinion that Carman was "America's foremost lyrist [sic]"[147] and Rufus Hathaway unabashedly placing Carman "among those men whose poetry is the shining glory of that great English literature which is our common heritage."[148] An honorary degree from McGill University in 1921 and special recognition of his value to the country that same year by the Montreal branch of the Canadian Authors Association further affirmed Carman's reputation. That Montreal scholars and writers conferred those honours was not lost on Maritime citizens, nor was it insignificant that as the new (unofficial) poet laureate of Canada Carman drew audiences of several hundred when he toured the west. The accolades kept coming with the Lorne Pierce Medal of the Royal Society of Canada (RSC) for Roberts (1926) and Carman (1928), and a flurry of book-length critical studies of their work by Odell Shepard, Cappon, Hathaway, and A.M. Stephens. Looking back, contemporary critic David Bentley notes that "both popular and critical acclaim came to Roberts and Carman on a scale for which their reception some thirty years earlier provides the only antecedent in Canadian literary history."[149] That acclaim, however, and the narratives it incubated, ended with the close of the 1920s.

For the central Canadian modernists of the 1930s, Charles G.D. Roberts, the erstwhile "Father of Canadian literature," becomes Charles "God Damn," the symbol of cultural fatigue and the "hypersensitive ... victim of his feelings and fancies."[150] E.K. Brown would reinforce that assessment by placing Roberts "in the very rear of the modern movement,"[151] thus condemning him to the previous century's exuberant, and by inference callow, idealism. Brown did the same with Carman, labelling his verse "jaunty," "cloying," and "soporific."[152] Especially curious, however, is the opposite trajectory of the fortunes of the central Canadian poets whose reputations Roberts and Carman had earlier eclipsed. At the exact time when the critical stock of the New Brunswick poets declines in the national narrative, so does the stock of the Ottawa school of the Confederation poets, namely Archibald Lampman and Duncan Campbell Scott, rise. They are described by Brown as "the two most powerful and satisfying poets of the period"[153] – and are subsequently promoted as avant-garde models of an early modernism. That Carman's and Roberts's exposure to the currents of modernist thought was much more pronounced and significant is dropped from the narrative, and historical fact, as Barthes describes,[154] conveniently evaporates.

But Brown was not the only storyteller. W.E. Collin had been the first to revise history when his groundbreaking *The White Savannahs* (1936) fixed a canon of Canadian poetry that included Lampman to the exclusion of Roberts and Carman (Roberts is not mentioned in the book, and Carman receives one footnote). Roberts's outrage must have been palpable, especially with regard to how Collin placed Lampman on a geographic periphery that in no way had impeded Carman or himself: "Lampman and his associates [presumably Roberts and Carman], who complained of the prevailing drought, kept themselves informed of the flow of ideas in the outer world by reading the great English and American monthlies and quarterlies."[155] Roberts and Carman, however, did much more than read from isolated outposts. They lived in the world's greatest literary cities, worked in senior capacities for leading monthlies and quarterlies in those cities, published in them, consorted with their owners and editors, and, at least in Carman's case, had more than passing influence on the intellectual development of the leading modernist poets of the new century (Ezra Pound, Robert Frost, and Wallace Stevens).[156] Nevertheless, those involvements were erased by the new generation of Canadian modernist critics, not because they were advancing modernism over an outdated Victorianism, but because they were promoting one group of Victorian poets (Ottawa's) over another (New Brunswick's). Collin's dismissal, then, becomes the start of a new narrative that equates the "cosmic consciousness" of the New Brunswick poets to "sympathy with trees and flowers"[157] and "the smell of the Canadian soil,"[158] thereby initiating a critical consensus that provincialism was the métier of the Fredericton poets. Leo Kennedy would echo the dismissal almost exactly when writing that "the domestic muse became paramour to a company of *poets hailing from the east coast provinces*, whose work was burdened with a prim Nordic consciousness and a second-hand Imperialism."[159]

A decade later, that view of New Brunswick writing was firmly entrenched. A.J.M. Smith's *Book of Canadian Poetry* (1943) had shifted the canon noticeably to exclude the New Brunswick poets, whose eulogy John Sutherland, the influential Canadian editor and one-time Saint John resident, delivered with cool detachment: "The firm of Roberts and Carman" can no longer maintain "that decayed faith, that shoddy and outworn morality, which blends in Canada with the colonial's desire to preserve the status quo."[160] Two influential critics (Collin and Brown) coupled with a new generation of poet-editors (Smith, Sutherland, and Kennedy) made straw men of the early Fredericton school, Smith famously writing in the introduction to the *Book of Canadian Poetry* that only the "isolated masters [of] Heavysege, Crawford, Cameron, Duncan Campbell Scott, and Lampman" approximated what poets offer to an understanding of the Canadian imagination.[161] Roberts and Carman were systematically demoted in the new narrative, made absent among a peer group that they had earlier mentored and, by all standards of their time, eclipsed.

The mid-century "literary" story of the nation being told by central Canadian writers and editors, then, followed the exact trajectory of the stories being circulated about the Maritime provinces. Not only had the centre shifted in those stories from the Maritimes to the Laurentian heartland, but the old cultural locus was being denigrated, its writers maligned, and their achievements belittled. So powerful and convincing was that narrative that even New Brunswick's literary critics, following their Toronto professors, fell in line, a young Desmond Pacey writing in 1950 that "the great mass of [Carman's] work lacks depth, originality, and distinction."[162] By mid-century, Maritime stagnation of thought and decadence of expression had been normalized, and Maritime intellectuals accepted the pronouncement as canonical truth and inheritance. The supplicant suitably mythologized, the best the region could hope for, mused David Alexander, was "a shabby dignity."[163]

That was the New Brunswick known to the mid-century Fiddlehead school, the New Brunswick that informed the urgency of their sense of cultural and narrative reform. As the oldest and most aristocratic member of the group (his ancestors were among the intellectual class at UNB), Alfred G. Bailey was especially impressionable, quickly coming to understand his role in not just literary and aesthetic terms but in federalist terms as well. His literary inheritance, education in socialism, and training in the material apparatus of heritage preservation would serve him well in undertaking the role of flashpoint for modernist energies at a rapidly expanding UNB. Not only would he challenge the new narratives of his region and its writers, but he would also precipitate a number of institutional, aesthetic, and intellectual measures to counter them. The final poem in his groundbreaking collection *Border River* (1952) gives a clear indication of his sense of the importance and enormity of the task before him (I quote it at length because of its relevance):

> Lest we revive the stormbound fortnights on the river reaches;
> the mud-flats at low water, hindering travel,
> waiting for the tide;
> the rocks at high that ram their whetted edges
> into the ribs and timbers, scattering
> sawdust among deceptive weeds;
> let us take inventory now that these days are upon us
> to pare the falsehood from our daily forecasts
> that acts of God may not disguise our blunders;
> that scribes may not write down our lack of skill
> the inevitable process of decayed nature:
> we should recognize these flats as the level of our ignorance;
> we should tamper with these weeds as we tamper with a tangled
>   theology;
> we must not wade at the flood nor swim at the dead end of the
>   ebb;
> we must not regard this reef
> as the impassable barrier of our most effete categories;
> and (to sum up) this mist
> spoken of formerly as the unquestionable Law
> we must know as the employed breath of professional
>   obscurantists
> keeping our bottoms forever impaled
> upon the shark-toothed rocks of disaster.[164]

The poem's final metaphor – "Guide to stormbound reaches of a tidal river" (61) – suggests that, just as tides rise and fall, so do fortunes and reputations, and so can they be reversed. The poem, then, signalled nothing less than a reformist call to arms to the region's cultural workers.

2

A.G. Bailey:
Bridging the Centuries

The long association of the d'Avray and Bailey families with the Roberts and Carman families is a factor in the literary tradition of Fredericton, and one of the influences on me, and on what I did here at this university [UNB].[1]

[Alfred Bailey] was the man who gave the University of New Brunswick its memory and made the place "a nest of singing birds." In his wake there are schools of poets, novelists, and magazines and publishers.[2]

In a remarkable early editorial, a young Alfred Goldsworthy Bailey, writing on the eve of his graduation from UNB, penned a short but rich statement of the critical principles that would guide his life. Published in the university's student monthly the *Brunswickan* in 1927, "Verse" is the closest that a normally guarded and privately political Bailey would come to enunciating a polemic. The editorial revealed his keen sense of cultural inheritance, his life-long grievance, and the means he would choose to resuscitate some of the pride of place that Confederation and subsequent nation-building policies had taken from his region.

We "should not only retain our present literary standard," he begins, referencing the efforts of the *Brunswickan*'s literary pages to buttress the return of the region's creative voice, "but should aspire to the excellence of our predecessors." Doing so, he insists, "is of the utmost importance. For we have a heritage to preserve; a heritage that, several years ago, sank to a low ebb, that left little to remind one

1   Alfred G. Bailey at UNB, c. mid-1980s.

of the glorious days when Carman and Roberts, as undergraduates, plied their pens for the pages of this magazine."[3] The observation would have remained provincial if left there – a young poet's histrionics merely serving the editorial needs of a student magazine – but its expansion into the realms of post-Confederation out-migration and strategic localism admits the statement to more serious consideration. "This Province," continues Bailey, anticipating the political narrative of New Brunswick for the next ninety years, "has produced great men, but few are here today. The culture of New Brunswick is in Toronto and Boston and New York. They are not here because the need of them is not felt and because there is no adequate field for their activities."[4] Positing that the reasons for this absence are both economic and educational, he concludes that it is the "educational deficiency" which is most acutely felt, that deficiency allowing a tawdry American culture to "flood this country" and "pervert [the] taste of the populace." The consequence is "too little pride in local achievement," he asserts, and the most serious fallout from that consequence is a perversion of value that assigns worth elsewhere, an action that contributes to the sense of cultural inferiority that all politically disenfranchised people experience. Using the example of Fredericton's statue of the Scottish poet Robert Burns, a poet "who never saw New Brunswick, and who was little in sympathy with the spirit of her people," Bailey wonders provocatively if "some local literary society [will] ... ever erect a monument to our own Bliss Carman?" While "the citizens of Toronto might do so," he avers, the chances of such a commemoration in Fredericton "seem very meagre."[5] New Brunswick readers are left to infer that their own sense of a past is rapidly diminishing, not merely from neglect but from competing narratives and a new culture of populist idolatry that concedes little to earlier glories and achievements. Nova Scotia's great son Joseph Howe observed the same change in socio-political sympathies two generations earlier, so it is not without coincidence that Bailey's editorial reaches into Howe's earlier work to express a New Brunswick version of an identifiable Maritime discontent.

I belabour the description of a young Bailey's polemic because of its revelations of future directions, both for the man and for the cultural corrective that he would prescribe. In that polemic is the sensibility of a late-generation New Brunswick Loyalist who in today's terms might be called hyphenated: certainly not American in the republican sense but neither unquestioningly British. Rather, in his early work, Bailey cultivates the persona of a post-revolutionary Loyalist, a sensibility that distrusts ethnicity without localism, that seeks to forge an independent identity across time and inheritance, and that sees clearly how unanchored allegiances lead to forms of colonization that erase history. As both a poet and historian, even a twenty-two-year-old Bailey could not abide any form of colonization, whether of sovereignty or narrative. The alternative was "pride in local achievement," an alternative that, in New Brunswick, meant returning to a time before Confederation had done its work. Only in that return, says Bailey in the last sentence of his editorial, could "aesthetic appreciation" be reborn. And it must be reborn, he stressed (with no concession to a future readership that would bristle against the terminology), "in the light of a purer eugenic ideal."[6]

To understand Bailey and what he would later bring to aesthetic and institutional renovation, one must turn to his ancestry and training, for it is in both that his sense of a living tradition and his own role in that tradition was first incubated.

HEREDITARY GENIUS AND "THE TRADITION"

Bailey lived and worked under expectations that came with being a member of the region's intellectual aristocracy. His family's fortunes had been won and lost, as had their influence in centres of political power, but what remained at Bailey's birth was the sense that his family was still consequential among the intellectual classes. The sense of civic duty that flowed from that encompassed both cultural and educational enterprise. To have inherited such a disposition while coming of age in a place where the turn from plenitude to supplication was the dominant narrative – though born in Quebec in 1905, he had an intimate knowledge of New Brunswick, living there until age nine and choosing UNB for his undergraduate education – meant that Bailey's life was certainly predisposed to cultural work from the start.

That sense of vocational inheritance becomes evident in the early pages of Bailey's memoirs when he places himself in a line going back to early colonial America. He thus begins with the Puritan preacher Peter Bulkeley, founder of Concord in the Massachusetts Bay Colony, who, along with Simon Bradstreet, Thomas Hincley, Joseph Dudley, and William Stoughton, were men of high intellectual and spiritual repute in the colonies.[7] Arriving in New England in 1635, Bulkeley became renowned both for his Puritan intransigence – he famously chastised Anne Hutchinson for being a Jezebel[8] – and for his poetry, which Cotton Mather praised as "competently good."[9] Clearly significant for Bailey, Bulkeley was an important scholar who enjoyed "[a] large place in Puritan literature ... in his lifetime and long afterward,"[10] a literary status that his most famous descendant, Ralph Waldo Emerson, turned into family narrative.[11] A.G. Bailey does not miss this connection, writing many years later that "the intellectual interests of the Emersons and Baileys are clearly traceable to [Bulkeley]," whose descendants included the "Baileys of the University of New Brunswick" as well as "Phoebe Bliss, who was, in turn, sister of Daniel Bliss, forebear of Bliss Carman and Sir Charles G.D. Roberts. These families, Baileys and Bliss's, so early connected, were to meet again and mingle in ways that had, in the fulness [sic] of time, a significance for the development of a Fredericton literary tradition."[12]

Especially germane to A.G. Bailey's sense of familial inheritance is the mention of his paternal grandfather's grandfather, the lawyer and editor Isaac Bailey, who, as an undergraduate at Brown University in Providence, Rhode Island, in 1812, wrote "a poem in which he prophesied that the genius of English literature ... would be reborn in America, a prophecy that was ... to be fulfilled ... as the *flowering* of New England."[13] "Flowering" would become a key word in A.G. Bailey's lexicon, prompting him to devote much of his undergraduate and graduate education to thinking about the socio-economic conditions under which cultural flowering and literary effervescence took shape. "Creative genius is a sociocultural product," he would later tell interviewer Travis Lane, as the fusion of ideas "occurs as a clustering in the population."[14] As Bailey would soon interpret it from anthropologists A.L. Kroeber and Gustav Spiller, that clustering must include a collision of artists and intellectuals, with each building on the other's ideas, if a society was to develop beyond a nascent parochialism "to great heights."[15] The genesis of that idea, too, had found its way to Bailey via a New England tradition, this one centred at Harvard in the teaching of Irving K. Babbitt, author of, among many other works, *Literature and the American College* (1908) and teacher of T.S. Eliot. (Bailey's later work would draw heavily on each.) Setting Babbitt's "new humanism" against John Dewey's "pragmatism," the two dominant approaches to late-nineteenth-century American education, critic Gail MacDonald attributes the former to the rise of a humanist tradition in early modernism that deliberately twinned artist and educator. Specifically, writes MacDonald, "education (or literature) should train citizen-leaders, set moral standards, derive those standards from a commonly accepted body of texts, inculcate respect for received wisdom and traditional values, identify an elite, and be valued for its own sake. Above all, the valorization of language defines the oratorical tradition, and this central value is strongest in its links to literary modernism."[16] ⓥ. *Conservative!*

For Bailey, that essential mix of the intellectual and artistic was a key feature of his ancestry and key to understanding the social history of creative effervescence, above called "flowering," in emergent cultures. It is no coincidence, then, that Bailey reserves highest praise for those in his New England ancestral line who model the characteristics of the artist-teacher. The first was great-grandfather Jacob Whitman Bailey (1811–57), the inaugural professor of chemistry at the United States Military Academy in West Point (1834), who was also a poet and translator of German literature. Rising to international notice in the cognate fields of microbiology and mineralogy, Jacob Bailey so impressed his colleagues that the famous German naturalist Christian Gottfried Ehrenberg named a diatom (*Stauronema Bayleyi*) in his honour.[17] He would later be elected president of the American Association for the Advancement of Science, a body that would circulate his poetry as a memorial at his death. Jacob's son and granddaughter – William Whitman Bailey (1843–1914) and Margaret Emerson Bailey (1885–1949) – were similarly endowed with professional and artistic aptitudes, the former a professor of botany at Brown University who published two collections of poems and odes, and the latter a popular novelist, teacher, and civic leader in Connecticut who knew poets Edwin Arlington Robinson and Elinor Wylie and who took a twenty-four-year-old A.G. Bailey to visit Mary Perry King, Bliss Carman's benefactor.

The most important of the ancestral figures that A.G. Bailey highlights, however, is grandfather Loring Woart Bailey (1839–1925), who came to Fredericton in 1861 on the recommendation of his Harvard chemistry professor Josiah Parsons Cooke. Loring stayed for a forty-six-year career in New Brunswick, doing pioneering work in zoology, botany, geology, mineralogy, and surveying.[18] According to his grandson, he studied under Asa Gray, Henry Wadsworth Longfellow, and Louis Agassiz at Harvard. Agassiz was the most influential, a Swiss naturalist who the American modernist poet Ezra Pound immortalized as a champion of close observation and clear expression.[19] Agassiz's methods of exposition were a model for Pound's poetics, for Loring Bailey's annotated typologies of natural science, and eventually for A.G. Bailey's method of ethnohistory. Most significant for the younger Bailey, however, was not that his grandfather had been tutored by one of literary modernism's pioneering stylists, or that his grandfather counted George Parkin as one of his students – Parkin was the renowned teacher of Roberts, Carman, and Francis Sherman, and first secretary of the Rhodes Trust – but that his grandfather held weekly meetings in his home where students, faculty, and prominent citizens (including Charles G.D. Roberts's father) discussed science and literature, thus putting into action the idea that society is best served when both these branches of knowledge occupy the minds of intellectual workers.[20]

That A.G. Bailey's other paternal line was equally illustrious in combining the artistic and intellectual merely reinforces the point about vocational inheritance. His great-grandfather, Joseph d'Avray (1811–71),[21] was educated at the French royal court, was a close friend and former teacher of Parkin and George Roberts (Charles G.D.'s father), and was founder of New Brunswick's first provincial normal

school, a man, said A.G. Bailey, who "as newspaper editor, chief super-
intendent of education, and professor of modern languages at [UNB]
... gave an impetus to scholarship that bore fruit in the creative
achievements of the poets."[22] "So my great-grandfather," deduced Bailey, "was a sort of grandfather of the Fredericton School of Poets."[23] To
the younger Bailey it must have seemed fated that Loring Woart
would marry Joseph d'Avray's daughter in 1863, thus bringing together in Fredericton two families whose paths had intersected elsewhere
for many generations. That strengthening of artist-scholar sensibilities, Bailey speculated, "provided the intellectual preparation without
which the poetry could not have been written."[24] In placing so much
emphasis on creativity, whether as a social, historical, or genetic phenomenon, and whether in the practice of artists, scientists, or teachers,
Bailey was moving toward the belief that only in advancing the creative, however widely defined, could the individual find an ethical
centre. The belief is later articulated in Bailey's poem "Colour Chart,"
which displays the high-modernist elliptical style for which Bailey
became known:

> The gold that guilds the goldenrod's petals
> raises man's sense of worth to a higher power
> than he is able to glean from other metals,
> gleam as they may steadfastly from hour to hour.
>
> Each colour is an act, blue is an act of grace.
> Red is a shiver as felt in a fever.
> Gold remains the glory of the face
> of earth, but green is the giver.[25]

As a boy growing into maturity first in Fredericton and then in
Quebec City and the village of Tadoussac on the lower St Lawrence
River, where his family summered, Bailey was well versed in the family legacy and preparing himself to fulfill his obligation to it, whether
as scientist, artist, or teacher. His father, Loring Woart Bailey, Jr
(1868–1943), who had been born in UNB's Old Arts Building, had
been taught by Carman, gone to Parkin's Collegiate School, and
delighted in reciting the poems of his close friend Theodore
Goodridge Roberts, younger brother of Charles. A banker by day who
aspired to be a published novelist,[26] he saw to it that all his children
were schooled in what he thought of as the family business, insisting

that they make frequent visits to the homes of their extended Fredericton family members, many of whom were leading figures at the university. (A.G. Bailey attended Charlotte Street School in Fredericton
for his primary schooling before moving to Quebec City to finish his
education.) Significant for Bailey's later development was not only
that his father knew and quoted the Roberts brothers and Carman,
but that he spoke reverently about UNB's mission and its professors.
English professor William F.P. Stockley was his favourite. Stockley was
a senator of the Irish Free State and a close friend of activist Douglas
Hyde, who founded the Gaelic League and who was credited, with
W.B. Yeats and John M. Synge, for spearheading the Irish literary
renaissance. Stockley reintroduced that activism to a New Brunswick
that had grown weary, observed Lorne Pierce, thus becoming an
essential figure for Francis Sherman and the other Fredericton poets.[27]
For Loring Woart Bailey, Jr, Stockley was the person whose example
his children would follow, for he taught that culture was what surrounded a person, not what was elsewhere.[28] His second son, A.G.
Bailey, learned the lesson well, noting later that

> friendships were very close in the small world of Fredericton. The
> children and grandchildren of Jonathan Odell, the Loyalist poet
> of the American Revolutionary War [and New Brunswick's first
> provincial secretary], were intimate friends of the Roberts,
> d'Avrays, Baileys and Carmans. The circle included James Hogg,
> the first to publish a book of poems on a local press, and Julia
> Catherine Beckwith Hart, the first native-born Canadian novelist.
> The posthumous volume of poems (1854) of Peter John Allen,
> neighbour and friend, contains a graceful tribute to my [paternal]
> grandmother, Laurestine [Mary d'Avray] ... [who] assisted at the
> birth of Bliss Carman.[29]

Family discussions of the Confederation poets and the history of
cultural achievement in New Brunswick were thus normal in the Bailey household, as was the more specific recognition of Fredericton's
long-standing centrality in affairs of the region. The Baileys were especially fond of citing W.G. MacFarlane's observation in that regard,
namely, that "each of the three nations who were settled [around Fred-
ericton] governed from there. Aucpaque [a Malecite nexus] was the
chief village of the Indians on the St. John. Fort Nashwaak was for a
time the capital of all Acadia, and now the celestial city is the seat of

government of New Brunswick."[30] The younger generation of Baileys took pride in the fact that Fredericton was the historical crossroads of vibrant traditions, and thus a locus every bit as accommodating to cultural achievement as Providence and Boston had been for their Brown and Harvard University ancestors.

A.G. Bailey's formal education at the High School of Quebec (earlier called the Royal Grammar School[31]) abetted that impression, its classrooms adorned with evidence of a still expanding empire. "In one of [those] classrooms," wrote Sandra Djwa in her biography of Bailey contemporary F.R. Scott, "was a large mercator map of the world showing all of the British possessions in bright red. 'The empire is my country, Canada is my home,' read the motto."[32] There, following a private school curriculum in which forms and masters (not grades and teachers) were the norm, Bailey read Shelley, Keats, Coleridge, Tennyson, Browning, and others from *Poems of the Romantic Revival* (1904), adding breadth to his literary knowledge of Roberts, Carman, and the earlier Fredericton poets. As importantly, he also read broadly in the area of colonial adventure, sampling Kipling and the work of Frederick Gustavus Burnaby, whose *A Ride to Khiva* (1876) stoked his interest in Asia and geopolitical affairs. The experience of that early education in one of the country's oldest English private schools affirmed the young Bailey's sense of an imperial citizenship that his upbringing in the English garrison of his mother's Quebec City instilled. "The house in which I was born," wrote Bailey in tribute to his mother, Ernestine Valiant Gale Bailey, "was built by my maternal grandfather's grandfather, Richard Goldsworthy, a builder and master of fortification, who came from Redruth in Cornwall to oversee the reconstruction of the walls of the citadel and city."[33] Four generations later, little had changed: "The front of [my] school faced ... the slope to the military fortifications of the citadel, and you could see the Union Jack," Bailey recalled. "There was no sense of a Canadian nationality in Quebec in those days ... We were British subjects with residence in Canada. In 1926 when I went abroad with my uncle I had a British passport."[34] His descent from New England Loyalists complemented that tradition, impressing on a young Bailey both a depth and a consistency of literary purpose. Bailey, after all, not only traced the tradition through family but could also source it "in the genius of English literature" that "would be reborn in America ... as the flowering of New England."[35] Neither the New England nor British side of that tradition equivocated about what was expected of young men of pedigree, a fact that gave Bailey an early sense of elite purpose and later disappointment with "Quebec's draconian language law[s]" that were blunting the "long-resident English-speaking families" of his beloved Quebec.[36] Such feeling for place was foremost in Bailey's mind when he told Robert Finch about the long and distinguished history of British gentry in Quebec society.[37]

It is not surprising, then, that, at seventeen, and with his headmaster's encouragement,[38] Bailey would become editor-in-chief of the *High School of Quebec Magazine* (1922–23), that role asserting an interest in cultural stewardship that his patrimony and earlier writing of poetry had anticipated (his first poems had been published in the above magazine in 1922). Interest in cultural leadership would develop further when, just published in the *Canadian Magazine*, he arrived at UNB in September 1923 as an undergraduate, initially struck by the refinements around him. Unlike other parts of the Maritimes, where "the short boom associated with the end of the First World War [had come] to an abrupt end," raising labour tensions to full boil,[39] Fredericton seemed relatively calm. In his early days there, living amidst the rich cultural heritage in his grandfather's house, where signed books by Parkin, Roberts, and Carman lined the shelves, he realized that Fredericton, too, had suffered – not industrially or materially, as other places had, but aesthetically. The "[Fredericton] literary tradition," he concluded, "had sunk to a low ebb," an especially troubling development because Fredericton, like Halifax, had been so central to its province's cultural health. In answer, he "dreamed of founding a magazine that would be the instrument of [a] revival." "I would call it," he proclaimed, "*The Fiddlehead* or *The Water Lily*."[40] Because production costs were prohibitive and mimeograph technology not yet available, however, Bailey had to begin with establishing the "Poets' Corner" in the *Brunswickan* in 1925. And, though the *Brunswickan* was then only a monthly magazine, Bailey's decision to start his cultural project there proved to be fortuitous, for he often laboured in isolation as literary editor while dreaming of better ways to cultivate an audience for New Brunswick literature. Hearing Charles G.D. Roberts read in Fredericton from the yet-to-be-published *The Vagrant of Time* (1927) finally spurred Bailey to action. Roberts's renown, coupled with the frustrations of finding literary material for the Poets' Corner, led him to bring together a small group that met weekly to discuss poetry. Comprised of contributors to his literary section of the *Brunswickan*, core members of "The Nooners" included George W. Mersereau, Dou-

2 *Brunswickan* staff at UNB, 1927. A.G. Bailey is in back row, standing, second from the left. Other members of Bailey's Nooners group in the photo are Dorothea Cox, back row, fifth from left, and George Mersereau, seated, third from left. Bailey's close friend Burton Keirstead is seated, second from left.

glas Sheldrick, Dorothea Cox, and Dorothy Gostwick Roberts, daughter of Theodore Goodridge Roberts.[41] Central to group discussions was the troubling decline in Fredericton's literary status, a decline made especially embarrassing by the legacy of past luminaries such as Odell, Beckwith Hart, and the Confederation poets. Bailey's editorial in the 1927 graduation issue of the magazine served to illuminate the group's dismay, though he later admitted that his intention in penning "Verse" was to be "deliberately pessimistic about the prospects of a Fredericton poetry revival, with a view to goading my successors into cherishing the tradition of Carman, and continuing that tradition in the present, but not with the idea of slavish imitation."[42]

Deciding to proceed by example, Bailey collected the poems he had written in high school and university and published them in a collection called *Songs of the Saguenay and Other Poems* (1927). No casual exercise of the ego, the effort was widely supported by the province of Quebec, which bought 500 copies for school libraries; by Canada Steamships

Lines, which sold copies on its steamers and at its hotels on the St Lawrence and Saguenay rivers; and by Quebec City's Château Frontenac Hotel, which sold copies at its newsstand.[43] It was also favourably reviewed in major periodicals, their appearance slightly predating the reviews that would aim vitriol at similar, late Victorian voices in Canada. The collection is significant not only for showing the emergence of a focused editorial intention – the desire to put work before a public in order to fill and address an aesthetic vacuum – but also for displaying a poetic style (though not a sensibility) from which the author would distance himself almost immediately. Remarkable in that regard is the fact that Bailey would republish none of his *Songs of the Saguenay* poems in *Miramichi Lightning* (1981), his authorized collected poems. Nevertheless, the early volume remains important for what it reveals about Bailey's sympathies to the previous century's Fredericton poets. Those sympathies are evident in the imagery and tone of each of the early poems. In "Ile Aux Morts," for instance, the gothic and pre-Raphaelite traditions, so evident in the poetry of Francis Sherman, are strongly present:

> One night upon this lonely isle,
> When all was dark and still;
> I lay in the lee of the lighthouse top
> And quaked with fear and chill.
>
> As I sat in the cold and shivered
> And listened with awful dread,
> I heard sepulchral voices calling
> And the wails of the walking dead.[44]

Likewise, Bliss Carman's lyrical cadences echo in many of Bailey's love poems, including "Micheline on the Saguenay" – "There was a smile you gave me / That was native to the land / Of wide and tossing oceans / And silver sifted sand" (9) – and "Solacia," first published in the *Brunswickan* in November 1925:

> But then the mist grew golden kissed
> And sped those dark alarms;
> Then Love with eyes as blue as skies
> Revealed her virgin charms;
> And ere I heard her raptured word
> I held her in my arms.[45]

Though it is understandable that one of Canada's most technically daring high modernists would choose to distance himself from this kind of apprenticeship work, these early poems establish an important affinity with what Bailey would later think of as an organic and still relevant "tradition." And it is precisely that preoccupation with "tradition" – specifically his embrace and refinement of a theoretical apparatus that would legitimize his sympathies with an earlier generation of New Brunswick poets – that characterizes his post-*Saguenay* development. The clue to that development is contained in his wish, quoted above, to continue a Carmanesque "tradition in the present, but *not with the idea of slavish imitation.*"[46] Separating tradition from imitation is a key qualification for Bailey, suggesting much about how he interpreted his social role as poet and intellectual, and what he did with the legacy he inherited. To make sense of the qualification, one must consider the disciplinary switch he made from English literature to history at the University of Toronto, as well as his discovery of T.S. Eliot's work, both of which were coincident with the start of his doctoral studies in Toronto in 1930.[47]

His disciplinary decisions reflected a liberalizing in his thinking rather than the usual graduate-school tendency toward compression and specialization. Even as an undergraduate at UNB, Bailey felt the need to move beyond the boundaries of his preferred subject – what he later termed "the evils of departmentalization"[48] – to equip himself to answer larger questions of history and sociology. While at UNB in 1926, for example, he and fellow student Burton Keirstead had petitioned the university's president, C.C. Jones, to revive the single elective course in modern history as part of the English Department's curriculum. Jones agreed and enlisted professor Leo Harvey to add the course to his English offerings. "Local aspects of imperial history were not neglected," reported Bailey, "and on one memorable occasion the professor took his class up some shaky ladders to the top of the dome of the Old Arts Building for a lecture on the Battle of the Nashwaak of 1696, the site of which, across the river St. John, was spread below us like a map."[49] Fascinated, as his ancestors were, by these macroeconomic processes of social and institutional evolution, Bailey gravitated toward graduate courses with the widest application, increasingly convinced of the truth of historian Arnold Toynbee's contention that "modern nations are not in themselves intelligible fields of study, but must be considered in the larger context of the civilization to which they belong."[50]

An early guide in focusing that interest was James J. Talman, a class-mate of Bailey's during his first year of MA study in Toronto. Talman's work examined the social development of Upper Canada, paralleling the approach that Bailey recognized from Wilfred Currier Keirstead's classes in sociology at UNB.[51] That such study was possible at the grad-uate level excited Bailey and filled his head with research possibilities, not the least of which touched his personal narrative: "To have lived during one's most impressionable years [in Tadoussac] in the visible presence of history had effects that would have been difficult to erad-icate had one attempted to do so. The windows of our country home looked down on the place where the Huguenot fur trader, Pierre Chauvin, in 1600 built the first house in Canada."[52] Bailey could also have added, and must have been thinking, that Tadoussac's colonial history included Jacques Cartier's first voyage of 1535, François Gravé Du Pont's first settlement in 1600, and Samuel de Champlain's first visit in 1603. The importance of that history, and of Tadoussac's strate-gic location at the confluence of the St Lawrence and Saguenay rivers, would become evident in every volume of creative writing and schol-arship that Bailey later produced.

It seems logical, then, that he would petition Professor Ralph Flen-ley to allow him to take a special course in the history of New France as an anchor for his MA work, and that he would eventually move from there, as a doctoral student, to what his University of Toronto professor Chester Martin[53] termed "historical sociology."[54] In typical Bailey fashion, intellectual and familial interests intersected, in this case bringing him increasingly to the study of history. He makes that trajectory clear in the essay "Retrospective Thoughts of an Ethnohis-torian," repeating his own experience of growing up amidst the ruins of New France (that repetition an important clue to the value he places on using the local as raw material for one's life work):

Champlain's monument on the Dufferin Terrace was a few hun-dred yards from the house in which I was born. As a boy I had often climbed the cliff that Wolfe had climbed, and our school's playing field was on the Cove Fields between the Citadel and the abandoned earthworks that had been thrown up for the defence against the besiegers, Richard Montgomery and Benedict Arnold, in 1775. I was aware not only of the great men and deeds of the French regime, but also of that period when Quebec, half English in population, was the largest builder of wooden ships in British

North America, an industry in which earlier generations of my mother's family had been involved. Our country house in Tadoussac stood opposite the Point des Alouettes, the long partly wooded point of sand and gravel on which Champlain had in 1603 made a pact with the Montagnais to aid them in their war with the Iroquois, an event which has been recognized as a turning point in the history of our country.[55]

With Martin, Harold Adams Innis, and the Royal Ontario Museum's T.F. McIlwraith,[56] "the leading professor of anthropology in Canada at the time" and the only one giving degree-credit courses,[57] Bailey "ended up with a kind of interdisciplinary tripos, unique then or since, comprising history, anthropology, and economics."[58] The intent, he told History Department chair George Smith, was to locate "the creative act ... that had raised man above low-grade culture"[59] to the various "flowering[s]" of civilization that his great-great-grandfather had spoken of at Brown University in 1812. Harold Innis, whose *Fur Trade in Canada* (1930) had come out at exactly the time Bailey began his doctoral work, modelled the critical methodology of using archival sources, travelogues, correspondence, missionary records, and commercial reports to reconstruct time, place, and causation, thus moving from the old practice of conjecture among learned gentlemen to a more robust evidence-based inquiry. The result was a PhD dissertation that Bailey titled "The Conflict of European and Eastern Algonkian Cultures, 1504–1700: A Study in Canadian Civilization" (1934), which later was published as a book of the same name by the New Brunswick Museum (1937) and reissued by the University of Toronto Press (1969). In keeping with Bailey's larger socio-historical ambitions, it examined the effects of first contact between Eastern Algonkian cultures and Europeans in the sixteenth and seventeenth centuries with a mind to understanding reciprocal exchange and devolution created by contact in New France. The scope, methodology, and subject matter of Bailey's project went against the prevailing co-adaptive theories of Bronisław Malinowski and Alfred Radcliffe-Brown, positing instead a new practice of ethnomethodology that examined how culture was constructed through everyday speech and material contexts. The pioneering approach contributed to the development of media ecology in Canada, a field later dominated by Marshall McLuhan and his intellectual heir Neil Postman at New York University.[60] Bailey's methodological advances also anticipated by more than two generations the work of John Ralston Saul and historical geographers like Cole Harris, who have sought to correct Canadian historical accounts by re-examining early records of first contact, in both instances concluding that influence moved in two directions.[61]

While engaged in this work of historical sociology, Bailey's encounters with proponents of American and European modernism – whether Professor Pelham Edgar's first wife drawing attention to the work of Henri Gaudier-Brzeska or Earle Birney introducing Jean Cocteau and the Dadaists via *The European Caravan* (1931) – caused him to start questioning his own creative writing. He began to feel that he "was out of touch with contemporary thought"[62] and "about 50 years behind the times,"[63] feelings reinforced by the reception of his second book of verse, *Tâo* (1930). Published by Lorne Pierce[64] in the Ryerson Poetry Chapbook series, *Tâo* displays the same, but matured, Romantic inclinations as *Songs of the Saguenay*, its verse influenced more directly by the work of Francis Sherman than of Carman, though Carman's lyricism and rhythms are present in many of the poems. "Love" is a representative example, its cadences Carman's but its colours and images those of Sherman, William Morris, and the early pre-Raphaelites: "OH, FEVER-RED is the moon tonight, / And the hills are a pallid brown; / But I am wreathed in a golden mist / And held in the arms of the stars light kissed / Where the hair on their heads hangs down."[65] Though the metrics are traditional, there is lightness in the movement of the poem that suggests, as it did in Carman's work, a yearning for a freer verse. Both that yearning and a desire to move beyond outmoded musical forms toward more suggestive visual imagery would preoccupy Bailey for the next decade. His more definably modernist poems of 1932–34 – "Best Seller," "Hochelaga," and "Rapproachment," all published in the *Canadian Forum* – would show almost no resemblance to the poems of *Tâo*, which mark the end of the period of Bailey's pre-Raphaelite aesthetic. *Tâo* was not widely reviewed, but the reviews that did appear were mixed, perhaps owing to Bailey's own ambivalence about the collection. Reviews by Margaret E. Lawrence in the *Times Globe* (Saint John, New Brunswick) and Augustus Bridle in the Toronto *Star Weekly* were favourable, though one by Edgar McInnis in *Saturday Night* was especially stinging. In that omnibus review, McInnis chastises Bailey and four other poets for "not [providing] enough real achievement to arouse any genuine enthusiasm." "It is very disappointing," McInnis says, to find "these volumes rather lacking in significance,"[66] a fact he attributes to the poets having nothing new to say. Bailey understood the message: poetic distinction is lacking because none of the poets have a distinct or definable individuality. Because McInnis was the type of poet-scholar whom Bailey admired (as a Rhodes scholar, he had won the Newdigate Prize at Oxford in 1925), Bailey took the advice and immediately set to work to follow it.

Hearing the American poet H.D. speak in Toronto in early 1931 helped that development, Bailey concluding that an accelerated reading program in modern poetry and thought was necessary. He returned to Edgar Lee Masters's *Spoon River Anthology* that Theodore Goodridge Roberts had lent him as an undergraduate at UNB (the book would later become important to Fred Cogswell). He also returned to the modern poems he had first encountered rather indifferently in E.J. Pratt's modern poetry seminar and in the pages of Harriet Monroe's *Poetry* a few years earlier. Remembering Pratt's reading of Arturo Giovannitti's "The Walker," one of the earliest socialist poems of the twentieth century, brought Bailey "closer to a new way of looking at things," the inference being that the problems of the present were as vital a subject for poetic treatment as were the "perfumed" memories of the past.[67] Temporary employment as a reporter with the Toronto *Mail and Empire* also reinforced his sense of the immediacies of the present, especially as those were mediated by the hard edges of urban poverty, crime, political indifference, and police brutality.[68] Bailey discovered how those themes could be handled in poetry by reading Robert Finch and A.M. Klein in the pages of the *Canadian Forum*[69] – and learned, also, as a newspaperman, how to write with more concision and objectivity.[70]

At roughly the same time, Bailey joined E.K. Brown and others in Toronto's "Nameless Society," a literary club of student poets and socialists (including Dorothy Livesay, Henry Noyes, and Stanley Ryerson) that met weekly at University College to discuss Canadian literature. One member would deliver a paper at each meeting that was then subjected to the uncompromising critique of Brown. Another member of the group would write up the minutes in verse form. At one meeting Bailey delivered a paper on Carman's musicality, praising "Low Tide on Grand Pré" for achieving "lyrical heights never reached by [Archibald] Lampman or [Duncan Campbell] Scott," but Brown soundly rejected the view, showing what Bailey would later describe as his "central Canadian bias" for the Ottawa school of Confederation poetry.[71] Bailey would also recall to Malcolm Ross that, despite Brown's misgivings, "we still loved ... Carman's poetry, although could no longer attempt to write, ourselves, in that way."[72]

After one of those sessions, Roy Daniells, a graduate-school class-mate, visited Bailey to share his recent (1931[73]) discovery of T.S. Eliot, reading "The Hollow Men," "The Love Song of J. Alfred Prufrock," and *The Waste Land*. For Bailey, the moment was transformative:

> I experienced the greatest excitement such as I had never experi-enced before and never have since experienced. All sorts of inchoate and previously ill-defined feelings and experiences sud-denly came into focus. One felt transfigured, and one can only think that the old symbols and intonations and meanings had become completely dead, that a great spiritual void had been cre-ated by a sense of the bankruptcy of the 19th century beliefs and standards, that the economic system under which we lived was in a state of disintegration, that the great urban wilderness of the modern world marked the sterility and death of our society. Eliot supplied the catharsis. He had pronounced an epitaph on the past. We felt that there was nothing more to be said.[74]

With Eliot as his aesthetic muse, Bailey was able to reinterpret the modern world and make sense of the work of Klein, Finch, Pratt, and Giovannitti that he had earlier encountered. He was also able to advance more daringly among contemporary poets and critics, read-ing W.H. Auden, Edna St Vincent Millay, William Empson, T.E. Hulme, Cecil Day-Lewis, and F.R. Leavis with new purpose. As arresting and final as Eliot's pronouncements were, however, they were not inter-preted by Bailey as a cul-de-sac. Rather, they were seen as evidence of the necessity of renewal: as an epochal sea change (Bailey called it "transmogrification") through which it was "necessary to pass," "incor-porate effects," and then "transcend."[75] Key to the process was tran-scendence, for the act of transcendence turned the ennui that some readers took from Eliot – that Prufrock-like sense of post-war inertia and despair[76] – into something productive. As Bailey told Roy Dan-iells, transcendence involved the conscious process of "pioneer[ing] without growing hard," thus reinterpreting the past through the new lens of the present.[77] Bailey went even further, suggesting in the same letter a practical poetics for the times: "Since we are confronted with 'problems,' isn't it the most important thing that we should take inventory? Yet nobody does. The economists are too busy with economics, the literati with verbs. I am all in favour of immediate implementation of an ethic." Robert Gibbs observed exactly that ethic in Bailey's practical poetics, poetics that created the conditions for "that late nineteenth-century local ferment [which Bailey] was trying to revive" in New Brunswick.[78]

If the work of Jean Cocteau, William Empson, and Virginia Woolf reflected the new realities of disintegration and ambiguity, it was Eliot's "Tradition and the Individual Talent" that provided the way forward that Bailey sensed but could not chart alone. Eliot's essay not only furthered Bailey's understanding of how the past could be made generative in the present – by, not ironically, turning from writing poetry to "an analysis of our disintegration"[79] – but it also became the theoretical means through which he twinned the demands of vocational inheritance with the needs of a provincial culture that had indeed sunk to a low ebb.

Published in 1919, four years after "Prufrock" appeared in *Poetry* (Chicago), Eliot's seminal essay anticipated what he would later call his "struggle against Liberalism." The heart of his argument was that "the struggle of our time is to concentrate, not to dissipate; to renew our association with traditional wisdom: to re-establish a vital connection between the individual and the race. It is, in a word, a struggle against Liberalism."[80] By "Liberalism" Eliot meant that which, in being reformist, claimed to be unique and terminally present. It was the assumption of Alfred Weber,[81] contra Gustav Spiller, that the work of art was the sole and unpredictable result of a mighty ego divorced from its larger contexts – and that ego's insistence that the allowances of the present trumped the past, turning it to crude anachronism. It was also the Lewis Morgan assertion of an evolutionary belief in history that considered the present as the sum of the past's fulfillments (Morgan, an early anthropologist, believed that history revealed the shift from barbarism to civilization[82]). In "Tradition and the Individual Talent," Eliot sought to correct those atemporal, Liberal views (today recognized as libertarian or neo-liberal) by identifying a "tradition," that aspect of the past that was always available to artists, no matter the eras in which they lived. Qualifying that that tradition "cannot be inherited," he said that it is obtained "by a great labour" which yearns to know both "the pastness of the past, [and] its presence."[83] This sense of a living history, he continues, "compels a man to write not merely with his own generation in his bones, but with a feeling that the whole of the literature of Europe from Homer and within it the whole of the literature of his own country has a simultaneous existence and composes a simultaneous order."[84]

The appeal to Bailey was immediate. What was especially germane was what we might think of today as Eliot's historical ecology: the idea that the historical record is not static, merely subject to what is added to and subtracted from it, but organic, the addition of any new element changing every other element by degree. New Brunswick culture after the Confederation poets was thus not just the old culture plus a handful of new poets, but an entirely different culture, which, of course, as Bailey knew, it was. As Eliot describes it, "the existing monuments form an ideal order among themselves, which is *modified* by the introduction of the new (the really new) work of art among them."[85] That "the past should be altered by the present as much as the present is dictated by the past"[86] was, for Bailey, an extremely powerful and useful idea. Not only did it encompass and make relevant all of his own disciplinary instincts and vocational dispositions – primary among them the belief that "man was only fully so as he entered as completely as possible into the cultural heritage of the race"[87] – but it also enabled him to believe that the local ferment he wished to recreate in the New Brunswick present could actually *change* the narratives of supplication and backwardness that post-Confederation mythmaking had assigned to his region. Fred Cogswell, one of Bailey's most attentive students, remembered that notion of renovation – of "reconcil[ing] the contrarieties of change and the persistence of tradition"[88] – as being central to Bailey's embrace of Eliot. As Eliot stressed and Bailey's own ancestral line of cultural workers confirmed, the key to social change was not to be found in the cultivation of one strong ego or artist, as Weber contended, nor, for that matter, in "extend[ing]" the literary ethos of the Confederation poets,[89] but rather in creating the conditions for the clustering of genius so that society might again rise to that flowering that his great-great grandfather had predicted. Integral in Bailey's reading and application of Eliot, then, was the "continual surrender of himself [the artist] ... to something which is more valuable,"[90] a suggestion that Bailey adopts as doctrine, pursuing, in private, the refinement of his poetic craft, and doing, in public, all he can to cultivate the ground for a critical mass of creative and intellectual talent. Bailey would therefore follow Eliot's dicta almost exactly in negating the "personality" of the poet for the "medium" of the poet's larger localism, that medium (a thing in itself discernible in history) extending back to Roberts and Carman, Emerson, Odell, Peter Bulkeley, and each member of the literary tribe since the time of Homer. New Brunswick was only on the margins, then, if its history and culture were silenced, a condition that Bailey felt qualified to address.

If Eliot's essay provided the enabling social theory, weekly lunches with Roy Daniells, Robert Finch, and Earle Birney (the "Diet Kitchen Group," so named after the restaurant on Toronto's Bloor Street where they met) provided the occasion for modernist poetic practice and, because of Birney, a marked shift in Bailey's politics, both important for what he would soon bring to New Brunswick. "These meetings, exercises and criticisms," recalled Bailey, who thought of them in the larger context of his "Nooner" and "Nameless Society" experiences, "were among the most valuable I ever took part in ... [for] following Eliot's dictum favouring constant practice so that our technique would be ready, like a well-oiled fire engine, when the moment of inspiration came."[91] Bailey admitted, too, that "these meetings gave me the idea ... for the Bliss Carman Society which I was to form in 1940 and which was to publish *The Fiddlehead* in 1945 and after."[92] In retrospect, though, it is clear that the Diet Kitchen sessions were most valuable in giving Bailey the political tools to mount his own kind of literary revolution. Though never a Marxist per se, Bailey moved to the left during this period in Toronto, persuaded by the measured arguments of the Fabians. Birney had much to do with that shift, even if he was more radical, proclaiming the merits of his beloved Left Opposition, a Trotskyite group that sought to implement revolutionary socialism in Canada and around the world. Birney's enthusiasms were not lost on Bailey, who, sympathetic to Eliot's and his own family's royalism, also had first-hand experience of the suffering of the masses (living in tarpaper shacks at the city dump) during his time as a reporter with the *Mail and Empire*. He also had watched the communist demonstrations in Queen's Park close to campus. Curious about those protests and Birney's pronouncements, Bailey attended the first organizational meeting of the League for Social Reconstruction in Toronto, then later in London gave a talk at King's Cross to Left Opposition members about "whether there had ever been a 'stage' of primitive communism in human history ... a view which had been taken up by Engels in his work 'The Origin of the Family.'"[93] The sum of those experiences opened Bailey's mind to the need for political as well as cultural reform, as did his subsequent associations with

J.S. Woodsworth and F.H. Underhill. As Anthony Pugh correctly suggests, Bailey's Toronto and London experiences must also have prompted him to question aspects of the bourgeois ideology held by "the intellectual elite of New England" from which he had come.[94] Bailey himself admits that the Marxist influences of Toronto and London could not be undone when he arrived back in New Brunswick.[95] Those influences, along with his memories of being in Harold Laski's class, furthered his confidence that change could as easily result from collectivist movements as from autocratic structures. Bailey remained, however, a social historian, his interest in impact zones of first contact and art always more dominant than his interest in ideology. He makes that distinction clear in his signature work on ethnohistory, *The Conflict of European and Eastern Algonkian Cultures, 1504–1700*.[96]

APPRENTICING FOR REFORM IN MATERIAL CULTURE

A day after their marriage in September 1934, Bailey and his wife, Jean Craig Hamilton, sailed from Halifax on the Red Star liner *Pennland* for Southampton, where he would then depart for post-doctoral studies at the London School of Economics and Political Science.[97] His research there was funded by fellowships from the Carnegie Corporation and the Royal Society of Canada (the latter fellowship stemming from a paper he had presented to the society in 1933 that Innis had arranged and from a letter of recommendation that W.D. Lighthall had written to society president Duncan Campbell Scott). Originally intending to work with the renowned Polish anthropologist Bronisław Malinowski, Bailey studied instead under Morris Ginsberg, one of the founders of modern sociology and editor of the influential *Sociological Review*. With Ginsberg's help, Bailey pursued "questions concerning the causes of the uneven contributions of different peoples to the advancement of civilization," an extension of his earlier queries into hereditary genius.[98] Ranging widely in the nascent fields of social history and cultural anthropology – work aided by Ginsberg's suggestion of Gustav Spiller's newly released *Origin and Nature of Man* (1931) – Bailey met and interviewed British historian Arnold Toynbee, who had just published the first three volumes of the monumental *A Study of History* (1934). Toynbee, who at the time was formulating his own thoughts on first contact and the clustering of genius, put him on to Vico, Spengler, Hegel, Henry and Brooks

Adams, and Adolf Reichwein.[99] The combination of those reading suggestions and Toynbee's ideas on cultural genesis and morphology led Bailey to conclude that "the great creative acts that had carried civilization on its upward course had occurred in the metropolitan centres rather than at the outposts and margins of civilization, and that the people in colonial areas derived almost all their material resources, their values and inspirations from such centres of creativity."[100] Soon after, Bailey applied the theories and forms of cultural creativity "to the development of literature and the arts in the Canadian provinces,"[101] articulating for the first time how he envisioned change in colonial or peripheral societies. If "to become fully oneself, one must first lose oneself ... in the vastness and infinite variety of the metropolitan processes," then colonial societies, Bailey inferred, "must imitate before they can successfully emulate."[102] In that conclusion was born the idea of "cosmopolitan regionalism" that would become a dominant way of looking at both the late infancy of Canadian literature and its first turns toward regional expression.

In what Bailey implied was his own cyclic pattern of far-reaching inquiry and return – that "thoroughgoing" process which enables the scholar "to cope with the hazard of parochialism"[103] – Bailey started from a defined New World (and New Brunswick) bias, examined and nuanced that bias through a rigorous program of interdisciplinary study, and returned to his original locus to make it the subject of his further inquiries. Familial inheritance may have been at the root, but the powers of his own intellectual curiosities, as well as his desire to legitimize the specific call of that inheritance, carried him to the point where he was prepared to continue the Bailey/d'Avray tradition. His poetic expression of the process is contained in the poem "Angel Gabriel," so named after the ship that carried Bailey's ancestors to the New World:

> the road that ran
> from the Wiltshire plain to Fredericton's hill [UNB]
> might be construed as sociological, but as we
> travelled over it, it became evident, at first
> however dimly, that something beyond awaited us,
> we did not know what to call it, but went forward to
> search for an answer.[104]

Fortune and "tradition" provided Bailey with the means to pursue that answer and to carry out the next phase of his work, this time in

New Brunswick. In the summer of 1935, a summer of widespread populist uprisings, including the Regina Riot, the coming to power of William Aberhart's Social Credit Party in Alberta, and the election of the Irish Catholic Allison Dysart in New Brunswick (that outcome thought impossible in a deeply Protestant province), Bailey accepted a position as assistant director and curator of the Department of Ancient and Oriental Industrial Arts at the New Brunswick Museum in Saint John.[105] In the region, as in the country, various grievances were fomenting, most fuelled, remembered Bailey, by the view that "the Maritime area had been wrenched out of the international and oceanic context ... [and] forced into a continental framework that was incompatible with its needs and welfare."[106] In New Brunswick, as elsewhere in the region, the Depression was acutely felt, and those feelings were wreaking havoc on an increasingly fragile détente between federal and provincial authorities. Not only was evidence mounting that the province had not been well served by Confederation, but vocal factions of the political class were starting to call openly for redress, calls that gave rise to the Rowell-Sirois Royal Commission on Dominion-Provincial Relations. Bailey's new position at the New Brunswick Museum was partly a response to the widely felt need for more provincial resources and autonomy. His appointment was also, however, the fulfillment of a promise made to him by John Clarence Webster and a result of the turn his post-doctoral studies had taken toward material culture.[107] That turn had been precipitated by his earlier work with T.F. McIlwraith and Charles T. Currelly at the Royal Ontario Museum in Toronto (like Innis, McIlwraith and, to a lesser extent, Currelly were doctoral supervisors), and it had become focused in 1935 when, following the advice of Alice Lusk Webster, John Clarence's wife, and the clues in Adolph Reichwein's *China and Europe* (trans. 1925), Bailey spent many hours studying the Chinese collections[108] at the British Museum, the Victoria and Albert Museum, the University of Leicester Museum, and the National Museum of Wales. As honorary curators at the New Brunswick Museum, Alice and John Webster would be important to Bailey's later work at the University of New Brunswick, particularly in regard to the collection, indexing, and storage of books and archival materials. Bailey, then, was not only equipped by the fortunes of pedigree and education to undertake the work of *literary* revival, but, because of his exposure to material heritage at a particularly strained period in New Brunswick and Maritime history, he would also function as a provincial leader in acquiring *cultural* resources for the purposes of reinvigorating provincial interest and study. He would see that work as being informed by a larger cultural activism that his exposure to Earle Birney's Marxism sparked.

Guiding Bailey in learning the methods of material culture in Saint John was John Clarence Webster (1863–1950),[109] one of North America's foremost medical doctors who had retired to his birthplace of Shediac, New Brunswick, when Bailey began his work at the New Brunswick Museum in 1935. As professor of obstetrics and gynaecology at Rush Medical College of the University of Chicago, Webster had had the opportunity and means to become an amateur historian, amassing, with his wife, one of the continent's finest collections of Asian art and Canadiana, which included a wealth of General James Wolfe and New France materials. Upon retiring to New Brunswick in 1920, Webster had become alarmed by the same loss of provincial pride and status that would later preoccupy Bailey. In a speech to the National Conference on Education and Citizenship in 1926, he openly "deplored the general stagnation and lack of enterprise in the Atlantic area in almost every field of endeavour," especially "cultural and educational standards."[110] In response, Webster wrote and published the pamphlet *The Distressed Maritimes*, which, in language and tones taken from Joseph Howe, "urged upon the people of the maritime provinces that 'the status of a nation is measured not merely by its material wealth, but by its contributions to science, art and literature, and by the evidence which exists of a widespread appreciation.'"[111] (Bailey's editorial polemic in the *Brunswickan* in 1927 echoed many of these concerns.) Webster's appointment as the New Brunswick representative to the National Historic Sites and Monuments Board of Canada focused his interest in material heritage on building the resources of the newly constituted (1929) New Brunswick Museum. He and his wife donated their extensive personal collection to the museum and then sought funding for its care, cataloguing, and promotion. They found that funding in a Carnegie Corporation education grant through which Bailey was first identified and then hired as curator.[112] As Webster wrote in a letter to respected provincial historian W.F. Ganong, "I thought that [Bailey] would be the very man to have with us. He could develop the department ... and could by lantern and other talks do much both for schools and for the public generally ... Then, I had in mind the association of Bailey with you if you are able to settle down to work in the museum."[113] The

Websters had received glowing reports on Bailey from their son Bill, who was a classmate in Harold Laski's course at the London School of Economics.[114]

From there, things moved rapidly. Bailey was hired and worked closely with the Websters for the next three years in Saint John, learning as much about public scholarship (Dr Webster was a tireless publisher of historical research) as about artifact preservation, archival practice, and cultural stewardship. Especially vital for the work Bailey would do in the province were the latter two, for Webster had been instrumental in overseeing the creation of the Public Archives of Nova Scotia and nominating D.C. Harvey as its first archivist. Harvey would publish "The Intellectual Awakening of Nova Scotia" in 1933, an essay that anticipated and was indeed a model for Bailey's "Creative Moments in the Culture of the Maritime Provinces" (1949). The echo of Harvey's work in Bailey's is not insignificant, Harvey beginning his examination with the statement that "for many years I have been interested in the controversy that has raged between the 'great man' and the 'spirit of the age' theories of history; between those who have argued that progress is due to kings and heroes, and those who have found in progress itself a dynamic force."[115] The point of comparison is not to suggest indiscretions of borrowing but to illustrate that, in associating with Webster's cultural activism, Bailey found an important mentor whose situational knowledge and networks shaped his own. In fact, a better guide to consolidating Bailey's inherited and theoretical knowledge, and a more committed advocate for social change, would have been impossible to find in the New Brunswick of the 1930s. That Webster's diagnoses of New Brunswick's ills paralleled Bailey's own – namely, that in having no sense of place and few remaining literary or scholarly touchstones, provincial citizens were "*déraciné*"[116] – directly shaped Bailey's future role as cultural worker.

In addition to caring for Dr Webster's collection of early Canadiana (rare books, manuscripts, maps, photos) and Mrs Webster's collection of Asian pottery and Middle Eastern art objects, Bailey began writing for the *Canadian Historical Review* and publishing guides to the museum's collections. He also expanded his network of provincial policy makers and leaders, many of whom opened their doors to him because of his last name. He met and corresponded often with A.P. Paterson, MLA for Saint John and New Brunswick's minister of federal and municipal relations. A leader of the second wave of the Maritime Rights Movement and "the main proponent of the compact the-

ory" of Confederation,[117] Paterson pushed Bailey to adopt his views of
provincial autonomy, attempting to convince the young scholar that,
under the terms of Confederation, the Canadian provinces had much
more power and autonomy than they were exercising – and almost a
moral imperative to treat the federal government as an instrument of
their wishes.[118] To entrench this view, Paterson implored Bailey to
write "a history of New Brunswick for use in our schools," a project
that carried added weight when Paterson became the first minister of
the newly independent Department of Education in Allison Dysart's
provincial government.[119] Though Bailey never wrote the provincial
history, and never adopted Paterson's compact theory, even though it
became "the official view of the New Brunswick government,"[120] he
did write "New Brunswick and Confederation: A Study of Provincial
Politics and Public Opinion 1864–1867" (1939). Though never published as a whole, this nine-chapter manuscript was later disassembled
for essays and articles in the *Canadian Historical Review*, *Culture and
Nationality* (parts of chapters 5–7), and the *Atlantic Advocate*.[121] Evident in the Bailey/Paterson exchange was the view of senior members
of the New Brunswick government that Bailey was the leading young
historian of the province, a view that was shared by the editor of *Canadian Business* magazine when describing Bailey, from Paterson's
account, as "the only person in Canada who understands the true
history of confederated British North America."[122] It was a view that
would pay dividends when Bailey sought a position at UNB.

One of the many tangible results of all this adulation was Bailey's
association with Fletcher Peacock in Saint John. A member of the New
Brunswick Museum's management committee, Peacock was principal
of the Saint John Vocational School from 1926 to 1937 and, beginning
in 1938, the first director of educational services for New Brunswick
(what would be called today a deputy minister). He was, then, Paterson's right hand in the new Department of Education, and thus a person of influence in the province. In his first report as director, Peacock
described an initiative that he had discussed with Bailey: namely, the
introduction of a number of creative components to the provincial
normal-school curriculum. As Peacock described it, the initiative
reflected both Webster's and Bailey's view that what actually "distressed" the Maritimes was a form of cultural philistinism that became
manifest in economic incapacity (a lack of entrepreneurial spirit) –
and that this should be addressed by aligning "liberal education in a
democracy" with "correct speech, creative writing and a cultural appre-

ciation of the fine things in Literature and Art."[123] The immediate result was the hiring of Elizabeth Sterling Haynes to bring creative education in drama and literature to the province. A tireless cultural worker who had spearheaded the push for community theatre in Alberta, Haynes hit the New Brunswick soil running, travelling eleven thousand miles to forty-nine towns in eleven counties, reported Peacock in his annual review.[124] Her impact was also (indirectly) Bailey's first measurable success in turning a social theory of cultural vacuity into a program of remedial action. The configuration of the province's bureaucracy at the time – the fact that the Department of Education had responsibility for cultural matters, a responsibility it retained until "culture" was siphoned off in 1975 – was perfectly suited to Bailey's background and training, and it would become especially useful for Bailey's subsequent cultural work in the province.

Equally important were Bailey's associations with members of Saint John's artistic community, who gathered at Ted Campbell's downtown studio at 147 Prince William Street.[125] Composed of Jack Humphrey, Miller Brittain, Julia Crawford, Fred Ross, Violet Gillett, Norman Cody, Betty Sutherland, Ruth Starr, and many of New Brunswick's leading artisans of the inter-war period, Campbell's group served as nothing less than "the fulcrum in the birth of New Brunswick regional art of the 1930s."[126] It was one of the few places in New Brunswick where a mix of writers, musicians, painters, actors, and teachers discussed avant-garde ideas about art – in fact, many of southern New Brunswick's leading artists of the time were associated with the group. In his cultured salon, Campbell quite consciously sought to replicate conditions of the Saint John of the late nineteenth century, when figures such as David Russell Jack, G.U. Hay, G.F. Matthew, W.O. Raymond, James Hannay, and William F. Ganong engaged in spirited intellectual debate in magazines such as *Stewart's Literary Quarterly*, *Acadiensis*, the *New Brunswick Magazine*, and the *Educational Review*. To walk into Campbell's studio was to be confronted with what a culturally confident and vibrant New Brunswick could be.

Bailey shared Campbell's interests and goals, but not his proclivities for histrionics and play. And he was too busy anyway to partake of merriment. During this time in Saint John, he envisioned himself in the role of cultural apprentice, having not yet gained full confidence in his transition from Victorian forms of verse. As a result, his involvements with the Campbell group were largely administrative: he

played a central role in the New Brunswick branch of the newly established (1935) Maritime Art Association (MAA), and he was president of
the Saint John Art Club and Friends of the Library Association. He
also delivered lectures ("The Artist as Historian, with Special Reference to Canada"), served on numerous MAA committees, and worked
at times closely with Nova Scotia's Walter Abell, who, like him, was
funded by the Carnegie Corporation to develop cultural and educational resources for the Maritime provinces.[127]

At one of the meetings of the MAA, Allan McBeath, another of the
occasional members of Campbell's group, told Bailey of a former student of his who was convalescing at the Saint John Tuberculosis Hospital. John Sutherland, future editor of *First Statement* (1942–45), said
McBeath, had been receptive to hearing about the modernist movement in literature and wanted more information from someone in
the know. Bailey obliged, visiting Sutherland in late 1937, reading
from Eliot's "Prufrock" and *The Waste Land*, introducing the ideas of
Pound and Gerard Manley Hopkins, and discussing his own recent
transformation under Eliot and Dylan Thomas. Not only was that
exposure "crucial to John Sutherland's development"[128] and "his first
contact with modern poetry,"[129] but it also heralded the role Bailey
was soon to play in New Brunswick as pioneering modernist teacher
and practitioner. Had Bailey stayed in Saint John and regularized his
contact with Ted Campbell's group, among whose active number
were the poets P.K. Page and Kay Smith, his own modernist poetics
would likely have emerged more quickly. As full-time assistant to
John Clarence Webster, however, and growing increasingly close
to senior members of the province's political class, Bailey's interests
became definably (and strategically) more cultural and pedagogic
than literary. It was fortuitous, then, that once cataloguing was complete Bailey was asked by the Websters "to use the Webster Collection
of Canadiana [to deliver extension] lectures on Canadian history" at
the museum and in the wider province.[130] That work took him to
Fredericton, where, Bailey concluded, "the Museum['s] wealth of historical material" could complement UNB's curriculum, which still
had "no course in Canadian History."[131] "As I was charged with the
task of extending the Museum's services to the educational institutions of the Province [*sic*]," said Bailey, "I could hardly neglect what
seemed to me to be the greatest need of all, namely a course in Canadian history which should serve as a credit towards a degree in the
provincial university."[132]

After one illustrated lecture to the York-Sunbury Historical Society in Fredericton, Bailey visited his old friend C.C. Jones, UNB president, whom he had earlier petitioned for revival of a course in modern history. He told Jones of difficulties at the museum between J.C. Webster and director William MacIntosh, and explained that the Carnegie Corporation Education Fund money that was paying his salary was coming to an end.[133] He wondered aloud to Jones, as he had to Webster and T.F. McIlwraith, if there might be a place for him at one of the region's universities, preferably Dalhousie or UNB. Jones was receptive, making what now looks like an astonishing deal (this was an era before higher-education commissions): if Bailey could use his high-ranking political contacts to convince the provincial government to increase its annual $35,000 grant to UNB, or at least agree to enlarge UNB's deficit capacity, Jones would ask the university's Senate to establish a history department and appoint Bailey to it.[134] After careful preparation, Bailey did just that, approaching New Brunswick attorney general John B. McNair with the idea. McNair, a Rhodes scholar and UNB graduate (BA 1911), liked the idea immediately, realizing that Bailey's extensive knowledge of provincial history could leverage grievance arguments against federal powers, always a feather in a Maritime politician's cap. McNair proposed the idea before cabinet, where it was grudgingly accepted (A.P. Paterson, curiously, spoke in opposition to it – not against Bailey, exactly, but against a position that would encompass more than his own view of a compact theory of Maritime history).[135] Regardless of that opposition, McNair's influence moved the vote and C.C. Jones kept his word. As "travelling lecturer" for 1937/38, Bailey was initially appointed as acting professor of British North American history.[136] He offered three lectures per week to the university without charge, commuting one day a week by train from Saint John. The lectures mirrored the ones he had been delivering in southern New Brunswick, those promoting history and the historian as public field and figure. As political historian Donald Wright explains, Bailey's lectures moved the discipline from its traditional focus on antiquarianism and amateur dabbling to the notion of history as constitutive of culture, thus always relevant: "The historian's aim," said Bailey, "should be not merely to supply reading material to titillate the jaded curiosity of an effete leisured class, but to direct his studies of the past towards the solution of our present economic and social problems."[137] That instrumental view had come to Bailey through Toynbee and Innis (who schooled historians to make sense of nations at the level of locales) and had been affirmed by D.C. Harvey, whose essay "The Importance of Local History in the Writing of General History" Bailey referred to repeatedly in his travelling lectures.

At a meeting of the UNB board a few months later (February 1938),[138] Bailey was permanently appointed as professor and head of the department – joking afterwards that he was, rather, "the head, body and tail of the department ... the first professor of history in the university."[139] Less than two years later, he started the Bliss Carman Society, forebear of the *Fiddlehead*. His move to Fredericton in 1938 marked the end of what had been an extraordinary and far-ranging apprenticeship.

The combination of Eliot's theory of a living tradition and Webster's guidance in using public education and material heritage to further enliven that tradition enabled Bailey to move from the abstractions of family inheritance and early intellectual interests to more concrete forms of cultural and institutional stewardship. Moreover, under the guidance of New Brunswick's senior bureaucrats, he had learned the necessity of extricating hereditary genius – "the uneven contributions of different peoples to the advancement of civilization"[140] – from social privilege, thereby preparing himself, with Birney's and Laski's help, to democratize cultural practice for the masses. Evidence of this was that he did not consider his time at the museum as preparation for a university appointment, but as an opportunity to align the resources of the museum with the longer reach of the university so that both New Brunswick and the Maritimes could benefit. "Creative genius," he later added in answer to the central question that he and D.C. Harvey had posed, was indeed "a sociocultural product,"[141] thus requiring that the "purer eugenic ideal" he had written about rather naively as an undergraduate be cultivated across wide social realms. Art and culture, in other words, should not just serve a leisure or creative class but should become the mainstays of a liberal education that seeks to reanimate entire populations. This belief in a rejuvenating eclecticism, as opposed to a narrow or ideologically driven theory (e.g., Paterson's compact theory of Canadian history) would come to dominate the cultural politics of the Bliss Carman Society, the *Fiddlehead*, and the many other institutional advances that Bailey would lead at UNB. It is perhaps fitting, then, that he would recite from memory the first stanza of Carman's song of renewal when recalling, in a 1985 interview,[142] this crucial time of transition from apprenticeship to practice:

Make me over, mother April,
When the sap begins to stir!
When thy flowery hand delivers
All the mountain-prisoned rivers,
And the great heart beats and quivers
To revive the days that were ...[143]

FROM APPRENTICESHIP TO PRACTICE: PROFESSING HISTORY AND ORGANIZING FOR CULTURE AT UNB

Bailey was for the first seven years of his career at UNB the only permanent member of the History Department. He taught courses in British,
American, Canadian, European, Latin American, and Chinese history,
as well as an introductory course in anthropology and a senior honours seminar ("Theory of History and Ethnology") that bridged what
for him were cognate disciplines.[144] Significant for UNB was the fact
that Bailey's anthropology course was only the second such credit
course ever given in Canada, the first one having been offered at the
University of Toronto. Considering his training, it is not surprising that
he placed as much emphasis on methodology as on content, introducing New Brunswick students to some of the first approaches in the
province to historiography and historical-research methods. Because
his teaching load was heavy – seventeen hours per week, including
Saturdays – he sought the company of high-functioning students to
ease his burden, as his great-grandfather Marshall d'Avray had done. By
1940, two years into his UNB career, that student outreach allowed Bailey to take a small but significant step toward his goal of literary renewal in New Brunswick.

The timing then seemed especially opportune to revive socio-
cultural fortunes in the province. Not only had the Rowell-Sirois Commission just released its report, promising significant redress of Maritime problems, but John B. McNair's twelve-year mandate as Liberal
premier of New Brunswick (1940–52) had also just begun. McNair's
tenure was especially significant in starting with the promise of
expanding and professionalizing the civic service, a move that was
widely thought necessary to bring the New Brunswick state into the
modern age. From there, McNair began reforming the provincial education system by passing the County Schools Finance Act, increasing
the salaries and pensions of teachers, reinstating vocational school

grants, and organizing financial-assistance programs for university and normal-school students. As one of UNB's best students of his generation – one who had earned a Rhodes scholarship to study abroad – McNair believed that education was key to New Brunswick's turnaround, an important consideration given that Canada would soon declare war on Germany in September 1939.[145] Despite global instabilities, there was reason for optimism about provincial prospects and reason to define that optimism in educational terms.

In December 1940 Bailey took up that spirit of renewal by organizing a few student writers into a group that he called the Bliss Carman Society. More his invited guests than a formal club, the society started meeting at his house for monthly and then biweekly evening sessions. Gatherings consisted of reading and critiquing the verse that members had written on pre-chosen subjects, Bailey often interjecting with the comment that "that has the makings of a poem." Original members were Robin Bayley, organist at St Andrew's Presbyterian Church, Linden Peebles, and Dorothy Howe, both undergraduate students.[146] (If the number was small, so was the pool from which they came, UNB having a student population of about three hundred at the time, many of whom were young men in science and engineering.) Bailey's wife, Jean, served as hostess, a role that became increasingly difficult as war rationing mounted.

In addition to starting the long climb back to literary respectability, the group sought to use formal exercises to improve technique, which Bailey had done with great success in Toronto with Roy Daniells, Earle Birney, and Robert Finch. The Bliss Carman Society manifesto that Bailey wrote at the time captured that aim in broad relief, vowing, first, to preserve and continue the "tradition [of Jonathan Odell, James Hogg, Barry Straton, and the Confederation poets]," and, second, to do so not as "slavish imitation" but as development "to the point of contemporaneity."[147] The manifesto reflected Bailey's Eliot-inspired thinking about how the past is integral in serving the present, hence the necessity of practice and formal experimentation to carry the tradition forward. Bailey was now in full possession of modernist ideas and ambitions, consciously using Eliot's and Pound's dicta to bridge his own and the previous century. The end goal, he told Bliss Carman Society members, was always to reanimate the past in the style of the present, a goal, writes James Johnson, that normalized the idea of "literary production as a cooperative social process" that was integrative rather than exclusionary.[148] No more grand egos or eugenic aristocracies, in other words, but rather creativity as a "sociocultural product" that builds from gradually expanding inclusion. Bailey's favourite formal exercise reflected that sense of fellowship, the exercise requiring each member in attendance to write the next line of a developing poem. The immediate result of such activities was a surge in poetic output in Fredericton, not only by volume but also quality. "The Society," Bailey told Janet Toole about his own creative output, "stimulated me to write more and better than I had ever done."[149] Many of his finest modernist poems ("The Unreturning" and "North West Passage") were written at this time, their images working at multiple levels to suggest Bailey's larger cultural aims. "North West Passage" is a good example. "He would come to his kin if he could and his fellows / would follow" reads the first line of Bailey's last stanza, echoing almost exactly what Eliot had written in "Tradition and the Individual Talent." "Ever and after his days the immutable journey / would challenge the skilled and the believing ... its promise the hope of a passage beyond it."[150] The society was just that passage, a way forward through the past. Continuity was key. And, though Bailey's position was liminal, as was his region and the status of its increasingly denigrated literature, he clearly felt that he was on a new threshold, as the poem "Discourse on Method," workshopped in another early society meeting, reveals:

When all is said, and each has had his say,
there's none deny the mole his sense to creep
by fractions upwards to the light of day.
He keeps his gains and has no need to weep.[151]

Borders, rivers, tentative movements, and teeming, restless seas thus adorn the Bailey imagery of this period, as do complementary metaphors of new growth in the verse of younger poets Bayley, Peebles, and Howe.

As word circulated in Fredericton of the society's vibrancy, its membership grew to include Elizabeth Brewster, Frances Firth, Jack St Clair Jeans, Margaret Cunningham, Eleanor Belyea, Robert Rogers, Donald Gammon, and Desmond Pacey – the principals, then, of the fledgling Fiddlehead group that would grow out of the Bliss Carman Society.[152] If the group's practice was "to criticize each other's poems without fear or favour,"[153] the intent behind that practice was definably humanist. "The lower animals can live by bread alone," said senior undergraduate student Margaret Cunningham in a December 1946 CFNB (Fredericton) radio broadcast,[154] "but man cannot. Without the great achievements of the human mind in the fields of philosophy, science, and poetry, man would be a contradiction in terms – he would be scarcely human. The greatness of a people such as the Greeks did not rest upon their commerce and industry."[155] "Economic prosperity is certainly necessary," agreed Robert Lawrence, a graduate student and occasional member of the group, "but if we neglect the things of the mind, we do so at our peril."[156] Feeling from the start that these ideas and the work of the group should be recorded for posterity, Bailey had duplicated E.K. Brown's Nameless Society practice of recording minutes, the content of which, in Bailey's hands, consisted simply of the poems under discussion at each meeting. It was the growing interest in formalizing that practice and circulating the contents of the "minute book" that gave Bailey the impetus to revive the "old idea of a magazine to be called *The Fiddlehead*."[157] If western Canada could have a literary magazine (Alan Crawley's *Contemporary Verse*, 1940–52) and central Canada could have two such magazines for new talent (Patrick Anderson's *Preview*, 1942–45, and John Sutherland's *First Statement*, 1942–45), then why couldn't New Brunswick have a similar instrument? The mimeograph technology that had not yet been developed when Bailey was a UNB undergraduate was now in standard use, and Bailey felt at least equal to (and a confidant of) many of the editorial workers at those magazines above, not the least of whom was Sutherland, a young man he had recently mentored in modernist ideas and practice.

Moreover, after 1942, the cultural tide had turned in the country in ways that were fortuitous for Bailey. For one thing, a new literary elite of critics and writers was forming, one comprised of young modernists well known to Bailey. His close friends Roy Daniells, Northrop Frye, and Earle Birney were part of that elite, each taking his place next to F.R. Scott and E.J. Pratt in professing new approaches to literary and Canadian studies. Those approaches were polemically expressed in E.K. Brown's *On Canadian Poetry* and A.J.M. Smith's *Book of Canadian Poetry*, both released in 1943. In the first, Brown made moot Matthew Arnold's argument about the absurdity of studying Canadian literature,[158] countering that the time had come to put critical resources to that effort. And, though he could barely resist looking down on what he was prescribing, Brown nevertheless advanced a convincing argument for national self-study that would provide "the spiritual energy to rise above routine," thereby ending a cultural malaise that had stemmed from a nation "not adequately believ[ing] in itself."[159] His clear identification of "the problem" – a deeply rooted puritanism sustained by the shame of being colonial – could be overcome in Canada by embracing a program of regional autonomy, the consequence of which would bring the local into high relief.[160] Such effort, Brown continued, does not come from "a succession of single great men, each arising accidentally, each sufficient to himself," but rather "by social conditions friendly to creative composition ... [by] a vital and adequate society."[161] That one of his old University of Toronto mentors had taken up his formula for cultural remediation reinforced Bailey's instinct that acting locally had both proximate and distant effects. In his mind, it was worth risking what Brown termed the chauvinism of the local[162] to avoid the erasure of the global, a calculation made easy by the fact that his grounding in modernist and sociological theory had equipped him to understand localism as something quite different from parochialism. It was that essential difference between localism and parochialism that Bailey worked a lifetime to demarcate.

Frye's 1943 *Canadian Forum* review of A.J.M. Smith's groundbreaking anthology *The Book of Canadian Poetry* further signalled that Bailey was on the right course. A sea change had taken place, observed Frye, and the canon was shifting accordingly. The high tones attached to "paint[ing] the native maple," which F.R. Scott had lampooned in the poem "The Canadian Authors Meet,"[163] were being replaced by the more erudite and metaphysical expressions of modernism. Yet, at the same time, the new poetry, as well as the reconsidered work of the past, was more immediate, more visceral, and less given to stagy exaltation: it was the witness of subjects (Smith's "coarse bustle of humanity"[164]) who had gone out into society to encounter the unvarnished truth and ugliness therein. Whether their inclination was toward the "native" or the "cosmopolitan," Canadian poets, said Smith in agreement with Brown, were now working consciously "to transcend colonialism."[165]

As if to punctuate the point, two final gasps issued from what Brown and Smith would have considered an expiring era. The first was the death of Charles G.D. Roberts in November 1943. With that death came the closing of the first chapter of the nativist tradition that Smith's work had identified.[166] The second gasp was Elsie M. Pomeroy's review of Smith's anthology in *The Maritime Advocate and*

Busy East five months later. As official biographer and devotee of Roberts, Pomeroy used the review, as she had used a speech to the Canadian Literature Club of Toronto in January 1944, to rail against modernism, taking particular aim at the work of Smith, Bailey, Ronald Hambleton, and Margaret Avison. Calling the title of Smith's anthology "pretentious,"[167] she groused that his treatment of Roberts and Carman had missed "the beauty and majesty" at the heart of their work,[168] lamenting that the clarity they brought to rarefied thought was being replaced by an impenetrable intellectualism. About "Ideogram," one of four Bailey poems in Smith's 1943 anthology, she wrote, "I haven't the slightest idea what it means."[169] Though sympathetic to many of Bailey's ideas about the New Brunswick masters,[170] Pomeroy's criticisms were the subject of "hilarity and derision" when read aloud by Smith at a party at F.R. Scott's house in Montreal that spring.[171] Making the situation worse was that the who's who of the new wave of Canadian poetry, the group whose style Smith had labelled "cosmopolitan" in his new anthology,[172] was in attendance, a body that included Patrick Anderson, Louis Dudek, Irving Layton, A.M. Klein, John Sutherland, Scott, and Bailey. Contrary to what she likely hoped, then, and despite the fact that her difficulty with modern allusiveness was not hers alone – even Smith himself, a pioneer of Canadian literary modernism, had difficulty with Bailey's poetry, asking him for "explanatory notes on IDEOGRAM and UNCROWNED" before publishing them in *The Book of Canadian Poetry*[173] – her review became the final statement on the closing of an era. The *Fiddlehead* sprouted at exactly this point in Canadian literary history – and it sprouted not solely to support a new cosmopolitanism but, as importantly, to modernize a provincial tradition. The point bears repeating in a New Brunswick context, for the province, already reeling economically and socially from the National Policy, was understandably reluctant to give up yet another feature of its Golden Age, this one aesthetic. A sense of loyalty, not necessarily to Roberts and Carman but to a bygone age that incubated their work, is one of the reasons that the Maritimes, as Glenn Willmott argues,[174] was so late in coming to modernism. Bailey's strategy to bring New Brunswick back to national prominence, then, was to reanimate not discard that past.

On 26 January 1945, less than a year after Pomeroy's screed and only months after the idea of a Fredericton magazine was discussed by Bailey, Edward McCourt, Norwood Carter,[175] and the Bliss Carman Society regulars,[176] Brewster, Belyea, Rogers, Firth, Cunningham, and

Gammon met at Bailey's St John Street house to put the idea of a literary magazine into action. They used Montreal's *Preview* as a model,[177] and were delighted when the first issue of their new magazine appeared on 27 February 1945. It was the same night that the page proofs of Pacey's *Frederick Philip Grove* arrived in Fredericton, thus a night to be optimistic about what seemed to be fomenting at UNB.[178] Gammon, a gifted student from northern New Brunswick and recipient of the Bliss Carman Scholarship for Poetry, was the first editor – and, from all accounts, the most energized of the early editorial workers. (The 26 January meeting was his first with the group.) He bought the printing stock, organized the inaugural issues, and mimeographed content, producing small, ten- to fifteen-page issues of the first six numbers (Feb. 1945–Feb. 1947), a task made difficult by the lingering embargo on paper earlier imposed by the Wartime Prices and Trade Board. As host and guiding seer, Bailey wrote the first editorial (a restatement of his 1940 Bliss Carman Society manifesto) and also sketched a drawing of fiddleheads, which Gammon took to Fredericton artist Lucy Jarvis for refinement and creation of a block print. The image appeared on the magazine's cover until 1967, its meaning, explained Bailey in the first issue, "said to be symbolic of the sun."[179] For the Indigenous Malecite of the St John River valley, the fiddlehead was nature's assertion of creativity, that symbolism of renewal capturing Bailey's belief that developing local cultural resources would reverse the social stagnation and "distress" about which he and J.C. Webster had written. It was therefore Bailey's vision of a modernist-infused localism, rather than the competing vision of "a New Province of the mind,"[180] that would become the editorial signature of the Fredericton magazine. To underline the point, the poems in the early issues of the *Fiddlehead*, observes James Johnson, "evince both a fidelity to literary modernism and a marked sense of impending cultural efflorescence." Fittingly, says Johnson,

> the themes and subjects of the poems included in the earliest issues frequently involve rebirth or regeneration: in [Donald] Gammon's "The Fiddlehead" the "fingers" and "leaves" of "a many fingered thought" "stretch" and "unfold" in the sun; in Robin Bayley's "Spring's Coronation," "Spring has this day / received / her crown" and now "walks the hills"; in Linden Peebles' "Day and Night at Wegesegum," at the edge of a "molten sea," a "golden rose" blossoms "in the east"; and in [Elizabeth] Brewster's "Only the

Subtle Things," "medalled heroes die" and "on their sunken graves there grows / the mute tenacious grass."[181]

These poems affirm the fact that the magazine's editorial intent was, first and foremost, the cultivation of local talent, an intent made clear by Bailey when he described the difference between "publication" and "private circulation" in the first issue.[182] In a letter to Earle Birney in February 1950, Bailey said that "I have never considered [the *Fiddlehead*] as constituting publication since the 'Fiddlehead' is a mimeographed sheet which appears only once or twice a year and is distributed almost entirely on the UNB campus."[183] Though this kind of admission might initially elicit thoughts of parochialism, Bailey's methodology was aimed more at elevating the local than closing ranks around it. Robert Rogers makes this point clear in a 1952 letter to Bob Gibbs. "Like the Elizabethan dramatists," he writes, "the founders of *The Fiddlehead* believed that good literature could be best developed by mutual criticism and mutual aid. Criticisms and suggestions of members of the poetry society have enabled me to produce better poems, and I feel that they have aided every other member of the group in the same manner."[184] Critic Andrew Moore interpreted that intention to mean that the magazine functioned "as a kind of printed writer's circle – albeit one of indeterminate circumference." The objective, Moore concludes, was "to promote Fredericton as a literary hub, to position the New Brunswick capital as a Canadian centre for creative arts"[185] – and therefore, by extension, to create the conditions that had earlier supported literary excellence. Subsequent editors from Fred Cogswell to Peter Thomas would circle back to that objective in their efforts to revivify the magazine, each mindful of Bailey's insistence that localism be fully present but never to the point of collapsing into itself or shunning that which is outside its boundaries. "Instead of trying to achieve identity by building a Chinese wall around one's home territory," Bailey advised, "one should open one's mind to all the winds that blow,"[186] a view that seemed sensibly attuned to the turbulent times in which these modernist pioneers were living. The implication was that smaller worlds are best served by studied rather than deferential openness (or opposition) to larger worlds, and that cultural colonialism is overcome by practised participation, not isolation.

That the magazine launched Brewster, Cogswell, Alden Nowlan, Robert Gibbs, Kay Smith, and a new wave of countless other New

Brunswick and Atlantic Canadian writers vindicates Bailey's belief that New Brunswick was the perfect incubator for an experiment in informed localism. Given its history of achievement followed by ridicule and neglect, the province needed to reassert itself in the face of new narratives of federalist ubiquity and might, but it had to do so in ways that were recognized by other narrative practitioners as being legitimate. Bailey found that legitimacy in the idea of an atemporal tradition that bridged the two worlds that he valued. If he could rid New Brunswick culture of the sycophancy of naive loyalties while also retaining (and refreshing) the focus on place, then the parochialism of otherwise well-meaning society ladies like Pomeroy would be trumped by the kind of heightened attentiveness and bold experiment that once characterized the literary work of the province – and New Brunswick would again be recognized as a pioneering cultural space. The Atlantic Canadian hybrid of "neo-provincialism" that later critic Terry Whalen identifies as being uniquely characteristic of the region's writing is therefore attributable to Bailey, though Whalen never credits Bailey with crafting that hybrid. A fuller knowledge of Bailey's stewardship corrects the oversight, however, for the blending of the native and cosmopolitan is found in Bailey's own poetic practices, in his reconciliation of the old and new cultures, and in the editorial signature he gave the *Fiddlehead*, the magazine that led to the groundswell of new Atlantic Canadian writing that Whalen rightly identifies. (Malcolm Ross identifies a similar debt to Bailey's notion of regional coherence in Bailey's essay "Creative Moments in the Culture of the Maritime Provinces."[187]) That hybrid, observes Whalen, contested "Atlantic colonialism" for "a new faith in home ... which trusts the cultural bearings of the region instead of uncritically consenting to bearings that beckon from down the road, over the pond, or across the border."[188] Furthermore, that new faith in home was not only "alert to roots, open to the wider world, [and] critically curious,"[189] but was alert with an unvarnished understanding of "the economic heritage of the region," an understanding that led "to fac[ing] its consequences squarely and ... exorcis[ing] its ghosts."[190] Herb Wyile uses the same reasoning in his 2011 study of Atlantic Canadian literature, arguing for "a more measured, qualified pride in the region's heritage in order to withstand the pressures of globalizing forces that increasingly wither that sense of historicity."[191] The region's two major critics after Bailey, then, each a generation apart, echo his prescription for cultural remediation, as does the trajectory of contemporary thought, whether expressed by American philosopher Kwame Anthony Appiah (*The Ethics of Identity*) or by Canadian political theorist Will Kymlicka (*Rooted Cosmopolitanism*). Both draw from the work of John Stuart Mill to develop parallel notions of "rooted cosmopolitanism," the only viable position, they argue, for subjects attempting to survive what Mill termed "the tyranny of the majority."[192]

Bailey was indeed ahead of his time in working out a modernist response to living under what sometimes felt like federalist occupation, and what is especially significant about his achievement is how attentive his response was to Maritime historical conditions. His was the response of a subject whose narratives are inflected and sometimes overwritten by legislation, policy, and other forms of state power. Understanding both the necessity of local expression to preserve identity and its ultimate futility in the face of power, that response worked creatively to reinvent itself so that localism would always be fresh, theoretically informed, linguistically daring, and alive to the ideological present. Bailey's neo-provincial hybrid, then, was very much of its place: such a hybrid was possible only in a locale that had moved from fullness to loss as New Brunswick had. The modernism of the Montreal and Toronto poets and editors was a different kind of response because it came from a different set of historical conditions. As E.K. Brown and A.J.M. Smith made clear in their 1943 works, that urban modernism was more reactionary and exclusionary than restorative. It made straw men of the New Brunswick Confederation poets in order to move the dial from the east to the centre of the country, thus championing Lampman and Scott. Its intent had almost nothing to do with recuperation, whereas Bailey's intent had recuperation as a primary objective. Not recuperation of the past, mind you, but recuperation of conditions within which fullness, both social and cultural, could return. It is not at all surprising, then, that Bailey had much higher ambitions than merely opening a forum for creative expression. His earlier study of the historical causes and sociological contexts of cultural vibrancy had identified habits of mind as being integral to creative production. He was indeed inculcating those habits of mind in his classes and editorial work, but his more ambitious plan was to effect institutional and structural change by positioning the university and the province to act as cultural stewards. UNB was small enough and Bailey was close enough to senior civil servants in New Brunswick to think that such an initiative could succeed. The *Fiddlehead* was thus only a first step in a larger plan of remediation.

When Desmond Pacey and Fred Cogswell joined the editorial board of the *Fiddlehead* in 1945, Cogswell's presence especially lifting the magazine to new heights, Bailey moved on to other initiatives, bringing to each the same sense of activist localism that had infused the magazine. And, as before, the intersection of his interests with social circumstances proved to be fortuitous.

FROM CULTURAL TO INSTITUTIONAL RENOVATION

By 1945, Canadian universities were on the eve of unprecedented growth. After the armistice in August 1945, returning Second World War veterans started filling university classrooms, lured there by the federal government's Rehabilitation Training Program, which subsidized veterans' tuition on the basis of time served overseas. At UNB, a large number of the 1946 freshman class of 350 students were veterans – and the size of that incoming class outnumbered that of the next three years combined.[193] UNB's new president, Milton F. Gregg, VC (1944–47), himself a decorated military man of the last two wars, was a strong advocate for veterans' education, building on his predecessor's work as chairman of the Committee on Post-War Problems of the National Conference of Canadian Universities. In that role, outgoing UNB president Norman MacKenzie spearheaded the veterans' subsidy tuition programs that incoming president Gregg endorsed. In fact, Gregg became one of the strongest advocates for post-war education in the country, insisting that UNB should do all that it could to accommodate the discharged soldiers. As a military man, however, Gregg "claimed no special knowledge of the task of running a university,"[194] a limitation that necessitated deputizing key members of his faculty, one of whom was the young star Bailey. "I had lots of ideas about curriculum," said Bailey, and "I suppose I talked too much."[195] Bailey's move to university administration and to positions of greater institutional influence occurred in that context, starting in 1946 when he became dean of arts. It was the first time in UNB's history that a dean had been formally appointed. Bailey had finally attained a position of some influence, taking his place at a table that his ancestry and mentors (Innis, Webster, Ganong) had prepared him for.

True to his program, he started with curricular reform, seeking specifically to find a pedagogic balance between "earning a living" and "living well." That balance, he argued, was essential to a university education that "transcend[ed] the purely vocational."[196] An introductory course on history and the social sciences (the precursor to UNB's long-standing Arts 1000) was made compulsory at this time, and courses in anthropology and sociology were added to the Department of Psychology and Education. Not surprisingly, the History Department received special attention. Bailey hired William Stewart MacNutt, who had just returned from war service in Italy as an infantry captain with the North Nova Scotia Highlanders. When MacNutt announced that he wanted to develop the field of Italian history at UNB, Bailey asked him to reconsider, encouraging him to focus instead on New Brunswick. MacNutt would eventually write a number of important essays on early-nineteenth-century New Brunswick and would author the definitive history of the province before Confederation, acknowledging his debts to Bailey in the opening pages. (The work remains the only substantial scholarly history of the province to date.) Bailey also groomed some of his best students to fill the department's ranks. Toby Graham, James Chapman, Murray Young, Steve Patterson, Peter Kent, and David Frank became the core of the department in later years, each pursuing research interests in Atlantic Canadian or New Brunswick history. To assist his students' transition to the professional ranks, while also cultivating their interests in provincial affairs, Bailey reactivated an idea he had proposed in a 1943 conference on Northern New England and the Maritimes. The idea, as he explained in a 1944 letter to J.B. Brebner, was to put his best honours students to work on New Brunswick projects, for "if New Brunswick is to enjoy a larger measure of social welfare, it is absolutely essential to attack contemporary and future problems in terms of their historic origins."[197] To operationalize that aim, he "drew up thirty thesis topics covering every aspect of the industrial, technological, political and cultural development of New Brunswick," asking that students research those topics and turn them "into pamphlet form for study purposes" across the province.[198] He had earlier won the support of his old friend Fletcher Peacock, director of educational services for New Brunswick, to fund some of the projects, but when funding fell through because of wartime austerity he approached the Rockefeller Foundation,[199] which put up $7,000 to buy the books, manuscripts, and archival tools necessary to do the research he had proposed. "The grants themselves were historic," Bailey recalled, "in being the first ever received by the University for research in the fields of concern to the departments in Arts."[200]

When historian George Rawlyk later observed the birth of "a new golden age of Maritime historiography,"[201] he was referring to a field of professional inquiry that Bailey's work had precipitated and shaped. In the opening editorial (1971) of the resurrected *Acadiensis: Journal of the History of the Atlantic Region*, editor Phillip Buckner agreed, setting forth an editorial policy that reflected Bailey's own critical parameters: "Devoted to focusing regional awareness, the journal will concentrate upon Atlantic Canada, but will include within its geographic scope not only the Maritime Provinces and Newfoundland but also Gaspésia and Maine with further extensions into Central Canada and Northern New England when these seem relevant."[202] Moreover, wrote Buckner, *Acadiensis* would have an interdisciplinary openness, its eclecticism inviting "contributions from anthropologists, political scientists, sociologists, or practitioners of any other discipline that will further our knowledge of the history of the Atlantic region."[203] Both in scope and critical method, *Acadiensis* captured Bailey's diverse ethnohistorical approach. The department he built and the seminal journal and biennial conference that department incubated became the country's unrivalled leaders in regional studies.

But an intellectual formation such as a university department or a faculty requires scholarly resources, the repository of which is the library. If scholars of repute were to come to New Brunswick and stay, if their work was to be informed by the latest developments in their fields, if graduate students and faculty were to create knowledge that went out into the world, and if UNB was to spearhead that larger cultural project that Bailey and Webster had hoped, then the UNB library needed immediate attention. Realizing the provincial and regional aims to which a first-class university library could be put, Bailey agreed to President Gregg's request that he become honorary librarian, a role that his great-grandfather Joseph Marshall d'Avray had occupied at UNB a century before (d'Avray was the first member of faculty to hold that position) and one that Bailey had trained for as a graduate student of William Stewart Wallace at the University of Toronto. An authority in Canadian history, Wallace was the university's chief librarian and a professor in the Toronto Library School.[204] In 1946 Bailey assumed a similar position at UNB, responsible for the library's management and expansion, a role that seemed a natural extension of his duties in the History Department, which was actually located in the library. He held the position until 1959.[205] In the days before administrative course release, that meant that Bailey carried a full teaching load in addition to being dean of arts, the university librarian, head of the History Department, and the guiding light of the *Fiddlehead*'s fledgling editorial board.

Despite that crippling load – and what must have been a tempting offer from Harold Innis to accept a permanent faculty position in sociology at the University of Toronto in 1946[206] – Bailey entrenched himself at UNB. His work there to build a modern research library was perhaps his greatest legacy, and it was certainly complementary to what he had done to construct a department specializing in regional history and to open what has turned out to be a lasting outlet for creative work (the *Fiddlehead* is now one of Canada's oldest literary magazines still publishing[207]). For him, a university library had as much symbolic as real value, which he emphasized in recalling Governor Thomas Carleton's description of UNB's original library in 1793. That library of the Academy of Liberal Arts and Sciences, wrote Bailey, was anchored by a collection of books that grew in consort with King's College and then UNB.[208] The university as material and ideological formation was inconceivable without its books, concluded Bailey, to the point that, without those, "it might well be asked how standards of education of a university level could be maintained."[209] As with the History Department and the literary magazine he founded, it was both UNB's lack of a modern research library and the potential that lack invited which captured Bailey's imagination. His stories of the former are nothing short of disturbing.

Shortly after arriving at UNB in 1938, he had been shocked to discover that valuable archival material on the library's top floor had simply been piled up in no particular order. More shocking still was that the piles had been receding from the door inward because the janitor was using the material as fuel for the basement furnace. Bailey immediately asked Josephine Rowan, one of his ablest honours students, to start cataloguing what remained, using a portion of the Rockefeller Foundation grant he had received to pay her.[210] On closer examination, he discovered that the library itself was in shambles. There were approximately ten thousand books, most uncatalogued, and those books had little relation to the fields in which UNB was developing expertise. Moreover, there was no research archive (text or artifact) of any type, the closest being the New Brunswick Museum and the Public Library in Saint John. Bailey concluded that students "couldn't do honours work properly, much less graduate work," and that UNB had "the poorest academic library in Canada."[211] More troubling was that that neglect seemed to be symptomatic of a larger malaise in the province about which he already knew. In this instance, however, neglect did not encompass literary production but the more consequential areas of historical awareness and cultural identity. The situation reminded Bailey of the stories that provincial historian W.F. Ganong had told him. Ganong had had similar experiences of the cavalier destruction of historical materials when he visited Old Government House and the Legislative Library in Fredericton. At Old Government House, which had been closed in 1890 and was being used for storage, Ganong watched a caretaker burning documents and emptying the province's historical records into the St John River. Exasperated, Ganong walked into town to commiserate with a friend at the Legislative Library, who told him of the visits of antiquarian book collectors who would arrive regularly, take what they wanted from the shelves, and pay the attendant on the way out. Moved to despair, Ganong hired a buggy to cart away as much of the Old Government House materials as he could. Unbelievable as the stories were, they corroborated other reports that Bailey heard from Dr W.C. Milner, another noted provincial historian, about the destruction of county court records. "When the clerk of York County died," Bailey recounted from Milner, "the records of York, Carleton, Sunbury and Madawaska were turned out on the Court House Square and burned."[212] Still other irreplaceable records were stored in stables, "the cows benefit[ing] more from their existence there than did the people of New Brunswick."[213] Such was the pride in provincial heritage in the late nineteenth and early twentieth centuries.

Bailey vowed to correct that practice at UNB. After hiring Josephine Rowan, he created a Historical Documents Room in the library where documents of provincial importance were placed for safekeeping. When the Honourable A.P. Paterson wrote to him complaining that the document granting provincial jurisdiction to the province of New Brunswick in 1784 could not be found, Bailey contacted the Dominion archivist for two copies of that order-in-council, giving one to the government and retaining one for his new research archives. Piece by piece, in painstaking fashion, he collected and catalogued the province's history, building a library and archives collections at UNB (the latter in default of a provincial archives at the time). To ensure that his work was sufficiently diverse, he recruited a faculty advisory committee to assist him. Consisting of Frank Toole (sciences), Desmond Pacey (arts), Foster Baird (engineering), and Miles Gibson (forestry), the committee charted UNB's disciplinary emphases and strengths, thereby laying the foundation for the university's research expertise. It is from that expertise that UNB built its modern disciplinary identity, which in turn created the capacities that informed the Fiddlehead moment. Significant in that development was Bailey's work with Lord Beaverbrook, the irascible and soon-to-be dominant force at the centre of UNB's library modernization.

Bailey and Beaverbrook were not strangers. Bailey's father and the pre-peerage Max Aitken (Beaverbrook) had been acquaintances in Fredericton and Halifax. Bailey's father, a banker and venture capitalist, had lent Aitken a sizeable sum of money, and at another time was summoned to a duel over the affections of a woman, both instances ending positively.[214] A.G. Bailey had met Beaverbrook in London in 1926 by arrangement of his father and got to know him personally when Beaverbrook became UNB chancellor (1947–64). One of Milton F. Gregg's final initiatives before leaving the university presidency in 1947 was to ask Bailey to serve as UNB's first point of contact for Beaverbrook, a situation that certainly benefited Bailey's plans for the library and archives. Thereafter, Bailey joined Beaverbrook's retinue whenever his "Lordship" was in Fredericton, usually for six weeks every year between August and October – his presence described by Pacey as akin to "a strong electric current flowing through the whole place."[215] For many years, Bailey and Beaverbrook met daily during this fall period, dining, discussing the province, attending sporting events, and spending long hours in Beaverbrook's vice-regal suite on the seventh floor of the Fredericton hotel that bore his name.

Bailey's genius in working with Beaverbrook was to don the persona of a manservant while steering Beaverbrook in the directions that UNB and the province needed to go. Having grown up himself in an aristocratic class, Bailey knew instinctively that flattery of an imperial sort mattered to Beaverbrook,[216] for "he was not always treated in a way that he had every right to expect."[217] Bailey also knew how important New Brunswick's Commonwealth connections were for Beaverbrook. Beaverbrook, after all, had begun funding the Beaverbrook Overseas Scholarships just after the Second World War,[218] and he had always been an advocate of international, specifically British, education for provincial students. One of the first things that Bailey did in that regard was to encourage Beaverbrook to strengthen the language around post-scholarship expectations, suggesting that part of the adjudication process should consider each candidate's utility to New Brunswick. The final language that appears publicly reflects Bailey's suggestion, pointing to "the likelihood of a career in New Brunswick" and the applicant's "usefulness to the New Brunswick community."[219] An early letter from Bailey to Beaverbrook illustrates the normal strategy employed to win "his Lordship's" endorsement, Bailey beginning by noting the kindness of Beaverbrook for agreeing to make copies of the Manners-Sutton correspondence for UNB. Bailey then goes on to the real purpose of the letter, which is to educate Beaverbrook about the matter at hand, in this case the value of the correspondence to New Brunswick. "[John Henry Thomas] Manners Sutton," Bailey says, "was Lieutenant Governor of New Brunswick from 1854 to 1861, and [his] dispatches to the Colonial Office and the Colonial Office replies are valuable sources of information on conditions in New Brunswick at that time."[220] Dozens of similar letters followed about dozens of other subjects, most noting what Bailey needed to enhance the UNB collection and, by extension, the interests of the province. The idea was not just to position UNB as a focal point for New Brunswick research, but more subtly to show that the province was at a crossroads of world affairs, thus meeting Beaverbrook's appetite for participation in a world beyond his native province. Bailey's pursuit and acquisition of the papers of Andrew Bonar Law, David Lloyd George, Arthur Hamilton Gordon, and Richard Bedford Bennett furthered those ends.

It was in a similar spirit that Bailey started lobbying Beaverbrook in 1947 to fund a wing on the library, a development that would win UNB "a deserved reputation for fostering original research, and by this means [enable] distinctive contributions to the intellectual development of Canada."[221] When Beaverbrook agreed to a $250,000 donation, Bailey became de facto project manager of the library's expansion, working with the engineering firm A.D.I. on everything from architectural design to shelving displays. To give the wing a provincial feel, Bailey insisted on bird's eye maple for the central reading room, soon-to-be named after Beaverbrook, and a fiddlehead design for the mezzanine floor and wrought-iron railings. While construction proceeded, Bailey worked with myriad assistants (many his former students[222]) to prepare book lists of materials, using Beaverbrook's money and overseas connections to amass a sizeable collection of print resources relevant to New Brunswick. Beaverbrook's minions and Bailey's students roamed all over England and Scotland to find books, many of which were discovered in antiquarian bookstores because they were out of print. "It was like the Battle of Normandy with Lord Beaverbrook turning out his spitfires," recalled Bailey.[223] Between 1947 and the opening of the new library wing in 1951, Bailey's team increased holdings to almost 50,000 volumes, a fivefold expansion from the late 1930s. With first editions of Dickens and Kipling, signed copies of the works of Winston Churchill and Lord Rosebury, and rare manuscripts by Thomas Jefferson, William Pitt, Admiral Lord Nelson, and Louis Riel (the latter written on the eve of Riel's execution), UNB's new Bonar Law-Bennett Library[224] became the centrepiece of the university and the most formidable library in the province – an institution, observed librarian Robert Rogers, that "would certainly transform this province and its people."[225] When Beaverbrook spoke of the achievement at a later dinner, he commented on Bailey's powers of persuasion, confessing that Bailey's eloquence in tying UNB's needs to those of New Brunswick had convinced him to put his money into the library instead of a new rink. "Thank God Alfie can't skate," he told the assembled guests.[226]

Beaverbrook rewarded Bailey by petitioning UNB president Albert W. Trueman for a six-month leave of absence on his behalf, for the work of the last four years had broken Bailey's health. The winter 1951 leave allowed Bailey to return to his creative work, the result of which was *Border River* (1952), one of the earliest modernist collections in New Brunswick. When Bailey returned from his leave in Arizona, Beaverbrook offered him the presidency of UNB, a position he felt free to fill as university chancellor. Bailey twice declined, Beaverbrook only relenting when Bailey said that he was better placed in staying close to his cultural work. As an alternative, the two came up with the idea of installing Colin B. Mackay, one of Bailey's former students (BA 1942) and an editor of the *Brunswickan*. Grandson of UNB classics professor Henry S. Bridges, whose daughter (Colin B.'s mother) was born, like Bailey's father, in the Old Arts Building, Mackay seemed bred for the position. He became president in 1953.

Bailey's work with Beaverbrook provides insight into one of the most important contributions Bailey made at UNB, namely, his work with successive university presidents to advance his cultural program in New Brunswick. Beginning with Norman MacKenzie (1940–44), Bailey enjoyed increasing success in convincing Milton F. Gregg (1944–47), Albert W. Trueman (1948–53), and Colin B. Mackay (1953–69) to assume greater custodianship of culture for the province. He argued that UNB's original mission supported that objective, identifying "principles of religion and morality" in the charter of King's College, UNB's earliest manifestation, that supported cultural and certainly community stewardship.[227] Not only, then, was the humanist role embodied in Bailey's ancestry, the Baileys and d'Avrays all institutionally rooted "public" intellectuals, but it was fundamental to his own view of the provincial university's role in an expanding and modernizing New Brunswick. UNB, he told incoming presidents, had a civic responsibility to serve provincial populations, whether through teaching, research, or community outreach. When Albert W. Trueman became the new president in 1948, that special feature of UNB's provincial stewardship had been clearly telegraphed, Trueman making it the centrepiece of his installation address: "Society has a right to look to Universities for intellectual leadership. The University must regard itself as a centre for the intellectual activity of the wide community it serves; and therefore must guard zealously the privileges and qualities which alone make possible the discharge of that function – its freedom of thought and utterance, its integrity, its moral courage, its enthusiasm for learning. But it must also have respect for and be responsive to the values of its community. Otherwise it cannot continue to live."[228]

The mid-century period of presidential succession at UNB illustrates the point that the "tradition," understood by Bailey, from Eliot, as the organic presence of the past in the everyday, was not just a quaint parochial feature of life in New Brunswick but one that could be turned to institutional strength. A final example from Norman MacKenzie's tenure is instructive. President of UNB from 1940 to 1944, he had left Fredericton to become president of the University of British Columbia (UBC), where he was to reconnect with and mentor a young Colin B. Mackay, whom he had known as an undergraduate student at UNB during the war. (Bailey had been decisive in sending Mackay, his history student, to UBC.) That relationship continued in Vancouver when Mackay was a law student,[229] culminating in Mackay's eventual appointment as president of UNB nine years after MacKenzie vacated the position. The necessity of continuity that Bailey recognized from Eliot as a first principle in the work of creative intellectuals was thus present in the succession planning that Bailey and MacKenzie oversaw, particularly, as MacKenzie told provincial artist Jack Humphrey, in the continuance of the work that they had done to turn UNB's Observatory into an Art Centre and then a Summer School for the Arts, to forge connections among southern New Brunswick arts communities, to hire artists in residence, and to position UNB as an incubator for the province's cultural work.[230] Pegi Nicol MacLeod, UNB's most outspoken practising artist, was unequivocal in her support of integrating the arts into the larger community, insisting, like Bailey, that the university and its presidents play a central role in this regard.[231] As incoming president, Mackay could do nothing less than assume the role of cultural custodian that Bailey had had a dominant hand in writing. It was therefore the triumvirate of Bailey, Beaverbrook, and Bailey's presidents that was responsible for building the institutional capacity to accommodate the province's embrace of cultural modernism. If that institutional insularity seems paternal by today's standards, it is because it occurred at the time of the gentleman scholar, the scholar who was called to civic leadership by his superiors and taught to exercise that leadership through service to society and institution alike. Considered in the context of his own intellectual inheritance and trajectory, the sense of a place-based living tradition that Bailey brought to and implemented at UNB was profound – so profound that the university's ultimate success in the role of cultural custodian in mid-century led Premier Louis J. Robichaud a decade later to want an equivalent institution of higher learning in New Brunswick to represent and shape the cultural aspirations of his own people, the province's Acadians.

Beaverbrook's usefulness to Bailey, however, was not over once Mackay became president in 1953. At Bailey's suggestion, the new Bonar Law-Bennett Library soon started doubling as a repository for Beaverbrook's and Sir James Dunn's sizeable collections of British and Canadian paintings, becoming an early iteration of a provincial art gallery. As wall space in the new library's Lloyd George Room and Beaverbrook Reading Room began to overflow with Beaverbrook's and Dunn's collections of paintings and engravings, Bailey saw an opportunity to shape another of the lord's schemes, lobbying him and new UNB president Mackay to build a gallery on campus that would complement what Lucy Jarvis and others were doing at the Observatory Art Centre. The larger campus gallery, argued Bailey, could become a focal point for regional and national art education. Opened in September 1959, the Beaverbrook Art Gallery would eventually be built off campus, and the plan to concentrate art education at UNB was scuttled because of Mount Allison University's earlier claim to that role, but Bailey laboured for years on the project, participating in the design and acquisition phases. Few New Brunswickers were as qualified as he was for the latter, his post-graduate training in material cultures placing him and a co-opted Colin B. Mackay at the centre of the enterprise. Bailey's correspondence with Beaverbrook in the mid-

1950s reveals his opinions of Joshua Reynolds, Thomas Gainsborough, Augustus John, Eugène Delacroix, Cornelius Krieghoff, and other masters whose works would eventually adorn the gallery. Bailey had a similar role in the plan to build a provincial archive for New Brunswick. Showing no inclination to work with J.C. Webster at the New Brunswick Museum in Saint John (Bailey claimed their strong personalities clashed), Beaverbrook discussed alternatives with Bailey and Mackay, who suggested that Fredericton would be the better site. In Fredericton, the archives would be close to the provincial university and the legislative heart of New Brunswick. In his role as foot soldier, Bailey scoured the country for an act of Parliament that would authorize such a venture, finding a model from Saskatchewan.[232] He then joined New Brunswick industrialist K.C. Irving, another of Beaverbrook's recruits, to draw up plans for an institution, working, as well, with his old friend J.B. McNair, now premier of New Brunswick, to involve bureaucrats in preserving historical documents.[233] Since McNair was also in Beaverbrook's inner circle, Bailey nudged Beaverbrook to advance his library and archives causes as provincial priorities with the premier.[234] The result was an increase in provincial resources for what was clearly seen as not just a university (UNB) but also a well-financed preserver and incubator of provincial heritage and culture.

By the late 1950s, Bailey had expended considerable energy in instituting multiple means to provincial self-knowledge and study. During his almost fifteen years as honorary librarian and the axis of UNB's Beaverbrook initiatives, the university's collection had grown to 90,000 books, the university archives and the provincial archives were proceeding apace, and UNB had finally acquired the intellectual resources "to go forward as a worthy member of the community of Canadian universities."[235] No less a figure than Malcolm Ross, founding editor of the New Canadian Library series, would comment that by working on multiple fronts Bailey turned UNB "from being a scattering of stray books to a fine, well organized and fully functioning modern university."[236]

A dynamic Faculty of Arts had also been established under Bailey's direction, and two departments in particular (history and English) were growing in size and reputation, their students winning prestigious prizes and scholarships abroad. Bailey had also witnessed the success of his students along the pathways he had forged. Katherine MacNaughton had published *The Development of the Theory and Prac-*

tice of Education in New Brunswick, 1784–1900 (1947), the first of the UNB historical studies that he had planned when applying for the Rockefeller Foundation grants years earlier. In his introduction to MacNaughton's study, Bailey was clear about UNB's role in provincial leadership – "[the university] would be recreant to its high calling as a disseminator of 'useful knowledge' if it remained indifferent to the reactions of its people to the exigencies of the physical and social environments"[237] – and equally assured that such research "will create an intellectual ferment without which there can be little hope of progress towards the realization of a better life for all."[238] With books by Frances Firth (on higher education in New Brunswick) and Dorothy Loughlin (on New Brunswick literary history) next in line for publication in the monograph series and with Beaverbrook's success in securing graduate fellowships for study of the historical relations between New Brunswick and Maine,[239] that hope was not unreasonable. On 15 May 1947 the hope took another step to being realized with the formal unveiling, at UNB, of the Poets' Corner of Canada monument honouring Roberts, Carman, and Sherman, the Fredericton school of the Confederation poets. Not only was Bailey the figure behind the initiative (proposing it to his old friend and mentor J.C. Webster, who was chair of the Historic Sites and Monuments Board of Canada), but he was also the same person who had earlier chastised New Brunswick for lacking the historical awareness to raise such a monument, speculating in his 1927 undergraduate editorial for the *Brunswickan* that Toronto would likely commemorate Carman before Fredericton.[240] The 1947 UNB that Bailey had had a hand in renewing had thus been inconceivable twenty years earlier – and Bailey's reading of a Charles G.D. Roberts poem at the close of the Poets' Corner ceremony especially sweet. When Bailey wrote in *The University of New Brunswick Memorial Volume* (1950) that his university "has come to occupy in many respects one of the foremost places among the smaller Canadian institutions of higher studies,"[241] he must have been thinking, not immodestly, of the distance it had come during his tenure.

And he must also have been thinking of how much his community had grown in realizing his most ardent hope that the New Brunswick of the present might be raised to the point where it could emulate the literary legacies of the past. In writing a letter of reference for Elizabeth Brewster, whose poetry he had nurtured and published, Bailey seems to mark this success in saying that her "original genius

3 Alfred G. Bailey reading a poem by Charles G.D. Roberts at the Poets'
Corner Monument unveiling ceremony, May 1947. *Left to right*: A.G. Bailey;
Major Barker, lieutenant governor's aide-de-camp; J.C. Webster; John B.
McNair, premier of New Brunswick; William G. Clarke, former lieutenant
governor of New Brunswick (1940–45).

in the field of literature ... shows every indication, if nothing befalls
her, of bringing the kind of lustre to this University which was
brought to it by Sir Charles G.D. Roberts and Bliss Carman."[242] His
work at UNB, specifically as it related to the founding of creative and
scholarly outlets – from the Bliss Carman Society to regionally
focused departments and research hubs – had advanced to the point
where each was autonomous and self-sustaining. It is no coincidence,
then, that he would invoke John Milton's *Areopagitica* when writing a
radio script about his Fiddlehead group in 1947: "Methink I see in my
mind a noble and puissant Nation rousing herself like a strong man
after sleep, and shaking her invincible locks; methink I see her as an
eagle mewing her mighty youth, and kindling her undazzled eyes at
the full midday beam."[243] By the 1950s, Bailey had indeed created the
conditions for literary and scholarly production in New Brunswick,

and those conditions were supporting exponential growth. In the eyes
of critic F.W. Watt, Bailey's cultural and institutional work had elevated him to "a Canadian nationalist pre-dating Margaret Atwood's kind
by forty years."[244]

Bailey would continue to work with Beaverbrook in the years
ahead, especially with regard to the construction of the Fredericton
Playhouse, but, by 1961, many of his objectives had been achieved.
And, though more administrative and creative work lay ahead (he
served as vice-president academic from 1965 to 1969, after which he
retired to his poetry), he was relying increasingly on the people he had
mentored to continue creating the conditions for an enhanced New
Brunswick. Significant among those people were Pegi Nicol MacLeod
and Lucy Jarvis, like-minded spirits in what Bailey called "the kindred
field of the plastic arts."[245] His UNB had always included such artists,
who were a constant reminder that ideas worth anything must be put
into action, whether in verse, paint, or some other medium. It was an
idea shared by Desmond Pacey and Fred Cogswell, both vital allies in
New Brunswick's Fiddlehead school.

More than any other cultural theorist or practitioner in New
Brunswick at mid-century, Bailey was aware of what Lenin described
as the structural phenomenon of internal colonialism, the state of
unequal relations between resource-rich, rural areas on a periphery
and the metropolitan centres that control those areas with capital and
law. He further understood that dependency and underdevelopment
were not natural or merit-based conditions, but conditions that resulted from policies and structures created for desired ends. With the
knowledge that regional "distress" was manufactured to create a
planned dialectic in Canada between the Laurentian core and the
areas peripheral to that core, Bailey undertook to remediate the
unequal status to which his province had been subjected. That involved
rediscovering nodes of "lustre" in New Brunswick history as well as
creating the means by which students, intellectuals, citizens, and
artists could assert provincial agency and explore identity through
cultural and scholarly work. Arriving at his task with a full theoretical
knowledge of the conditions necessary for creative and intellectual
ferment, he laboured for a career "to hand on, and to improve upon,
inherited knowledge and belief,"[246] thereby enabling New Brunswickers to take their place as equal citizens in the larger federation.

Joseph Howe had done the same in Nova Scotia a century earlier,
finding "the real stamina of [his] country's character ... in habits, feel-

ings, and moral and intellectual cultivation."[247] The means of achieving egalitarian citizenship for Howe and Bailey were thus similar, and did not in any way include humble acceptance of the consolation prize of a "shabby dignity."[248] Rather, only by cultivating difference – what Benedict Anderson would later call "creole nationalisms,"[249] in which centralized models of governance are altered for the periphery – would independence of means through a self-sustaining common vision be assured. Mounting programs of imaginative reconstruction in province and region were necessary, as Howe, too, advised: "A wise nation preserves its records, gathers up its muniments, decorates the tombs of its illustrious dead, repairs its great public structures and fosters national pride and love of country by perpetual references to the sacrifices and glories of the past."[250] As Howe and Bailey knew from history, all great periods of the past had at their core a vibrant life of the mind and spirit – and if the Maritimes were to aspire again to those heights, a rebranding of the idea of place must be central, especially if the myths circulating hold that place to be defeatist, wedded to old ideas, and resistant to change. "[Howe] went beyond the view that experience of the arts had only an aesthetic value," said Bailey. Rather, the arts "not only refine our senses and faculties, but [are the means] through which our character, and self-knowledge, [is] heightened."[251] Bailey's late-career poem "Reflections on a Hill Behind a Town" captures that belief, putting knowledge of the human arts at the centre of the reformist enterprise that he and Howe shared:

> knowledge was in itself a good
>   and would bear issue
> in season, as did the earth around us
> and keep us whole.[252]

3

Desmond Pacey:
Reducing the Nation to Order

Without a body of critical opinion to hearten and direct them Canadian
writers are like a leaderless army ... The critic-militant is required for this;
not a very engaging fellow, perhaps, but a hard worker, a crusader, and useful withal.[1]

Don't be discouraged, Des. Your day will come, when the essential
services you've rendered and are rendering to Canadian criticism will be
recognized.[2]

After the fulminations of Rhodenizer, Logan and French, and Lorne Pierce,
I felt the time had come to look at Canadian Literature with a kind of
classical calm – and that is what I have tried to do.[3]

Between 1936 and 1939, as he was apprenticing in the archival and
academic fields that he would soon shape to serve provincial ends,
A.G. Bailey amassed notes for a project that was quite distinct from
the material custodianship and university lecturing that were preoc-
cupying him. That project was a book of Canadian literary criticism
that anticipated A.J.M. Smith's introduction to *The Book of Canadian
Poetry* (1943). And, though most of his notes for the book have been
lost, and the book itself never written, there does exist a repurposed
précis for the text that served as an essential point of entry into New
Brunswick for Desmond Pacey, who arrived to teach literature at UNB
in 1944.

Bailey's précis, entitled "Style of the Canadian Culture," addressed
the composite identity of Canada at a period of transition from a Vic-

4 Desmond Pacey at UNB, 1968.

torian to a modernist aesthetic. Smith's controversial introduction to
The Book of Canadian Poetry would later deal with the same divide
between the "native" and "cosmopolitan" traditions – evident, for
Smith, in the movement from a "fetish for the exalted subject" toward
a "metaphysical" commons of ideas, wit, and social criticism.[4] Predictably, Bailey's earlier thinking distinguishes itself from Smith's in
being more tolerant of the nativist traditions in Canadian poetry. The
difference is key. For Bailey, and later for Northrop Frye, those nativist
traditions were not nostalgically historicist but embedded in a Canadian sensibility that is an amalgam of multiple human geographies:
the historical and contemporary, the continental and European, and
the settler and Indigenous. That amalgam, argues Bailey, constitutes
the "deep-seated attitudes, beliefs, and habits" of the Canadian personality.[5] Especially important, he adds, is that that mixture of traditions in the Canadian personality is accompanied by dreams of abundance that register as a belief in "magnificent distances" that an
unexploited wilderness and continental immensity first offered to settlers. For Bailey, those dreams and registers still inhere "in a shrinking

and barricaded world" and are therefore still relevant in an age of modern disillusionment.[6]

While citizens "are conscious of [that] Canadianism which shapes their attitudes," however, they are also, continues Bailey, "at a loss to shred the fabric into its constituent elements."[7] Here, he implies, is a task that a national critic must undertake. Once the Canadian style is accepted for what it is, "there remains only the task of defining this outlook before proceeding to explain its persistence in Canadian literature."[8] The task is the same for the poet and critic: "to comprehend and communicate to his readers the spirit of ... [those] immensities."[9] Bailey concludes by saying that "few Canadians [poets or critics] have risen to the occasion,"[10] the inference of which, again, calls to writers and scholars to undertake a pan-Canadian critical project that will correct the errors of hasty and ill-formed judgments. The last few lines of Bailey's précis are especially germane to how Pacey would define himself at UNB: "The rub is not in the continued use of these ['images of infinitude as emotive symbols of an ahistorical national consciousness'] in place of the increasingly employed exact curvature of urban and industrial imagery, but in the task of firing the images of 'extension' with the requisite 'intensity.' When this is achieved in greater measure Canada will come into possession of an idiom of mete quality and proportionate to the landscape, which, with imperial vision, it has made its own."[11]

In this somewhat elliptical reference to the dangers of embracing the past or present as solitudes without understanding their mutuality in the contemporary mind, Bailey was no doubt thinking of what Pacey would later describe in a letter to Louis Dudek as "the fulminations of Rhodenizer, Logan and French, and Lorne Pierce."[12] Those "fulminations" and their aftershocks warrant brief consideration if the ground of Pacey's entrance into Canadian studies via the Fiddlehead ethos is to be understood in context.

The important and, in most cases, pioneering critical texts that set the tone for Canadian literary studies of the post-Confederation period emerged in quick succession in the 1920s. Most extended the Arnoldian view (Tory, nationalist, and culturally elitist) of the anthologies of the previous century. Indebted especially to E.H. Dewart's *Selections from Canadian Poets* (1864) and W.D. Lighthall's *Songs of the Great Dominion* (1889), these early critical studies sought to present the nation's literature as coherent, place-based, and derivative of (yet conflicted about) colonial models, whether American or British. Ray Palmer Baker's *History of*

English-Canadian Literature to the Confederation (1920) is the most interesting and idiosyncratic of these studies, for it made concrete an idea that
not only upset post-Confederation thinking about Canada but also
prompted a flurry of books which refuted that idea. Baker's thesis suggested that Canada's most significant pre-Confederation writers, and, by
extension, the early Canadian "style," displayed continental and republican biases that are evident in the Loyalism of Joseph Howe and T.C. Haliburton, whose characters struggle openly (consider Haliburton's Sam
Slick) with the contradictions of being pre-Revolutionary Americans in
a Nova Scotia given to rejecting the progressive ideas of frontier republicanism. Clearly heard by others, Baker's larger implication was that
Canada's literary turn to British Victorianism in the work of the Confederation poets was a retrograde move that invited the sort of self-
reifying topocentrism against which later critics such as E.K. Brown and
A.J.M. Smith would react.[13] (Fred Cogswell would later refute Baker's
hypothesis, claiming that the attitude "toward social morality by the sup-
porters and opponents of puritanism contributed more than any other
single factor to the failure of nineteenth century poetry in the Maritimes
before Roberts."[14]) For Baker, the seemingly paradoxical import of republican ideas via the Loyalists served to universalize our literature and
efface, for a time, the enervating Toryism that Confederation institutionalized. Given the east coast's participation in the North Atlantic pre-
Confederation seaboard economy, Baker's observations seemed reasonable at the time, for the movement of people, commerce, and ideas did
in fact twin eighteenth-century Canada and the United States in ways
that Confederation never duplicated or allowed.

However accurate Baker's observations may have been, the critical
studies that rapidly followed challenged his reading of history and
influence, the concentration of those arguments overdetermining a
particular reading of Canada. Archibald MacMechan's *Headwaters of
Canadian Literature* (1924) assailed Goldwin Smith, Baker's ideological fellow, for "sympathies [with America]" that "were strangely imperfect,"[15] taking as truth that the republicanism of the Canadian sensibility that Smith and Baker observed put them in "irreconcilable
opposition" with "the Canadian people."[16] Seeking a coherent identi-
ty-consolidating device, "MacMechan's argument," noted E.D. Blodgett, "depends implicitly upon [the] fact ... [that] Confederation
invests geography with a meaning it could not otherwise possess,"[17]
thus remaking Canada in opposition to the powerful southern neighbour from which many of its early citizens came.

Critical studies by J.D. Logan and Donald French (*Highways of Canadian Literature*, 1924), Lionel Stevenson (*Appraisals of Canadian Literature*, 1926), W.A. Deacon (*Poteen*, 1926), Lorne Pierce (*An Outline of Canadian Literature*, 1927), and V.B. Rhodenizer (*A Handbook of Canadian Literature*, 1930) take similar positions. In each, literature is approached not just as mirror but also as shaper of patriotic national identity. Stevenson is clearest in defining that identity in a preface fittingly called "A Manifesto for a National Literature," which asserts that "an instinctive pantheism" informs our best literature, a pantheism that "recognis[es] a spiritual meaning in nature and its identity with the soul of man."[18] While it may seem dismissive to classify these early critical studies under one umbrella, their consonance in identifying a nationalist, conserving, coherent, imperial, and non-continental "instinct" in Canada provides some insight into the overdetermined aspects of our criticism against which the critics of the 1930s bristled, A.J.M. Smith characteristically describing Logan and French's book as "uncritical and badly written."[19] Unwittingly, the somewhat haphazard if well-intentioned nature of these critical studies of the 1920s bespoke a clear message: not only was Canadian literature ready for renewal, but so was Canadian criticism.

The call was indeed heeded in the next decade and a half in the work of W.E. Collin (*The White Savannahs*, 1936), A.J.M. Smith (*The Book of Canadian Poetry*, 1943), and E.K. Brown (*On Canadian Poetry*, 1943). Re-canonizing the literature to exclude the two principals of the previous century – Roberts and Carman, as previously stated, are ignored in *The White Savannahs* – Collin led the way by moving Canada's literary heritage to the centre of the country, effectively changing a half-century of literary history to suit an emerging modernist aesthetic that aligned more favourably, he thought, with the Ottawa rather than Fredericton school of the Confederation writers. E.K. Brown followed by placing Roberts "in the very rear of the modern movement,"[20] condemning him to a nineteenth-century provincialism that Collin claimed Archibald Lampman managed to escape.[21] Echoing Collin, Brown performed a geographic shuffle that promoted Lampman and Duncan Campbell Scott, "the two most powerful and satisfying poets of the period,"[22] at the expense of Roberts and Carman, who are assigned to the backwater of New Brunswick. The same pattern repeats with Smith, who declares that only the "isolated masters [of] Heavysege, Crawford, Cameron, Duncan Campbell Scott, and Lampman" offer lasting insight to an understanding of the Canadian imagination.[23]

To A.G. Bailey, as established in the previous chapter, this forceful realignment of the literary record begged to be addressed. Bailey knew from Toynbee that history was a cumulative field, subject to all manner of flow and disruption, but he also knew from Marx that, once subsumed by more powerful narratives of relevance, old centres or figures of authority are repurposed as lackeys in unflattering materialist dramas. Though he was in sympathy with Brown and Smith as far as the need for a renovating modernism in both literature and criticism, Bailey was not nearly as bombastic or willing to sacrifice history on the altar of the present. Like Eliot, he held modernism to be as much about conserving as adding to tradition, not by "a slavish imitation" or "a complete break with the past" but by "develop[ing] [the past] to the point of contemporaneity."[24] At the same time, Bailey felt that Eliot's modernist dicta were too broad and exclusive, for "the whole of the literature of Europe from Homer"[25] smacked of the sort of Eurocentrism that looked down on New World achievement. Eliot's further dismissal of "the fluid haze of Swinburne"[26] was, in addition, no causal comment, for Bailey knew that Swinburne's fanciful conceits powered Fredericton's Confederation poets as surely as did Shelley's. Eliot's critique of Swinburne and William Morris embodied the idea that the past was never just the past, even in the hands of those loyal to it, but that it could become a straw man in service to those repurposing history for their own ideas. Modernists whose exuberance erased the past and radical localisms, or were selective about the past for arguments of advancement, were, in Bailey's view, simply careless and poorly informed. What was needed was a strong, independent *Canadian* critic who had the classical background and rooted loyalties to work against those tendencies, one of the most insidious being the emerging centralist notion that the home of the Confederation poets had become hopelessly lost in nostalgia and indigence.

Bailey turned this need into a rallying cry in the years before Pacey arrived at UNB. In academic talks, public lectures, and closed-door sessions with the university's senior administrators, he lamented the lack of a contemporary literary criticism that dismantled easy assumptions about the nation rather than reifying it in the past or fetishizing it in the present. He lamented the absence of a criticism that, like modernism itself, was historically inclined, classically evaluative, and formally as well as intellectually daring. In the process, he advocated strongly for a criticism that treated eighteenth- and nineteenth-century expression as judiciously as twentieth-century work, for he understood the Canadian sensibility to be a composite field that melded British, American, French, and Indigenous pasts. His views about such a criticism accommodated the fact that scholarship was as important as creative work in the maturing of the Canadian voice and intellect. While his motive was partly to encourage a criticism that would bring less animus or unqualified cheerleading to a nineteenth-century literature he valued – that hope partly dashed when he read Smith's assessment of the Fredericton Confederation poets[27] – it was also to encourage the wider cultivation of intellectual ferment that he had long sought. It is clear that he understood from his own sociological studies that what was good for Canada was also good for its federated parts, including New Brunswick.

In what now appears to be a sophisticated form of cultural reasoning, Bailey's appeal for a modern Canadian criticism was therefore another way of activating localist studies that would benefit New Brunswick. An address he delivered in the early 1940s makes this thinking and his strategy clear. "Our position as a province in a large dominion of a vast commonwealth of nations must be considered," he begins. "Our varying allegiances to London and Ottawa and elsewhere has [sic] made our loyalty eclectic, and has [sic] dulled the keen awareness of contact with our own soil. I think we should proceed to discover ourselves."[28] The logic is obvious if not stated directly: precisely *because* New Brunswick loyalties are "eclectic," with provincial identities layered deeply within an amalgam of other symbolic and imaginative touchstones, the revivification of the province through closed and myopic study is untenable, susceptible always to accusations of provincialism. Rather, he concludes, "we should seek through study and well thought-out programmes to bring before our minds the best in contemporary art. But we must make it our own."[29] In other words, a working space was needed in New Brunswick for figures like Pacey and Cogswell to develop critical personalities that were broad (national), focused (local), and atemporal (interested equally in the historical and contemporary records). Bailey had articulated the problem, thought through a number of solutions, and extended an invitation for a national critic to join the cause; it would be up to Pacey, the successful candidate, to find a way to fit within the discursive field that Bailey had created. The difference between his entrance into the mid-century

Fiddlehead moment and Bailey's was stark: Bailey had entered a New
Brunswick milieu through generations of family inheritance; he had
apprenticed with Canada's and New Brunswick's leading scholars, cultural workers, and writers; and, from that, he had arrived at UNB in
1937 as a celebrated alumnus, one with a clear plan to recreating the
conditions that would enable his province to reassert its literary and
cultural signature. When Pacey arrived at UNB in 1944, Bailey was well
along in instituting his plan. Pacey, however, had no such long acquaintance or ordained entrance. He had arrived in Canada via Britain and
New Zealand, he had no connections or loyalty to New Brunswick,
and he had not yet worked out a career path that would take him
through Canadian literary studies. When he arrived in New Brunswick
in the fall of 1944 as the second choice of two short-listed candidates,
he entered a narrative and professional space that Bailey was in the
midst of creating. In effect, he entered Bailey's world.

    Which is not to say that Bailey dictated the terms of Pacey's profes-
sional trajectory, but only that the most nuanced understanding of the
need for such an appointment – and the ends to which it could be
put in New Brunswick and Canada – was largely Bailey's. Perhaps
that is why, after conferring with UNB president Norman MacKenzie
in the winter of 1943, Bailey suggested a short list of two candidates
to replace English Department head Edward A. McCourt, who had
grown tired of the east and was seeking a position at the University of
Saskatchewan. (Bailey's list originally included three names, the last of
which, UNB graduate Malcolm Ross, was dropped early because of perceived political radicalism related to wartime activities.[30]) Bailey's first
suggestion was Hugh MacLennan of the Classics Department at
Lower Canada College (Montreal), a young man he had met at the
British Museum a few years earlier. Bailey and MacKenzie were admirers of MacLennan's *Barometer Rising* (1941), its sense of new, post-
imperial beginnings having had particular resonance for Bailey and
special relevance, as well, for a Canada that was rapidly gaining confidence from its wartime efforts. Both had also listened to MacLennan's
October 1942 "Twelve Million Neighbors" CBC Radio broadcasts for
the Community Schools Program of the Rural Adult Education Association and both knew of MacLennan's success in winning a Guggenheim Fellowship to write what would soon become the best-selling
Two Solitudes (1945).[31] For Bailey and MacKenzie, MacLennan was
one of Canada's most promising young academics, especially appealing because of his Maritime roots and his desire to escape the

drudgery of teaching Latin at a boys' school in Montreal. Born and raised in Nova Scotia and educated at Oxford and Princeton, where he specialized in Roman history and the collapse of provincial towns, MacLennan was exactly the kind of rooted scholar/writer who was likely to champion the region's causes while also putting the region at the centre of the pan-Canadian critical project that Bailey thought was so vital. MacLennan's letter of application to McCourt expressed the kind of internationally informed fidelity to place that Bailey sought: "I firmly believe," wrote MacLennan, "that no novelist can create first-class work except out of his own background. No matter how universal his work may be, it must have this root."[32]

The finer details of what transpired next have been lost to history, extant letters and fragments suggesting that, after some initial hesitation by MacLennan, MacKenzie and Bailey conferred again in early July to formalize the process, this time bringing Pacey's name forward. (MacKenzie had gotten to know Pacey during the previous summer.) It appears safe to assume that, with the completion of *Two Solitudes* pressing upon him, MacLennan felt obligated to fulfill the terms of his Guggenheim Fellowship and complete the novel he had proposed – and, in a broader sense, that he was still trying to figure out if his destiny was that of a writer or academic. With the commercial and critical success of *Two Solitudes* – the novel sold out completely on the day of its launch, Leo Kennedy calling it "the GREAT Canadian novel" in a review in the Chicago *Sun*[33] – that question would not be answered until MacLennan accepted a position at McGill in 1951. But the episode remains a tantalizing one for speculations about the direction of literary studies in Canada had the MacLennan/Pacey story turned out differently. How might Canadian (and Maritime) literary history have been different if the country's foremost novelist of mid-century had found a home in New Brunswick?

Speculations aside, Pacey won the day with testimonials from E.K. Brown, A.S.P. Woodhouse, E.J. Pratt, Pelham Edgar, and Roy Daniells, all intimates of Bailey. When Pacey arrived in Fredericton from Brandon College in the middle of September 1944, Bailey was there to greet him as much as tutor him in the poetics of the region's history and need.

THE COMMONWEALTH'S PERIPATETIC BOY

William Cyril Desmond Pacey was born on 1 May 1917 in Dunedin, New Zealand, a coastal city on the country's south island that he

would always consider home. Long after leaving as a child, an adult
Pacey still talked about the penguins on St Clair Beach and about the
sand and surf that formed his earliest memories. Desmond's father,
Rifleman William Pacey, was an engineer with the New Zealand
Expeditionary Force. He was descended from the Pacy-sur-Eure clan
of the Eure River (west of Paris) two hundred years before Charle-
magne, and his modern ancestry was scattered around Nottingham,
England, the home of the family's most famous figure, the Reverend
Robert Lowe, rector of Bingham.[34] Filled with wanderlust, a young
William Pacey and his bride, a gifted singer, had found their way to
New Zealand, where, with his wife expecting their first child, he
joined the Expeditionary Force in November 1916, six months before
his son Desmond was born, and seventeen months before he was
killed on the battlefield in France on 27 March 1918. The circumstance, not surprisingly, led to his son's strong aversion to war and to
an unusually close bond between mother and child. And, though
Desmond Pacey would eventually forge a strong connection with a
stepfather in Canada, he was always, in real and symbolic ways, father-
less, a condition that prompted him to establish very close relationships with some of the older men he encountered during his studies.
It was for those mentors, and to please a mother who had lost so much
while investing so selflessly in their enterprise together,[35] that he
strove to excel academically and seek a professional status that he
eventually found in New Brunswick.

In 1924, on her only child's seventh birthday, a widowed Mary Elizabeth Pacey moved back to England from New Zealand, the move, she
later said, aimed at giving her son the best education he could receive.
Her people were tenant farmers in the Midlands, and so her return to
central England with her son was as much to provide him with emotional stability as to equip him with a good British education. Training
in maternity and midwifery at the Jessop Hospital for Women in
Sheffield, she began her nursing career in the Stanton Harcourt district
of Oxfordshire.[36] Being a widowed woman with a child made finding
nursing positions difficult, however, and the utilitarian conservatism of
her parents grated against her freedoms. Desmond Pacey's early years
were therefore spent in transit as his mother moved between nursing
districts and rooming houses seeking an elusive permanence. Even
summer holidays were spent chasing temporary work assignments.
Mother and son found stability where they could, often in church communities around Oxfordshire, where young Desmond was a choirboy

at St Michael's and later a student at Magnus Grammar School in the East Midlands town of Newark-on-Trent, Nottinghamshire. The footholds of church, school, and maternal doting instilled in young Desmond a lifelong love of church music, a deep faith, a sense of gentlemanly conduct (learned early and well by the only sons of single mothers), and all the pleasures and escape of solitary reading, each tied to the work he would undertake as a literary critic.

Magnus Grammar School, the most formative of his early schools, was a boy's academy oriented toward classical foundations in the early forms. Deeply class conscious, its students received introduction to Latin and Greek and, as importantly, learned about the social corridors along which their lives could reasonably expand. (In an early draft of a memoir about his move to Canada, Pacey recalled his delight in discovering "that the outstanding boy in [my new Canadian] school – the one who would have been known as Head Boy in my English school – was the son of the school janitor[,] [something] that could never have happened in England."[37]) Though he arrived late at Magnus (September 1928) and stayed only three years, leaving the school in the spring of 1931, young Pacey made a strong impression on his masters and peers – so strong that the Newark *Herald* would cover the story of his academic success in Canada three years after he left Magnus. Citing his high-school record in Canada as one "never equalled in the school during the last quarter of a century," the *Herald* story touted Magnus's responsibility for Pacey's academic preparation, conceding only that his entrance scholarship to Magnus revealed aptitudes of a high order.[38] Buried in the school's interest in one of its distant boys was the most significant thing that a young Pacey took away from Magnus: that sense of abiding fraternity – sociologists call it anthem-attachment – that one develops in accord with school and chums. Even as an adult, Pacey remained in contact with a few of his Magnus classmates and insisted that his own children experience the English system at some point in their educations, as much for the sport and camaraderie as for the instruction.

The full story of what happened next – of what brought mother and son to Canada in 1931 – is sketchy, except for the knowledge that Mary Pacey had met a Canadian farmer and travelled to Canada to visit him, whereupon they became engaged. With prospects still poor for anything but itinerant nursing work in Nottinghamshire, she decided to move permanently to Canada with her son, arriving in Montreal aboard the *Duchess of Richmond* on 18 September 1931. For fourteen-year-old

Desmond, the move to the farthest western reaches of the Commonwealth was another in a long series of upheavals, this time to a foreign
country (in his British schoolboy's mind still a colony) that had only
been glimpsed imaginatively in the pages of *Chums* and the romances of
G.A. Henty and R.M. Ballantyne. What he encountered in Canada, however, was nothing like what he had imagined or anticipated.

Arriving in Hamilton, Ontario, on a fall market day, he was taken
aback by the bountifulness of the harvest, noting years later how different that sense of abundance was from the "bleak, dour" market
town of Newark he had just left.[39] To the impressionable boy, the welcoming bounty of the land seemed to match that of the people, whose
unqualified embrace also startled him. "I loved the informality with
which these new Canadian friends picked up the cobs [of fresh corn]
in their hands," he recalled, "and the warmth and gaiety with which
that first meal was conducted. From the very first I became aware of a
quality in Canadians which has never failed me – their readiness to
accept an immigrant, a stranger, and to make him feel at once that he
is welcome and at home."[40] Those impressions would be redoubled in
the days ahead, especially in his new school. When Principal T.J. Hicks
of Caledonia High School greeted him warmly, promising him that
honest work would surely open unlimited horizons (maybe the University of Toronto, Hicks said, and then, perhaps, Oxford or Cambridge), a young Pacey felt "the first burgeoning of hope," as much sur-
prised as thankful that his English schoolboy's cap, knickers, and
accent did not get him the schoolyard beating that he had expected.[41]
What was essential about that experience of inclusion is the sense of
forward optimism it instilled in the young man. The Canada he
entered was exactly the Canada that Bailey had defined in "Style of the
Canadian Culture": a country in which wilderness and immensity registered as dreams of abundance, providing both room to grow and
support in that growth. It was clearly a nascent country, beckoning
anyone who wished to come forward to participate in its development. If it could only outgrow its lack of self-confidence, Pacey later
mused, it "will become one of the truly great nations of the world."[42]
In his first weeks and months, he became convinced that Canada provided a special sort of opportunity: a talented young man and a
nascent country could grow together. Even as a boy, Pacey knew that
everything was possible here. That view became the hope that powered him for an entire career and that lent itself to the title of his only
novel (unpublished), *The Land Is Bright*.[43]

In his three years at Caledonia High, Pacey excelled academically. Rising at five each morning, he milked cows and did barn chores on his stepfather Boulton's Glanford Station farm, then took a bus or hitchhiked the six miles to school. The Boulton farm had no indoor plumbing, wiring, or any of the amenities of homes in Hamilton, fifteen miles northeast, but it did provide the first feelings of lasting rootedness that Pacey experienced. He graduated in the spring of 1934 with the school's top marks, achieving first-class honours in ten provincial exams and a second in two. "During my twenty years in this school," wrote principal Hicks, "I have not had a more diligent student, nor one as deserving of a scholarship."[44] On the strength of that record, Pacey was accepted to Victoria College (University of Toronto[45]) with three entrance scholarships, one the prestigious Moses Henry Aikins Scholarship in General Proficiency. Years later he wrote about the feelings of a boy in similar circumstance in the story "The Field of Oats." The once naive, now happy farm boy contemplates his own move to a big-city university from the family farm, understanding for the first time his "strong stirring of affection for the field[s]." In the story's moment of insight, the boy realizes that "though he had put a lot of himself into those [provincial] examinations there was more of himself in this field. His roots were here. This was where he belonged. For the first time he really knew."[46] And so must have Pacey known at that time that he had become Canadian and would always prefer a rural to an urban home.

He arrived in Toronto in September 1934 with a great need for guidance, which was initially provided by George S. Brett, former head of philosophy and recently appointed dean of graduate studies (1932), who recommended that his own academic stream, modelled after Oxford's *Literae Humaniores* or "Greats," was the most liberal of the options on offer and thus a good choice for a Moses Henry Aikins scholar. Pacey followed Brett's advice, entering what was known as the Philosophy Course (English or history) at the denominational Victoria College, a stream that enabled him to read widely in philosophy, literature, and history in an atmosphere that affirmed his Methodist traditions. Though increasing numbers of University of Toronto faculty were advocating for a more secular curriculum for undergraduates, the denominational system was firmly in place during Pacey's years, Victoria College still centred at Emmanuel, its United Church school of theology, and a lingering Methodist spirit still strong from the college's earlier days. Brett proved to be a good if distant guide.

His philosophical orientation was toward science and psychology, a perspective that was manifest in what one of his students described as "a form of dynamic pluralism" that rejected idealism for more instrumental, grounded inquiry.[47] It was that grounding in the realm of utility that students found so liberating, some, like Northrop Frye, who had arrived at Victoria five years before Pacey, displaying as much interest in popular forms (Hollywood and Charlie Chaplin) as in high culture (Oswald Spengler and William Blake). This early culturalist approach was further abetted by English professor J.D. Robins's interest in folklore. Students of Brett and Robins were therefore not only part of a progressive liberal-arts experience but also witnesses to early efforts to present cultural and practical inquiry as legitimate fields of study. In fact, Brett's students saw those efforts unfold before them in the pages of the interdisciplinary *University of Toronto Quarterly*, founded just three years before Pacey arrived and often central in academic discussions.

Brett proved most helpful to Pacey, however, in recommending a supervisory relationship with the Harvard-educated Walter T. Brown, who had been lured back to Toronto from Yale in 1932 to become principal of Victoria College. Brown was less trenchant than Brett and considerably warmer, given to championing his students in personal and spiritual, not just intellectual, ways. A brilliant student from the southern Ontario farming town of Lakefield, he was sympathetic to precocious undergraduates like Pacey who had followed similar rural pathways to higher education. On the strength of Pacey's scholarships and first-year grades, Brown made a point to get to know the young man, advising him, as he had advised Frye,[48] that acquiring a credential in the ministry would serve as a foundation for all other learning. His great modernist colleague, E.J. Pratt, was proof of that, a poet not just of emotional mastery but of intellectual range. Having come from Yale and experienced the close-reading approach of the Berkeley Divinity School, Brown thus complemented Brett's method of "dynamic pluralism," insisting that his students read broadly but selectively to make learning relevant in a rapidly changing world. His students were therefore widely read in classical history (Greek and Roman), English, French, "religious knowledge," philosophy, and anthropology, while also schooled in the formalist methods of the Berkeley Divinity School. Pacey followed suit, narrowing to English only in his third year.

One of the many benefits of working under Brown was entering his orbit, which included Pratt, Robins, Roy Daniells, Frye, E.K. Brown,

Robert Finch, Earle Birney, and a number of other left-leaning figures interested in Canadian literature and in the recently renovated *Canadian Forum* magazine, its profile changing rapidly under publisher and socialist Graham Spry during Pacey's first two years at Victoria. And, though Principal Brown was, at least publicly, a model of conservatism in the United Church, his catholicity of spirit on campus opened students to all manner of possibility, including the quite daring notion (in the 1930s) that Canadian literature was a fruitful area of study. That notion, championed especially by his colleague Pelham Edgar, became a signature of the college, influencing the careers of Daniells, Frye, and Pacey, and affecting the direction of the college's student publication *Acta Victoriana*, which, under Frye's editorship in 1932, recommitted to a focus on Canada. It was on Brown's advice that Pacey entered Roy Daniells's class on Canadian and American literature in his third year, a class taught by Daniells, assisted by Frye,[49] and wholly influenced by Edgar, who became a mentor to Pacey in Edgar's last years of a long and distinguished career (Edgar retired in 1938).

A long-time friend of the Confederation poets, Edgar was the unchallenged dean of the discipline, having just published *The Art of the Novel* in the year before Pacey arrived. It was Edgar who built the university's most influential English Department in a century, hiring Pratt, Robins, and Frye; it was Edgar whose interest in French Canada paved the way for our contemporary understanding of Canadian biculturalism; it was Edgar who pioneered and popularized Canadian literary studies in an age of still lingering anglophilia; and it was Edgar whose critical style Pacey and other foundational critics of mid-century came to emulate. It was also Edgar's fascination with T.S. Eliot and D.H. Lawrence that introduced a whole generation of students, including Daniells and Bailey, to modernist ideas. If he annoyed his more austere colleagues with his informalities – classics professor C.B. Sissons recalls Edgar lecturing to undergraduates with his dog tied to the leg of his desk[50] – students delighted in his congeniality and high ideals. Frye dedicated *Fearful Symmetry* (1947) to Edgar, the man, he said, who had practically introduced him to Blake in his eighteenth-century course.[51] The Edgar whom Pacey encountered a few years after Frye was equally formidable, an Arnoldian who believed in the same reciprocity of art and society that Bailey would insist upon at UNB. A decadent society, Edgar told students, produced decadent literature in the same way as a literature of fine and noble sensibility strengthened a society's values. Intellectual workers in the arts must therefore be mindful of their roles as social arbiters, their declamations moving the social register up or down. His students, remembered Frye, learned that they were social agents with responsibility for the health of the commons, not merely oracles of taste or fanciful opinion. As such, Edgar insisted that his students work to effect social change through cultural means, opening themselves particularly to the worlds from which they had come. The idea became revolutionary for Pacey and his cohorts, Frye considering it one of the great lessons of his undergraduate training. As Frye put it, "[Edgar] learned from Shelley ... that great culture is also completely provincial, that it is as racy of the soil as a fine wine, and can only grow where there is a powerful sense of locality."[52]

No less important for Frye and Pacey was a critical stocktaking that Edgar was working on in Pacey's last year at Victoria. Published in the July 1939 number of the *University of Toronto Quarterly*, Edgar's "Literary Criticism in Canada" beckons to aspiring critics of a fledgling Canadian literature. While there is "a considerable volume of literary criticism in this country," the essay begins, "it would be unwise to say that much of it is of outstanding merit."[53] The call to arms is deliberate, for Edgar, like A.G. Bailey, was seeking to create "[a] critically receptive public" and a body of professional literati who could inculcate literary values. When the critic's work is done well, Edgar asserts, we "cannot fail to create the buoyant and sustaining atmosphere which Matthew Arnold associated with periods of creative expansion."[54] When Pacey heard the same language and logic from Bailey six years later, he recognized it instantly.

Edgar's "Literary Criticism in Canada" was also influential for identifying some of the fruitful avenues that Pacey's later scholarship would follow. Edgar persisted in the view that Roberts was still relevant, despite the recent critical opinion of W.E. Collin's *White Savannahs* (1936) and the *New Provinces* (1936) anthology of poetry that Edgar's close friends Pratt and Finch had been instrumental in producing. His good-natured approach to Collin's biases – "the plan of his book necessitated that his enthusiasm for younger writers should be balanced by a hostility equally enthusiastic to the work of their predecessors"[55] – reveals a clinician's calm that Pacey would adopt in sorting candidates for his canonical judgment. An additional lead that Pacey pursued (perhaps the more significant) is found in Edgar's comment that "Frederick Philip Grove is another writer of established reputation" who warrants closer study.[56] In everything from the frankness of tone to the necessity of annual stocktaking, a need that Pacey would begin to address in his sweeping essays of the 1950s ("Literary Criticism in Canada," "Areas of Research in Canadian Literature," "English-Canadian Poetry, 1944–54," and "The Canadian Writer and His Public"), Edgar's critical imprint is detectable. Even in the area of mentorship, Edgar's more advanced students became Pacey's closest guides.

Roy Daniells, who began as an instructor at Victoria in the year that Pacey arrived, was particularly important in that regard. Just as he had introduced A.G. Bailey to literary modernism via Eliot's poetry four years earlier, Daniells also introduced Pacey to modernism and Canadian literature. (Bailey and Pacey never crossed paths in Toronto, Bailey leaving in September 1934 for post-doctoral study in England just as Pacey was arriving to begin his undergraduate degree.) Daniells, who taught Pacey from 1934 to 1937 (including the second-year English honours course), befriended him in residence and worked with him in the Dramatic Society and on the editorial board of *Acta Victoriana*. Lifetime correspondent, emotional supporter, godfather of his first-born, and, in Pacey's description, "chief architect of my career,"[57] Daniells nudged Pacey toward studying a Canadian literature that could only be made better by the involvement of competent critics. In that action it was clear that Edgar's views had infused the English Department, filtering down to graduate students and new instructors like Daniells, who in turn passed them on to undergraduates. For Daniells, as biographer Sandra Djwa relates,[58] the application of Edgar's ideas to a neglected literature was bound up in larger narratives of escape from dogma. Just as the Plymouth Brethren doctrine of his father suppressed Daniells's intellectual freedoms, so did colonial dogmas suppress the freedom to explore new modes of expression (modernism) and new areas of interest (Canada). The study of Canadian literature and that literature's struggle to modernize was therefore emancipating work, thought Daniells, work that invited the independent thinker and pioneer. For Pacey, the intellectual roadmap that Edgar and Daniells offered aligned exactly with his own sense of the open horizons of a nascent Canada.

That aspect of classroom instruction found complement in the larger university of the 1930s, where social activism was on low but steady boil. The lead-up to the Spanish Civil War was attracting faculty comment, Daniells and Birney writing poems of protest for the *Canadian Forum*, Frye publishing increasing numbers of socialists in *Acta Victoriana*, and high-profile professors like Frank Underhill and

Eric Havelock gaining notoriety and, in Underhill's case, censor for comments about capitalism's complicity in global injustice and unrest. Pacey's philosophy professor G.S. Brett was also active, joining a large group of University of Toronto faculty who wrote a public letter condemning police actions in stopping a Fellowship of Reconciliation committee from holding a meeting on campus. Ever attentive to Christian citizenship, Toronto Catholics added their voice in the pages of the diocesan papers the *Catholic Register* and *Social Forum*. As the decade progressed so rose the political vitriol. Just weeks before Pacey's arrival on campus, Underhill spoke at the annual Couchiching Conference, saying that the British Empire should be assigned "to the scrap heap" and that "[Canada] went into war blindly because we swallowed the British propaganda about democracy."[59] Even the normally reserved Methodists at Victoria College were incensed by what another war would do to the country's poor, their reactions contributing to a growing evangelical sentiment that echoed earlier expressions of the Social Gospel.[60] King Gordon and Eugene Forsey gained prominence as pioneers of a new political party, the Co-operative Commonwealth Federation (CCF) at this time, joining Toronto professors Harry Cassidy (social science) and Joseph Parkinson (political economy) as architects of the Regina Manifesto. Methodist minister-turned-activist J.S. Woodsworth also started visiting the Victoria campus, supporting the fledgling Anglican Fellowship for Social Action and Fellowship for a Christian Social Order.[61] Though tepid by later standards, this bubbling activism nevertheless garnered administrative concern, university president Henry John Cody opining that "the chief sponsors of socialism in this part of the country are members of the staff of Victoria College."[62]

As Richard Allen correctly observes, however, social reform is never a political anomaly in a denominational context.[63] Rather, for the colleges that were under Toronto's charter, including Victoria, social reform was thought of as God's work, with the advancement of either moral order (Protestant) or social justice (Catholic) held up as the exalted labour of educated men. For the evangelical "clergyman-professors" at Victoria College,[64] social service was instinct and creed. It was their calling, regardless of disciplinary profession, and the provision of that service was the criteria by which each felt he would be judged. This was the common ground on which the Methodists and United Church faculty of Victoria College stood – and, in fact, the common ground of all Protestant churches since the founding of the

Social Service Council of Canada in 1914. All were missionaries for reform, plain and simple. And it is precisely on that point where the Arnoldian ideas of an incongruous Pelham Edgar (a free-thinking, high-spirited, imbibing Anglican at a Methodist-turned-United college) come into full relevance for Daniells, Frye, E.K. Brown, and Pacey.

Put simply, the stricter Methodists at Victoria may not have approved of Edgar's informalities and his drinking, but they were completely in accord with his literary and critical values. Like them, he believed in what Matthew Arnold called the "special utility"[65] of striving toward perfection. Intellectuals should not be privileged members of an elite class given to the liberal temptations of fancy, but rather models of social action and change. "The true business of the friends of culture," wrote Arnold, is "to spread the belief in right reason and ... to get men to try, in preference to staunchly acting with imperfect knowledge, to obtain some sounder basis of knowledge on which to act."[66] But "right reason" alone is not enough, explained Edgar. Arnold's "strong doing"[67] must also be present – to the extent that the educated citizen must adopt a missionary zeal to convert "Philistines" and "Barbarians"[68] from the baseness of Parliament and the marketplace. Where does one find that combination of perfection, right thinking, and strong doing? In the most rarefied expressions of literary culture, of course, which, wrote Arnold, embodies "moral and social passion for doing good."[69] And so Edgar, like his more overtly evangelical colleagues, encouraged his students to go out into the world as apostles of culture, using culture in all forms ("the best which has been thought and said") to model the finest Hellenistic ideals. "Those who work for this," he quoted Arnold, "are the sovereign educators."[70] For Edgar's students, whether Lorne Pierce, Daniells, Brown, Frye, or Pacey, that teaching was gospel: "Their generation [sought] the kingdom of God in the ordinary necessary professional labour that Canada needed."[71]

Arnold's nineteenth-century idealism is easy to scoff at today, but it was in full force in the hallways and classrooms of Victoria College in the 1930s. Students there, like Pacey, did not study literature or philosophy for personal edification but to apprehend the right sort of values – and, once they did so, they were obliged to convert others in order to "help [society] out of [its] present difficulties."[72] For Daniells, Frye, and Pacey, the idea was unassailable. Each may have chosen a slightly different path through culture, but all followed the premise that to educate was to convert – and conversion the path to social reform. Those lucky enough to engage in this work were the high priests of truth. Their authority was inviolable, and, as missionaries, they were in a hurry. Frye's famous quip – "I know Blake as no man has ever known him"[73] – stems from that urgency. The college's motto inscribed in Old Vic's Romanesque arch reinforced the message: "The truth shall make you free." The emotional suffering that each experienced (documented in biographies of Daniells and E.K. Brown, and evident in the private correspondence of Pacey) reveals the costs of that belief for men whose quite natural feelings of unworthiness were amplified by this underlying proselytism.

The last thing of significance that Pacey absorbed from his undergraduate training in Toronto was his field of interest. Influenced as he was by events around him, that field was inevitably *Canadian* literature. Not only was Canadian studies a burgeoning interest of his English Department professors, but a groundswell of Canadian patriotism also surrounded him at the university. In Hart House, paintings from Group of Seven artists A.Y. Jackson, Fred Varley, Tom Thomson, Lawren Harris, J.E.H. MacDonald, and Arthur Lismer covered the walls. Hart House theatre sets often bore the imprint of those painters, Lismer frequently visiting the theatre in his role as educational coordinator at the Toronto Art Gallery. There was also a direct line of connection between art and literature at Victoria. English professor J.D. Robins insisted that his students avail themselves of the wider expressions of art, requiring that they visit the Toronto Art Gallery and Mellors Fine Arts store, where large inventories of the Group of Seven were on display. Artists such as Pegi Nicol, whom Pacey would meet again in Fredericton, frequented the galleries. Helen Kemp, Frye's soon-to-be wife, was hired by Arthur Lismer to lecture to groups at the Toronto Art Gallery and coordinate inter-gallery loans. As in New Brunswick, local galleries were seen not just as repositories of other forms of artistic expression but as sites of energy that were perfecting localist enterprise. Likewise, in scholarly communities, *New Provinces* (1936), the first anthology of modern Canadian poetry, was receiving a lot of attention, as was Pratt's *Canadian Poetry Magazine* (1936–43). Just as boldly, the *University of Toronto Quarterly*, the *Canadian Forum*, and *Acta Victoriana* were rising up to meet and shape the expectations of an increasingly sophisticated Canadian intelligentsia. In April 1936 the *Quarterly* began its first instalment of the "Letters in Canada" series, an annual stocktaking of Canadian literature that would morph into the *Literary History of Canada* a generation later. Each of those magazines was making Canada its primary focus, the latter two in often provocative ways. Pacey partook directly of that trend when he became editor-in-chief of *Acta Victoriana* in 1937.

Though still an undergraduate, he was deeply influenced by what he witnessed at Victoria. His four years there were some of the most dynamic of the college's history. Public intellectuals and churchmen were defying convention to speak against injustice. Canadian nationalism was in the air, legitimizing new fields of Canadian study. Bolstering this ferment was a sense of urgency informed by a nineteenth-century idealism that infused educational culture. This "very appealing mixture" of "[Christian] Socialism, Imperialism and Nationalism," wrote Frye, contributed to "mak[ing] Canada sturdier than England and more coherent than the United States."[74] As Pacey had hoped, Canada was indeed on track to "become one of the truly great nations of the world."[75]

This enthusiasm for Canada found expression in an essay that Pacey wrote in his last year at Victoria and published in the *Cambridge Review* in December 1938. Along with the clues it provides to his mentors' influences, "At Last – A Canadian Literature" reveals some of Pacey's later expository style, a style learned well from Pelham Edgar and E.K. Brown. Central to the essay's argument are two ideas that Pacey rehearses in print for the first time: the declaration of neglect as a motive for critical attention and the statement that, being colonial for so long, Canada has not yet produced a mature literature. The first idea is delivered with a sense of youthful bravado that Pacey never quite outgrows. "It will no doubt come as a surprise to most of my readers," he writes, "to learn that there is someone who has the temerity to believe that the foundations of an essentially national literature in Canada are, if not laid, at least in the process of being laid."[76] To construct neglect in that way was to create opportunity, which Pacey would do for the first decade of his career. It was a well-learned rhetorical trick from his mentors that he perfected early. At the same time, the defensiveness that was evident in statements of neglect had to be tempered, which is why he always twinned the notion of neglect with the admission of want: "Canadian literature, and Canadian culture generally, suffered, during the last century and for the first two decades of this, from the fault of being 'derived.'"[77] Pacey thus casts off Carman, Lampman, and Scott as imitators of Wordsworth and William Cullen Bryant. Their work, he writes, is a monotonous hybrid of Canada and the English Lake Country.[78] Much better is the poetry of Pratt, the fiction of Morley Callaghan, and the critical prose of the *Canadian Forum* – better because of the "ruggedness" of Pratt, the realism of Callaghan, and the wide-eyed "keenness" of the *Forum*.[79] Again, while the essay is indeed precocious for an undergraduate, its ideas are Edgar's and Brown's, particularly those that will appear in the first chapter of Brown's not-yet-published but widely discussed *On Canadian Poetry* (1943). The importance of the essay is not its originality, then, but what it reveals about the ideas that Pacey chooses to extract, the most important of those being Brown's notion, shared by Bailey, that "[a] great literature is the flowering of a great society, a vital and adequate society."[80] Pacey was displaying early that, like Eliot, he was adept at synthesizing and popularizing the ideas of others. And thus, while not original – he would later dismiss the piece as "adolescent in its uncritical enthusiasm" and naive in "fail[ing] to do justice to our older poets"[81] – his Cambridge essay provides at least the glimmer of how he would begin to see and present himself to a public readership.

True to the Victoria College creed, he would perceive himself as a high priest of culture, someone who believed not only that a Canadian culture did exist but that that culture needed an emissary to bring it into full expression. In accepting that role, Pacey presents himself as a new Adam, the person who names, categorizes, and evaluates that which is essential to an emergent and better Canada. His early work is unequivocal about the fact that he would do this to rid the world of ignorance while claiming for Canada a merit that colonial mockery denied. Between the lines of the essay is evidence of a view that he had heard Frank Underhill and other left nationalists declaim: that Canada was better served by its own citizens than by the opinions of those from supposedly superior places. Pacey may have sought the Old World legitimacy and romance of a British apprenticeship (he published "At Last – A Canadian Literature" while in his first year at Cambridge), but he bristled at the haughtiness of superiority. In that attitude, he was Canada's and New Zealand's child, at home in a Commonwealth of self-governing Dominions striving to rid themselves of colonial status. As both a twenty-one-year-old and a mature critic, he belonged to a Canada that he was a participant in creating. Though imitative of the ideas of his mentors, the first essay he published suggests that his undergraduate training at Victoria College was far more significant for what he would become than his brief time at Cambridge. Cambridge was status and calling card, with some romance and nostalgia thrown in, but Victoria College was where a lifetime's ideas were first sown.

His time abroad at Trinity College, Cambridge (October 1938 to June 1940) was focused on acquiring the credentials to teach in Canada. Finishing with an undergraduate record at Victoria that approached Frye's – Pacey won two gold medals and the governor general's silver medal for the best honours degree – he narrowly missed a Rhodes scholarship, finishing second to Alan Jarvis, who in 1955 would become director of Canada's National Gallery and whom Robertson Davies later used as the model for the suave Alwyn Ross in *What's Bred in the Bone* (1985). Shaken by the outcome, Pacey concluded that "perhaps it is a sign that God has a job for me in the ministry."[82] His disappointment was tempered by support from professors Pratt, Robins, and Edgar, who assisted Pacey in applying for a Massey Travelling Fellowship, which allowed him to study at Cambridge.[83] But that did not dampen his interest in the ministry, the utility of which Walter Brown had instilled in Victoria students. While at Trinity, Pacey also studied the philosophy of religion and church history at Westminster [Presbyterian] College. He would later continue that work with a view to ordination in the Faculty of Theology at United College, Winnipeg, in 1942. His primary pursuit at Cambridge, however, was a course of English studies at Trinity College under the direction of Brian W. Downs, his thesis project considering the influence of French fiction on the English novel from 1880 to 1900. Though certainly not Canadian, the project reflected the interests of Pelham Edgar and E.K. Brown, the latter of whom had done similar work in his own graduate studies at the Sorbonne in the late 1920s.[84] Pacey's graduate studies produced two 1941 articles, "Balzac and Thackeray" in the *Modern Language Review* and "Henry James and His French Contemporaries" in *American Literature*. Some other work from this period at Cambridge was later published, but upon returning to Canada in 1940 Pacey resumed his first interest, Canadian literature, telling Roy Daniells that his graduate study had simply broadened the context for work in Canada.[85] In that admission, Edgar's signature was again present, for in the influential essay "Literary Criticism in Canada" he had insisted that exposure to international writers and trends was necessary to prevent Canadian criticism from "grow[ing] up in a void."[86]

With a Cambridge PhD almost in hand and letters of reference from E.J. Pratt and the renowned British critic E.M.W. Tillyard, whose students at Jesus College Pacey tutored, Pacey accepted a job in May 1940 at Brandon College in Manitoba.[87] His mentor Roy Daniells, who was head of English at the University of Manitoba (1937–46), had also written in support.[88] Pacey and his wife, Mary Carson, whom he had met as a fellow student at the University of Toronto (Annesley Hall) and married in 1939, moved to Manitoba to take on the new teaching role, quickly immersing themselves in a large social circle that included Sinclair Ross, author of the soon-to-be-published *As For Me and My House* (1941). After seeing Pacey perform in Noël Coward's *Hands across the Sea* at the Brandon Little Theatre, Ross befriended Pacey, urging him to return to a focus on Canada, particularly the west, and also to revisit his creative work. Pacey did both, writing more short fiction than criticism during his early years at Brandon. (At Ross's suggestion, Pacey also secured the services of AFG Literary Agency in New York in 1941 to place his creative work in magazines.)

Of considerably more consequence, though, was Ross's interest in Frederick Philip Grove, which spurred Pacey to revisit the reading he had begun under Pelham Edgar in Toronto. Pacey's first letter to Grove was written on 15 January 1941 to prepare for a radio talk he was giving on CKX (Brandon) entitled "Manitoba in Fiction." Daniells had organized these broadcasts, called "Canadian Sketches: Our Non-Taxable Wealth," a year after arriving in Manitoba, their intention to create a series of "University on the Air" shows. Grove, a kindred wanderer,[89] was to be the focus of Pacey's broadcast, so he wrote to the author for information about his life, aims, and literary influences. Grove responded enthusiastically, sending an early version of "The Seasons" and then the autobiographical "Life of a Writer in Canada," which became *In Search of Myself* (1946). The contrasts between Grove's youth among the European literary aristocracy and his later life as an itinerant teacher and farmer in the United States and Canada both fascinated and misled Pacey, the result of which was the actual start of a critical career rooted in Canadian concern.[90] Of course, as the Canadian critical establishment now knows, Pacey's work on Grove would be severely compromised by Grove's congenital lying, as Douglas Spettigue put it, but the fault of that rests as much with Grove as with Pacey's uncritical acceptance of received truth. That the critical community in Canada took the opportunity to lambaste Pacey for shortcuts and other scholarly misdemeanours was reflective of the same set of generational dynamics that had turned Leo Kennedy and A.J.M. Smith against Roberts and Carman: in short, by the late 1960s, Pacey had become the establishment figure that new critics felt compelled to unseat. His reign, some felt, had gone on too long, and his authority could be too brash. In the clarity of hindsight, circumstances of the Pacey/Grove debacle are easier to read. In 1941 Pacey was a young critic eager to establish himself. His mentors and a burgeoning cultural nationalism had convinced him that he was operating in a nascent field. Those same mentors, notably E.K. Brown and Pelham Edgar, had always spoken highly of Grove, especially about how his work unsettled Canadian puritanism. (*Settlers of the Marsh* [1925], Grove's first novel, was banned by the Winnipeg Public Library and put on restricted access in Toronto for moral wantonness.) More consequentially, however, Pacey was working at a time when the gentleman's covenant was firmly in place; that is, when the best source of information about a writer was the writer himself. Pelham Edgar had followed that credo when working on Roberts, as had A.J.M. Smith and F.R. Scott when working on their contemporaries. It was simply the way research was conducted before the critic metaphorically killed the author. That Pacey would not have believed Grove, especially his written record, is inconceivable – and, again, as much a blight on Grove for falsifying that record as on Pacey for trusting the word of an accomplished artist. By the time Spettigue arrived on the scene, the methods of criticism had changed dramatically.

That explanation is not meant to defend unreservedly a young critic's judgment, but rather to place that critic fairly in his own time. Pacey had no reason not to believe Grove, and those who made much of the apparent indiscretion of doing so were targeting Pacey more than his research practices. What makes this clarification necessary, as George Woodcock was first to observe, is that Pacey, more than any figure in his generation of pioneering Canadian critics, produced the work and attained the status that invited challenge.[91] When Pacey arrived at the University of New Brunswick in 1944, four years after his first academic post at Brandon (and a year from the launch of his book on Grove), he was on a path to establishing a reputation that would become ripe for overthrow.

The year before arriving in New Brunswick, Pacey was found medically unfit to join the war effort. Though terrified by war, he had allowed his name to stand for the air force, as much to honour the memory of his father as to find some relief from what was becoming a stultifying Manitoba existence. (Though less dramatically recounted, Pacey's final year in Brandon was not that different from Frye's time in southwest Saskatchewan.[92]) Relieved of combat burden, Pacey accepted a part-time job under John Grierson and newly installed chair Norman MacKenzie (UNB president) at the Wartime Information Board (WIB) in Ottawa. (University professors were so poorly paid that many taught summer school or took part-time jobs to survive.) While there, Pacey edited "Canadian Churches and the War" and worked to improve the WIB's Religious News Service,[93] thus fulfilling his obligation to the war effort. It was his publication of the essay "The Humanities in Canada" in 1943, along with MacKenzie's encouragement that he consider the position at UNB, that set the stage for his move to New Brunswick, the content of that essay likely serving as source material for his interview in Fredericton. Written five years after "At Last – A Canadian Literature," "The Humanities in Canada" is a much more mature assessment of the wider field of humanities that Pacey occupied at the time.

Speaking to one of MacKenzie's greatest concerns – the need to make preparations for returning war veterans – "The Humanities" is an instrumental call to arms to universities to show social leadership in directing this vast and needy human resource. Social workers, teachers, ministers, scientists, and even technical workers will be required in record numbers, Pacey argues, and all will need prerequisites in the humanities. For humanities faculty, this need will provide an unprecedented opportunity to add "moral" dimension to undergraduate training, thus preparing people "not only for a living, but for life."[94] Again, Pacey borrows purposefully from Pelham Edgar and E.K. Brown, arguing that, despite the shattering of idealism that a second global war has wrought, "it is still not too late to hold with Matthew Arnold that the designs of the Eternal are really with the humanities."[95] The 1930s' social evangelism of the Protestant churches is now clearly Pacey's, as is the desire to shape university resources to serve it, a combination of activist Christianity and democratic socialism that A.G. Bailey must have found both familiar and appealing. To achieve such moral and social outcomes, Pacey's essay applies the general ideas of the United Church's Commission on the Church and Industry (1932)[96] to the university sector, advocating for integration of cognate academic units, inter-faculty roundtable conferences, university-wide curriculum planning, regional university cooperation, scholarly associations, annual meetings of disciplinary bodies, and national associations of faculty and administrators. In all these endeavours, Pacey suggests, the model should be that of the Canadian Historical Association, which applies its "energies chiefly to the Canadian field."[97] Besides the quite remarkable prescience of such advocacy (all of those bodies now exist in SSHRC, ACUTE, MPHEC, ACS, and other forms[98]), the suggestion of a shared aim is the focal point. It is an aim, qualifies Pacey, that uses the New Critical approach to scholarship – academic inquiry should borrow from scientific methods "to analyze a poem as a chemist analyzes a strange compound"[99] – but does not end in the dispassionate analysis (the "practical criticism") that I.A. Richards and his Cambridge ilk espoused. "Surely this much at least is certain," emphasizes Pacey: "that the humanist will not save himself by aping the scientist."[100] Rather, the humanist will save himself and society by application of the conviction that "in the field of human relations[,] knowledge is inescapably bound up with judgement, and all judgement of human behaviour must ultimately be moral."[101]

Pacey provides elaboration of this key point in an August 1944 letter to Roy Daniells, which responds to Daniells's comments about his Grove manuscript. In that letter, Pacey repeats the hard line of his 1943 essay, clearly decoupling critical rigour and professional friendship. "I hate the back-slapping atmosphere of Canadian literary circles," he writes, and therefore "I was determined not to pull any punches out of deference to Grove's feelings. We are not going to get anywhere by that." He continues in the same letter: "E.K. Brown may ignore the faults of Pratt's Dunkirk – but wouldn't it be much better for Pratt if its faults were pointed out to him?"[102] The critical aesthetic is easy to detect. First, critic and author do not stand together, as in earlier eras, but apart (and this despite the fact that critics may rely on authors for biographical information, a consideration that should further inform the reading of the Pacey/Grove debacle). Second, critics are not subordinate to authors but equal, that status affording a licence to correct. "The true critic," Pacey writes elsewhere, "does not merely reap the benefit of the creative writer's exertions, but guides him and instructs him in the course of those exertions"[103] – so much so, he later tells Irving Layton, that the critic shares an essential creativity with the writer.[104] And third, the compass for critics is not friendship, loyalty, or a "tender-hearted" humanism,[105] but a higher moral order that works for the betterment of society through artistic excellence. Thus defined by Pacey, a true humanism is beyond the personal as the personal is normally conceived. That view of what the Portuguese term *compadrio*, or creative co-parenthood, would set Pacey up for much pain and misunderstanding in his professional

career, but it is important to understand that that ethic was rooted in
the circumstances of his youth and apprenticeship: specifically, in a
near-evangelical faith in Arnoldian cultural idealism; in a hard-won
self-reliance borne of the absence of a father; and in the commitment
to a nascent country that had taken him in and, he believed, needed
his services to realize its true measure. As he wrote in his later book
on Grove, we must get over the adolescent belief that subjecting "our
social fabric to critical scrutiny is ... a form of treason."[106] His loyalties
were therefore transcendent – and he was, not to put too fine a point
on it, often hated for that.

The gossip between authors sometimes revealed that hatred. In a
letter to Marian Engel, for example, Hugh MacLennan railed against
Pacey for evaluative criticism: "What I find intolerable about Pacey is
his smugness, and his apparent assumption that his own personal
tastes, and the declaration of them, add up to legitimate, creative criticism." More consequential is the supposedly collective view of opposition that MacLennan expresses, namely, the view that "[Pacey's]
patronizing attitude toward all writers except Grove irks most of us in
the profession."[107] The extent to which that view was as universal as
MacLennan claims is uncertain, but what is not uncertain is Pacey's
unpopularity among the "North Hatley" Montreal modernists of
MacLennan's larger circle – and that is important because it developed into a schism between modernist groups in Montreal and Fredericton that furthered the earlier belief that nothing of worth, and certainly nothing modernist, ever happened east of Quebec.

When he arrived at the University of New Brunswick to become
head of the English Department in September 1944, a twenty-seven-
year-old Desmond Pacey was well along on his way to being both consequential and controversial. He was a committed Canadianist who
had rejected the dispassion but not the rigour of the New Criticism,
taking it for granted, remembered soon-to-be student Fred Cogswell,
"that the teaching of literature ought to stress a broad humanity based
upon sincere expression rather than upon intricacies of form."[108]
Pacey was also encouraged by, but not yet confident in, early promises of success. He knew that he wanted a more dynamic environment
than Brandon's, and that he and his growing family needed a place to
put down roots, but he was also aware of being untutored in the
rhythms and customs of the eastern provinces. Going to New Brunswick would be starting over. To A.G. Bailey, one of two people most
responsible for his hiring, Pacey must have appeared to be unrefined

matter, for Bailey sought someone in English who would complement what he was doing in history and the arts. Had Pacey been farther along in his career or buoyed by the early successes of a Hugh
MacLennan or full of his own opinions about the Maritimes, he may
not have taken as readily as he did to Bailey's project. That he was
young, ambitious, impressionable, and shared an uncanny alignment
with Bailey's own trajectory (same University of Toronto circle, same
sense of cultural activism, same experience of British graduate education) proved fortuitous, as Bailey and his group of New Brunswick
nationalists soon discovered.

PROCLAIMING NEW BRUNSWICK FROM CANADA

Pacey's early days at UNB were tantamount to a conversion. He rapidly took to the city, its people, and setting, often contrasting Fredericton and the St John River with Brandon and "the muddy Assini-
boine."[109] Finding the city's tall, majestic elms and circling pines
reminiscent of the old world charm of Cambridge, he told correspondents of the quality of "sparkling clarity" that emanated from
river to town and campus.[110] He was equally enamoured with the
townsfolk he met. The first was his University Avenue landlady, Mrs
Mersereau, whose son graduated from UNB in 1927, studied at the University of London, and was serving as a colonel with General Eisen-
hower's staff in France. Son and daughter, also a UNB graduate, knew
"Alfie" Bailey, about whom the widowed Mrs Mersereau spoke reverently as a member of the city's aristocracy. The depth of a tradition
anchored at UNB and fanning out to the wider world impressed Pacey
immensely. Pacey also found an early friend in the Reverend H.T.
Jones, minister of Fredericton's Wilmot United Church. Though
older, Jones would become another of the clergy that Pacey counted
as his closest friends. It was "Alf Bailey," however, whom Pacey wrote
most effusively about. "I liked him immediately," he told his wife two
days after he arrived, adding that Bailey was a close friend of Roy
Daniells and Jerry Riddell, a University of Toronto lecturer whom
Pacey had met through Daniells and Pratt. Pacey's near-identical comment to his wife and Daniells – that "I should guess that [Bailey] will
become my best friend here"[111] and "I am sure he will be my closest
friend here"[112] – is significant for not only establishing the early connection between both men but also for echoing the well-known sentiment of a local literary idol, Lucy Maud Montgomery. In fact, it is

not inconceivable that Pacey, always an admirer of children's literature, had read *Anne of Green Gables* as an introduction to the region.

Pacey's early letters from UNB indicate that he hit the ground running. He and Bailey met often, either at the daily 4 P.M. tea in the
librarian's office or in the evening at Bailey's home, which Bailey had
opened to Pacey until his wife and children arrived. Pacey was delighted with Bailey's circle, finding the "CCF-ers ... the most alive of the lot"
and the scientists full of wide-ranging humanist interests. They are "all
youngish, all leftist, [and] all interested in ideas," he remarked.[113] Two
initiatives were hatched immediately, both by Bailey. The first was to
bring a small group of arts and science faculty together for evening
discussions of curriculum and ideas – to recreate, in other words, the
energy of E.K. Brown's Nameless Society sessions. The second initiative was to partner with Bailey to build the English and history departments along parallel lines. Pacey's English Department in a university of six hundred students consisted of himself and two others,
Frances Firth, a graduate teaching assistant who lectured four hours a
week to freshmen, and the poet Elizabeth Brewster, who marked
essays as Pacey's undergraduate assistant. Firth and Brewster were
members of Bailey's Bliss Carman Society. To ensure that both initiatives were undertaken with a New Brunswick focus, Bailey steered
Pacey toward the library's Rufus Hathaway Collection, which became
Pacey's special possession. Describing the vast collection of Canadian
literature, letters, periodicals, and manuscripts as "my greatest joy,"
Pacey told Daniells only two weeks after arriving in Fredericton that
it had become his "inner sanctum."[114] When he discovered that Lorne
Pierce had brokered the collection's move to UNB after Hathaway's
death in 1933, Pacey, who was working closely with Pierce on his
Grove book, took it upon himself to become the collection's de facto
guardian. "No one has made any use of it yet," he told his wife. "There
is so much to do, I don't know where to begin."[115]

Bailey's strategy was nothing short of inspired. He not only gave
Pacey an entrance to a special field of study that paralleled the localism of his prairie work on Grove but also provided him with an
untapped resource of research materials in which to work. Where
Hathaway had been the collector, Pacey would become the critic. That
the collection's focus was the Group of the Sixties (also known as the
Confederation Poets), with almost complete representation of Carman and Roberts, simply concentrated Pacey's subsequent work on
what Bailey felt was neglected. By good luck and design, and, of

course, Fredericton's centrality in Canadian letters in the preceding decades, Pacey was handed an entire research career in his first few weeks at UNB. For a University of Toronto-educated Canadianist, the opportunity could not have been better, and Pacey immediately responded. He got to work devising an honours course in Canadian literature built around the resources of the collection. He also learned as much as he could about the New Brunswick and Maritime literary traditions, using the Bliss Carman Society meetings as evening seminars, where he took notes and asked questions. He also proposed to President Milton F. Gregg, who had mistaken him for a student, a new semi-annual series of lectures that would be hosted and published by UNB. Modelled after the Alexander Lectures in Toronto, the "Roberts Memorial Lectures," Pacey said, would "stimulate criticism and research in the field of Canadian literature, and ... enhance the prestige of this university."[116] Despite the fact that his wife and children were still in Ottawa, where Mary had just given birth to their second child, Pacey felt so buoyed by his first month at UNB that, in British schoolboy fashion, he penned a school song:[117]

On a hill-top
Stands a college
Which is known as U.N.B.
For her students and her faculty
She is famed from sea to sea.

    Raise your voices
    Sing her praises
    In devoted loyalty
    That her glorious name may ever remain
    Hail U.N.B.!

Where the maples
Blaze in splendor
Stands our university
In our hearts and in our memories
She's enshrined eternally.[118]

Pacey, to repeat, had been converted. The town and university, its resources and potentials, all suited his temperament. He would henceforth channel his considerable energies into UNB, New Brunswick, and the regional heritage that surrounded both. His adoption of Bailey's project seems hasty only if his background and need for stability are not considered. His comment to President Gregg that his first exposure to UNB had convinced him to become "an ally in the fight to restore the humanities" suggests clearly that Bailey had found one of his deputies.[119]

But restoration of a local tradition for Pacey could never be what it was for Bailey, whose inheritance was in the New Brunswick soil. Instead of championing the familiar, then, Pacey's work complemented Bailey's by defining the conditions in which a regional literature could again flourish. That focus starts to appear in Pacey's post-1944 work, "The Novel in Canada" the first example of his transition from an early criticism of defensiveness and hyperbole to a more nuanced dialogue with readers that admits its "incompleteness but [that is] hopeful that its formulation may encourage further analysis."[120] Pacey was beginning, in other words, to write himself into Bailey's project. Premised on what was then the irrefutable fact that Canadian poetry had advanced well beyond Canadian fiction in quality and critical appeal – Collin's *White Savannahs* (1936), Scott's *New Provinces* (1936), Pratt's *Canadian Poetry Magazine* (1936–43), Smith's *Book of Canadian Poetry* (1943), and Brown's *On Canadian Poetry* (1943) spoke in unison about that superiority – Pacey's essay seeks a critical redress for fiction, and none too soon. Though Sara Jeannette Duncan's *Imperialist* (1904), Stephen Leacock's *Sunshine Sketches of a Little Town* (1912), Grove's *Settlers of the Marsh* (1925), and Morley Callaghan's *Strange Fugitive* (1928) had pushed Canadian fiction beyond the sentimental and didactic, the nineteenth-century tradition of historical romance was still dominant in the 1940s. Preferring to avoid considerations of the contemporary scene, those romances championed the distant and exotic in grand rhetorical styles meant to moralize and instruct. The result was a utilitarian, even puritan, literature of uplift that circumvented the increasingly urgent questions of the Canadian present. Pacey's essay highlights, then divides, those two fictional traditions. Fiction, he argues, must rid itself of a preference for historical fancy and "[deal] in an adult manner with life as it is lived *here and now*."[121] What that meant specifically was for novelists to drop the "shallow romanticism" of an otherwise talented Mazo de la Roche and explore instead the ideas and sociology of "the contemporary Canadian scene."[122] "We need to see the festering sores in our social body," Pacey wrote, "as well as its areas of healthy tissue." No more "sugar-coated tracts or novels of escape."[123] The call was both *modernist* in suggesting greater awareness "of the technical advances" of James Joyce, Marcel Proust, and Franz Kafka, and *localist* in concluding that the problem of fiction's late bloom in Canada was the result of the country's history and size. Anticipating Frye's great insight into the difference between Canadian identity and unity (the first involving the work of culture and the imagination, the second of politics[124]), Pacey laments that "Canadian society ... is a peculiarly difficult society to reduce to order."[125] His inference is that, while a strong national consciousness reflects a country's maturity, the only means of achieving that maturity in a country as diverse as Canada is by enabling a similar consciousness of its regions. He would make the point even more strongly in *Creative Writing in Canada*, wondering "whether there is any such thing as a national literature apart from its regional components."[126] No Canadian, he insists, "can be fully aware of Canadian society who has not ... read Haliburton on the colonial society of Nova Scotia, Stephen Leacock on the big cities of Quebec and the small towns of Ontario, Grove on the pioneer days of prairie agriculture, Pratt on the building of the Canadian Pacific Railway, or Morley Callaghan on the urban life of Toronto in the nineteen-thirties."[127] Adopting the view of his new colleague Bailey – that "instead of trying to achieve identity by building a Chinese wall around one's home territory, one should open one's mind to all the winds that blow"[128] – Pacey differentiates an inward-looking provincialism from an outward-seeking localism, advising that "when a strong regional consciousness is supplemented by an equally strong consciousness of the world beyond the region ... the need is felt to interpret [the] region to others."[129] Echoing his friend John Grierson, he proposes that, in a federation as manifold as Canada's – where different regions are akin to foreign countries – novelists should strive to "interpret the various regions to one another."[130]

Pacey's essay warrants the foregoing attention because of how it positioned him as critic to do his subsequent work. The essay makes clear that, in choosing fiction as a critical territory, he intended to undertake pioneering work in a genre that few critics had taken seriously, a genre that he shrewdly perceived as the ground of post-war national definition. Ryerson's spring 1945 catalogue later corroborated the point, claiming that Pacey's *Frederick Philip Grove* and E.K. Brown's *On Canadian Poetry* each constituted a "definite and distinguished beginning" to literary reinterpretation in Canada. (Ryerson's editors might also have said that the publication of Pratt's *Collected Poems* in 1944 marked an important turning point, for the country's foremost modernist poet was starting to look back on a career that was reaching its zenith, the implication of which suggested new beginnings.) Pacey, of course, knew from his Cambridge professor I.A. Richards that the "practical criticism" brought to bear on poetry in earlier decades was applicable to fiction. Literary innovation was not genre-specific and the state of Canadian fiction in the 1940s demanded the attentions of the strong-minded critic that Bailey sought. Pacey welcomed the role, and, as he had done previously, created or at least heralded the critical vacuum that would accommodate him. "Basically the job of the literary critic in Canada," he said, "is still that pioneer task of clarifying the historical background, sorting out biographical and bibliographical details, [and] seeking to arrive at preliminary evaluations and interpretations."[131] In that vein, he took a bold opening position, following Bailey's lead in resisting what the most persuasive recent criticism had identified as the "chauvinism" of the "local second-rate"[132] to make way for a more comprehensive consideration of Canada as a special political entity: a constellation of regions that fiction, the most democratic of genres, was ideally suited to address. Variously informed by his experience of a sprawling Commonwealth, by his knowledge of three distinct regions of Canada, and by his association with Bailey and the Bliss Carman Society poets, this definably "regionalist" position may have put Pacey at odds with prevailing critical sentiment but it also put him on the leading edge of a new decentralized thinking about Canada that would grant agency to the country's divergent parts. It was by this means that Pacey found his way into the Fiddlehead critical aesthetic, and that aesthetic, in his hands, shaped the direction of Canadian literary criticism for two generations.[133]

Pacey's first major pan-Canadian project, *A Book of Canadian Stories* (1947), brings that emphasis into focus.[134] Evident by virtue of simply undertaking the project is his understanding of the correlation between a robust criticism and available texts. Where primary texts are not widely accessible, he states, it must be the critic's job to supply them. And, if Pacey had uneasy relationships with publishers, it was often because of the haste with which this mission had to be accomplished in a country with scant publishing and research capacity. (In this haste, Pacey's impatience is no different than Lister Sinclair's in promoting Canadian theatre, Arnold Walter's in establishing a Canadian opera school, or Gweneth Lloyd's in staging Canadian ballet.)

Evident in the anthology, as well, is Pacey's rethinking of the federated conception of Canada. Rather than the nation being the first
among equals, and the accompanying criteria for a national anthology being that which captures unifying principles, the federated parts
of Canada have primacy in Pacey's selections, the idea being that
the nation is visible only through the matrix of its distinct societies.
The stories chosen present that matrix: the myths of Canada's First
Nations; the Atlantic of Haliburton, Roberts, Will R. Bird, Norman
Duncan, and Thomas Raddall; the Ontario of Susanna Moodie, Stephen Leacock, and Mazo de la Roche; the west of Grove and Sinclair
Ross; and so on. Rather than try to represent a coherent Canada, the
stories that Pacey chooses capture differences in eras and aesthetics
(romanticism and realism), differences in sociology (rural and urban),
differences in ethnicity (Indigenous and settler), and, of course, differences in geography. The goal of such a configuration is clearly identified by Pacey as a move toward national maturity, the means to
which is greater self-awareness. By "self-awareness," he says in the introduction, "I do not mean ... the kind of awkward involution which we
speak of as 'self-consciousness'; I mean the intelligent and purposive
comprehension of one's *nature and circumstances*."[135] Literature is vital
to maturation, he later writes, because "the chief function of literature
is to stimulate awareness, to produce a sensibility open to the maxi-
mum possible number of responses. This awareness should include
an awareness of one's own self, of one's physical environment, of one's
immediate social environment, of the total social environment of the
human race, of man's relations with the whole physical universe, and
of man's relations with God. Now all literature to some extent serves
to keep open all these channels of response, but only one's own literature can fully open up the first, second[,] and third."[136] Pacey's selections were indeed intended, then, to interpret the country to its citizens. Where Bailey's project was to restore a region and province to
their former confidence and cultural maturity, Pacey's was to expand
that self-possession to the country as a whole.

What emerges from the anthology and its justifications are a series
of emphases that would form Pacey's critical signature, the means by
which he intends to make the changes in Canada that Bailey wishes
to make in the region, both those complementary of a place-based
consciousness. Showing the influence of Bailey and Pelhan Edgar,
Pacey first favours a constant circling back to history to determine the
social conditions from which literary excellence materializes. Pacey

identifies Joseph Howe's *Novascotian* and John Gibson's *Literary Garland* as models in that regard. Both, he concludes, were responsible for the literary advances of their time and both should be emulated today. Pacey develops this idea further in 1947 when scolding Northrop Frye for taking William Blake out of his milieu and placing him in the realm of Eliot's universal imagination. "I agree," Pacey says in commenting on Frye's *Fearful Symmetry*, "that you cannot altogether explain a writer's art in terms of his personal Selfhood and historical circumstances, but ... I am quite convinced that you cannot safely ignore these things altogether and consider him in the abstract."[137] Like Bailey, then, Pacey has much to say in his work about the cultural and material infrastructure that complements production – and, from that, about how place and circumstance imprint themselves on the imagination.

Pacey's introduction also makes it clear that he is writing to instruct and cultivate a readership. He presumes his readers are untutored in the regional literatures of Canada and thus intuits his role to be more guide than seer. He explains to readers, for example, that, though "Haliburton is called, with some justice, the father of American humour, it is in Addison and Swift, in Johnson and Goldsmith, that we must look for the sources of his art."[138] Derived from his training in the United Church ministry, which taught clergy to bring biblical teaching to laity rather than stand aloof in pulpits as interpretative intermediaries, this critical methodology would lead Pacey to write or edit *Creative Writing in Canada* (1952), *Ten Canadian Poets* (1958), *Our Literary Heritage* (1966), *Selections from Major Canadian Writers* (1974), and many other glosses on our literature. Those books and his many essays offer the introductory assessments of the literary docent. They consider influence, social context, biographical import, and other factors that situate texts to initiate comprehension. It was only by this method, he believed, that he could cultivate a readership that would be open to the reception of literary values. In this regard, the scope and tone of Pacey's work parallels that of the modernist Ezra Pound, whose many anthologies and ABCs of reading were intended to save readers from crawling through the dross to get to the best of what was thought and said. George Woodcock understood that exactly when contrasting Pacey and Frye: Frye the greater analytical, original, and imaginative critic, and Pacey the "descriptive and appreciative commentator."[139] Both roles were necessary, thought Woodcock, and neither more important than the other, though

Pacey's role of gathering and sorting was less glamorous in a McLuhanesque age of critical celebrity.

Also characteristic of Pacey's critical practice in the anthology and other work of this period is an unusual inclusiveness. Though he was trained in the white, male, anglophone environs of gentleman scholars and churchmen, Pacey's editorial choices reached beyond those worlds to recognize the achievement of francophones, Indigenous peoples, and women, the last two groups receiving critical treatment in the anthology.[140] It is the place of women in particular that warrants comment, for the notion has become popular that a sort of critical misogyny was a Pacey trait (Carole Gerson, for instance, accuses Pacey of a modernist bias for virility in his critical language about Lucy Maud Montgomery[141]). What critics are sometimes reluctant to admit, however, is that all writers are shaped by their times, and just as Frye's private declaration that literature is "mainly for the benefit of women"[142] did not make him a misogynist, neither did Pacey's strong opinions and robust critical language reveal a disrespect of women. The evidence of his anthology and later work is clear on the point. Prominent in the anthology are stories by Susanna Moodie, Marjorie Pickthall, Mazo de la Roche, Mary Quayle Innis, and P.K. Page. Central, too, is Pacey's admiration for those writers. Moodie is described as "an excellent observer of the follies and hardships of pioneer life";[143] Pickthall as suffusing her work "with tenderness and pathos, with simple piety and reverence";[144] Roche and Innis as exhibiting "grace and élan,"[145] "[d]eft[ness], intelligen[ce], sincer[ity] ... [and] power."[146] And, while it is true that he aims unsparing judgment at some of their weaknesses, that judgment is no less pointed than it is for Gilbert Parker, Charles G.D. Roberts, and other men, Parker receiving the comment that "his best work is only superior journalism."[147] In that sharpness, Pacey was an equal-opportunity critic, showing no discernible gender bias. If he admired a work's literary merits, he praised it; if not, his language could be unmercifully harsh.[148] His often-original treatments of Frances Brooke, Julia Catherine Beckwith Hart, Moodie, Catherine Parr Traill, Isabella Valancy Crawford, Pickthall, Pauline Johnson, Roche, Ethel Wilson, Gabrielle Roy, Miriam Waddington, Dorothy Livesay, Jay Macpherson, and Elizabeth Brewster attest to a pioneering critic who did exponentially more to advance the literary cause of women in Canada than did his contemporaries W.E. Collin, A.J.M. Smith, and E.K. Brown. His sense of the uneven playing field for women and the consequence of that for production and quality is writ large in his personal correspondence and often manifest as a negotiation with editors to increase female representation. His exchanges with Lorne Pierce to include Dorothy Livesay and P.K. Page in *Ten Canadian Poets* are one such example, their eventual exclusion in favour of historical benchmarking a source of regret.[149] To repeat an earlier point, Pacey's loyalties were transcendent, and he was often hated or misunderstood for that.

The final emphasis in the anthology that bears scrutiny in the wider context of a Fiddlehead aesthetic is Pacey's preference for a literary realism that had grown in consort with modernist experimentation in Canada in the 1920s. Bound up in his belief that such realism was both functional and revelatory in a country of vast geographic differences – enabling citizens to learn about themselves and each other, and the country to mature accordingly – this preference also reflected the Fiddlehead school belief that the creative work of locales was enhanced when borders opened. Consequently, wrote Pacey, "a greater effort to approach [foreign] models with detachment and discrimination [is needed], absorbing the best that they have to teach and modifying it in the light of our own peculiar situation."[150] In making this statement, Pacey was articulating what would soon become a Canadian mantra: that, said Mavor Moore, "we can look closely and clearly at these other peoples because there is a little of each of them in us ... but we stand slightly to the cock-eyed side of each: a perfect position from which to observe – even to observe oneself."[151] Learning from the avant-garde styles of distant modernisms was therefore as beneficial for provincialisms as for the nation those provincialisms constituted.

But there is more to Pacey's preferences for the ordinary and familiar – for the "festering sores of our social body" over the shallow fictions of historical romance – that he had not yet worked out in 1947, and perhaps never did fully explore or admit publicly, though it is apparent as backdrop in his creative writing. His stand against romance was not a ploy to marginalize women or a manifestation of distaste for a generic form suddenly out of fashion but rather an effort to temper an expression of imperial history that his upbringing, training, and immersion in Bailey's New Brunswick had disavowed. Put simply, he didn't want to live as a colonial in harness to a set of beliefs and traditions that were touted naively without examination. He was too well read for that and too independent of spirit. As an immigrant, he desired the fresh start that only a new country could provide, which is why he persisted in seeing Canada as either nascent or in need of cultural remediation. The useful metaphor he would soon apply to the country's need is of a field lightly harvested: "Our operations in it may be compared to those of a harvesting machine which merely removes the heads from the grain: we still have to examine the soil in which the seed grew, and to investigate the processes of growth."[152] This view of critical adolescence, however, did not put him at odds with Bailey and the Bliss Carman Society poets who knew of earlier achievements. While it is true that he could never occupy the Canada and New Brunswick that they did, he could occupy the "new provinces" conception of a modern Canada as a full and equal citizen. Besides, their ideal region was never the nineteenth-century place of Roberts and Carman, but, as Bailey had always made clear, a *contemporary* place alive with the same vitality and national significance. Thus, while restoring the region to its former state of cultural confidence served their interests, expanding that robustness to the country as a whole served Pacey's.

Romance could never accomplish that because, as Pacey understood it from I.A. Richards and T.E. Hulme, romance depended on the deus ex machina of an external force for resolution. The gods, the state, or some other form of benevolence had to intercede in romance. Realism, on the other hand, held that personal endeavour could lift one out of circumstance and trigger change. From different directions, then, Pacey and Bailey arrived at the same conclusion: that, while the emotional and nostalgic elements of romance were indeed seductive, realism's more powerful lenses were needed to extricate Canada and New Brunswick from the structural circumstances that had led to their stagnation. The whole of Canada seemed to be moving in this direction. By the mid-1940s, to take just one example, the National Film Board had reconstituted itself around Canadian filmmakers whom Grierson and his British peers had trained. As a result, a Canadian style was emerging that used the documentary form to interpret reality in ways other than how Grierson had. Gudrun Parker's *Listen to the Prairies* (1945) and F.R. Crawley's *Four Seasons* (1947) were pioneering ways to evoke landscape as psychic condition, and Donald Fraser's *Look to the Forest* (1950) began the examination of resource destruction and husbandry that were so central to the Canadian experience. These filmmakers were re-examining previous representations of the real, even if that exposed the festering sores of a broken society. Bailey, of course, had foregrounded those sores in his own poetry, writing of the barns "empty of grass," "the wrecks of tugs," and other "graphs of decay" that blotted the regional landscape.[153] For him, as for Pacey and others, romance offered either evasion or escape into a wistful status quo that perpetuated backwardness and self-loathing. Pacey's career-long interest in Haliburton, Howe, Grove, and Major John Richardson as republican more than historical figures advances from this thinking,[154] as does his affinity with Irving Layton, who described himself and Pacey as Canada's "horses of realism."[155] Al Purdy would also take note, lauding Pacey for "upholding the non-mythologic and straightforward approach to writing poetry."[156]

What emerges from this belief in realism, particularly as it applies to inducing agency, is Pacey's effort to decentralize the post-graduate landscape in Canada, a landscape made uneven (and thus the country's regional or remote universities subordinate) by the dominance of A.S.P. Woodhouse and the University of Toronto. The decoupling of upper-level English studies from Toronto is of a piece with Pacey's view of a modern Canada and is expressed to Daniells as exasperation with an Ontario-centric arrogance that is out of step with a mature federalism. "I think we are better away from the place [Toronto]," he tells Daniells in a letter. "I'm sure it's much more provincial, for all its surface cosmopolitanism, than Winnipeg or Fredericton."[157] Pacey takes similar aim at Louis Dudek and McGill, dressing down Dudek for oversights in *Canadian Poems 1850–1952* and following that up with the now-familiar decentralizing refrain that "the fact that you do not know [of the *Fiddlehead*] seems to me symptomatic of the parochialism and obliqueness that exists in literary circles even of the most advanced sort."[158] Pacey is obviously working here to divest Canada of its nodes of power, while partnering with Bailey to reinstitute some of that power on an eastern periphery. This becomes clear when Pacey invites Lorne Pierce to the unveiling of UNB's Poets' Corner of Canada monument honouring Roberts, Carman, and Sherman. Finding himself in the middle of Bailey's work with Beaverbrook to establish UNB as the country's leader in regional studies, Pacey tells Pierce of his efforts to amass all manuscripts, letters, and books of the three Fredericton poets for the library, declaring the hope that "this university may become a centre for the study of Canadian literature."[159] The claim is backed by the evidence of Pacey's graduate supervision, the bulk of that furthering a pan-Canadian project rooted in New Brunswick: Robert Lawrence's descriptive bibliography of manuscript materials in the Rufus Hathaway Collection (1946) and the efforts of an entire MA class to "chart the course of Carman's literary reputation," to "analyze the Literary Garland as an index of Canadian literary and intellectual trends," and to "analyze the treatment of nature in the poetry of Roberts and Carman."[160] For Pacey, the seemingly natural claim of Woodhouse and the University of Toronto to lead advanced literary study in Canada made every other university in the country susceptible to that institution's view of the discipline while also taking authority away from universities that were becoming regional incubators. In this, once again, is the view that Canada is not reducible to its major urban centres, no matter how socially or culturally consequential those are.

Pacey's efforts to add critical dimension to a maturing, decentralized Canada fell directly in line with Bailey's hope that New Brunswick would again become a centre of literary concern in the country. In the decade ahead, Pacey supervised theses on the pre- and post-Confederation novel; the poetry of Carman, Roberts, and Sherman; drama in New Brunswick; Anglo-French literary relations in Canada; early Canadian children's literature; and other topics too numerous to list. By 1960, he had supervised fifteen MA theses on Canadian literature, nine MA theses on New Brunswick and Maritime literature, and had several doctoral dissertations on Canadian subjects at varying stages of completion.[161] As well, he had been pushing members of his department to develop expertise in the literatures of the Commonwealth, purchasing library resources in the areas of Caribbean and South Pacific literature. By the early 1960s, one of the first doctoral dissertations in the country on West Indian fiction had been undertaken at UNB.[162] Pacey not only was writing the critical narrative of Canadian literature, then, but, with a constant stream of graduate students who would become the leading Canadian critics of the next generation, he was also steering critical studies in Canada. Taking a page from Bailey and Woodhouse, he hired his best students as colleagues,[163] trusting that his signature would be evident in their own work and supervision. Canadian critic John Moss's study at UNB under Fred Cogswell and Robert Gibbs reflected that critical genealogy. Both Cogswell and Gibbs had worked under Pacey and shared his belief in the importance of initial spadework, a belief manifest in Moss's co-founding of the *Journal of Canadian Fiction* and later creation of essential readers' guides to the Canadian novel. Pacey became so serious about his pedagogical evangelism that he brought Daniells into a scheme to break Woodhouse's monopoly on doctoral education in Canada. In the planning stages since 1953, the idea was to position UNB to offer a PhD in English, starting with the department's strength in Canadian literature.[164] Over the course of a number of years and proposals, the idea was adopted by UNB and UBC, each accepting doctoral students by 1959.[165]

It was a Fredericton-based Pacey-the-humanist more than Pacey-the-specialist who summoned the energies of other Canadians to take up the cause of Canada amidst the hegemony of "English" literary studies. Believing that "the humanities must be restored to something approaching the position which they once occupied"[166] and that "as Canadians we have a special right and responsibility to investigate our own literary history,"[167] he oversaw a flood of new bibliographies, scholarly editions, anthologies, biographies, literary and intellectual histories and sociologies, comparative studies, reputational analyses, and other correctives to the colonial presumption that Canada had no interest in or capacity for its own culture. He persisted in employing the wide view – national but not nationalist – and always with a mind to the needs of the general reader so that reader could grow into mature citizenship. His much-discussed and later ridiculed *Creative Writing in Canada* (1952) must be read in that light. It was conceived to provide orienting markers similar to those in J.K. Ewers's *Creative Writing in Australia: A Selective Survey* (1945) – and not the unifying metaphors of garrison, Wacousta syndrome, or survival that other critics employed to franchise "Canada." Taking his cues from Bailey, Pacey was expansionist not reductionist, always suspicious of the "labels and pigeon-holes" of academic criticism.[168] In fact, while unhesitating in offering his views on merit, he never identified a work, author, or set of conventions as being distinctively Canadian. His sense of the country and its histories as manifold prevented that, even if he did believe that some reduction to order was necessary if Canadians were to make sense of themselves in their own peculiarly diverse milieu.[169] His efforts to reduce the nation to order while also allowing for its diversity anticipated and complemented the work of the Royal Commission on National Development in the Arts, Letters and Sciences [also known as the Massey-Lévesque Commission] (1949–51). That commission's working assumptions of Canada as both embryonic and worthy of state mechanisms for self-determination paralleled Pacey's, and its recommendations about formalizing a national research infrastructure, funding universities and artists, and centralizing a national broadcast system reinforced what he had already written about a Canada that was "quicken[ing]" toward the future.[170] Pacey and the commission seemed to be standing on the cusp of fulfillment, each working toward a Canada whose "future," wrote Pacey, "is certain to be greater than her past."[171] The considerable social momentum generated by the Massey-Lévesque Commission transformed the country, legitimizing the work of intellectuals and artists and placing them in the vanguard of national self-definition. Critics like Pacey whose work addressed the nation rose to prominence in the new Canada that Massey-Lévesque envisioned. By the mid-1950s, he was among a small number of the country's most influential commentators, a critic who was teaching Canadians how to read not only their literature but also their country. When F.R. Scott, chair of the Programme Committee of the Royal Society of Canada, wrote to him in October 1955 proposing a Canadian literature panel of Frye, Birney, and Pacey, his status as one of the deans of Canadian literature had been cemented.

However, with the country paying attention to his declamations, Pacey pivoted, turning his considerable energies back toward his home territory. The Confederation school of Roberts and Carman, always of interest because of the Hathaway Collection, began to occupy much of his time, as did his contemporaries, a school of poets he began referring to as "the Fiddlehead Group."[172] He not only defended both schools – lobbying aggressively for their inclusion in the anthologies of Dudek, Smith, Ralph Gustafson, and Raymond Souster – but also started to promote a form of affirmative action behind the scenes. "We should consciously try to counteract the tendency to assume that all valid Canadian performance occurs within the Montreal-Ottawa-Toronto triangle," he wrote to A.R.M. Lower, president of the Royal Society of Canada. "If there were two equally qualified candidates [for induction into the RSC] in Halifax and Toronto, and only one could be elected, I believe Halifax should be given the preference."[173] Such need for levelling had been a Pacey drumbeat for decades, but it re-emerged when a May 1954 encaenia event to plant a scarlet maple on Bliss Carman's gravesite, as per his wishes in the poem "The Grave Tree," was ignored by the national arts media. Pacey and Bailey were incensed, Pacey's introduction to the *Selected Poems of Sir Charles G.D. Roberts* (1955) stating what had to be done in response.[174] Efforts must be made, he explained, to "rescue Roberts' reputation from his too fervent admirers on the one hand and his too bitter detractors on the other."[175] Even though he was angry that his work to convince Canadians of their diverse identity was not having much effect in the nation's centre, Pacey's "classical calm" was on dis-

5 Planting a maple tree at the grave of Bliss Carman in Forest Hill Cemetery, Fredericton, May 1954. *Left to right*: Mrs John Palmer, standard bearer; Louis R. Seheult, Department of Forestry; A.G. Bailey, dean of arts and head of History Department; UNB President Colin B. Mackay; and Desmond Pacey, English Department.

play, that calm a reasoned alternative to the kind of cheerleading that he considered naively colonial, narrowly dismissive, or geocentric. As he told V.B. Rhodenizer, he admired the "traditional" expression of the Group of the Sixties as much the "'metaphysical' poetry" of the Canadian modernists. "I am an eclectic rather than a traditionalist or a modernist," he said, "and as such, I suppose, I deserve and can expect to be fired on from both sides!"[176]

Joke about it as he might with Rhodenizer, that view of diverse democracy reflected his belief in decentralization as an avenue to national maturity and, importantly, was a signature of the Fiddlehead group's alternative modernism, a form of rooted cosmopolitanism that was open to all manner of expression as long as that expression was "written well."[177] Pacey, of course, had gleaned this notion chiefly from Bailey, who, in *Border River* (1952), had collapsed the differences between the native and the cosmopolitan, but it was Pacey who wrote the first articulation of the idea in an early draft of an essay about New Brunswick literature:

> The editorial policy of *The Fiddlehead* has been and probably always will be eclectic rather than aggressively avant-garde or rigidly traditional ... Endorsing the revolt against the decadent romanticism of the late nineteenth century, its editors have written and championed a poetry in which the intelligence is at work to discipline the feelings, in which words and rhythms are used with restraint and functional cunning, in which a sense of place is complemented by a sense of time, and in which a balance is maintained between the particular, concrete fact and the general, universal truth. *The Fiddlehead* has always been ready to welcome the experimental in form, but only when the experimental form was conceived functionally and not as a mere end in itself. It has been equally ready to welcome the traditional forms when the same condition was observed. It has been hospitable to social satire, but has not rejected love and nature lyrics simply because they have been relatively unfashionable in recent years.[178]

Entirely in agreement with Pacey's rejection of the New Criticism for its indifference to "historical criticism and the significance of biography,"[179] this model of cultural democracy made room for spatial plurality in a post-war nation that was reconstituting itself around urban growth poles at the centre of the country. Pacey believed that, if the nation were to be turned purposively toward the future, however, Canadian writers and intellectuals had to recognize that their literature, like their country, was federated and contiguous and thus could be both regional *and* cosmopolitan, an allowance that would free them to express "both [their] place and [their] time."[180] That areas on the edge of the nation such as New Brunswick were structurally disadvantaged from participation in urbanized dynamism by small and distant populations meant that Pacey, like Bailey before him, had to turn his attentions inward. When the real impact of marginalization became evident to him in the mid-1950s, he began working on both theoretical and practical fronts to level the field.

In the first instance (the theoretical), he formulated a theory of cultural emplacement in Canada in which the centres of Montreal, Toronto, and Fredericton (he would later add Vancouver) are prominent. Beginning in the mid-1950s, and a central trope in the revised edition of *Creative Writing in Canada* in 1961,[181] this preoccupation with nodal centres of literary ferment informs much of Pacey's mature critical writing and is quietly cheered by Bailey, who offers reminders that "UNB is certainly the other centre of the enterprise [of Canadian literature]."[182] As a complement to this view of emplacement, Pacey becomes vocal about the turn Canadian criticism is taking toward the ahistorical. He chides Dudek and Michael Gnarowski, editors of *The Making of Modern Poetry in Canada* (1967), for perpetuating a Victorian myth of progress that makes straw men of the writers of the past.[183] "The whole complex of ideas that leads us, in the name of a fictitious progress, to denigrate the work of a really profound poet such as Archibald Lampman is anathema to me," Pacey writes. "The besetting sin of Canadian criticism today is not deaf traditionalism but blind modernism, the myth of the up-to-date."[184] This view must surely put to rest the thinking of critics like Donna Bennett who accuse Pacey of "the Victorian sense of historical continuity and evolutionary development."[185] Pacey had no such belief or interest in applying evolutionary logic to culture, and, if he did, Bailey would have corrected him swiftly. In fact, as his opposition to New Criticism and "deaf traditionalism" often shows, Pacey broke with many of his peers, including the modernists, in rejecting the notions of temporal superiority or growth. Critic Philip Kokotailo is helpful on that point, contrasting Pacey's non-evolutionary view of Canadian writing with that of Smith, Frye, and Sutherland,[186] and correctly citing Pacey's intentions, expressed in *Creative Writing in Canada*, to study "the *quality* of Canadian writing" rather than its growth.[187] "It's time for less heat and more light," Pacey confirms in reviewing *The Making of Modern Poetry in Canada*. "Now we should be patiently examining the best work that has been done – and not merely the work of the moderns, but the work of Roberts, Carman, Scott."[188] That the more deliberative and free-ranging criticism of the 1970s and 1980s emerged from this view becomes clear in the historicist emphasis of the Canadian Historical Association, which, in the criticism of Maria Tippett and Ramsay Cook, contests the popular idea that "English Canadians wrote better plays, novels, and poems, composed better music, and produced better works of art after the Second World War than they did before it."[189] Canada's new wave of literary critics expressed the same opinion, Frank Davey observing that the "emergence of Canadian poetry in the sixties and seventies ... into an unprecedented variety of idiosyncratic forms may owe at least a small debt to Desmond Pacey."[190] Again, in trading the dominant metaphor of evolution for evaluation, Pacey was ahead of his time, opening channels for reassessment and experiment that knew no temporal boundaries.

In the second instance (the practical), Pacey broadened his commitment to building local cultural capacity, joining Bailey and Beaverbrook in acquiring library and archival materials, planning Maritime writers' conferences, exploring the feasibility of a regional Atlantic university press, promoting the work of visual artists in Lucy Jarvis's Observatory Art Gallery, and becoming the de facto publicist for provincial art exhibits and the UNB Art Centre. Paul Arthur, managing editor of *Canadian Art*, was so impressed with Pacey's commitment to the local art scene that he invited him to take on the role of associate editor for the Maritimes, which he did. Some of the subsequent interpretative work done in the province in the 1960s was Pacey's. Paralleling this effort was Pacey's desire to put the resources of his English Department to provincial use. He appealed to UNB president Colin B. Mackay for a linguist "who could do a great deal of useful research into the speech habits and dialects and pronunciations of New Brunswick, the ballads and folk stories, the impact of French or English speech on the North Shore [of the province] and vice versa."[191] Through Bailey's association with D.A. Middlemiss, director of curriculum and research for the New Brunswick Department of Education, Pacey received an appointment to the province's English Curriculum subcommittee. Tasked with instructional reorganization of the grade 7–12 curriculum, the subcommittee's objectives reflected Pacey's influence (he was the only academic on the committee) and were clearly evident in language that sought to enhance imagination and spirituality, elevate Canadian literature to equivalency with British and American, raise consciousness of the best that has been thought and said, provide opportunities to develop creative abilities, cultivate awareness of the two founding languages, and broaden the study of literature to include social, intellectual, and historical elements.[192] After the subcommittee tabled its work, and its recommendations were accepted, the provincial English curriculum, first piloted in Fredericton secondary schools, changed beyond recognition – and it retains today much of the language Pacey brought to it half a century ago (literature, for example, provides "a unique means of exploring the spectrum of human experience").[193] The "creative restlessness" that resulted from this wide-ranging work put Pacey at the centre of what William Patterson called "the 'golden noon' of renascent criticism, music, art, and scholarship in [New Brunswick]."[194] And it emboldened Pacey's wish to bring his own department closer to the province's English teachers. Over the next few years he sent university lecturers into more than twenty schools in all parts of New Brunswick to offer advice, resources, and practical help.[195] Attempting to duplicate the success of Elizabeth Sterling Haynes's trips around the province in the late 1930s, these visits aimed to cultivate literary sophistication and local knowledge, not recruit future students.

Being able to shape local outcomes so directly prompted a further fine-tuning of Pacey's critical writing, which began revisiting his earlier interest in the historical relationship between the social and the creative in Canada. But it did so this time in ways that anticipated the creative and cultural-economies discourse of Charles Landry, Richard Florida, and other political economists several decades later. Pacey's essay "The Canadian Writer and His Public" (1957) reflects this change by drawing attention to the Canadian Copyright Act, small magazine polemics, literary prizes and symposia, professional concentrations of various types, the effects of cottage publishers, and other stimulants to production. In this spirit, Pacey and his old friend Roy Daniells begin exchanging letters about the relationship between literary magazines, Pacey expressing interest in the provincial stimulus seeded by *Stewart's Literary Quarterly* and the *New Brunswick Magazine*.[196] To make concrete the co-dependency of the social and the creative, and to underscore the university's centrality to that relationship, Pacey increased pressure on UNB president Mackay for more provincially apposite academic appointments and for larger research and travel funds, equating those expenses with the social relevance of institutions.[197] To ensure that Mackay understood UNB's significance to national letters, Pacey invited Daniells to deliver a special Founder's Day talk on the role that UNB played in Canadian literary history. He also endeavoured to professionalize creative writing, seeking and receiving the support of the Canada Council in 1964 to institute the first writer-in-residence program in the country at UNB. (It did not hurt Pacey's cause that UNB's former president, Albert W. Trueman, was the first director of the Canada Council [1957–65].) In the years ahead, Norman Levine, Dorothy Livesay, Alden Nowlan, and other notable Canadian writers went to UNB as working artists.[198] Never again, Pacey told Mackay in a letter, should a writer suffer in penury and obscurity as Frederick Philip Grove had.[199] So certain was Pacey that the conditions and momentum for literary ferment had been created in the region – the conditions seeded by Bailey and the momentum generated by himself and his peers – that he told a student conference on writing that "if we do not in this or the next generation produce a literature worthy of the name the bulk of the blame will lie upon ourselves rather than upon our public."[200] The key to restoring any region's literary reputation, he told students – and by so doing, elevating the country – was hyphenating cosmopolitanism and place: that is, turning to the "immediate environment" while remaining open to the "great masters of the past."[201] If a writer "plants himself indomitably on his instincts," he said, quoting Emerson, "the huge world will come round to him."[202] Hence his exasperation conveyed to James Reaney, one of the organizers of the 1960 ACUTE conference, that "not a single Maritimer [is] on the programme."[203]

The Fiddlehead school's belief that "regional accuracy and universal validity" are not only reconcilable but integrative became the Pacey creed. "Are [the regional and the universal] incompatible in the Irish poetry of Yeats, or the Wessex novels of Thomas Hardy, or the Russian plays of Chekhov?" he asked. "Rather than seeing the strong regional particularities of this country as an obstacle to great art, I see them as an advantage."[204] So, too, was the case with universities: when they assumed roles commensurate with their responsibilities to the immediate environment, which included not just their locales but also their pasts, Canadians would start seeing themselves "steadily" and "whole."[205]

Changes in Pacey's professional status were coincident with what he would have thought of as a sharpening, not narrowing, of his critical focus. After he was elected to the Royal Society in 1955, his trajectory veered toward the local, starting in 1955/56 when he replaced Bailey as acting dean of arts (Bailey was in Toronto as the Innis Visiting Lecturer). A year later (1957), Pacey was courted by Ryerson Press to replace Lorne Pierce as editor-in-chief, but he declined, writing to his parents that the "sense of belonging to something in which you sincerely belong is worth more than money."[206] Grateful that he had remained at UNB, Bailey recommended that Pacey be promoted to dean of graduate studies, which he was in 1960. In the final years of his career, Pacey replaced a retired Bailey as vice-president academic (1970) and then took on the simultaneous role of acting president in 1972/73. When he was offered the presidency of Brock University in late 1973, the offer coming less than a year after being denied the permanent presidency of UNB (a snub he took very personally), Pacey declined, unable to see himself leaving the university where he had grown to national prominence. He told Daniells that "life here is amply fulfilling, and ... the pleasures of family and friends are superior to those of power and prestige."[207] He had become rooted in New Brunswick, having found in family and community the centre that his mother had always sought for him. In many ways, he was the first and became the most prominent of the figures brought to New Brunswick by the conditions that Bailey had created. And as both neared the end of their careers at UNB, Pacey stayed closely attuned to Bailey, alert always for clues and directions. A typical late instance of this can be found in a Bailey letter to Frye in 1965 about how the Canadian climate and landscape affected T.E. Hulme's outlook.[208] After an exchange with Frye, Bailey brings the matter to Pacey, who later writes to Daniells "trying to assess the qualitative effects of ... [how] our response to these climactic conditions shaped our psychology, our sociology, our values."[209] The result appears as Pacey's call for more study of Canada's literary sociology in "Areas of Research in Canadian Literature: A Reconsideration."

It is perhaps fitting, then, that Pacey's final articles were written on Brewster, his much-admired student (*Ariel*, 1973); Grove, his long-held subject (*International Fiction Review*, 1974); and Bailey, his mentor, friend, colleague, and enabler (*Canadian Literature*, 1976). It is also fitting that the last of these articles appeared a few months after his death in July 1975. Its title was simply "A.G. Bailey," a monument to the man who was so integral to his becoming. The article was the first sustained treatment of Bailey's work and, true to Pacey's approach, displayed no tendency toward encomium, only the dispassionate analysis of the careful clinician. Published forty years ago, it is still among the most succinct critical statements written about Bailey, one of the country's major modernist poets. Northrop Frye captured Pacey's importance in a short memoir written for circulation among editors of the second edition of the *Literary History of Canada* (1976). (With Frye, Bailey, Daniells, Claude Bissell, and Carl F. Klinck, Pacey was a founding editor of the first edition of the *Literary History* [1965], having discussed the idea of a survey of Canadian culture – one undertaken collectively by the humanities side of the Royal Society – with Klinck years earlier.[210]) In remembering Pacey's many achievements, Frye noted his friend's courageous pioneering work, his success in building "one of the most prominent centres for the study of Canadian literature" in the country,[211] and, most significantly, his vision for both Canada and Canadian humanist studies. "The *Literary History [of Canada]*," wrote Frye, "may be regarded as an extension of his survey," particularly "*Creative Writing in Canada* (1952) and *Ten Canadian Poets* (1958)." For Frye, Pacey had become one of "the dominant figure[s] in Canadian literary history,"[212] a view corroborated by Bailey, who observed that "[Pacey's] *Creative Writing in Canada* (1952) should be grouped with two other works, namely E.K. Brown's *On Canadian Poetry* (1943) and A.J.M. Smith's *Book of Canadian Poetry* (1943), as well as with Malcolm Ross's editorship of the *New Canadian Library*, as having marked the coming of age of the modern movement in English Canadian literature."[213] That Frye, at Bailey's request, delivered the inaugural W.C. Desmond Pacey Memorial Lecture at UNB in March 1981 was appropriate, then, as was the fact that Fred Cogswell, Pacey's best student, would take up his work as the next and most influential member of the Fiddlehead school.

4

Fred Cogswell:
Internationalizing the Local

Eager to clothe our nakedness, we prize
Our neighbour's cloaks, regardless of their size,
And find too late what suits them well, on us
Appears inane or else ridiculous.
O Canadians, when will the truth be known,
No other coat can fit you save your own,
Tailored by Time's needle, measured by Need's tape,
Nine cloths stitched into one coherent shape?
Work then to serve our most immediate needs,
Words serve for binding thread as well as deeds.[1]

I saw who you really were:
one of Rider Haggard's or A. Merritt's
astonishing narrators,
pipe-smoking, bookish men who settle down
comfortably
at colleges as quiet as this
to write of their descent into the Moon Pool
or of following Ayesha, She Who Must Be Obeyed,
into the Palace Of The Spirit Of Life in the caves
of Kor.[2]

In an address delivered in the late 1970s to a Royal Society-sponsored symposium on "Nineteenth-Century New Brunswick," Fred Cogswell described the intellectual space that had been created for him in the Fiddlehead group. "Every tradition," he said, "is, in reality, a movement that has finally succeeded in enlisting majority support. Movements

6 Fred Cogswell standing in front of the Poets' Corner
Monument, UNB, December 1990.

arise when enough members of any society feel the pressures of a tradition to be cramping or inadequate, and when their efforts to put
something else in place of it coalesce into a unified point of view."[3] His
paper proceeded from there to adapt the methodological system used
in A.G. Bailey's "Creative Moments in the Culture of the Maritime
Provinces" to a consideration of similar patterns of social development
in New Brunswick. Considering himself in that line of development,
Cogswell stressed that his own first volume of poetry (*The Stunted
Strong*, 1954) attempted to "combine local character with traditional
form ... to show that the words 'modern' and 'intellectual' and 'univer-

sal' were not necessarily incompatible with the words 'traditional' and 'emotional' and 'regional.'"[4] As is now clear, Cogswell was recalling Bailey's overarching dictum that a New Brunswick modernism could both preserve and embellish an important local tradition – not as "slavish imitation" but "to the point of contemporaneity."[5]

Cogswell was thus attaching himself to a particular socio-cultural movement in New Brunswick that Bailey had initiated, proving, in the rather casual way he spoke of it, that what once was the revolutionary idea of modernizing New Brunswick was now normative. As critic, he had fully absorbed Bailey's dominant form of cultural analysis (the historical sociology of Toynbee and Innis) to examine New Brunswick as an organic field, and as a creative writer he was extending Bailey's supposition that particularities of time and place could be brought to the point of contemporaneity. What Cogswell could not have known fully at the time, however, was the extent to which both his thinking and practice were embedded in the "unified point of view" that had coalesced around Bailey. By the time Cogswell arrived at UNB in 1945 as an undergraduate, Bailey's ideas had indeed become normative in the work of the Bliss Carman Society and *Fiddlehead* poets, in the teaching of Pacey and other members of the English and history departments, in the institutional thinking of UNB presidents Norman MacKenzie and Milton Gregg, and in the provincial desire (informed by John Clarence Webster, Beaverbrook, and Premier John B. McNair) to use post-war momentum to repurpose New Brunswick society. Cogswell's role in the Fiddlehead movement, then, must begin with a consideration of inheritance and move from there to an examination of what he did with what he inherited.

The first point to be made is how seemingly different Cogswell was from his two principal mentors, Bailey and Pacey. Unlike Bailey, he had come from no intellectual or social aristocracy, and unlike Pacey, his rootedness in the province was deep. More typical New Brunswickers than Bailey or Pacey, the Cogswells knew the province in their bones, having been stewards of the soil for generations. As a result, Fred Cogswell had no need to trumpet provincial fidelity or compensate for a lack of that fidelity with nationalist histrionics. For those reasons he became one of Bailey's special projects: a brilliant New Brunswick student who would either succeed or fail in the cultural milieu that Bailey had shaped for just such a new generation. Pacey had "come from away," to use the local expression, in 1944, an orphan seeking permanence and thus given by circumstance to ready embrace. Had Bailey's project been otherwise defined, Pacey would likely have gone in other directions. But coming from New Brunswick, Cogswell was different. If repurposed localism as trust and vocation didn't capture *his* imagination, then Bailey's work was more theoretical than transformative. Cogswell (and fellow New Brunswick students Elizabeth Brewster, Robert Gibbs, Robert Hawkes, and Allan Donaldson) would be key, and were groomed accordingly. Under Bailey's watch, and under the leadership of Webster, Beaverbrook, and other influential native sons, there was no bias against talented young New Brunswickers. That lookdown would come later.

NURTURED BY SURROUNDING SOIL

Fred Cogswell's maternal ancestors were Westmorland and Kent County Acadians.[6] Frederick Walter Leblanc, his maternal grandfather, was a charming, riotous character who returned to the province of his birth with the anglicized name "Fred White" after being adopted and educated by an American family in Boston. A veterinarian with a nose for shenanigans, he married Marie Elizabeth Girouard from Bouctouche, the first Acadian woman in the province to receive a university degree.[7] Her line descended from an illustrious French family that had arrived in Port Royal in 1642. Seeking to uphold that status, Marie's father, Gilbert-Anselme Girouard ("le Petite" to his friends), became a community leader.[8] He was elected Conservative MP in 1878 and 1882 in the federal riding of Kent, and he was one of the principal organizers of the First National [Acadian] Convention in July 1881 in Memramcook.[9] His passionate defence of Acadian heritage and rights would become a touchstone for his grandson Fred, who, a century later, would become one of Canada's pre-eminent translators of Quebec and Acadian literature.

Fred Cogswell's mother, Florence Antionette, the first child of Fred White and Marie Girouard, was born in 1900 in Rivière-du-Loup, a small community on the south shore of the St Lawrence River where her parents had fled to escape the shame of a shotgun wedding (they had eloped the night before Marie was to be married to another man). They later settled in the tiny farming community of Bath in western New Brunswick and had a large family. In Bath, Fred White became known as a lively spirit who played musical instruments and made up folksongs about the area. Over time, however, the quotidian demands of being husband, father, and breadwinner became too much for Fred,

so, in a peak of desperation, he staged his own drowning in a river near
Plaster Rock and fled to the east coast of the province where he
assumed a new identity. To feed her family, Marie taught music in local
schools and gave private lessons to wealthy families in the area, but
prospects had changed for her children. Even before Fred's stunt, it was
clear from his shenanigans that all her children would have to make
their own way. Knowing this, Florence left as a teenager to marry the
much older Walter Scott Cogswell, a Baptist farmer of thirty-four from
Bath's neighbouring village of East Centreville.

Walter Cogswell's ancestral line was as firmly rooted in New Brunswick as his wife's, though it was less flamboyant. He was descended
from prosperous wool merchants in twelfth-century Coggeshall
(Essex), England, and his New World chapter began when John and
Elizabeth Cogswell and their eight children immigrated to the Massachusetts Bay Colony in 1635 aboard the *Angel Gabriel*, the ill-fated
ship that had been commissioned for Sir Walter Raleigh's final
voyage across the North Atlantic.[10] When the ship went down in an
August storm off the coast of Maine, taking all their possessions, the
Cogswells made their way to Ipswich, Massachusetts, a town of like-
minded Puritans east of Boston that guaranteed a generous land grant
(this was the age of the Great Migration of Puritans seeking religious
freedom in the New World). In the early 1760s, a branch of the
Cogswell family that had been on the losing end of a dispute over
John Cogswell's inheritance moved north to what was thought to be
the more civil British colony of Nova Scotia.[11] The deportation order
that Governor Charles Lawrence had issued in 1755 created the conditions for British North Americans to reclaim western Nova Scotia
(now New Brunswick) from Acadians – and the rising militancy
among republican colonists seeking to cut ties with a distant Britain
made the prospect attractive to American settlers wishing to remain
loyal to their British roots. The vanquished line of the Cogswells, then
living as merchant farmers in Connecticut, took the opportunity,
crossing the porous border with a wave of New England Planters and
establishing a landholding in the northwest corner of Wicklow Parish
that soon became known as Cogswell Settlement. The East Centreville farm that Walter Cogswell inherited from his father, William,
was near the original settlement. It was registered in 1810, became
the site of the marriage of Florence White and Walter Cogswell in
November 1916 (and the birth of their first son, Fred, in November
1917), and is still in the Cogswell family more than two hundred years

later. A symbol of constancy in the face of change, the farm in what is now Carleton County, New Brunswick, is the "surrounding soil" that Fred Cogswell would describe in his most important early poem, "New Brunswick."[12]

Part of the legacy of that "surrounding soil," however, and always prominent in Cogswell's portrayals of Carleton County farm life, was narrowness. "Valley-Folk," the poem that, with "New Brunswick," frames his first collection *The Stunted Strong* (1954), minces no words about that claustrophobic narrowness:

O narrow is the house where we were born,
And narrow are the fields in which we labour,
Fenced in by rails and woods that low hills neighbour
Lest they should spill their crops of hay and corn.
O narrow are the hates with which we thorn
Each other's flesh by Gossip of the Grundies,
And narrow are our roads to church on Sundays,
And narrow too the vows of love we've sworn.[13]

That Cogswell chose to open his first published collection of poems with that rather unflattering portrait of his neighbours was no accident. He was born into a kind of narrowness against which his values, poetics, and cultural ethos would be shaped. Living with an uncommunicative, older father, a man who laboured endlessly on the land while pushing against the technological innovation that would unburden him, was a formative experience, as was witnessing the unfulfilled companionship of his parents' marriage. Growing up in a part of rural New Brunswick where aggressive parochialism upheld church, crown, and ethnicity's darker sides also informed what he would become. "The nearest thing to a sustained intellectual address we heard was the sermon," said an older Cogswell.[14] Which is not to say that the East Centreville of the 1920s was dull or fatigued. A short drive from the American border, it was a frontier town alive with rum-running, cross-border trade (legal and illegal), provincial police, and, as an ad in the *Observer* of 19 June 1952 testified, "old fashioned, sin condemning, soul winning, Christ exalting" revival meetings,[15] that combination creating what poet/journalist Alden Nowlan called "a Dickensian gusto."[16] The county's paper, the *Carleton Sentinel,* ran ads for two general stores, a bank and farm-supply depot, a drugstore, and a small but opulent opera house where travelling shows and weekly movies played with piano accompaniment. There was also a nearby rail line, the St John River Valley Railway, a school, and town buildings where doctors set up clinics to treat and vaccinate locals, an important service given the smallpox outbreak that gripped the adjacent towns of Bristol and Florenceville in the weeks after Fred Cogswell's birth.[17] For all the frontier bravado, however, or perhaps because of it, there was also an abundance of intransigence and secrecy, some of that owing to the fact that the Centreville area was tightly garrisoned – that is, both geographically fortified and socially isolated. Squeezed between an international border on the west, two major river systems to the south and east, and a sizeable mountain range to the north that separated Carleton and Victoria counties, Cogswell's village was a territory unto itself. For Woodstock political maverick Dalton Camp, that garrison incubated a mentality that ranged between individual dissent and outright hostility, the outward signs of which were fierce conservatism, defiant self-sufficiency, and distrust.[18]

Fred Cogswell's mother's story provides insight into how that garrison shaped the populace. Florence was a French-speaking Acadian, her mother, Marie, a frequent visitor to the East Centreville farm, and the Cogswell home a waypoint for Acadian cousins travelling from their New England outposts in Massachusetts and Connecticut to Bouctouche for summer festivals. Yet rarely did Fred and his siblings hear their mother speak French, for Carleton was a brazenly English county, one of the few Canadian strongholds for the anti-French, anti-Catholic Ku Klux Klan (KKK) in the early decades of the twentieth century. Two weeks after Walter and Florence were married in 1916, the following threat appeared in the *Carleton Observer*: "K.K.K. The three K's might stand for the Ku-Klux Klan. Whether they do or not you will learn in a few days."[19] Such tactics became commonplace in Carleton and Charlotte counties as political cudgel. Tensions came to a head in the late 1920s when, with the backing of Charlotte County MLA James S. Lord, the Orange Order staged a series of marches in protest of Regulation 32, which affirmed the goal of bilingual education in New Brunswick.[20] Hooded Klansmen burned crosses in the fields near Centreville to support Orange Order efforts, warning French Catholics to temper their expectations of reform. The intimidation continued until the 1935 provincial election, when the Klan went after Liberal candidate-for-premier Allison Dysart,[21] a Roman Catholic from Kent County. "If Dysart is elected," said flyers circulated throughout southwestern New Brunswick, "Rome will rule."[22] Because of those pressures and overt threats to people in mixed marriages, Florence rarely gave voice to her French or Catholic ancestry, accepting instead the Protestant fundamentalism into which she had married and in the midst of which she lived. For her son Fred, however, those silences and denials were paramount in the peculiar sociology of his youth. As recreated imaginatively in *The Stunted Strong*, his boyhood in rural New Brunswick was anchored in a powerful paradox: an undeniable love of place tempered by a simultaneous exasperation with its parochialisms.

So how does one emerge from such narrowness? Cogswell provides an answer in an early essay on Moses Hardy Nickerson, a nineteenth-century Nova Scotia fisherman and editorial writer whose rise seemed to parallel his own. "How does one explain this love of learning on the part of a boy who grew up out of contact with formal schooling," asks Cogswell, "and who, as soon as he could pull an oar, accompanied his father and brothers to the fishing grounds?"[23] "The answer," Cogswell posits, is twofold. First, it lies in inheritance – in the knowledge passed down from fathers to sons "that in their veins ran the blood of men who had been somebody and who had stood for something big"[24] – and, second, in the radicalness of religious fundamentalism, which instills "honest independence and non-conformity"[25] as chief virtues.[26] Cogswell's own formative period is best understood as a process of coming to terms with that inheritance and radicalness. His upbringing was thus characterized by various forms of imaginative transport, which he would later describe as yearnings for the "wider regions where the river goes."[27] He spent considerable time at the nearby farm of his uncle and aunt, whose openness to new ideas was fresh and exhilarating, particularly when compared with his neighbours who, he later recalled, "would never dare / To let new things contaminate the head."[28] When Cogswell was eight, his uncle gave him a crystal set from which he fashioned a crude but functional radio, its signals opening his world exponentially. He watched the birds, catalogued flowers, and collected moths and butterflies; he also played baseball and read everything in his midst, showing unusual aptitudes for mathematical calculation and the kind of defiance that was publicly condemned yet secretly admired (he once took up the devil's cause in Sunday school, claiming that the fallen angel's questioning of authority had not received its proper due in the Abrahamic and Thomistic traditions). His memory was also enormous. Protected by a mother who realized early that her precocious son's best chance in life was escape from the rural farm, and worried over by a reticent father who believed that his son's malocclusion and resulting speech impediment made him unsuited for the wider world, a young Fred Cogswell learned to reconcile the opposites around him. He therefore became as familiar with the Bible and the Imperial Dictionary (the only books widely available in his village) as with the standings and statistics of the Boston and New York baseball teams that he and his father followed on the radio. It was the same at the one-room schoolhouse he attended across the road from his family's 200-acre farm. He watched and listened, absorbing everything around him, yet played the requisite fool so as not to offend his peers. "A teen-aged oaf, I sang off-key," he wrote looking back, "And they would clap in ridicule. / The fool they needed then was me, / Paying back for my marks at school."[29] Such was life for precocious boys in rural New Brunswick. For him, there would be none of the European tours or New England visits that had rounded and "finished" A.G. Bailey.

By age ten, he had repeatedly read his school's Everyman edition of *The Vision of Piers Plowman*[30] as well as E.S. Creasy's *Fifteen Decisive Battles of the World*, the *Anglo-Saxon Chronicle*, and the *Celebrated Speeches of Chatham, Burke, and Erskine*, the latter of which would be important in sharpening his debating skills. He also devoured Book II of Palgrave's *Golden Treasury*, the standard anthology of verse in North American classrooms of that time. His writing began when he started scanning the forms of the Victorians to make sense of their metres, then trying to express his own ideas in those disciplined measures. For a boy who showed signs of mathematical genius, the play with forms built a determination to bind ideas to structure, thus advancing formalism in an age of free verse. A young Cogswell, of course, would not have known that his technique, far from naive, was an example of the "contemporaneity" that A.G. Bailey's modernity both encouraged and demanded, that formal discipline "following Eliot's dictum [of] constant practice so that our technique would be ready, like a well-oiled fire engine, when the moment of inspiration came."[31]

In the animal stories of Charles G.D. Roberts, the historical fictions of Walter Scott and Gilbert Parker, and the adventure romances of Rafael Sabatini, James Fenimore Cooper, Alexandre Dumas, Robert Louis Stevenson, Edward Bulwer-Lytton, and Henry James O'Brien Bedford-Jones, which came to him in serial form in the pages of the *Pictorial Review* and the *Star Weekly*, Cogswell found further alternatives to his rural isolation. In those first books, he told colleague David Galloway, he discovered worlds "more satisfactory ... than the social and other experiences which I was having in the settlement where I lived."[32] The reliance on literature for escape would later define Cogswell's views of his own entrapment in the still colonial world of his youth: "The Loyalists of New Brunswick and Ontario led a double life: they experienced monotony and hardship on the outskirts of civilization; but when they wrote novels and when they read them, their thoughts centred on exciting adventures among English lords, ladies, dukes and duchesses, leading a life of luxury, intrigue and idleness. In their fiction at least no gentleman had to sweat for a dollar, and no lady had to pine in solitary seclusion for the lack of gallants."[33]

When he graduated in 1934 from Centreville Superior School, Cogswell was a jumble of contradictions. Awkward yet gregarious, strong yet gentle, rooted in the quotidian yet awash in romantic escapes, he was a young man whose unusual sensibility had been incubated in an illiberal parish environment that was as suspicious of outsiders as it was contemptuous of their ideas. It was a place where young men apprenticed in courage and denial in order to stay on the family farm. A misaligned figure like Cogswell, an aspiring poet who collected butterflies, should have been eager to leave, yet he would hold East Centreville close for the remainder of his life, loyal to his family farm, his folk, and the Carleton County earth. His true inheritance, then, was provincial, quite unlike that of the well-bred A.G. Bailey and the peripatetic Desmond Pacey. His enrollment in Fredericton's Normal School just a few months after graduation illustrates the point, that decision a tentative step into the wider world that was still close enough to East Centreville that he would be near to his inheritance. The risky choice of teacher education for a young man with a speech impediment is best understood in those terms – that is, as a compromise that satisfied his mother's wish that he leave, his father's hope that he stay, and his own allegiance to the soil from which he had come.

His next five years were mostly vocational, starting with teacher training and advancing through a number of temporary commitments that would give him a life off but near the farm. Had Cogswell come from wealthier circumstances, he would certainly have attended university, for his marks were as good as Pacey's (he came fifth in the province in his exams); however, UNB did not have the scholarship money that the University of Toronto did, and Cogswell's parents, unlike Bailey's, had no institutional standing. Desperate, he had written to UNB president C.C. Jones shortly after graduation, explaining that "my parents are hard-working honest people and through no fault of their own have found themselves unable to help me very much, owing to the depressed agricultural conditions."[34] Scholarship money, however, was not forthcoming, and so Cogswell would have to make his own way, beginning in Fredericton. An early experience there would affect him profoundly and consolidate his thinking about the jumble of contradictions that he had become.

In his first year at Normal School, as he recalls in the poem "It Began in 1935," Shanghai-born V.K. Wellington Koo (Ku Wei-chün) visited Fredericton. A decorated foreign-service diplomat – he had represented China at the Paris Peace Conference in 1919, had been a founding member of the League of Nations, and even for a time (1926–27) had served as acting premier of the Republic of China – Dr Koo was a well-known anti-imperialist whose resistance to the territorial ambitions of the West had been the subject of his PhD thesis at Columbia[35] and later, because of his influence at the Paris Peace Conference, resulted in China not signing the Treaty of Versailles in 1919.[36] Koo's response to that imperialism informed his message to audiences around the world, including in Fredericton. To counter imperialism, he argued, China must open itself to the world, negotiating with foreign powers to unwind the treaties that infringed on its sovereignty. That view, which became the position of the Kuomintang, China's pre-communist Nationalist Party, advocated building alliances over military aggression, national isolation, and cultural exceptionalism. China, Koo said, was but one country in a league of nations, that simple yet eloquent statement expelling the either-or absolutes that Cogswell had learned in school and church.[37] "What ideas were," Cogswell concluded on that day, "so life was. League / Became the deepest principle I held / And which held me."[38]

Koo's idea of "a greater league"[39] (in its simplest iteration, openness) turned Cogswell's mind to Chinese thought, triggering a lifelong fascination with Eastern philosophy – a fascination that he would share with Bailey. He read busily for the next few years, immersing himself in Lin Yutang's *The Importance of Living* (1937) – his introduction to Taoism and the ecologies of interconnectedness – and in Tom MacInnes's *The Teachings of the Old Boy* (1927) and Arthur Waley's *The Way and Its Power: A Study of the TAO TÊ CHING and Its Place in Chinese Thought* (1936). In each, Cogswell found alternatives to the narrow evangelical Christianity that marked his upbringing. Their "more rational education"[40] taught him to find meaning in simplicity, in silence and reverence, and in release from the anxieties and desires of modernity. "Out of opposites came complements when / Yin and Yang together created league," Cogswell wrote: "Two forces were its key."[41] At age eighteen, then, Cogswell took his first steps out of the biblical world that had held him in thrall.[42] Taoist tenets would inform his ethics thereafter and colour his unusually democratic approach to editing and publishing. What Chinese thought taught him was that stewardship without "league" was militancy, thus fraudulent.

As liberating as that breakthrough must have been for Cogswell, it also made his first teaching positions in small Carleton County schools difficult. His sympathy for his inattentive charges and his reluctance to maintain discipline made his employment temporary. As he later confessed to one of his students, his "emphasis on the individual worth of students was an *avant-garde* style for that time [that] came hard up against ... 'institutional warfare.'"[43] Rather than face another year of itinerant teaching, he enrolled in the Carleton County Vocational School in Woodstock to study clerkship, hoping to follow Dr Koo's example by putting commercial skills toward a career in the Canadian diplomatic service ("anyone who could write shorthand, operate a typewriter and knew something of office routine," said Centreville-born vocational school graduate Robert Tweedie, "stood a reasonable chance of finding a job"[44]). Cogswell left the vocational school in 1939 with a commercial diploma but no job. Instead, he took a handful of poems to Woodstock's most decorated literary son, the dentist and amateur archaeologist George Frederick Clarke. Recognizing him as the young poet who had published "Poland," an antiwar poem, in the *Telegraph-Journal*, Clarke found great promise coupled with great insularity of experience in the poems, a disjunction that prompted him to suggest that Cogswell spread his wings. With few prospects at home and no response to the foreign-service application he had made or the Treasury Department post he had applied for a few months earlier, Cogswell followed Clarke's advice. Against his mother's wishes, he enlisted in the army in early 1940, taking a consequential step into the wider world.

His aptitudes for accounting and management systems eventually brought him to the Canadian Forestry Corps, where he became a staff sergeant in charge of lumber inventories for the war effort. In effect, he oversaw timber harvesting and shipping for mines and railways.

Stationed first on a large working base in the northern Scottish Highlands near the city of Inverness, then transferred to a unit west of Aberdeen, Cogswell interacted with people from vastly different backgrounds than his own. He also travelled when on leave, visiting the libraries of the region and availing himself of books and opportunities offered by the Canadian Army Education Services. The experiences of travel, education, and interaction were transformative, accelerating his drift to the political left and giving him insight into a European perspective that was the opposite of his own. Not only was Europe enlivened, he said, by "the associations writers and musicians and people generally have with their history,"[45] but rural New Brunswick, he learned, was comparatively empty, its "uniformity of opinion" as vigorously protected as it was ultimately enervating: "I grew up in an anachronistic enclave of Canadian society, and I still remember the shock, after joining the Canadian Army in 1940, which I experienced in encountering views of life and people so markedly different from those I myself held, and which I assumed (because the clergy, the teachers, and my neighbours held them too) were universal. This very uniformity of opinion ... presented an image of God, Nature, and Man that seemed to supply the answers to people's needs to such a degree that there was no desire ... to deal with points of view that were considered abnormal, amoral, or in any significant way different from the norm."[46]

Cogswell made opportunity of that difference, as had other members of the Fiddlehead circle. He befriended intellectuals in the rank and file, followed them to the lectures that British universities opened up to enlisted men, and turned his own poetry to activist ends. Meeting his future wife, Margaret Hynes, while on furlough abetted that movement. An Irish nurse stationed at an Exeter infirmary, she was the daughter of an Irish Republican Army member who had been killed by the British. When Cogswell returned to New Brunswick in August 1945 at age twenty-seven, he was not only married and soon to be a father, but, like many of his fellow servicemen, he was more worldly and much less biddable than the rural youth who had left.

He also had a focus that he had never had before, enrolling immediately as a veteran at UNB and partaking of a post-war momentum that would carry him as far as he needed to go. His point of entry could not have been more opportune. UNB's outgoing and incoming presidents, Norman MacKenzie and Milton F. Gregg, had been vocal proponents of Privy Council Order No. 7633 (1941), which mandated rehabilitation training programs for armed-services personnel. Altered by the new Department of Veterans Affairs to become the Veterans Rehabilitation Act in 1945, the legislation gave family-graduated living allowances, tuition waivers, and loan guarantees to discharged Second World War veterans – and, as importantly, provided institutions like UNB with federal grants proportional to the number of veterans admitted. The act not only smoothed the re-entry of young men and women into Canadian society after the war, but also furnished the capital that built the nation's universities. Between 1945 and the early 1950s, over fifty thousand veterans took advantage of subsidized university education, their numbers comprising upwards of 50 per cent of the enrollment at some universities.[47] In the manner to which he was accustomed, incoming UNB president Brigadier-General Gregg mustered Bailey and his other UNB lieutenants to open the university to the flood of incoming vets.[48] Gregg and his team subjected all curricula to immediate review and began the process of repurposing parts of the campus and town to house and educate military freshmen. Army tents were erected next to the Old Arts Building, surplus bunks were bought and placed in lounges and common areas, and a former basic training centre on the town's exhibition grounds was designated as Alexander College, a self-contained facility for married student veterans. Dalton Camp's description of the college's students as having "matriculated from Ortona or the Schelde Estuary, or from a corvette, or from a bomber squadron" is apt.[49] Named in honour of British field marshal and Governor General Alexander of Tunis, the college was a rough barracks – its atmosphere wavering "between primitive and shoddy," remembered graduate student Heath Macquarrie[50] – but it provided the chance for some five hundred veterans to attend university. They took first-year classes there and enjoyed a variety of on-site amenities, including a gymnasium, rink, barbershop, grocery store, counselling centre, and even a small, nine-bed hospital.[51] "Although you can't spread your bread with a college diploma," wrote Camp, "neither can you build a nation without trained men and women."[52] The sentiment informed the ethos of Fred Cogswell's UNB and Alexander College experiences.

The university itself was a changing space, adapting rapidly to liberalizing social norms. Harold Adams Innis mused about the excitements and dangers of this era in an impassioned convocation address to the UNB community in May 1944. Universities must adapt, he told graduates, but must be careful to maintain their core values of humanistic scholarship lest they yield to business, bureaucracy, and government. Their mandate can no longer be that of the gentleman scholar and his paternalistic benefactors, warned Innis, echoing the social Christianity that Bailey and Pacey would have recognized from Toronto, but neither should it open itself to the corruption of scholarship by commercial interests. The freedoms of a long tradition of academic inquiry must at all costs be defended against social incursion.[53] A then left-leaning Dalton Camp described the challenge eloquently in a comment that Cogswell would have roundly endorsed:[54] "We must become tough enough and calm and wise enough to parry superstition with fact, contradict propaganda with logic, and confound hatred with benevolence. It seems to us that the universities are crowded because the people who must pay the consequences are determined on having a crack at searching for the truth."[55] Indeed, Alexander College's young men and women, many newly married with infants in tow, were not the naive rural youth who had left New Brunswick a few years earlier. Their payback from a grateful nation was not just institutional accommodation but the expectation that the nation's ruling classes would listen to what they had to say.

In the Faculty of Arts that newly appointed Dean A.G. Bailey led (his term started in 1946), what they had to say was idealistically humanist, a humanism that balanced historical awareness, local application, and justice for all. That balance was reflected in the rights-seeking liberalism of Camp's May 1947 valedictory address, which, echoing Innis, warned of the dangers of post-humanism: "In a thoroughly mechanized society, we stand to be manufactured in the image of the machine ... In a society so lavishly proud of its techniques in mass production ... the independent and inquisitive mind finds itself compressed, confined, bounded on all sides."[56] And the balance was also reflected in the justice-seeking exasperation of Cogswell's "Ode to Fredericton," a 1948 poem that called attention to the gulf between town and gown populations in a still parochial Fredericton. Prompting Cogswell's poem was a late-1947 incident in the capital city in which two black students, one a veteran, were denied service by four barbers because of the colour of their skin. Vernon Mullen, student editor of the *Brunswickan* and also a veteran (Royal Canadian Air Force and prisoner of war), published a supplement to the paper condemning the incident. His editorial, entitled "Pharisees and Publicans," accused locals of "unchristian racial discrimination," saying that "the same fine citizens of Fredericton who contribute large sums to

'Christianize' the poor 'heathen,' who are considered to be solid pillars of our churches, but who refuse to sit in a barber's chair after a Negro has had his hair cut there, are no more Christians in the true sense of the word than the 'heathen' they want to convert."[57] The next month's edition of the *Brunswickan* (January 1948) carried Cogswell's well-known "Ode to Fredericton," which satirized Fredericton's purity:

> White are your housetops, white too the vaulted elms
> That make your stately streets long aisles of prayer,
> And white your thirteen spires that point to God
> Who reigns afar in pure and whiter air,
> And white the dome of your democracy –
> The snow has pitied you and made you fair,
> O snow-washed city of cold, white Christians,
> So white you will not cut a black man's hair.[58]

Cogswell excelled at UNB because he discovered there a freedom to write and think in this way without constraint, a freedom that was reflected in the veterans' determination "to win the peace."[59] Winning the peace demanded political changes that he and his peers were willing to attempt, whatever the risks. The first order of business was to overthrow the "archaic 'Family Compact'" of UNB's Student Representative Council, thus achieving fair representation for the majority veterans.[60] The second was to line up behind the political party that provided the greatest likelihood for economic and social change. For many of UNB's veterans, that party was the CCF. Taking his place, then, in a movement that historian Ian McKay described as "the most solidly left-wing cohort in Canadian history,"[61] Cogswell emerged at UNB as a committed socialist. Having followed Harold Laski's talks on the BBC's Wartime Broadcasting Service and having been steeped in European ideas that "had to a great degree ended ... the kind of political naïveté" that had characterized his youth in New Brunswick,[62] Cogswell formally joined the CCF in 1946. He helped his friends Vernon and Dana Mullen with the provincial CCF paper, *True Democracy*, which was assembled and printed in Fredericton, and he began writing commentaries for local radio station CFNB. In the same way that the Liberal Party took note of Dalton Camp's work in the *Brunswickan*,[63] so did the CCF leadership take note of Cogswell, inviting him to become a writer in support of fellow student Murray Young's CCF candidacy in the 1947 York-Sunbury by-election. In the aftermath of that election, Cogswell accepted an appointment as provincial secretary of the CCF.[64]

His reasons for accepting were twofold. First was a desire to quiet the voices at UNB that were spouting increasingly aggressive anti-CCF rhetoric. One such voice was coming from the Department of Economics and Political Science, where the Tory chairman, J. Richard Petrie, was talking loudly about socialist sympathizers. About one left-leaning faculty colleague in particular Petrie boasted that "if we have another war my first patriotic act will be to get a Sten gun and shoot that old bugger."[65] For young socialists striving to "win the peace," not to mention the veterans who had just come from standing in front of such guns, these were reckless words indeed, but they were the lesser of Cogswell's motivations for formalizing his political brand. More determinative was a troublesome propaganda campaign being waged by Liberals and Conservatives against the CCF in his home turf of Carleton County. Appearing in weekly editorials and broadcast in fiery radio addresses, that campaign warned farmers of the socialists' plan to nationalize food production, in effect equating socialism with communism for the purpose of worrying New Brunswick farmers about their birthright.[66] Conservative premier-in-waiting Hugh John Flemming, MLA for nearby Juniper, beat that drum loudly, warning rural New Brunswickers that a vote for the CCF would turn the province into another Russia.[67] For Cogswell, such deliberate manipulation of truth – not for power but more perniciously to turn citizens against their own interests – was another form of the religious autocracy that he had rejected, and especially similar in how it preyed upon the uneducated and impressionable. In anger, he wrote the draft of a poem that he would only release years later. "There's no freshness in vocabulary," he wrote about Flemming's speeches, "Which puts a cause above adversity."[68]

It was in the midst of Cogswell's growing cynicism with such attitudes and tactics that A.G. Bailey, his history professor, invited him to play a more integral role in the *Fiddlehead*, thus rescuing him from the conspiratorial narrows of provincial party politics. Bailey had noticed Cogswell two years earlier; in fact, the young man had finished at the top of his introductory survey course and, with Desmond Pacey, was one of the first people outside the Bliss Carman Society to join the board of the fledgling *Fiddlehead* in 1945. By late 1947, Cogswell and Bailey were well acquainted, the topics of their conversation centring on common ancestry and on Chinese thought –

Cogswell's Taoism aligning exactly with Bailey's view that identity was discovered in openness, not behind self-imposed walls. Surprisingly enough, their New World ancestors, John Bailey and John Cogswell, had both been on the *Angel Gabriel*, the ship that had gone down in rough seas off Pemaquid Point, Maine, in August 1635. Thereafter, as A.G. Bailey was fond of relating, the Bailey and Cogswell families intermingled for the next two hundred and fifty years, moving across the border between New England and Nova Scotia/ New Brunswick.[69] Bailey's interest in that common ancestry warrants examination, for it points to how he saw both his larger Fiddlehead project and Cogswell's role in it. The utility of the happenstance, he explained, was not to be found in a tenuous nepotism – "Reanimation of the dead," Bailey wrote, is "helpful only to a point"[70] – but rather in how history moves randomly by chance and instinct (accidents of travel, passenger manifests, weather) toward future outcomes. For Bailey, then, ancestry was order and providence – as M. Travis Lane would observe, "a genetic working out in the present of the patterns of the past as part of a still living web"[71] – and Cogswell a point of intersection and opportunity. The final lines from "Angel Gabriel" are worth repeating in this context:

And so to be
"burst in pieces & cast away in ye storme" was
not the ultimate adventure; the road that ran
from the Wiltshire plain to Fredericton's hill
might be construed as sociological, but as we
travelled over it, it became evident, at first
however dimly, that something beyond awaited us,
we did not know what to call it, but went forward to
search for an answer.[72]

In 1947 the abstractions of ancestry became emphatic. Bailey convinced Cogswell to recommit to his studies and warned him of the consequences of leftist politics in an aggressively centrist New Brunswick – a New Brunswick that, quite extraordinarily, extended tolerances to the far-right KKK in Carleton and Charlotte counties while at the same time singling out the CCF in those areas as "a 'destructive factor.'"[73] The full implication of Bailey's warning would come a few years later in 1950 when Cogswell was shortlisted for a Rhodes scholarship. The first question put to him at the Saint John interview concerned his politics: specifically, when was he going to drop his CCF sympathies?[74] From that point forward, Cogswell was a private leftist, as he explained in letters to Pacey and Bailey. "I have decided henceforth to be a teacher," he told Pacey, "not a politician."[75] And to Bailey: "The air about England is blue with political arguments; as pointless and as heated as political arguments always are."[76] "I myself am well out of it."[77]

To steer Cogswell to cultural instead of political ends, Bailey arranged for him to work with Robert Rogers to co-edit the *Fiddlehead* (Donald Gammon had resigned as editor to study library science in Toronto). Cogswell cut his editorial teeth on the seventh issue, December 1947, co-editing the next two issues with Rogers until taking sole charge of issues ten and eleven (fall 1948 and spring 1949). Cogswell was ready for the challenge. In classes from Bailey, Pacey, Alec Lucas, and David Galloway – and in courses in Latin, French, and Spanish – he was advancing from his earlier imitation of poetic forms to more sophisticated studies of symbolism and allusion.[78] Lucas and Galloway precipitated his move toward American and French literature, Lucas suggesting that he examine southern American modernism, specifically the work of the Fugitive Poets (John Crowe Ransom, Allen Tate, and Robert Penn Warren) for its agrarian sensibility. In parallel fashion, Galloway guided his study of the early French Romantic Alfred de Vigny[79] as well as what he termed "the visual grammars of William Blake."[80] Cogswell, in turn, shortened his own poetic forms as a result of Blake's iconography and Bailey's suggestion that he renew his interest in the Chinese haiku. As importantly, Cogswell had adopted a greater seriousness about his work that his association with the Bliss Carman Society writers, now affectionately called the "Poetry Club," demanded.[81] "There were only about ten people allowed in the [society] when I first entered it," Cogswell recalled, and "none of your poems were in [the *Fiddlehead*] unless everybody approved of them. So, for the sake of shining at the meetings, and for the sake of getting one's poems published, one was on one's very best poetic behavior."[82] Cogswell's first poems in the *Fiddlehead* reveal this more considered practice and, as importantly, his accord with Bailey's larger New Brunswick project. Like the others in the Poetry Club, he could not help but absorb Bailey's teachings, which had coalesced into a definable ethos. "If you are exposed to a group of people who develop a certain sensibility ... and technique" and if you "have been given massive encouragement," Cogswell told an interviewer in 1973, "you will usually pick it up."[83] So it was with Bailey's poetics, at least at the outset: Cogswell accepted that "poetry had to be clear and hard, and had to avoid abstractions"; that it had to be written in contingent form, should avoid clichés, and be scrubbed of emotion.[84] By 1947, the obscure little-magazine publishing credits that Cogswell had accumulated for literary companionship and affirmation had dimmed in the rear-view mirror. So had his novice poetic technique learned from the models in Palgrave's *Treasury*.

Appearing in the fourth number of the *Fiddlehead* (February 1946), Cogswell's "Prisms" and "The Man Who Climbed and Came Back" provide evidence of his new orientation. Each poem entertains Bailey's notions of ancestry while also articulating an interest in the Taoist concept of "league" that Cogswell and Bailey regularly discussed. "All things converge in me," begins the second stanza of Cogswell's "Prisms":

> All things diverge from me,
> All things flow through me,
> And flowing through me are never the same;
> As glass is a refraction and directs the sunlight,
> So I myself refract,
> Directing the course of events.
>
> I am a prism through which life pours,
> But I am only one of many ...
> If anything were original in the beginning
> Or at any other time,
> They are not now.
> And what they were and are and will be
> Is beyond my power of telling.[85]

Not only is the poem modernist as Bailey and A.J.M. Smith defined modernism – "a poetry of ideas," wrote Smith in his groundbreaking anthology[86] – but the poem explicitly introduces the concept of plurality that Cogswell would soon turn into an editorial ethic of eclecticism. The key idea in the poem, then, is not that things converge but that they *diverge*. Convergence is a nineteenth-century Whitmanesque notion: the poet/thinker as Shelley's "unacknowledged legislator of the world." Divergence, by contrast, is fragmenting and democratic, allowing for the presence of multiplicities outside of a gifted or heroic brain (the great man) that filters those – and allowing, as well, for an infinite variety of such filters. The allusion to Ralph Waldo Emerson's concept of the "transparent eyeball" is also evident in the poem, suggesting Cogswell's close reading of the New England transcendentalists (and, again, Bailey's guiding hand). For Emerson, the transparent eyeball, like the prism, absorbs the light around it, gaining understanding of nature's profusions: "Standing on the bare ground, – my head bathed by the blithe air, and uplifted into infinite spaces, – all mean egotism vanishes. I become a transparent eye-ball; I am nothing; I see all; the currents of the Universal Being circulate through me; I am part or particle of God."[87] Cogswell's poem asserts a similar openness and yielding to greater forces "beyond [the poet's] power of telling." That the speaker of the poem is "only one of many"[88] – one of many conduits that others enter and flow through – means that he must remain open to what he cannot immediately understand. That openness marked a key difference between Bailey's two principal lieutenants: Pacey setting out from the start to be the declarative mind that interprets (the peripatetic spirit that seeks in such definition a home), and Cogswell intent on being an absorbent prism through which various lights flow to their own eventuality. With no need to create for himself a home or authority beyond his "surrounding soil," Cogswell could (and would soon) become the vessel through which others created their own imaginative spaces. As the complementary poem "The Man Who Climbed and Came Back" reveals, his place was on the ground in New Brunswick in service to a larger humanity there. He thus embodied cosmopolitan rootedness. Though his poem's subject climbs, he always comes back to earth:

He climbed.

He did not even know
The path he took.
The valley where he was
Restricted him
With opaque barriers:
Any upward way (he felt)
Would give a clearer view,
And so he climbed
For one brief day.

But nightfall brought him back ...

He stayed among us in the valley
And worked beside us in the fields,
Grave and proper like the rest
He never spoke about his climb.[89]

Readers of Maritime literature may recognize Ernest Buckler's David Canaan between the lines of Cogswell's poem – Buckler's *Mountain and the Valley* was published in 1952, six years after Cogswell's poem – and will appreciate both the utility and validity of a Cogswell-David comparison. David's clear-eyed redemption at the end of Buckler's novel is found in ecumenical openness, specifically in the act of giving an "absolving voice" to the family and friends whose demands had earlier confounded him.[90] Cogswell's mission will be the same. He will be a prism through which lights merge and diverge. He will help others find voice, those voices an antidote to "the tick, tick, tick, of emptiness" that David Canaan feels in his rural place.[91] For Cogswell, filling emptiness with voice would become sustaining faith and editorial creed, both sourced, perhaps surprisingly, in a tradition of radical Baptism that he would express in non-doctrinal ways. "The matrix of the earliest impressions are always the deepest," remarked Cogswell, despite the fact that "that cultural imprinting is broadened through reading and the experience of living."[92] Cogswell, then, could no more shed his religious conditioning than Pacey could. Each brought his formative sense of moral rectitude to his work: Pacey the belief that service to excellence in creative endeavour fulfilled higher moral and social purposes, and Cogswell that service to the artist, as opposed to the art, met the same objectives. In Fred Cogswell's case, the faith was differentiated and personal, "The faith that what men built will not fall down, / That though it [may be] bad, yet good may come of it."[93]

Cogswell had indeed learned his lessons well. UNB had deepened his political acuity and honed his poetics. He had internalized "league" to understand the opposing forces of the human drama and had begun using poetry to work out his ideas, hence the similarity of his early *Fiddlehead* poems to the more mature work that appears in *The Stunted Strong*. His *Fiddlehead* poems often speak of growth and yearning: seeds and desires pushing through "stubborn soil" to "where sun shines / And blue winds are."[94] Yet desire always returns to earth, finding nothing to sustain it in skies. The poem "Acceptance," published in the *Fiddlehead* in 1947, makes that clear – and is Cogswell's clearest articulation of a direction, if not a vocation:

> Like a caterpillar
> Pursuing its fellows' thread
> Around a saucer's rim
> No more my thoughts traverse
> The circle grooved by myriad minds
> Skirting mystery mountains.
>
> Here in my narrow valley
> I shall sit at ease
> And eat the wholesome fruit,
> Knowing all roads escaping
> Turn back on themselves.[95]

Cogswell will thereafter consider this "narrow valley" the middle path where yearning gives way to yielding. Real growth, he discovers, is in service not flight. "It is better / to be a well-placed / candle / than a blazing sun," he would later write: "to illuminate / without distortion / the empty spaces / between and around / what is normally seen."[96]

When he completed his BA in 1949, Cogswell had a clear vision to the future. With hopes for a later role in Bailey's larger Fiddlehead project and on the strength of a stellar undergraduate record – he had won the Bliss Carman Medal in 1946 and 1947 and the prestigious Douglas Gold Medal in 1948 (previous recipients were George Parkin [1865], W.O. Raymond [1901], and Elizabeth Brewster [1945]) – he began his MA at UNB, working under Pacey's supervision to write a thesis on the Canadian novel. Submitted in March 1950, "The Canadian Novel from Confederation until World War One" became a model for Pacey's *Creative Writing in Canada* (1952).[97] As envisioned by Cogswell, the work's original intent was to "present a well-balanced historical survey of the Canadian novel, in which every author would appear in his appropriate chronological and regional niche together with a summary of the pertinent facts of his life, a list of his principal novels and a few generalizations about their literary qualities."[98] That objective was deemed "too 'thin' to serve either the University or myself,"[99] however, and so Cogswell opted instead for select treatments of overlooked works by William Kirby, Gilbert Parker, Sara Jeannette Duncan,[100] Susan Frances Harrison, Robert Barr, and Norman Duncan.

Not partial or tentative as graduate work often is, Cogswell's MA thesis is both a work of mature literary criticism and a portal to understanding his eventual role in the Fiddlehead triumvirate. Just as his early poems in the *Fiddlehead* reveal an ecumenical spirit that had rooted itself in (and, indeed, reconciled itself to) a particular locus, so is Cogswell's first work of scholarship revealing for what it says about his literary apprenticeship and the cultural values that will shape his career. Falling under Pacey's tutelage, the thesis focuses on realism, not surprisingly, but on a type of realism that is of special interest to Cogswell: namely, realistic fiction in which "the reader's experience, insofar as there is common ground between them, is of equal validity with the writer's."[101] Cogswell posits that in fiction of that kind there is evidence of an artistic maturity that moves the larger culture to an "awareness of itself,"[102] which is integral for any society's emergence from colonialism. At least on the surface, this idea restates Pacey's notion in the introduction to *A Book of Canadian Stories* (1947) that, as "the intelligent and purposive comprehension of one's nature and circumstances,"[103] self-awareness brings individuals and nations to maturity because it places humans in their own environments, for good or ill. While not new, then, Cogswell's premise is in line with the Bailey/Pacey belief that renovation of a tradition begins in confrontation with rather than escape from one's own circumstances.

What Cogswell saw clearer than Pacey, though, and where his study of realism differs, was that Canada's Confederation moment was the symbolic start of the country's long and often difficult journey *into* itself. Pacey certainly understood the federated nature of Canada's geopolitical identity, the evidence of that in his selections for *A Book of Canadian Stories*, but he did not approach the personal and spiritual dramas underlying federation as deeply as Cogswell did. Cogswell is thus able to write of Norman Duncan's *Way of the Sea* that, though "man's mortality and the limitations of his body doom to futility all the efforts his indomitable spirit can devise,"[104] the great accomplishment of Duncan's novel lies in its avowal of humanity's "dauntless optimism."[105] Despite "the disparity of the conflict" between "the Great Antagonist" (Nature) and humankind, and despite "the insignificance of his achievement,"[106] the human, concludes Cogswell, presses on with virtues of "strength, loyalty, endurance, and courage,"[107] those virtues revealed most acutely in confrontation with one's own immediate, not national, circumstance. The pursuit of realism for Cogswell, then, was not an effort to align himself with a formal means to national maturity or with a mentor's critical aesthetic, but rather a fascination with a particular form of literary expression that laid bare the spiritual dramas in which all Canadians, in their different regions, were engaged. Examining that confrontation with immediacy was the role of the critic, he concluded. When mapped onto Bailey's cultural sociology – evident in Cogswell's view that the Canadian predilection to use culture to escape "from the unpleasant realities of a harsh existence"[108] created the puritanism that E.K. Brown and Bailey lamented[109] – realism is presented in the thesis as the means to spiritual growth (a growth that takes artists out of the evangelical narrows of puritanism into more enlightened spiritual realms). The critic's role in that growth is pastoral, Cogswell insists, akin to a care that shepherds, comforts, and defends. On this point, the differences among the three Fiddlehead principals are easily discernible: realism, for Bailey, a means of re-energizing for cultural renewal; for Pacey, a means to national maturity; and for Cogswell, a means to personal and spiritual growth. While all three believed, like Eliot, that the sum of literary outputs was organic – that "the tradition" could be shaped by human intention – Cogswell emerged as the figure most invested in localizing that effort, for he believed that it is in immediate circumstance that one discovers oneself. His swerve from Bailey and Pacey in a 1961 article made that plain. "Bailey's 'Creative Moments in the Culture of the Maritime Provinces,'" he wrote, "is ingenious and attractive," and "Pacey's *Creative Writing in Canada* ... [is] indebted to it,"[110] but "Bailey's thesis ignores the moral and religious ferment of the Maritime provinces, the slackening of which was necessary before significant poetry could be developed."[111] For Cogswell, realism was the portal through which one transitioned from the institutional (romance and religion) to "fearless expression and free inquiry" of the self.[112]

Cogswell's aptly named poem, "Statement of Position," brings his poetic and critical visions together, such that "each from each [the critic and the artist] may take his natural food":

> So sustained
> I feed upon the fruit of lives I feed
> And need not look behind to fear of salt,
> Nor forward to terror, knowing no drought
> Of water, dearth of earthy fare will fret
> The man whose journeying need is justified

Not in new road nor record-breaking climb
But by a humbler kind of pilgrimage.[113]

The "humbler kind of pilgrimage" is similar for the poet and critic in
Cogswell: each works in service to expression that advances individuals, wherever they are. The significance of that view for Cogswell's
later editorial eclecticism cannot be overstated, for as early as 1950 he
became increasingly strident in voicing the opinion that the *Fiddlehead* "is not quite catholic enough."[114] Though he was rooted in New
Brunswick and anchored in a mentor's project that sought to return
to New Brunswick some of the cultural achievement of the past, his
study of realism had impressed upon him that localism was diffuse
because encounters with immediate circumstance were innumerable
and diverse. His own creative and critical attentions to the province
did not contradict that belief, but simply reflected the fact that New
Brunswick was the space of his own becoming. He agreed with Bailey that all life exists in its own circumstance and that each circumstance is culturally determinative (Bailey would express that sense of
ecology in the magnificent poem "The Muskrat and the Whale"). In
Cogswell's mind, this meant that localism and eclecticism were not
incompatible. Again, his verse provides a useful gloss. "O Canadians,"
he pleads, "when will the truth be known, / No other coat can fit you
save your own / Tailored by Time's needle, measured by Need's tape,
/ Nine cloths stitched into one coherent shape? / Work then to serve
our most immediate needs, / Words serve for binding thread as well
as deeds."[115]

To ensure that there would be no confusion about what he meant,
Cogswell wrote an explanation of that view of localism for Don Gammon in July 1950. Meant to clarify the lines he delivered at a Poetry
Club gathering ("Communist, capitalist, socialist to boot, / All who
never saw trees for the wood)," Cogswell's explanation was another
attempt to refine his developing theory of eclecticism. About the second line above, he wrote: "[There is] a tendency in modern society to
emphasize unities rather than differences, to search for the One rather
than the Many, to ignore individuals and individual relationships in
their particular form in favour of generalizations, to put concepts
above precepts. Because of these tendencies we have great emphasis
upon ideologies, whereas every ideology is only an abstraction or gen-
eralization of phenomena which makes it not only a half-truth ... but
also takes from it the essence, the greater part of the color and joy of

life which lies in an appreciation, ungeneralized, of particular incidents and things."[116]

Cogswell carried this outlook to the University of Edinburgh in
1950. Unsuccessful in getting the Rhodes that would have sent him to
Oxford – he joked that New Brunswick Liberal premier J.B. McNair,
himself an Oxford man and Rhodes scholar, would not tolerate a
CCFer at his beloved university[117] – Cogswell chose a Scottish university that was close to his wife's family in Ireland. His PhD topic was
officially registered as "The Concept of America in British Literature
of the Romantic Period," but its actual intent was to examine the
motif of the noble savage in the Romantic imagination.[118] The topic
gave Cogswell the latitude to continue his work in history and literature, particularly in the Bailey stream, while also pursuing his interest
in "America" as utopian myth and symbol. Beginning with *The Inter-
lude of the Four Elements* and the work of Sir Thomas More, his sweeping survey of British literature brought him to two important discov-
eries, each influential in his later work. The first find was John Logan
(1748–88), the controversial Scottish poet/preacher who had attended
the University of Edinburgh, gave public lectures on the philosophy
of history (now the field of historiography), and ended his career editing London's *English Review*. Logan's examinations of history and
sociology as twin forces mirrored Bailey's approach to cultural systems and affirmed the superiority of social over "events" history for
understanding what Logan called "the people."[119] "Poetry, philosophy,
the fine arts, national manners and customs," Cogswell quoted from
Logan in the same letter, "result from the situation and spirit of a people." Logan's early ethnographic studies provided yet more reason for
Cogswell to consider his own "valley folk" as being in the forefront of
cultural movements. While such folk are not contributory agents of
official culture, Logan argued, they inhabit culture's deep biases as
social participants and thus are worthy of careful study. That idea, of
course, aligned exactly with Cogswell's belief in the legitimacy of
their voices.

The second figure of special interest during Cogswell's doctoral
study was the Scottish novelist John Galt (1779–1839). A contemporary of Logan, Galt was equally committed to exploring the agrarian
sensibility of the Scottish folk, a preoccupation that Cogswell found
to be common when going through archival records of the *Scots Magazine* of the mid-eighteenth century.[120] Galt's early work was coincident with that of the better-known Scottish novelist Walter Scott,

and may even have served to humanize Scott's more fanciful romantic imaginations.[121] Galt had been a favourite of Beaverbrook, who
spoke highly to Bailey of *Annals of the Parish* (1821), Galt's examination of rural Scottish life as seen through the eyes of the Reverend
Micah Balwhidder.[122] As a realistic account of rural manners and a
slowly obsolescing agrarian economy on the cusp of the Industrial
Revolution, Galt's novel was an early treatment of rural folk that
Cogswell would later emulate in *The Stunted Strong*. What Balwhidder witnesses is similar to what Cogswell records as the effects of
rapid social change on a rural population. Galt's work was therefore
extremely useful to Cogswell as a creative dramatization of the
Innis/Bailey theory of historical change, wherein society and culture
shift with alterations in wealth, circumstance, and dominant forms of
production.[123] Cogswell's later agitation with publishers who overlooked works of literature that explored those historical processes
hearkens back to his fondness for Galt's work and underscores his
commitment to individual lives, often rural, that are altered by forces
over which they have no control. Hence his affection for Grove's
novel of small-town boom and bust, *The Master of the Mill* (1946).[124]
What Cogswell found troubling in the omission of such works from
the literary canon was the loss of Galt's vision that societies can be
both progressive and stable if, as Balwhidder remarks at the end of
Annals of the Parish, the "large and liberal experience of goodness"
accrues as much from the people as from the technocrats. "It was far
better," concludes Balwhidder, "that the weavers meddled with the
things of God, which they could not change, than with those of the
King, which they could only harm."[125] In other words, societies thrive
when progress and tradition partake of the other's virtues. When the
weavers deny tradition, however, the spinning jenny leads rapidly to
a large-scale cotton industry that replaces the king's authority with a
machine economy that brings degeneration. Brought up as a farm
boy in a garrisoned rural county not unlike Galt's fictional Scottish
midlands, Cogswell likely read Galt's work as a parable of his own
father's life.[126] The history of provincial peoples, Cogswell knew, was
rife with examples of moral and social disorders that followed historical change. Cogswell would later make Galt the prime subject of
study during a 1959–60 sabbatical to Scotland sponsored by the
Nuffield Foundation.

If Bailey's echo is evident in Cogswell's Scottish studies, his actual influence was direct. He suggested authors and emphases (from

Vico's *New Science* to Trevelyan's *English Social History* to Robert-son's *History of America*) that appear throughout the Bailey/Cogswell correspondence of 1950–51. Bailey was instrumental, in part, because Cogswell's supervisor, William L. Renwick, was not – absent for long periods, Cogswell complained, to paint the French coun-tryside.[127] As Regis Professor of Rhetoric and English Literature at Edinburgh, and one of the architects of the School of Scottish Stud-ies in 1951, Renwick would have seemed the ideal supervisor, but he was unable to provide the mentorship to which Cogswell had become accustomed. Cogswell's most important graduate work, then, like Pacey's, was done at the MA level. What the two-year term in Scotland provided was a period of intense, uninterrupted reading in eighteenth-century literature, very important later for his neo-classical formalism, coupled with immersion, once again, in Euro-pean culture. Cogswell wrote effusively to his friends about the quality of the radio programs, plays, and poetry readings he heard. He saw plays in London by August Strindberg, Henrik Ibsen, and John M. Synge, and he attended the Royal Lyceum Theatre in Edin-burgh to see Beaumont and Fletcher's *Knight of the Burning Pestle*, George Bernard Shaw's *Pygmalion*, Thomas Kyd's *Spanish Tragedy*, and Shakespeare's *Winter's Tale* (with John Gielgud).[128] He also placed his poems in British journals, publishing in the *New States-man and Nation*, *John O'London's Weekly*, *Nine*, *Chambers's Edinburgh Journal*, and *Poetry Review*. At the suggestion of the editor of the lat-ter, he sent a manuscript to the Hand and Flower Press, though it was eventually returned. He had fulfilled, then, the wish of George Parkin, George Foster, and Beaverbrook that intellectually gifted New Brunswickers study abroad to learn about European values and culture. "To become fully oneself," said Bailey, "one must first lose oneself … in the vastness and infinite variety of the metropolitan processes."[129] Bailey, Pacey, Donald Gammon, Robert Gibbs, Mar-garet Cunningham, Elizabeth Brewster, Allan Donaldson, and Ger-trude Gunn followed that trajectory, all studying abroad. The world beyond New Brunswick was an essential finishing school that enhanced what native sons and daughters could do in the province. That larger world made an informed localism possible. As under-stood by Gibbs, it ensured that "any aspirations to the heights of Par-nassus" would be met – and extinguished – so work at home could be undertaken with requisite focus and sophistication.[130]

"POEM PUBLISHED IN THE NATIONAL CONSCIOUSNESS": COGSWELL'S FIDDLEHEAD, 1952–67

When Cogswell returned to New Brunswick with a PhD in the summer of 1952, he was almost thirty-five years old. Six months earlier he had written foreign-service exams in London for the Canadian Department of External Affairs, still thinking that a diplomatic career might be an option.[131] Pacey had been supportive, writing a glowing letter to the Civil Service Commission and assuring potential employers, including UNB president Albert Trueman, that Cogswell's speech impediment was not a detriment. But Cogswell was still worried, volunteering to accept a probationary appointment at UNB contingent on students being able to comprehend him.[132] He need not have been concerned; the extent of Bailey and Pacey's involvement in his academic preparations meant that a position would be waiting for him at UNB. But good timing was also on his side, that timing integral as well to the more general Fiddlehead moment in New Brunswick history.

As John Sutherland had observed in the *Northern Review*, "the phenomenal development of Canada during the last war, relatively greater than that of any country in the same period, gave a marked impetus to poetry as it did to the arts generally."[133] Coupled with the exponential rise in post-war university enrollments, the expansion of university physical plants, and the increasingly normative view that Canada's success in a new world order was tied directly to the education of its young people, Sutherland's sense of "an excitement" would prove fortuitous for Cogswell and his peers in the Bliss Carman Society. Simply put, it was a good time to be a newly minted PhD, especially in the humanities. In June 1951, a year before Cogswell had returned from Scotland, the Massey-Lévesque Commission had released its report. The report was nothing less than the blueprint for a post-war Canadian identity project, one that clearly articulated a partnership between the federal government and a growing university sector in fostering cultural preservation and development. The Canada Council for the Arts, the National Library, a National Historic Sites and Monuments policy, a new National Gallery, and many other arts and educational interventions, including federal programs of financial aid for universities, were at the forefront of the commission's report. As much a response to American cultural imperialism as an attempt to compensate for the tiny domestic market for Canadian books, magazines, music, and film – so tiny that, the year before the commission was mandated, English-language publishers in the country "had issued a mere fourteen books of fiction and thirty-five works of poetry and drama," an "output [that] was far lower than at the turn of the century or during the 1920s"[134] – the commission recommended a sweeping program of social engineering to reverse the cultural philistinism that E.K. Brown had lamented in *On Canadian Poetry* (1943). The experience of another global war had added urgency to Brown's lamentations. If Canada were to inhabit the world stage with determination equal to what it had shown in the two wars, it had to become more than a British colony or an American appendage. It had to acquire an identity as an independent nation – and the responsibility for that had to be shared at federal, provincial, and local levels.

If ever there was an opening in Canada (including New Brunswick, thanks to the efforts of Bailey and John Clarence Webster before him), the Massey-Lévesque report provided it. For one thing, it supplied an imprimatur of approval for the work Pacey was doing with the release of *Creative Writing in Canada* in 1952. Pacey's book was exactly the sort of orienting device that Massey-Lévesque called for, the book offering qualitative judgment so that Canada could showcase and differentiate its best literary work from that of Britain and America – and also address the question of whether or not Canada had a national literature.[135] The commission's report also justified the material work of Bailey's students: Donald Gammon, (legislative librarian for the provincial government); Frances Firth (UNB archivist); Eleanor Belyea (UNB head of cataloguing); Robert Rogers (UNB assistant librarian); and Elizabeth Brewster (student of library science at the University of Toronto). Getting the country's textual and bibliographic history in order was a key recommendation of the commission,[136] and it became a top priority of Bailey's protégés.

The commission's report would also open a pathway for Cogswell. As one of Bailey's most attentive students, he did not have to be reminded of the cultural vacuity that had driven Charles G.D. Roberts, Bliss Carman, and other New Brunswickers to New England publishers and magazines. Nor was he indifferent to the crisis and opportunity in front of him, the crisis identified in the Massey-Lévesque report as contributing to "our slow growth as a cultivated community" and the opportunity as using little magazines and presses to enhance "the cultural life of our country."[137] The enfeebled *Fiddlehead* proved the point. In Cogswell's absence, the magazine, once so vibrant, had foundered, losing part of its audience accordingly. The gap between the last issue he edited (spring 1949) and the next issue (March 1951) was two years. Though Gammon and Rogers stepped in to edit three issues between March 1951 and March 1952 – Rogers telling Cogswell that he even saw the potential for a quarterly[138] – it was clear that the magazine needed permanent leadership if it was to sustain what Bailey had begun. With the Poetry Club regulars occupied in library and archival work, Cogswell stepped in to take charge. Immediately after returning, he joined Rogers in co-editing issues sixteen and seventeen (November 1952 and February 1953), then took the reins of the magazine by himself for issue eighteen (summer 1953). Though he could not have foreseen that he would edit the magazine by himself until 1967, he did have some sense that he was making a long-term commitment to the editorial and publishing side of Bailey's project. His distance from Fredericton had at least made that clear. He now saw Bailey's project as a source of motive energy that had created the space for the emergence of a number of "critic-militant[s]"[139] who would confer legitimacy on national letters. Bailey, the prime mover behind that energy, was well established at UNB when Cogswell arrived in 1945 – and by 1952 he was diverting his energies to institutional and creative ends, having just released the poetry collection *Border River* (1952). Pacey, the first critic-militant who had come in 1944, had hit the ground running – his book on Grove fresh off the press when Cogswell enrolled as a first-year student – and by 1952 he was taking his place as one of the authorities on Canadian literature. The role of editor/publisher in Bailey's project – the proverbial third leg – was open and suited Cogswell's interests. That role complemented the recent establishment of Brunswick Press (1951), the Fredericton publishing wing of the mid-century Beaverbrook/ Wardell media empire. With momentum for national and local publishing on his side, Cogswell knew he would have the freedom to take the *Fiddlehead* and the larger Fiddlehead project in any direction he wanted. That the provincial electorate at exactly this time installed Hugh John Flemming as the new Conservative premier of New Brunswick added potency to his thinking about the magazine, for Flemming was the old Carleton County nemesis he had battled from inside the CCF five years earlier. Still appalled by some of the extreme right-wing views he had heard in Britain – particularly the opinion of "one Conservative acquaintance" who so resented "being taxed to feed the 'scrub population'" that he "advocate[d] sterilization of the poor"[140] – Cogswell began his editorship of the magazine with a determination that it would become unlike any other Canadian magazine and unlike the province in which it existed.[141]

To ensure that it would, he supported Rogers and Gammon in the changes they had started to make. Expansion drove the agenda: the frequency of publication would increase to three times a year (perhaps four) and fuller information would be provided about contributors, each of those changes announced in issue fifteen (July 1952). More significant was the change announced in the next issue, November 1952. An editorial statement in that issue invited contributions from outside the Bliss Carman Society,[142] thus ushering the magazine into a wider realm and changing its purpose. No longer would the magazine circulate privately in order to cultivate local talent toward the goal of a New Brunswick renaissance, but it would become a more public and precarious thing, potentially unrecognizable from what Bailey had intended. In effect, the Chinese wall around the *Fiddlehead* was coming down. When he took the helm of issue eighteen in the summer of 1953, Cogswell inherited a magazine that had broken free from its original moorings, yet another circumstance that proved fortuitous. Robert Gibbs had been the most vocal in the Poetry Club to articulate the need for change, commenting in a letter to Robert Rogers that the magazine needed new direction: "Do you get the feeling when you are reading through the Fiddlehead ... that you've read it all before in other words – somehow I feel that a certain attitude towards life expressed in poetry has become academic – the accepted and established attitude. I hope we'll be able to grow away from that tendency and write more *truly* from our own vision."[143] Not only, then, had many of the original Bliss Carman Society members gone on to other pursuits, but the magazine's content had become circular, which Rogers descried as a fall into "a more conservative tradition."[144] Cogswell felt that opening the magazine to outside contributors addressed that problem, but he insisted that that opening must not alter the core editorial principles of "mutual criticism and mutual aid."[145] Thus, while the purpose of the magazine would change, its editorial ethos would not, at least in the short term. Cogswell's *Fiddlehead* would continue to be a teaching journal, devoted to not only apprenticing authors but also apprenticing editors. That ethos was key to the magazine's longevity. As a teaching journal, editorial succession would be embedded, as it had been for Cogswell. The reason the magazine had passed effortlessly from Gammon to Rogers to Cogswell, all of whom were competent editors, was because, under Bailey's guidance, the editorial function had been shared. Cogswell was already schooled when he took the helm, able to recognize literary talent and defend the merits of his decisions. It is for those reasons that Cogswell felt confident in making the changes he did to *Fiddlehead* issues eighteen and nineteen.

Those changes were both cosmetic and structural, reflecting the input of professional printers from Brunswick Press, a Beaverbrook-owned subsidiary of the Fredericton *Daily Gleaner*. The first and most noticeable change was a new look. More like the *Dalhousie Review* and *Canadian Forum* than an 8½ x 11-inch mimeographed in-house circular, the magazine under Cogswell's direction acquired a table of contents, advertising, and issue-specific pagination, as well as improved layout, formatting, ink, and stock. A new poetry-review section also materialized – Alec Lucas and Desmond Pacey reviewed Bailey's *Border River* and Brewster's *East Coast* respectively – as did the outside contributors that the sixteenth issue had invited. Saint John modernist Kay Smith, Ralph Gustafson, and Dorothy Roberts, niece of Charles G.D., appeared in the magazine for the first time. Dorothy Livesay, Al Purdy, Robert Finch, Miriam Waddington, Daryl Hines, Wilfred Watson, Terence Heywood, Martin S. Dworkin, and Jay Macpherson appeared soon after, the start of an influx of respected poets from Canada and elsewhere. The names, however, did not matter, as significant as they would have been to marketing the magazine to a national audience. Cogswell stressed the point in a letter to James Boyer May, explaining that though "'names' may be important ... we prefer not to collect them." "All poems received," he continued, "are reprinted and distributed to the editorial board minus the names. As a result, we have turned down poems from such Canadian poets as Louis Dudek, Phyllis Webb and James Reaney, whose names at the moment would have been most useful to us."[146] Cogswell was signalling the formalization of the practice of anonymous review that became rigorous at the start of his tenure. Though anonymous review had been used in various forms since the early days of the magazine, Cogswell institutionalized the practice when he became editor, a task that he felt "preserved a certain artistic integrity of judgment."[147] After a first reading to weed out the weakest, he would retype every poem he received and create a scoring sheet with the titles of poems listed in the left column. The poems and the scoring sheet would then circulate among Pacey, Lucas, Galloway, Rogers, Bailey, and whoever else was on the editorial board at the time. Board members would assign an A, B, or C grade to each title, then Cogswell would aggregate the scores and make selections based on what would fill sixteen pages, the magazine's length in that period. Short poems were preferred to long ones in order to feature more poets. Only the best work made it to publication, and that work had to have the support of at least four of six editors. There was no other way in. The magazine's content alone, Cogswell felt, would ensure its success, and in very little time it did, a normally prickly John Sutherland telling Cogswell that "it is a relief to read [the *Fiddlehead*] after some of the drivel that has been getting into print these days in the Canadian magazines."[148] California editor James Boyer May was even more complimentary, stating that the *Fiddlehead* was "accomplishing what *Poetry Chicago* was vainly trying to accomplish"[149] and, in so doing, was rising to a "leading position internationally."[150] In a short time, apprenticing poets started seeking Cogswell's advice, an emergent Al Purdy inviting Cogswell's thoughts on what he could do differently and ranking him with Arthur Bourinot, Northrop Frye, and B.K. Sandwell, all respected Canadian editors.[151] Word soon spread that the *Fiddlehead* was publishing important work.

This striving for excellence must be considered in the larger context. In order to be taken seriously, Cogswell knew his magazine's content had to be of the highest quality. Otherwise it would be viewed as confirming the still widespread myth that nothing of substance ever came from New Brunswick. Operating within Bailey's project, Cogswell, then, had no choice but to be a discriminating editor.

Overshadowing the significant editorial, production, and distribution changes in *Fiddlehead* issue eighteen was the larger symbolism of the death of Theodore Goodridge Roberts a few months earlier in February 1953, a passing that marked the end of the magazine's infancy. At Cogswell's request, Bailey paid tribute to Charles G.D.'s younger brother in the issue, acknowledging the enlivening spirit of the nineteenth-century Confederation tradition in New Brunswick. Cogswell and Robert Rogers also secured outgoing UNB president A.W. Trueman's help in rearticulating the double objective of Bailey's cultural project, a restatement of purpose that Cogswell thought necessary for the new audience coming to the *Fiddlehead*. Trueman's foreword "officially" opened the pages of the magazine "to poets anywhere in the English-speaking world" – an opening, the president said, that would "enrich the contribution which [the *Fiddlehead*] has been making" –

7 UNB President A.W. Trueman and members of the editorial committee of the *Fiddlehead*, May 1953. *Left to right*: David Galloway, English Department; Alec Lucas, English Department; A.W. Trueman, president of UNB and honorary president of the Bliss Carman Society; A.G. Bailey, dean of arts, head of History Department, and chairman of editorial committee; Fred Cogswell, English Department, and editor of the *Fiddlehead*; A. Robert Rogers, assistant librarian and business manager of the *Fiddlehead*; and Desmond Pacey, English Department.

while also reminding new readers that the magazine "is the natural outgrowth of a literary tradition which has its roots in the early history of this country."[152] Fittingly, an insignia for the Poets' Corner of Canada appeared on the inside front cover, where it stayed for many issues. Thus, though the magazine looked new, had a new editor, and was pivoting toward an experimental openness, its fundamental purpose remained intact (more proof of that found in Rogers's request that Trueman enlarge and clarify his "statement about the spirit of the Loyalists"[153]). The only change to that purpose that Cogswell would oversee was its wider application: the magazine aimed to cultivate local writing by showcasing national and international talent. To repeat an earlier point, the change as Cogswell saw it would not dilute New Brunswick localism but expand it, for locales were as diffuse as the writers who came from them. It that regard, Cogswell's *Fiddlehead* would carry the imprint of his two most influential mentors: it would take the core logic of Bailey's formula for local renewal and franchise it, thus stimulating the national development that was always Pacey's primary goal. In breaking out of its UNB cocoon, the *Fiddlehead*, an instrument of New Brunswick context and design, was starting to circulate across Canada.

The work of growing the magazine to meet this new challenge was intense. Cogswell and Rogers sent more than two thousand letters to schools, publishers, trade magazines, newspapers, booksellers, writers' groups, English departments, and university libraries to stimulate interest. Three hundred complimentary copies of the magazine were given away as enticement to fellow editors and poets selected from the *Canadian Who's Who*, all in the hope of securing notice or review in North American periodicals. Even the membership of the Beaverbrook Canadian Foundation was solicited. In less than a year, the *Fiddlehead*'s subscription list grew "from 30 to more than 175."[154] A large part of that increase was attributable to the demise of *Contemporary Verse* (CV), the British Columbia magazine edited by Alan Crawley and managed by Floris McLaren. By the end of 1952, *CV* had reached its end, having been at the forefront of Canadian poetry for eleven years (and thirty-nine issues). In early March 1953, Rogers wrote to McLaren on Bailey's suggestion, asking if she would make *CV*'s subscribers' list available to the *Fiddlehead*. (Rogers, Bailey, and Cogswell had lived through the loss of *Poetry Commonwealth* a couple of years earlier, regretting that they had not made a similar request of the British editors at that time.) This request seemed more reasonable because Bailey and Crawley had known each other, at least by correspondence, since the early 1940s. Bailey had spoken highly of Crawley to Poetry Club members, admiring his tours of Canada, his radio broadcasts, his presentation to the Massey-Lévesque Commission (he and John Sutherland were the only little-magazine editors to present formally), and his cultivation of a left-leaning[155] modernist poetic – a poetic that, in Crawley's words, invited a poetry that was "sincere in thought and expression and contemporary in theme and treatment and technique."[156] *Contemporary Verse*, as Louis Dudek would observe a few years later, "was concerned only with publishing 'good poetry'" and "was not a fighting magazine with a policy."[157] Because that was the balance that Bailey had sought for his own little magazine in New Brunswick, Cogswell and Rogers thought of the renewed *Fiddlehead* as a continuance of *CV*, their interest in the latter's subscribers' list ensuring that "*Contemporary Verse* has not passed."[158] Though "the untimely demise of Contemporary Verse creates a vacuum," admitted Robert Rogers to Kay Smith, "it is our hope that we may be able to go some distance toward providing a medium of expression for Canadian poetry through our programme of expansion."[159] Precisely because the *Fiddlehead*, too, "was not a fighting magazine," Crawley and McLaren agreed to Rogers's request, sending their list of roughly three hundred subscribers to Cogswell in April 1953.[160] Poet Miriam Waddington passed the final judgment on the transition in a letter to Cogswell a few months later, observing that like attracts like and that, in the natural order of things, "creative centers move geographically."[161]

The subtler point, though, should not be missed. Being progressive without being combative or polemical was a quality of editorial temperament built into the *Fiddlehead* that contributed to its longevity. Always the shrewd observer, Robert Gibbs noted this in a letter to Pacey, adding the "hope that the editors [of the new *Fiddlehead*] won't be overcome by the loftiness of their aims and that they'll leave the magazine open to *genuine* poetry rather than what is important. What seems to be the trouble with a lot of little magazines I've looked at here [Cambridge] is that they're so concerned with being important, being intelligent and up-to-date that they often fail to be genuine."[162] A significant part of Cogswell's challenge, then, was to maintain the magazine's middle path – its editorial modesty – in a small-magazine environment characterized by the fiery polemics of A.J.M. Smith, John Sutherland, and Louis Dudek. Whether Cogswell knew it or not at the time, and it seems that he did, editorial modesty was another of the qualities that would ensure the life of the magazine long after *First Statement*, *Preview*, *Northern Review*, *Contact*, *CIV/n*, and the avant-garde magazines of the 1960s and 1970s ceased publication. Was Gibbs repeating the Bailey ethic or was he observing a simple truth about cultural enterprise when he said to Pacey in defence of that modesty that "I'd rather have a few lines of Wilfred Owen than a whole volume of Ezra Pound"?[163] Whichever it was, his sense of what was lasting proved accurate. Being progressive without being combative or polemical – cultivating what Al Purdy confirmed was "a middle course between traditionalism and ultra-modernism"[164] – was bred into the magazine's DNA. What Cogswell defined as "modified traditionalism" became the magazine's "official" line, defined as follows by Cogswell to fellow poet and editor Arthur Bourinot: "One cannot uproot a tree after twenty centuries and put it in completely new soil, and it seems to me that [is what] some of the more modern extremists are doing to the language today. We cannot abandon without losing more than we gain what long generations of English poets have worked out in technique and thought. Obscurity in modern Canadian poetry has provided every bit as big a curse as had imitation and colonialism in late nineteenth and early twentieth century poetry."[165]

Cogswell's own, much discussed poetic forms of expression are best understood in those terms, as is his separation from the kind of abstract creative work that Bailey was producing. "It seems to me," continued Cogswell in the same letter to Bourinot, "that the cardinal principles of art [–] simplicity, economy, clearness of outline, etc. [–] ought to apply to poetry as well as to painting and music – more so because of the rational content which must be present in a poem." In keeping the magazine in a middle channel away from turbulent ideological waters, Cogswell was enhancing its robustness and working to cultivate a more receptive audience for poetry in Canada. Convinced that the *Fiddlehead* could do for poetry what the more experimental urban magazines could not, he took on editors of the popular domestic presses to win back a place for modern verse at the centre of national culture, essentially mirroring Bailey's own objective. His admonishment of the editorial board of Montreal's *Family Herald & Weekly Star* is one of many examples of this strategy. Angered by that paper's dismissal of Canadian poetry for its obscurity, he sent a copy of issue nineteen of the *Fiddlehead*, pointing out that only two of the issue's poems (both by Robert Gibbs, curiously) "demand above average literary knowledge for elucidation."[166] His defence was not of the magazine he edited but of Canadian poetry in general, and his objective was to open the field. Subscriptions from all over Canada and the United States continued to rise.

As the *Fiddlehead*'s popularity and readership grew, however, so did costs. With circulation climbing to five hundred in late 1953 (half subscribers and half complimentary) – and with a goal of one thousand subscribers in three years – Cogswell was forced to consider cheaper production and distribution alternatives. Complicating matters were British import restrictions that blocked sales of magazines not printed in that country, thus effectively closing a market to a New Brunswick coterie intimately tied, because of Beaverbrook, to British libraries and universities. When Brunswick Press would not lower its print rates, Cogswell sought advice from fellow editors, one of whom, James Boyer May of *Trace*, suggested Villiers Publications. A London (England)-based press, Villiers used the influential Hollywood magazine *Trace* as a North American aggregator, advertising its services to other small magazines through *Trace* and promoting those small magazines in turn. For the *Fiddlehead*, finding such an aggregator was ideal, for *Trace*, commented Cogswell, "delivered reviews, ratings, and samples of *avant garde* work, and it took a refreshingly catholic interest in all changes then going on in the international world of poetry."[167] The result was immediate: production costs dropped, even with overseas airmail between Fredericton and London, and the *Fiddlehead* was "inundated with material."[168] Poets of national and international repute sent material. In Montreal, London (Ontario), and Hamilton, the *Star*, *Free Press*, and *Spectator* carried editorials and reviews praising the magazine, and awards started accumulating. In 1954 Dorothy Livesay's "Lament" (issue nineteen) won the President's Medal from the Governor General's Awards board for the best poem published in Canada in 1953, and the esteemed American magazine *Poetry Public Letter* recognized six poems from the *Fiddlehead* as among the best published in North America in 1953. That number was "the most given to any magazine," wrote Cogswell.[169] Stanford University Press's annual anthology of *Best Poems* and Borestone Mountain Poetry Award winners would also feature *Fiddlehead* work in 1956, 1957, and 1958, circulating notice of the magazine even farther afield.

In the years ahead, the *Fiddlehead* grew in proportion to the size of its readership and number of contributors. Poems got longer and the pool of poets more diverse. The number of poetry books it reviewed also increased, that expansion taking the place of discussions that Bliss Carman Society members used to have about the craft. In reviews, poetry was analyzed, debated, classified, and treated as an object of serious study, thus fulfilling poet Raymond Souster's hope that Canada would encourage "a franker discussion on the directions poetry is to take," preferably in "a poetry mag with daring and a little less precious an attitude [than *Northern Review* and *Contemporary Verse*]."[170] Next to the quality of the creative work, the seriousness of the reviews gave the magazine the authority of a national poetry workshop.

In the February 1955 double issue, which marked the *Fiddlehead*'s ten-year anniversary, Cogswell provided the evidence of a decade of growth: "Our subscriptions have increased by 658.064%. Last year over 600 poems were received, of which we printed forty-nine. Our bank balance ... now stands at $62.20."[171] Though small by today's measures, those numbers convinced Cogswell "that the next ten years of *The Fiddlehead* will eclipse the glories of the past."[172] With Sutherland's *Northern Review* about to cease publishing, a circumstance that would make the *Fiddlehead* the most important poetry magazine in the country, two other instances boded well for Cogswell's prediction of future success. The first was that, with the exception of Rogers, Gibbs, and Cogswell, who still contributed poetry, many of the founding poets of the magazine were no longer appearing, replaced by a new generation of poets whose names would become familiar in the 1960s and 1970s (Milton Acorn, Gwendolyn MacEwen, Robert Kroetsch, Karen Connelly, Pat Lower, Michael Ondaatje, Brian Bartlett, and M. Travis Lane, to name a few). As Cogswell had hoped, the magazine was becoming an incubator for national talent. If local poets were to emerge, they would have to emerge in competition with the country's (and the world's) finest. "The best chance for Canadian writers," Cogswell told Dorothy Livesay, who criticized the *Fiddlehead* for "not adding to our cultural self-consciousness,"[173] "is to produce work that can compete with English and American."[174] In saying so, Cogswell was advancing an approach to local cultivation that suited Bailey's aims perfectly, if obliquely.

The second thing that boded well for the *Fiddlehead*'s future was the expansion of its mandate into small-press publishing. In 1954 Fiddlehead Poetry Books (FPBS) was launched, its first title being Cogswell's own *The Stunted Strong*, "a small book with a large significance" wrote Pacey.[175] Modest in design and girth at sixteen or so pages, books in the series were intended "to give the public a chance to read the work of new Canadian poets" (copyright page). Apart from the fact that its inaugural number, *The Stunted Strong*, was a creative turning point for Cogswell – who confided in a letter to Arthur Bourinot that the poems "are my first attempt in a campaign to restore greater consideration to classicism (the subordination of detail to the over-all effect) as opposed to the baroque and even rococo state in which so much of modern Canadian poetry has developed"[176] – the intention behind the chapbook series was indeed significant for what it said about the evolving Fiddlehead project. It said, first, that the project was opening toward the personal and turning away from the intellectual, a move that favoured Cogswell's poetics of direct speech over Bailey's metaphysical modernism. It also said that the project was becoming a place for an aesthetic of classical, unadorned speech for a new generation of not-yet-known Canadian poets. In a later letter to Cogswell, Prince Edward Island poet Milton Acorn saw this poetics of the personal, what he called a "social vision," as a "main line of Canadian poetry" originating in the east, suggesting that Cogswell edit a special anthology of such poetry "called MAINLINE ATLANTIC."[177] The twinning of magazine and press thus became utilitarian: the *Fiddlehead* would find those new voices and Fiddlehead Poetry Books would introduce them more amply to a reading public. Cogswell's faith in that public drove the initiative, as he told Floris McLaren. "I have a theory," he explained, "that as there are so many thirsting to become poets, there must also be even more who would like to read poetry in Canada."[178] That Fiddlehead Poetry Books was the first series in Canada to be funded by a university meant that Cogswell had the resources to shape a poetic canon that broke free of the high-modernist experiment and allusiveness that closed the door to so many readers. As Pacey observed, the chapbook series, with Cogswell's book as model, was conceived as a different kind of venture – as a "poetry of our people by our people for our people."[179] Cogswell confirmed that sense of the personal in an earlier letter to Purdy, sending drafts of the sonnets that would become the sixteen poems of *The Stunted Strong* and arguing, as he had done toward different ends in his MA thesis, that the *Fiddlehead* would become a place for poetry that concerned itself chiefly with people in the ordinariness of their circumstances. Purdy liked the idea, noting the "peculiar topography" evident in the varied personalities of his friend's sonnets.[180]

In the years that followed, Fiddlehead Poetry Books would introduce some of the country's pioneering confessional poets, including Alden Nowlan, Al Purdy, Don Gutteridge, Frances Itani, and Joy Kogawa, all of whom placed voice and personality – Purdy's "peculiar topography" – at the forefront of their art. When Cogswell could not publish complete volumes of the confessional poets he admired, he published special issues of the *Fiddlehead* instead, as he did in devoting a 1963 issue of the magazine to *58 Poems by Milton Acorn* and a 1969 issue to Alden Nowlan. Those and other special issues of the magazine deploy attendant critical voices in unique ways, the criticism informal, non-academic, and appreciative as if to match the tone of the work being considered. Take, for example, Edward Ives's opening to his essay on Nowlan: "If there is such a thing as the average reader of contemporary poetry," he begins, "I can almost qualify. I read poetry for the just plain hell of it nowadays, and I don't know any poet whose work I read with more pleasure than Alden Nowlan's."[181] One cannot imagine special issues overseen by Louis Dudek, Dorothy Livesay, or even Raymond Souster as being so informal. By foregrounding personal responses to poetry, however, Cogswell was reaching into the middle audience in an effort to deinstitutionalize art. Nowlan would echo the idea a decade later when he told John Metcalf of his hope that "*if* there comes a time that truck drivers read poetry, mine will be the poetry they'll read."[182]

In cultivating an audience for poetry and seeding a literary culture in Canada, Cogswell's chapbook series carried the distinct Fiddlehead imprint to a larger reading public. That imprint was cast not in the form of a fighting manifesto but in what Pacey identified as a series of editorial dispositions that reflected Bailey's teachings about modernism: "realistic sympathy," "ironic appreciation," "refusal of sentimentality," "directness," and "unremitting honesty of vision"[183] – in other words, a disposition that welcomed all manner of voice and personality as long as those were accessible and realistically drawn, "spring[ing] simply and validly," wrote poet Ralph Gustafson, "from [their] sources."[184] A final statement from Cogswell – perhaps his fullest description of that poetics – will make this important point clear and dispel the popular notion that it was Purdy who carried this conversational emphasis into Canadian poetry. In a letter to Lawrence Holmes that responds to what critics said were the flat lines of *The Stunted Strong*, Cogswell wrote that

> words bare of imagery and couched in the rhythm of prose become[,] perhaps paradoxically, the greatest poetry if used dramatically in a poem so as to bring to a head all the emotional forces and tensions that have been slowly created by the other elements in the poem which come before ... This same ability to invest prosaic statement with the grandeur of feeling and circumstances is what I consider the true organic use of language and occurs in both poetry and prose ... Simple language at a sublime crisis in literature has always this advantage. It brings home to the

reader the human relevance of the literature, and he feels it not as a work of art but as a touching upon life, like meeting his sorrowing or happy neighbor earlier in the same day.[185]

The "large significance" of which Pacey wrote, then, referred not only to the launch of a new publishing venture but also to the fact that Cogswell had assumed full control of the Fiddlehead project and its editorial dispositions. In gaining control, there had been no power struggles or angry public resignations, but rather a divestiture of responsibilities that Bailey's openness of spirit made seamless. By the *Fiddlehead*'s tenth year, Bailey's two principal literary lieutenants, Pacey and Cogswell, had become firmly established, both having apprenticed under his tutelage and each applying the lessons of that tutelage in his own unique way. Though very different in temperament, they were similarly modern: both rooted in New Brunswick and open to the world, yet always working to advance the province's interests in what each believed was an asymmetrical federation. The lasting coherence of their unity of purpose is one of the remarkable legacies of Bailey's project, made all the more extraordinary because its energies supported cultural endeavour for so long, defying the conventional wisdom expressed in the *Tamarack Review* that "there are no literary quarterlies in the English-speaking world that are practical in the long run."[186] The *Fiddlehead*, of course, continues and Fiddlehead Poetry Books, edited and managed solely by Cogswell from 1960 until 1981, continues as well under the imprint of Goose Lane Editions.[187]

For the sake of efficiencies, Cogswell assumed increasing control of the magazine as his editorship advanced. By 1957, his pool of anonymous reviewers was narrowing and the effort of retyping each poem and coordinating arm's length reviews too time-consuming. Believing his energies were better expended in providing a generous ear to poets, he undertook a project of correspondence with Canadian writers that snowballed in the mid-1950s. As the *Fiddlehead*'s first reader, he read upward of five thousand poems each year, responding to each poet as time allowed with at least a short note of constructive feedback.[188] In addition, he took sole responsibility for proofreading, financial management, printing, subscriber relations, and circulation of both the magazine and Fiddlehead Poetry Books, a workload that, when added to his heavy teaching duties, would have broken most people. The prospect of growth alone must have been daunting, for the more effort he put toward building contributor and subscription-distribution lists so did his subsequent work increase. But increasing work was not the only problem. The large number of American authors published in the *Fiddlehead* was attracting notice, prompting some of Canada's leading literary figures to question Cogswell's motives. Earle Birney, long a friend of the New Brunswick poets (though stung by a review that Pacey gave of his anthology *Twentieth Century Canadian Poetry*[189]), wondered on CBC radio if the *Fiddlehead*'s fondness for American poets was limiting opportunities for Canadians. Northrop Frye did likewise in his 1957 retrospective on Canadian poetry, suggesting that the *Fiddlehead* was at risk of becoming "a dumping ground for otherwise unpublishable American stuff."[190] These criticisms echoed comments that Cogswell was hearing from Miriam Waddington and Dorothy Livesay, poets whose work he had encouraged. "I am rather lost, baffled, by the magazine," said Livesay in a letter to him about the *Fiddlehead*. "I think it important, when we have none other, for a Canadian magazine to be Canadian!"[191] Cogswell was undaunted, convinced of the truth of Bailey's supposition that literature is made better, and local work stronger, when walls and other protections come down. He was convinced, too, that all cultures go through periods of hyper-nationalism, as Canada was doing in the post-Massey-Lévesque 1950s. In fomenting the local and regional through exposure to the international, Cogswell's *Fiddlehead* was displaying its modernist provenance while also preparing the ground for other magazines to follow. Despite its editorial modesty, then, the *Fiddlehead* was daring in the lengths it went to seed local and national talent, a commitment that Cogswell reiterated in an autumn 1958 editorial called "Restatement of Policy." In that editorial, he repeated what he had said to dozens of correspondents over the years, including Americans: that "we are interested in publishing poems, not poets."[192] What made the cut was published, regardless of the nationality of the poet. The idea was to model excellence, not trumpet an abstract nationalism that had done little to promote New Brunswick's interests.

If the *Fiddlehead*'s daring strikes an ironic note – a New Brunswick instrument, after all, is not supposed to prefigure the avant-garde or be anything *but* modest, preferably parochial – that is because of how deeply embedded Canadians continue to be in urban-centric myths of federation. Andrew Moore saw that semiology vividly when observing that, for the proto-nationalists of the late 1950s, the *Fiddlehead* "was both un-Canadian and too provincial: its international content called the magazine's Canadian identity into question, and, as a New Brunswick publication, its capacity for literary discernment could not be trusted by the nation's more sophisticated, more cosmopolitan centre."[193]

Confident in his New Brunswick mission, Cogswell became increasingly comfortable with and less defensive about the contradictions that his magazine's success garnered. If the *Fiddlehead* was open to a wide array of voices, then he had to accept both criticism and difference, for those too were part of the national conversation, as were the embedded biases of a hardening centre-margins perspective. And, if the ultimate goal was to raise the coin of New Brunswick writing by exposing it to the best models, then the exasperations of nationalists had to be endured. (Poet Jay Macpherson took the opposite position of Waddington, Livesay, and Frye in denouncing Cogswell for what she perceived as the magazine's narrowness, thus illustrating the arbitrariness of the national conversation: "Is there any group in the country," she asked Cogswell in a letter, "who could take such pride in being so provincial?"[194]) In a series of letters that touched on this confusion about what the *Fiddlehead*'s position actually was vis-à-vis the nation, Alden Nowlan posed a revealing question: "How can [Irving] Layton write about Lachine, Que., Westmount, De Bullion Street and Mount Royal and *not* be a regionalist, while I'm a regionalist because I write about New Brunswick?"[195] By the time Nowlan's question came, Cogswell's answer was well rehearsed. "The only answer is guts," Cogswell had earlier confided to American poet Gil Orlovitz. "Loneliness, frustration, and near madness, and perhaps appreciation in the end for the wrong reasons," he said, are the prices that artists and visionaries pay. "Jesus Christ is a case in point," he ended, qualifying that "you are not Jesus Christ but Gil Orlovitz."[196] His advice, repeated to Pacey and Nowlan in later years, was to soldier on as "a proud outsider."[197] He would take the ridicule, confident that the project he shared with his mentors was advancing for the good of the province and nation. As others around him would later confide, he was not alone in battling this paradox, UNB historian William Acheson telling him that the *Canadian Historical Review* wouldn't publish his demographic analysis of Charlotte County, New Brunswick, because it was too provincially focused but that it would publish his article on commerce in 1820s York, now part of Toronto. Commiserations aside, what Cogswell likely could not see completely was the embedded contradiction of his project's grand experiment. The discordance of editorial daring and modesty, coupled with the tactic of seeding the local by showcasing the international, was difficult for outsiders to comprehend. Thus, without the fuller context of Bailey's activist reading of provincial history and the many excitements fomenting on the UNB campus, outsiders concluded that Cogswell was a disloyal nationalist bent on squandering an important cultural birthright. Being so close to his project, he probably could not see this quite reasonable assumption, and thus he soldiered on as he attended to his wounds.

Perceived in hindsight, the contradictions (daring/modesty, local/international) fade away. What Cogswell passed on to editors who followed him was, in fact, a much more expansive sense of catholicity than he had inherited from Bailey and Bliss Carman Society members. The magazine that had become his in the 1950s and 1960s – so distinctly, Bailey observed, that "in a sense he refounded it, working almost single-handedly ... until he became a national father-figure to nine-tenths of the poets in Canada"[198] – did not war against itself to contain contradiction, as some central Canadian editors wanted to believe, but rather opened itself to what polyvalence could generate and achieve. In doing so, the *Fiddlehead* was local *and* international, a place for new *and* established writers, and modest *and* daring in its editorial temperament. And the magazine would continue to adapt. It started publishing fiction in the fall of 1959 as a condition of Canada Council funding, and by the time Robert Gibbs took over editorship in 1971 its length was averaging 120 pages, but its core values would remain intact in the post-Cogswell era. When Cogswell relinquished editorial control of the *Fiddlehead* in early 1967, the face and tone of the magazine changed to reflect new editor Kent Thompson's playful bombast, as it did again in the summer of 1981 when Peter Thomas reinstituted a more strident localism, but those were tonal changes that did not affect the magazine's abiding catholicity, a catholicity that Cogswell, now considered "the greatest *animateur* of them all,"[199] defined in a 1965 editorial. In that editorial, he attributed his desire to publish "the technical, emotional, and intellectual range of verse-writing as practiced in the English-speaking world" to a faith in what that literature could teach others: namely, how it "put other poets in mind of possibilities that may be further explored and perfected" and how it "may encourage deserving little-known verse writers by being put before the public side by side with the work of established poets."[200]

Reflecting his reading of literature for its narratives of the personal, Cogswell placed himself among those artists and editors who benefited from what eclecticism enabled. "Throughout my writing career," he stated in 1980, "I have tried to get so far beyond style that any number of styles would always be at my service."[201] In other words, his own creative work was tied directly to the stylistic choices that other writers modelled. "I felt that if somebody reading the magazine who liked [style] A would see some good in [styles] B, C, and D, his taste would be broadened accordingly," he told David Galloway.[202] Accordingly, opening the magazine to "'a potpourri of types, attitudes, ideas and sensibilities'" created the conditions for writers to learn "'something other than what they were doing.'"[203] And so later editor Don McKay had it exactly right when, on the magazine's fiftieth birthday, he observed that the *Fiddlehead* "placed attention ahead of direction, broad aesthetic range ahead of selective listening."[204] The magazine, under Cogswell's stewardship, had indeed become a model of attentiveness, an absorbent prism through which various lights flowed to their own eventuality. That openness, however, and its position on the nation's periphery as "a proud outsider," did not limit the magazine's sense of itself or its role in raising the local literary standard. *Fiddlehead* editors and scholars considered New Brunswick as good a place as any for a pan-Canadian literary enterprise and believed that the province's literature, as in an earlier era, had important things to contribute to the national conversation. Why couldn't New Brunswick become a national hub for creative arts? Poet Tom Wayman, whose early work was published in the magazine, understood that it had – and against the odds. "A magazine that lives so long so successfully is itself a kind of great poem," Wayman said, "'a poem published in the national consciousness.'"[205]

"SPORANGIA ECLECTICA"

Editor Don McKay's Latinization of the *Fiddlehead*'s editorial disposition – "sporangia" referring to a live receptacle that generates non-differentiating spores in ferns and lower plants – was well chosen, but of course it applied as much to the larger Fiddlehead project as to that project's most visible instrument. Like Bailey and Pacey, then,

Cogswell worked on multiple fronts, even as he entered the final
phase of, and then left, his magazine editorship.

After a 1959–60 sabbatical year in Scotland and England studying
the literary maverick John Galt, he rededicated his energies to Fiddlehead Poetry Books, which, as mentioned, had suffered in his absence.
Determined to keep the small press viable as a New Brunswick complement to the magazine whose editorship he had relinquished, he
assumed sole ownership upon his return, running the press out of his
office in the UNB English Department (and later his home) until 1981.
In the twenty years that he was sole owner and publisher, Cogswell
brought out the works (often the first collections) of writers who
would become the leading poets of the 1960s and 1970s, creating in
that effort what emeritus critic George Woodcock said was "a literary
ambiance ... of a kind that had never existed in this country before."[206]
The actual numbers behind that ambience exist today only as apoc-
rypha, for Cogswell was too busy with the mechanics of publishing to
attend to recordkeeping; however, the evidence suggests that approximately three hundred FPBs were produced,[207] the time, expense, and
effort of the enterprise an expression of Cogswell's commitment to
New Brunswick and Canadian poets. Well known is the fact that he
subsidized the production of many of those collections out of his own
pocket. Less well known is that at five hundred copies on average
printed, and with a price of fifty cents each, his efforts to publish
other writers added some 150,000 works of affordable literature to the
country's inventory, an astounding feat of cultural stewardship that
prompted critic and teacher Dennis Lee to wonder how he could ever
"make decent acknowledgment of that."[208] In retrospect, the significance of Cogswell's achievement was as much in the effort as it was in
the numbers. As he explained in an interview, he saw and filled a need
without fearing the enormity of the task: "'[I responded to] the situation into which publishing had fallen ... We had literally hundreds of
poets, but the commercial publishing houses in Canada, for financial
reasons and lack of a reading market ... only undertook to publish a
relative few, and those few over and over again ... So I felt there was a
great need for small presses, particularly a small press that was eclectic ... and [not] the organ of [a] coterie.'"[209]

The first Cogswell-owned FPB publication undertaken was *Five New
Brunswick Poets* (1962), a collection that featured his work along with
that of Brewster, Gibbs, Nowlan, and Kay Smith.[210] Publication in a
literary magazine was merely the first step for a writer, he told Alden

Nowlan; publishing a full collection was necessary for proper national notice and credibility. Nowlan agreed, writing to Cogswell that similar publishing initiatives "originating in Toronto and Montreal have been instrumental in attracting attention to the poets in those centres."[211] The press, then, like the magazine, arced back to local concern. Cogswell was again serving a provincial interest as a national publisher. And, again, the national response to what he was doing, perverse as it was predictable, strengthened his sense that he was on the right track.

In a review in the *Canadian Forum*, George Bowering declared that "a restful conservatism" marked the work in *Five New Brunswick Poets*, the tone of the collection distinguishing New Brunswick as "the least urgent poetry scene in Canada."[212] Only in the work of Nowlan, he said, was there energy in excess of the provincial lack. Eli Mandel was equally uncomplimentary, finding in the collection "a terrific sense of guilt" and "timidity" as well as "pain, paralysis, self-hate, tormented love, and a good deal of worry."[213] "No fireworks" here, he concluded.[214] Finally, Kenneth McRobbie and Milton Wilson beat the same drum in observing "a permanent depression" and a "darkness greater than light" in the work of the post-war New Brunswick poets.[215] Cultural centres had shifted once again, as had literary tastes. The kind of modernist-inspired realism that characterized the Fiddlehead signature – "direct treatment of the 'thing' whether subjective or objective" and use of "absolutely no word that did not contribute to the presentation"[216] – was being supplanted by new forms of bombast and abstraction that recast the Fiddlehead school's human-centric modernism as rearguard conservatism. By the 1960s, said Bowering in his review, "energy" was becoming synonymous with "western" virility and thus completely antithetical to "the bloodless retreat from life" that characterized the modesty of Kay Smith and Elizabeth Brewster.[217] New Brunswick was again being sent to the back of the line, the place where E.K. Brown had put Charles G.D. Roberts: that is, "in the very rear of the modern movement."[218] Phyllis Webb's abstractions suddenly had more depth and erudition, the Tish group more pizazz, and Ontario's archetypal myth poets greater relevance for a country yearning to discover itself between the shadows of two empires. Cogswell and Bailey, who had been witness to the plasticity of literary fashions before, reacted as they had done previously by fortifying themselves in their own discursive space. Both buried themselves in the work of the developing *Literary History of Canada*, Cogswell taking on expanded roles in writing about settlement patterns and literary activity in the eighteenth- and nineteenth-century Atlantic provinces. The more his region was disparaged, the bolder were his efforts to place it more prominently in the national narrative.

It was at this point in his career, having established a national reputation as an editor, that Cogswell took a turn reminiscent of Pacey's: he became more visibly a Maritime nationalist, especially in his critical work. His appearances in magazines, on CBC radio broadcasts, and at national conferences were dedicated almost solely to Atlantic Canadian study. He worked on E.J. Pratt, Thomas Chandler Haliburton, and Joseph Howe, all important Atlantic Canadian writers, but he also gave equal attention to Arthur Sladen, Alexander Rae Garvie, Amos Chandler, May Agnes (Fleming) Early, and Peter John Allan, lesser-known New Brunswick authors who were as good technically, he said, and "far superior in realism," to the canonical writers of the period.[219] His critical work of the time hinged on the fact that something vital was missing from earlier accounts of Canadian literary history. And so he dug into old newspapers, periodicals, and publishers' logs in libraries and archives, finding in the literary voices he discovered a worldliness and finesse that, though at times uneven, rivalled that of Byron, Tennyson, and the best English poets.[220]

Significant in this turn from editorial eclecticism to scholarly localism was the extent to which Cogswell drilled down into the work he discovered, displaying in the process a frankness of opinion that was opposite to the avuncular manner he had cultivated as an editor. He became, like Pacey, an unsparing critic of boosterism, critical timidity, and canonical entitlement, often blaming his own evangelical religious tradition for "inhibit[ing] the fearless expression and free inquiry upon which the greatest literature depends."[221] While this radicalism may have suddenly become noticeable in his critical work, however, it had always been a part of Cogswell's sense of the role of an intellectual – and thus radicalism as independence of thought and frankness of opinion had centrally informed the tenor of the reviews section of the *Fiddlehead* under his editorship. When he fully took the reins of the magazine in issue eighteen, Cogswell was as uncompromising in demanding critical rigour as he was in overseeing creative excellence. The first-ever review in the *Fiddlehead* reveals the point, Alex Lucas's assessment of A.G. Bailey's *Border River* effusive with equal measures of praise and criticism. Despite the reverential treatment that "Dr Bailey" enjoyed as founding visionary and elder of the

Fiddlehead group, Cogswell did not hesitate to publish Lucas's assessment that "*Border River* suffers from obscurity. Sometimes the images are esoteric, or the gaps between them are too wide, and they become forced and puzzling. Sometimes, also, the poetic fires are too heavily banked with learning, or the poems are almost entirely lacking in feeling."[222] In his own reviews, Cogswell is equally blunt. In reviewing Pacey's *Creative Writing in Canada* in the next issue, he serves notice that even his closest mentors are not above unsparing appraisal in his magazine. Pacey's book, he writes, "suffers from the defects of interim reports. Classification and description predominate over interpretation ... It is, too, I feel, more reliable in dealing with the earlier strata than it is in judging the complex structure of our modern literary formations."[223] His conclusion is that Pacey is a better and more enthusiastic lecturer than critic.

What is important to understand about Cogswell's critical radicalism and how it is expressed in his measured praise of Pacey's work is the extent to which that radicalism and praise open the door to his own deeper consideration of the Atlantic region's writers. In other words, the critical position he enjoys as renovator is possible only because a figure like Pacey had preceded him – a literary historian, that is, whose sense of critical urgency manifested itself in breadth of coverage over depth of analysis. In the eyes of many people around him, Cogswell was challenging the work of his mentors in order to take that work to its next level, thus aiming to energize the field of Atlantic Canadian literary study by correcting previous errors of emphasis and judgment.[224] Where Pacey was the nation's literary historian, Cogswell saw room to become the region's literary critic, differing from his teacher in moving beyond pointing to what was good and bad (and why that was) to focusing instead on the significance of both in the regional context. Cogswell thus saw as much critical utility in what was bad as in what was good, each reflecting important aspects of provincial taste and, as importantly, the sort of conditioning that tends toward abasement. Louis Dudek observed the difference between the two approaches in lauding Pacey's "usefulness" as an initial sorter of literary facts while preferring how Cogswell was systematically "demolishing the theories of [his] Dean [Bailey]."[225] Dudek understood Cogswell to be doing exactly what a modernist-trained critic should do: he was following Pound's insistence that "the proper METHOD for studying poetry and good letters is the method of contemporary biologists, that is careful first-hand examination of the matter, and continual COMPARISON of one 'slide' or specimen with another."[226] Cogswell, too, was working from slide to slide, building on previous knowledge to nuance critical understanding. What few in the Fiddlehead circle likely knew, and what makes a not-insignificant aside, is that Pound arrived at this method of critical modernism from the teachings of the Swiss naturalist Louis Agassiz, who, as earlier noted, had taught A.G. Bailey's grandfather (Loring Woart, Sr) at Harvard and influenced the style of the elder Bailey's critical writing. Was it for that reason that Bailey and Pacey encouraged Cogswell in his method of scholarship, even if that scholarship was critical of them? Whatever the reason, both did, Pacey going so far as following his former student in more focused New Brunswick study. Especially noteworthy in that regard is that Pacey took from Cogswell's criticism the opportunity to reprise some of his earlier opinions of Carman, Roberts, and Grove. Cogswell's turn to scholarship was therefore important for symbolic as well as for practical reasons, not the least of which was the development of his own critical positions on the literature of Canada's eastern provinces, those positions consolidated in his shared editorship of the groundbreaking *The Arts in New Brunswick* (1967).[227] That he modelled unsparing discernment as both editor and critic should not be surprising, for he, like Bailey, was primarily interested in provincial outcomes.

The last two of Cogswell's major initiatives as editor and critic attest to the essential localism at the heart of the Fiddlehead project. The first was his encouragement and care of Alden Nowlan, the finest humanist poet he had encountered. The second was his turn to literary translation, an effort that brought him back to his own lineage while also serving to uncover a significant part of the New Brunswick literary tradition that had been blacked out by English history.

Cogswell and Nowlan discovered each other in American little magazines, where both published their early verse. Finding first a Canadian, then New Brunswick, then Carleton County connection – Nowlan was a young journalist who had been working for the Hartland *Observer* since early 1952 – Cogswell became intrigued, as Nowlan had been by Cogswell's book *The Stunted Strong*, reprinting the Fredericton *Gleaner* review of that work in the *Observer*. They began corresponding in 1955 and soon after Nowlan's poetry started appearing in the *Fiddlehead* ("All Down the Morning," "Resurrection," and "My Famished Fathers Bartered Belief for Bread" in issues twenty-seven, twenty-eight, and twenty-nine [February-August 1956]).

Cogswell was struck by the biblical tones of Nowlan's verse as well as its brute honesty about sexuality, family violence, the contradictions of faith, and the precariousness of childhood in rural life. But he was struck, especially, by Nowlan's treatment of the forms and expressions of puritanism that had fuelled his own small-town compendia of social manners in *The Stunted Strong* and *Descent from Eden*.[228] Almost immediately, Cogswell understood that Nowlan, more than himself, was the poet who had managed to bring into verse the dark puritanism at the heart of the Maritime character. That realization was echoed by Pacey in the second edition of *Creative Writing in Canada*, where, after acknowledging Nowlan's indebtedness to Cogswell, Pacey states that the younger poet "possess[es] a confidence in the validity of his perceptions that Cogswell is inclined to lack."[229] Cogswell could not but agree, for raising puritanism to its highest point of visibility was paramount, he felt, if the people of his province were to understand themselves. As he had written earlier, puritanism was so endemic that it "maintained a position in the intellectual life of the Maritimes [and] impinged upon the views of ... Presbyterians, Methodists, and even Anglicans."[230] And, though it had been silenced briefly in the Confederation-era work of Roberts, Carman, and George Parkin – Parkin, Cogswell believed, found in the British pre-Raphaelite movement an alternative to censorious moralism – an enervating puritanism still hung heavy in the rural New Brunswick air. Nowlan's ability to invoke that aspect of moralism in poetry was unique, thought Cogswell; but it was his ironic rendering of it while preserving the essential dignity of its proponents (and his compassion for them) that was remarkable. Nowlan's was thus a literature of the provincial soil that was unmatched in the region.

Declaring him "a poet of similar order to the American poet Robert Frost,"[231] Cogswell gave Nowlan full access to the resources he had built and to his own attentions. He sent books and magazines that stood in for the modernist schooling that Nowlan had not received. He introduced him to the who's who of Canadian and American verse, gave him postage to cover the cost of sending out his work, and suggested publishing venues of greater merit than those Nowlan had been frequenting. He also gave constructive feedback and praise to the apprenticing Nowlan, ensuring that those in his wider literary circle, which, at that point, was most of Canada, knew about this fledgling writer in New Brunswick. "Fred Cogswell was more than the first poet I'd ever met," recalled Nowlan; "he was the

first person I'd ever met who read poetry ... I was twenty-four years
old and, in one sense, I had never before had anyone to talk with."[232]
So integral was Cogswell's encouragement that Nowlan credited it
with inspiring the start of his mature work, writing that "the best
poems I wrote that fall [after meeting Cogswell] are the oldest that I
still take seriously."[233] With Cogswell's support, Nowlan had found
his poetic voice, embarking on a series of "village" portraits and
vignettes that showcased the particular and oftentimes peculiar
accent of New Brunswickers. In 1958 Cogswell published Nowlan's
aptly titled *The Rose and the Puritan* as a Fiddlehead Poetry Book, thus
granting the young poet the legitimacy of a first collection. Nowlan
was, through the Fiddlehead apparatus, launched.

Cogswell remained central in Nowlan's life until the latter's death
in 1983. He wrote dozens of letters to granting agencies on Nowlan's
behalf, kept Nowlan's name circulating in academic and publishing
circles, and acted as editor in helping Nowlan collect and place his
work. In 1966 Cogswell edited a collection of Nowlan's stories for
Crier Publications in Dartmouth, Nova Scotia, but the press folded
before the stories came out. Clarke Irwin published *Miracle at Indian
River* two years later to much acclaim. Cogswell was also instrumental in installing Nowlan as UNB's third writer-in-residence in 1968.
(Nowlan followed Norman Levine and Dorothy Livesay, then was
replaced by John Metcalf in 1972–73 because the Canada Council did
not support writers on a continuing basis.) The efforts that Cogswell
expended to establish Nowlan as writer-in-residence were typical of
his care. To begin, Cogswell approached Richard Hatfield, premier of
New Brunswick and a fellow Carleton County resident, to ask that
provincial money be given to UNB to support Nowlan's permanent
residency. Though unprecedented, a taxpayer subsidy would serve "as
a cultural service to the province," Cogswell wrote.[234] Cogswell further
lobbied Hatfield by coordinating letter-writing campaigns in which
influential members of the province wrote to Hatfield about Nowlan's importance. Cogswell then convinced the heads of English
departments and libraries at UNB, St Thomas University, and the New
Brunswick Teachers College to make literary and cultural appeals.
The result was a permanent position for Nowlan as consultant in
Canadian Studies at UNB, a role that came with the expectation that he
would "study the library's holdings and act as a liaison between the
library, faculty and students."[235] Obviously, Bailey and Pacey, still the
library's key champions, were on board.

As writer-in-residence, Nowlan became one of the leading figures in continuing the Fiddlehead tradition in the post-Bailey/Pacey/Cogswell years, a fact that Cogswell predicted in his letter to Hatfield when he pointed to Nowlan's role in already "inspir[ing] and help-[ing] the work of such good young writers as Joseph Sherman, Terry Crawford, Louis Cormier, Al Pitman [*sic*], Bernell MacDonald, Eddie Clinton, and Elizabeth Rodriquez."[236] Just as Bailey had worked to ensure the continuance of the first phase of his project, so did Cogs- well lay the groundwork for the next Fiddlehead generation. Both were single-minded in creating the conditions for a re-emergence of literary excellence in New Brunswick, so when a figure such as Alden Nowlan materialized, a figure of national and soon-to-be internation- al importance, the Fiddlehead apparatus mobilized quickly. In many ways, Nowlan was the fulfillment of the shared goal – indeed, as Cogswell was now telling his legion of correspondents, "the best poet the Maritime Provinces has produced since the time of Roberts and Carman."[237] In him, and with the apparatus that had been created to nurture and launch such an extraordinary local talent, Bailey's vision had been realized.

But there was one final aspect of provincial attention that Cogswell thought necessary if New Brunswick were to rise again to national sig- nificance: that was to bring the work of the province's French- language writers into the light. The reasons were obvious. New Brunswick was not only one-third French and, since 18 April 1969, the only officially bilingual province in Canada,[238] but French lan- guage and culture had profoundly informed the heritage of the province, including that of the Bailey and Cogswell families. To deny that heritage was to ignore a feature of the province's uniqueness and thus to abandon the strategic localism at the centre of the Fiddlehead project – not to mention the reformist character of Cogswell's own cultural activism. His interest in French literature and translation was therefore complex, stemming from personal, political, provincial, and ethical convictions.

After retiring from the editorship of the *Fiddlehead* in early 1967, Cogswell took a sabbatical leave (partly in Montreal) to immerse him- self in French. In Quebec, the Quiet Revolution was threatening to become more boisterous with the release of the first volumes of the Laurendeau-Dunton Royal Commission on Bilingualism and Bicul- turalism, and in New Brunswick Acadian premier Louis J. Robi- chaud's Program of Equal Opportunity was disrupting the social calm. When an anonymous letter appeared in the Irving-owned *Tele-graph-Journal* in the fall of 1965 accusing Robichaud of "Robbing Peter to Pay Pierre," and then a series of "derogatory" editorial cartoons depicting the premier as a decadent King Louis XIV of France appeared in the Irving-friendly (and soon-to-be-Irving-owned) Fred-ericton *Daily Gleaner*,[239] Cogswell became convinced that English-speaking citizens had to come forward to defend the interests of the French in New Brunswick. For him, this anti-French, pro-industry (pro-Irving) campaign against fair-minded reform was an exact replay of the ideological battles waged by the Conservative Hugh John Flem-ming against farmers' interests in Carleton County many years earli-er. Why was a country that claimed to be so cosmopolitan at its Expo '67 world fair being so retrograde with its own citizens? And why had he been so complicit in the problem, submerging his own French her-itage for so long? He was no different, he concluded, from the major-ity of English intellectuals in New Brunswick, who "made little attempt to understand [their] French neighbour[s] and still less of an effort to use [them] as subject[s] for serious literature."[240] By 1967, Cogswell knew he must act in defence of his own and his province's French heritage.

After returning from Montreal, he spent the remainder of his 1967–68 sabbatical year translating the poetry of modern Quebec, an undertaking that brought to English readers a selection of thirty-eight writers, including the now-but-not-then familiar Alain Grand-bois, Hector Saint-Denys Garneau, Rina Lasnier, Anne Hébert, Gas-ton Miron, Gatien Lapointe, and Marie-Claire Blais. Cogswell's *One Hundred Poems of Modern Quebec* was published by Fiddlehead Poet-ry Books in 1970 – published, that is, the year after New Brunswick became officially bilingual and the year before Antonine Maillet's groundbreaking *La Sagouine* was released.[241] With his first forays into French translation completed, he started to read Acadian literature in earnest, convinced that introducing the French sensibility to English readers in New Brunswick would buttress tolerance through under-standing. It also became clear that the needs of French writers in New Brunswick were more acute than in Quebec, where culture was already central in public discussions. In the fall of 1969, the Montre-al journal *Liberté* had devoted a full issue to Acadian literature,[242] the first such treatment of its kind for Acadians. Both the national and francophone response, however, was surprise that such a community existed. When Cogswell considered the creative and political energies of the new wave of Acadian writers against the backdrop of their virtual anonymity, even inside their own province, his path was obvious. That he saw in a modernizing Acadie a response to the manipulations of anglophone New Brunswick industrialists also fuelled his interest, as did the gathering of cultural momentum toward what appeared to be another distinct movement in the province. "By a reorganization of the tax structure and the administrative base of the school system," he wrote, Louis Robichaud was altering the structural levers of power in New Brunswick to serve social and cultural over commercial ends, a first for a province that had always bowed to imperial and monetary might.[243]

But there were also aesthetic appreciations. His admiration for the sincerity of Acadian artists' "personal" as opposed to "doctrinaire or dogmatic conviction[s]"[244] matched his admiration for Alden Nowlan's similar frankness and mirrored the foundational humanism at the core of the Fiddlehead project. Unlike modern poetry in Quebec, where *ennui* (boredom) and *néant* (existential nothingness) dominated,[245] modern poetry in Acadie was generative and life-affirming, not mired in the cruel ironies of being alive but elevated by grand statements about growth and vibrancy. "I envy these Acadian poets," he wrote, "who are able still to speak for themselves in their own way and at the same time speak in tune to most of their peers without violating the reality of their time and their place."[246] Cogswell's final hope, repeated many times after in his discussions of the Acadian community's arrested development, was that "no myths as simplistic as those of 'Evangeline' and 'the Lord's chosen people' will ever arise again in Acadia to support the inherent laziness of the human spirit."[247]

To ensure that they did not, Cogswell became a national champion of the new wave of Acadian poetry, translating, teaching, and circulating it until he died. His capstone contribution was the collection *Unfinished Dreams: Contemporary Poetry of Acadie* (1990), co-edited and translated with Jo-Anne Elder.[248] With his translations of the Quebec poets, his translations of Acadian writer Herménégilde Chiasson,[249] and his mentorship of the province's leading translators (Elder was twice nominated for a Governor General's Award for literary translation), Cogswell not only introduced French literature to English readers in New Brunswick and across the country, but he also dedicated much of the latter part of his career to intercultural awareness in Canada. And, while his support of Acadian literature and hope for a vibrant Acadie are now commonplace among the province's cultural workers, Cogswell was the first in the post-war intellectual class to formulate a critical response to French literature in New Brunswick. He did so as the province's foremost English-language critic – in the early days of the Acadian literary renaissance – because he saw in the Acadian trajectory the same place-based modernism that had fired the Fiddlehead school. The new wave of Acadian poets in Moncton, like the English modernists in Saint John and Fredericton, were working to loosen the shackles of puritanical oppression imposed by church and state, Catholicism and conservatism. To Cogswell and Bailey, it must have appeared that a small army had joined the cause. New Brunswick might, after all, regain its status as a literary lion, a province where artists speak variously and in different languages but in personal and direct voices, those voices tutored by national and international models but incubated on New Brunswick soil. That the first anglophone in New Brunswick to give his full support to Acadian literary aspirations (and, more generally, to foster a culture of literary translation) was a Baptist from Carleton County is a testament both to Cogswell's vision and to the inclusiveness of the larger Fiddlehead project.

In his cognate work with the Canadian Humanities Association (1967–72), the Independent Publishers' Association (1971–76), and the Association of Canadian Publishers (1976–79), Cogswell joined like-minded cultural nationalists to lobby government for more attention to Canadian publishing in both languages, one result of which was a 1972 Canada Council initiative to offer the first substantial programs of financial support for Canadian publishers. When the Literary Press Group formed in 1975, Cogswell was again involved, for he had long been an advocate for a separate body that would speak for literary publishers in Canada. In partnership with the Canada Council, the Literary Press Group became instrumental in raising awareness about Canadian literature across the country and stimulating a renewed sense of national purpose in the literary arts. For those reasons, Cogswell would be central in the formation of the Atlantic Publishers' Association in 1978. Yet this life's work of building capacity for artistic expression and excellence was not solely rooted in a politics of cultural nationalism, provincial or otherwise. Rather, Cogswell believed in supporting individuals, especially those silenced or on the margins. As he said to Alden Nowlan, he wished to use his position of privilege as a university professor to make it possible for others to find publishing venues in a still rural and colonial country, a country, moreover, that was curiously susceptible to coteries and manifesto-inducing "clubs."[250] Cogswell told David Galloway in 1985: "I have taught and enjoyed a reasonably good living. Many other people with whom I have come into contact have chosen to take [the] other road. That is why they have been poor and needed help, and they have been more out-and-out poets than I have ever pretended to be, and because they are such, I have valued and respected very much the kind of thing they were doing, very often even though it was not terribly fashionable, nor terribly appreciated and sometimes not even terribly good. What I respected most of all, I think, is somebody who is capable of giving in a big sense, rather than a small sense, to that which he or she believes is worth giving to."[251]

That view qualifies what he had written to Richard Ashman years earlier about why he was "remarkably patient with contributors." He said it was because "several writers who I [had] secretly dismissed as hopeless have come up with quite respectable poems and won acceptance." "I have come to the conclusion," he confessed to Ashman, "that anyone who [has] it in him to try can miraculously enough produce a poem if he tries hard enough and long enough. In this world of conformity, I have great respect for even the rudest attempts at poetry. Wretched as they often are they are signs of the resurgence of the human spirit."[252] Long-time Fiddlehead school associate Robert Gibbs had it exactly right, then, when he described Cogswell as a "Great coated / lover of poets more than of their poems."[253] Cogswell saw their hunger and courage, and he put himself in service to the spirit that drove them.

The last poems Cogswell wrote before he died in 2004 spoke of the injustices of a bureaucratized world that imposes and institutionalizes its structures, a world where power thwarts the masses as it enriches the few. The unpublished poem "Pelagius and Augustine" is particularly salient in that regard. The poem puts the two medieval thinkers (Pelagius and Augustine) in counterpoise, suggesting that in the battle for moral authority the Celtic monk Pelagius lost to the more austere Augustine, a one-time disciple of Mani. As a result, the freedom to love, serve, and choose that Pelagius celebrated became overshadowed by the self-denying Manichaeism of Roman fatalism. From the third century forward, Cogswell believed, Augustine's Manichean views of good and evil, righteousness and original sin, sexuality and hell dominated Western thinking. Cogswell writes of their differences as follows:

Pelagius gave human love and all
He felt would pay God's debt, prayer and thought
From all he was. They never were enough
To suit the morning star of Augustine
In a Roman religion. There was no
Saint Lucifer more powerful than he.[254]

To the end, Cogswell expressed profound beliefs in the freedom of the imagination and the moral rightness and imperative of service. With Christianity gone off the rails, the creative impulse, he felt, was the only truth and thus must occupy the work of humanists and intellectuals alike. The literary translation that he was most proud of was his translation of the poem "Art" by Theophile Gauthier. Its last two stanzas might stand as Cogswell's epitaph, for they speak not only to art as a human impulse but to those forces and people who enable art:

The gods themselves are dead.
Great verse, stronger than brass,
   In their stead
Lives on and will not pass.

Write, sculpt, paint, use the knife.
May your floating visions come
   To life
In the hardest medium.[255]

It was advice that the post-Bailey/Pacey/Cogswell generation followed in continuing the Fiddlehead ethic – and it was what carried Cogswell through a long career as poet, editor, publisher, critic, teacher, mentor, and translator. He was indeed "great coated," as Robert Gibbs described him, his coat "large and commodious ... for souls and bodies and keeping them / together out of the cold as many as he can."[256]

The Fiddlehead Project:
Pioneering a Canadian Post-Colonial

All the greatest subject matter is free to the world's writers. Of course the tone of a work, the quality of the handling, must be influenced by the surroundings and local sympathies of the workman, in so far as he is a truly original and creative workman and not a mere copyist ... By all means let our singers preserve to the sweetness which they gather a fragrance distinctive of its original. It is true we have much poetical wealth unappropriated in our broad and magnificent landscapes, in our seasons that alternate so swiftly between gorgeousness and gloom, in the stirring episodes scattered so abundantly through parts of our early history; but let us not think we are prohibited from drawing a portion of our material from lands where now the very dust is man.[1]

I think you will find our verse somewhat different from that of CONTACT and CIV/n. It seems to me that it reflects something of the difference one senses about the Maritimes and especially about New Brunswick when one returns from Central Canada or elsewhere.[2]

The foregoing chapters have illustrated that culture is a production, not a naturally occurring attribute of place or an inheritance of class. And, while it is true that an individual may inherit a proclivity for cultural work, as A.G. Bailey did, that individual must also apprentice thoroughly and work on multiple fronts if cultural outcomes of any worth are to be achieved. Such was the belief of New Brunswick's Fiddlehead modernists. Each understood that a cultural environment was built – and could be built in any locale – and that the creative energies generated from those constructions could revivify whole

8 Founding editors and poets at Memorial Hall, UNB, for the *Fiddlehead*'s 25th
anniversary, May 1970. *Left to right*: Donald Gammon, Elizabeth Brewster,
A.G. Bailey.

communities and regions. Their belief in the latter principle of place-
based renewal made them unique in Canada. Poet Elizabeth Brewster
conveyed that when observing that, though the Fiddlehead phenomenon was "part of that mid-forties ferment which was responsible
for *Preview* and *First Statement* and [A.J.M.] Smith's anthology and
E.K. Brown's book," Bailey's guiding hand ensured that it was the only
flashpoint of its kind tasked explicitly to "create a new Province."[3]
Brewster's recollection of Bailey's pun on the *New Provinces* (1936)
anthology of modern poetry is revealing. It signals clearly that modernist energies for him had the power to alter locales as much as traditions, but that they must do so, at least in already denuded places
like New Brunswick, without denigrating earlier achievement, which
A.J.M. Smith's rejected preface[4] to *New Provinces* had done. Rather,
Bailey's "new Province" would emulate the literary status and authority, but not the style, that Roberts and Carman had brought to nine-

teenth-century New Brunswick, a province that had led the way in mythologizing Canada as colony and nation.

The implication of that particular view of social reform admits this study to the location-of-culture debates that have swirled since the 1994 publication of Homi K. Bhabha's book of the same name. Providing yet more evidence to dispel the resilient myth that modernism is urban, avant-garde, intellectual, formalist, and a violent break from an unwanted past, this study of New Brunswick's Fiddlehead modernists shows that modernism can also germinate in non-metropolitan locales; have humanist and moderate, even conservative, aims; and be socially transformative at the same time as being aesthetically disruptive. In that sense, while the urban Canadian modernism that has attracted the widest critical comment did not veer far from British-American canonical modernism – Ken Norris notes "elaborations rather than radical departures from the Modernist tradition"[5] – New Brunswick modernism was much more ambitious in its reformist agendas. In wanting to regain for New Brunswickers a seat at a national table that had been lost because of imaginative reconstructions of the country, the Fiddlehead modernists took on not just a cultural program but a much larger identity project that had historical, political, social, and economic dimensions. They were, in that regard, the bolder revolutionaries. They were not, to put it bluntly, bourgeois: not fatigued by a staid tradition or lack of venues for alternative expression, but deeply frustrated by the limitations that forced supplication and its attendant narrations had placed upon their region. The "shabby dignity"[6] that federation had consigned to the east had become so enervating that nothing short of a series of provincial Marshall plans would address it. Bailey's work in the context of J.C. Webster's, D.C. Harvey's, Beaverbrook's, and Joseph Howe's of an earlier generation must be viewed in that ambitious light. Their projects were not just progressive or modernist but definably post-colonial in how they sought to change provincial agency under federal configurations of power and narrative. The Maritime provinces had been so emptied of infrastructure, capacity, and spirit that they had become dependent wards of a distant, colonial state, a state whose various commissions and exasperations had reduced them to the kind of Orientalist subject identified by post-colonial theorist Edward Said. By being endlessly studied, diagnosed, and treated as ailing or broken, the Maritimes had actually become *defined* by the languages and practices of equalization. That dominant discourse of want had first removed cultural agency from the region, then reconceived the region, in a construction that was essentially an action of control, as anti-modern (Leo Kennedy's territory of "a second-hand imperialism"[7]). Said's work on this kind of discursive operation is useful because he was theorizing not solely about the relationship between the Occident and the Orient but about how that relationship models more general institutional constructions of difference. To study, to diagnose, and to represent symbolically a people or a region in a "have-not" discourse is, said Said, to maintain firm political control.[8]

For Bailey and his associates, literary innovation was not enough to address this imperial operation or to restore any real or lasting dignity. Cultural workers in the region had to attend to history, curricula, archival preservation, bibliography, and a host of other determinants of social health before the literary could be considered. That is why Brewster was careful to qualify that the *Fiddlehead*, as the most visible symbol of the project, was "in the Maritime tradition."[9] Louis Dudek did the same when placing the magazine in its wider geo-cultural context,[10] recalling Joseph Howe's hope that regional difference could be cultivated for the good so that "we may come to be one people, living under different forms of government ... but knit together by a common policy."[11]

The first thing to understand about mid-century New Brunswick modernism, then, is that it was socially and politically reactionary before it was culturally reformist. Luke Gibbons's work on the comprador's (or foreign agent's) role in Ireland during the early Enlightenment phase of European history is helpful in understanding the primacy of a political rather than cultural response to supplication, for the backwardness assigned by rulers to subjects on the periphery of empire, said Gibbons, "is not always superseded by progress, but may in fact be produced by it."[12] In other words, the so-called "losers of history"[13] are as likely to be manufactured by the benevolent forces that purport to bring relief as they are already compromised, an operation that *demands* political response. Canada's urban centralists and policy makers will not want to hear that, assuring themselves that this view of history-as-grievance and policy-as-cudgel is now a sleeve-worn trope, but the fact remains that the motive energy for Maritime modernism coalesced in the post-Confederation decades as a regional response to increasingly obvious disparities. New Brunswick is a case in point. Because the provincial effects of Confederation were so different than in other parts of Canada and the region, the modernism that took shape to drive reform in the province was of a more reactionary kind than the Canadian modernism we know about from urban critics. A comprehensive and generous definition of modernism must therefore include consideration of not just where the movement takes root but in what longer historical context and for what purposes. Modernism is thus itself a discourse whose first function is adaptability.

By the 1920s, almost a half-century after the introduction of Macdonald's National Policy in 1879, two things had become clear in the Maritimes: first, that reorienting the axis of trade from seaboard (north-south and Empire) to overland (east-west and continental) had fundamentally changed the regional economy; and, second, that the region had become subject to narrative reconstruction as a result. Stories of failure or inadequacy normalized a certain Maritime condition and attitude that historical circumstance seemed to abet. In New Brunswick, especially, high-profile endings dominated the headlines. In 1922 George Parkin, the mentor of the province's most celebrated poets, died, followed four years later by Francis Sherman. Bliss Carman would die a few years after that, his reputation having sunk to that of quack and populist. Two years before Carman's death, Charles G.D. Roberts made a final tour of Canada as president of the Canadian Authors Association. The ardent admirers that tour attracted became immortalized in F.R. Scott's 1927 poem "The Canadian Authors Meet," a satiric lambasting of the dusty pomposity increasingly associated with New Brunswick's Georgian versifiers. Scott's poem was an uncomplimentary eulogy that closed New Brunswick's literary chapter. Making that close irrevocable was the end of the post-First World War boom that had brought a temporary relief to the province's economy. As before, wrote historian David Frank, Maritimers boarded the "Boston boats and the westbound trains," outmigration a metaphor for the high-profile deaths that had seemed to close the province's literary authority.[14] Those who stayed became Confederation's losers, their circumstance – "caught between their penury [and] the 'new' federalism's promise of employment and social security"[15] – creating space for opposite stories of growth and vitality elsewhere in the country.

That dialectic served to divide Canada and its people into geo-political zones that were presented, in Derridean terms, as fixed binaries: rich/poor, receptive/passive, ebullient/flat.[16] Whole regions of the country were placed on the right or wrong side of history. Whole regions were assigned the right or wrong dispositions toward the work of building the nation. Lamenting the lack of a fighting spirit down east, Frank Underhill best articulated the centralist view of the have-nots, concluding with a shrug, in a comment quoted earlier, that "as for the Maritime Provinces, nothing, of course, ever happens down there."[17] The centre had indeed shifted, and the eastern provinces had been dismissed. At the level of the sentence, the dismissal reverberated with condescension, Underhill's parenthetical "of course" indicating clearly that in consolidating power at its urban growth poles Canada was achieving a natural harmony that Confederation's wisdom had decreed.

It is precisely in that cultural operation that New Brunswick comes into sharpest focus, for the province's inadequacies highlight how a nation narrates itself into existence. Simply put, New Brunswick's failures had begun to function performatively in order to coerce and educate. In fact, the condition of the province and the larger region in the 1920s – thrust into shabbiness and supplication, eulogy and nostalgia – served as an object lesson for Canadians. Moreover, in the larger narrative of nationhood, New Brunswick had become a resonant subtext. It was that part of the Confederation story that was understood but rarely discussed, thus functioning integrally as a component of every story's (and every sentence's) larger meaning. The province and its metaphors of inadequacy were thus akin to what narrative theorist Roland Barthes called the "*non-sentence*" that "accede[s] to the sentence."[18] If we extrapolate from Barthes's theory, New Brunswick was therefore both "*outside the sentence*" and "*before* the sentence," acting as a "predictive syntax" in the larger story of the nation.[19] As a failed state – a signifier of social unrest, economic collapse, and bad management – the province was essential to the national story of "peace, order and good government" that informed the British North America Act of 1867. The federated nation needed New Brunswick's failure to showcase other provinces' – and thus the federation's – successes. In semiotic terms, the province was thus both outside and inside the narrative of the nation. Not only, then, was New Brunswick's role essential to the national story, but, in a Barthian sense, the national story was *dependent* on New Brunswick – dependent, that is, on New Brunswick as a sign of the subaltern in a larger and otherwise propitious semiotic system.

As self-evident as the tropes constructed around the province's subaltern status may appear to be, however, as constituents of narrative sign systems they are "arbitrary historical inventions"[20] that have no extradiegetic basis in fact – they are, in other words, only partially reflective of historical events and therefore have no truth outside story. Considered in this light, the nation comes into clearer view. As a constellation of regions, provinces, and locales, the nation is not just a diverse narrative field – not just a patchwork of stories of infinite difference – but more consequentially a narration itself: a way of speaking history, of representing populations, and of addressing imagined listeners on matters ranging from sovereignty to social health. Thus understood, the Maritime conditions as they have been narrated in Canada are discursive *mis*representations, but misrepresentations that are as natural a symptom of federation as are the other fictions that we tell to make sense of the arbitrariness of the borders and policies that define us. There can be no truth to those fictions except in their function as signifiers – and no truth to what is attributed to people outside the action of attribution. As constituents of narrative, all New Brunswickers are at once Canadians, Maritimers, provincial residents, and more; and just as centres of artistic fervour take root, flourish, and inevitably move elsewhere, so do the deeper grammars that inform all fictions, including our own, shift.

A.G. Bailey's importance to the Fiddlehead project and to New Brunswick and the Maritimes more generally was in understanding that semiotic action: that all narrations are both ambivalent and necessary. His province was thus being enunciated in a larger fiction of two founding nations (England and France), two powerful empires (Britain and America), and ever-more-assertive western protagonists who were as impatient with central Canada as easterners were. If Bailey was the first, he was also, by graduate training, the most well informed of the Fiddlehead group to understand the historical dynamic impelling that narration. Realizing that his region was small and economically insignificant, and that his province was marked by differences that had hardened into sectoral tribalisms, he understood that he could not mount an ideological campaign to match that of the Laurentian powers. The only ground open to him was to work at the level of the sentence – in effect, to appropriate the sentence to destabilize an already unstable narration. Today's post-colonial theory provides the critical tools to make sense of the strategy he used. Specifically, he sought to contest narration by following what Homi K. Bhabha later said was a process of "articulat[ing] [the] archaic ambivalence that informs modernity."[21] To begin, Bailey would teach New

Brunswickers a *new* language of modernism, drilling them to the point of perfection in the use of that language so they could narrate a local agency that was not derivative of urban or Laurentian forms. That narration would challenge the presumed ubiquity of the state narration (namely Confederation) and expose the arbitrariness, thus disrupt the authority, of Confederation's pan-Canadian modality. Only in that way could his province and region participate again as equals in the nation. His genius was in knowing that the unstable fictions that narrated his province's relational identity could be supplanted only by other fictions that were localized, personal, and outside the official timeline that the Confederation, modernist, and other state narratives had mapped onto Canada. He somehow knew that he would have to remake New Brunswick as a sovereign subject that stood outside those stories and timelines as they were normally narrated. Again, contemporary literary theory illuminates what Bailey was intending. "At times when the State takes reality into its own hands, and sets about distorting it, altering the past to fit its present need," said post-colonial writer Salman Rushdie, "then the making of the alternative realities of art, including the novel of memory, becomes politicized."[22] And so was a similar memory project formulated in Bailey's mind. Differently nuanced and articulated, his "New Brunswick" would illuminate the "ambivalence that informs" the Enlightenment project that was post-Confederation Canada. (And predictably, the Laurentian narrators most invested in the liberal idea of a Canadian Enlightenment would object the most strenuously, as Louis Dudek, George Bowering, Frank Davey, Brian Trehearne, and others did.)

T.S. Eliot's ideas on modernism gave Bailey the entrance he needed. Those ideas licensed an approach to literary history that enabled Bailey to both retrieve the past and locate it in the oppositional dualisms that Canada was narrating. The sense of what we now understand to be the Derridean "trace" that informs deconstruction – that aspect of narration that unsettles the easy distinctions made between opposites – allowed Bailey to begin from the premise that modernism, as shaped most recognizably in Canada by the first- and second-generation poets at the centre of the country, was neither ahistorical nor a happy accident of like-minded urban intellectuals. Rather, as Bailey would come to understand, the modernism practised by A.J.M. Smith, A.M. Klein, F.R. Scott, Dorothy Livesay, and other twentieth-century Canadian pioneers had its roots in the classicism and erudition of Charles G.D. Roberts, the bohemianism of Bliss Carman, the cosmopolitanism of George Parkin, and the polemics of pre-Confederation small-magazine journalism in Saint John, New Brunswick. The rhetorical operations that were staged at the centre of the country "to debase or subordinate [that] writing,"[23] which Derrida later described as the treatment of the secondary on which the primary reluctantly relies, illustrated to Bailey the primacy of New Brunswick's literary authority and the itch that that authority continued to inflict on a nation that had footnoted New Brunswick in its westward quest – yet desperately relied on the footnote to complete the story. Bailey's insistence on the importance of New Brunswick's nineteenth-century literary culture was thus not merely an attempt to jog historical memory but to call attention to an *interdependence* of regions that was the real character of the federated country. Why shouldn't New Brunswick's nineteenth-century achievements be credited with laying a foundation for Montreal modernism? If the coupling of incongruous regions that was Canada could be anything resembling a nation, it must first be based on an equality of those regions, something that the Confederation fathers had written into the British North America Act of 1867. As a student of epochal history, Bailey knew better than others that movements and societies result from accumulations, migrations, mimicries, and swerves. To attempt to countermand the past by overlaying timelines that started in 1867 or peaked in 1927 with the *McGill Fortnightly Review* was to misunderstand the construction of a present that is always contiguous, thus always in opposition to authorial intention and always, by nature, ambivalent. That is how Bailey *found* New Brunswick most distinctly in the discursive spaces where it was hidden (and the more wilfully it was buried or ignored the more vibrant it appeared to him). Such was his precocious understanding of what Jacques Derrida would later conceive of as "trace" and "supplement." As both Derrida and Barthes would declare, neither story nor sentence ever rids itself fully of the subtexts that resonate within it.

The accusations of provincialism aimed at New Brunswick writers by early modernists such as E.K. Brown, A.J.M. Smith, and Leo Kennedy seem quite different in this light. Thus illuminated as operations of narrative, those accusations appear as competing fictions that mask insecurities clearly visible in amplified polemics. Bailey did not formulate his project to respond directly to those provocations because he understood that the louder the accusers were the more obviously unsure they were of their ground – and, paradoxically, the more in agreement they were with his own aims. What their denunciations masked actually benefited his own project, which is why he and the Fiddlehead modernists remained close to individuals like Louis Dudek and John Sutherland, whose provocations sometimes felt like the bare-knuckled variety. Perhaps not surprisingly, the exception to this tolerance among Fiddlehead modernists was Desmond Pacey, who parried willingly with Dudek, Layton, and Sutherland. Was that because Pacey's connection to New Brunswick was cultivated rather than inherited, thus the most tenuous? This simply raises the question and does not imply that his loyalties were insincere, even if they hadn't come from the soil in the same way that they had for Bailey and Cogswell. Their resilience to provocation, though, was different by inheritance, not degree; they, more than Pacey, had a provincial identity that was never a distinct thing and therefore could never be shaken by opposition.

That said, a central tenet of Fiddlehead modernism was its engagement with what Bailey called "the vastness and infinite variety of the metropolitan processes."[24] Fiddlehead modernism, then, was not nativist in the pejorative sense of the word, nor did it trade in the tribalism of identity politics so pervasive today. Rather, as Bailey and his peers practised it, strategic localism was outward looking, freeing individuals most fully when engagement with the outside world became operative. "To become fully oneself," insisted Bailey, "one must first lose oneself [in vastness and infinite variety]."[25] This lesson seems especially important in an age when populist leaders are trading unscrupulously in false nostalgias of white ethnicity, working-class piety, closed borders, and rural innocence, in effect altering history by peddling fraudulent stories of becoming. Bailey and his associates in the Fiddlehead project not only knew better but understood the consequences of a reduction to the insular. They knew that, without exposure to contemporary poetics, "New Brunswick" as content would always be perceived as provincial, for the animus aimed at the province's authors tilted heavily toward dated styles of versification and expression. The Bliss Carman Society was founded as an incubator in which to cultivate a new kind of modernist aesthetic that met that challenge, an aesthetic that was rooted in "surrounding soil," as Cogswell described it,[26] but at the same time, as Bailey qualified, "open to all the winds that blow."[27] In being both rooted/local and cosmopolitan, Fiddlehead modernism acknowledged what today's literary critics now hold to be true: that modernism as emancipating practice need not be a tool of displacement. That is, it need not work in opposition to or be exclusive of that which it seeks to both celebrate and reform. Its territoriality, then, transcends the European, metropolitan, and Anglo-American as surely as its applications become hybridized and plural. In short, modernism is not incommensurate with rurality or other non-metropolitan configurations of population or class.

While today's generation is comfortable with that more plastic definition of modernism, it bears remembering that the movement, as originally carried out in Canada, was not inclusive. First- and second-generation modernism in Canada was assertively male, sourced in what were thought to be male dispositions for logic that best positioned literature to compete with the authorities of technology and science. Early modernism was also paternalistically urban, part of a larger socio-political effort to concentrate intellectual resources at the centre of the nation in an attempt to normalize the idea of a Canada united unshakably across gargantuan space. Fiddlehead modernism was of a different kind, its hybridization of the urban and rural (the cosmopolitan and distant) a precursor not only to the rise of a self-conscious literary regionalism in Canada but also to the assertion of regional identity in the larger mosaic. Fiddlehead modernists were certainly not the first to conceive of the cultural richness embedded in regional difference – one need only consider Bailey's numerous early references to Thomas D'Arcy McGee and Louis Riel – but they were the first organized school of writers in Canada to put into practice the aesthetics of a reformist movement whose pioneers bore almost no resemblance to themselves.[28] In so doing, they were the first school to take a measure of the robustness of the Confederation experiment. In testing whether a federation of discordant provinces was sturdy enough to withstand local and regional assertion, they were not seeking the end of a confederated Canada but pushing the limits of what Canada could be – striving, as Bailey wrote in "Confederation Debate," for the dream of living "in peace and / freedom / with mutual forebearance, / speaking in half the languages of Europe / and Asia, / with rights grounded in law."[29] That distinction is critical, for they believed that a monochromic federalism could only be reductive and coercive, thus unable to withstand the "flaws and biases," the "fierce factional strife," and the "political disunity" that characterized a naturally dissonant Canada.[30] Accordingly, they hybridized modernist aesthetics to create forms and capacities that were appropriate to the peculiarities of their own history and place. The alterity they sought was a republican Canada of regions, voices, ethnicities, and locales, not a manorial Canada of centres and margins. It was toward that end that each worked to shape a modernism that would address what had become an asymmetrical social and cultural landscape in the country. Fiddlehead modernism was therefore conservative in embracing the first principles of federation as mutuality *and* reformist in upholding the political ideal of a constellation of self-governing regions that itself was a composite of the many empires and world views that had created it.

In embracing a characteristic of modernism that Ernest Hemingway anticipated when describing the movement as "a moveable feast,"[31] Fiddlehead modernists influenced Canadian literature's first turns toward a distributive regional expression. For later generations of writers who deliberately identified place-based affinities, the necessity of openness to worlds larger than their own had become normative. The real implication of that engagement with vastness, expressed by Bailey in the caution that one should never attempt to "achieve identity" by fortifying oneself in the familiar,[32] meant that the cultural colonialism that E.K. Brown and Pacey so lamented in their criticism could be overcome only in study and emulation of distant models. The real job of the Canadian modernist, stressed Pacey, is thus to absorb "the best that [distant masters] have to teach" while "modifying [that teaching] in the light of our own peculiar situation."[33] The post-Fiddlehead "neo-provincialism"[34] that critic Terry Whalen later identified as being uniquely characteristic of Maritime writing is sourced in that openness, which split creative attentions between home and abroad in order to bring the best back while also casting a "steady eye" on denigrations from elsewhere lest those attempt to narrate inferiority.[35] But the reach of Fiddlehead modernism into Canada (as hybrid and plurality) was not solely regional or literary. At the heart of the Fiddlehead group's experiment with rooted cosmopolitanism lay an acceptance of the socio-political advantages of multiculturalism that did not become commonplace until the post-Pierre Trudeau era. The New Brunswick modernists established early in their opposition to urban modernism that it was only by cultivating "creole nationalisms," as Benedict Anderson later termed such hybrids,[36] that the colonial subject could move to the front of the sentence – and that Canada, widely dispersed across languages, traditions, and geographies, could work as a nation. Borrowed from else-where and reworked in the image of the places where they were imported, those hybridized forms ensured that a theoretically and aes-thetically informed localism, whatever its constituents, would always be linguistically relevant and adept at responding to those majority speakers who control the narrative by positioning the subject in unstable and untenable ways.

Bailey's secondary genius at rallying students and colleagues to New Brunswick's need ensured that these new ideas would be translated into practice. Moreover, the extent to which his two principal lieutenants modified and amplified the regional inflection at the core of his project suggests not just the diverse application of his thought but also a fun-damental elasticity that sustained it. Pacey's staging of the nation as an unwritten tableau is but one example of that elasticity, which accom-modated his desire to present himself as an original Adam who would define Canada via the realist depictions of distinct nationalisms that he chose. Bailey's reading of the nation as a dynamic social field did not clash with the practical criticism that Pacey had picked up from I.A. Richards at Cambridge. Rather, the combination of the two seeming opposite critical approaches – Bailey's socio-cultural and Richards's textual – positioned Pacey to narrate into existence a syncretic Canada that returned literary authority to New Brunswick (and granted it else-where) as surely as it decentralized authority from the urban interiors. Reading the distributed cultures, languages, and geographies of the Canadian mosaic as a text, Pacey could not have come to a different conclusion. For him and the generation of critics he mentored, Bailey's rejection of an exclusionary, rather bourgeois urban modernism for a hyphenated, attentive modernism that was socially and culturally reflexive invited not just a new kind of critic but whole new programs of critical work. The "Canada" Pacey saw through Bailey's prism was thus a much more complex country than most had seen – and there-fore an exciting country in which to be both a literary pioneer and an agent of social improvement.

Pacey's career-long emphases on realism, decentralization, and clin-ical assessment of artistic quality extended that unique Fiddlehead modernism. Realism, he insisted, must drive narration so the truth of diversity would supplant the myths of uniformity and centralization, thereby enunciating a Canada that is a patchwork of distinct and often competing societies. So it was with his ideas about the decen-tralization of publishing and higher learning. Because Canada was *not* reducible to its major urban centres – in fact, the more dominant regional profile of the country was rarely discernible in those centres – no one university or publishing house should serve the nation. In instances where one did, the Canada distributed across distances and differences was misrepresented, fetishized, or coerced into adoption of a single vision, which critic Wilfrid Eggleston observed in A.R.M. Lower's and Pelham Edgar's separate characterizations of New Brunswick's "sterile soil."[37] The alternative to the monotone of centralization was cultivation of expertise in numerous locales, which would open Canada to the kind of total field attention that the Fiddlehead project modelled. To repeat an essential earlier point, "it's time for less heat and more light," Pacey wrote in reviewing Louis Dudek and Michael Gnarowski's *Making of Modern Poetry in Canada*: "We should be patiently examining the best work that has been done – and not merely the work of the moderns, but the work of Roberts, Carman, Scott."[38] Standard by the 1970s, that insistence on opening the field across temporal and spatial axes was key to democratizing culture and criticism in Canada.

The fact that Fiddlehead modernism was institutionally situated certainly helped. Bailey began his work in museums, later using university libraries and archives – and, of course, the boundless energy of young minds – to advantage. While academia would seem the natural place to embed a program of cultural reform, universities of the 1940s and 1950s had to be managed in careful ways to accommodate the social missions of research, activism, and local stewardship that we associate them with today. Bailey and Pacey were at the forefront of that effort in a mid-century Canada that increasingly looked to universities as instruments of social change. And, though they were obviously not responsible for the post-war expansion of the country's higher-education sector, they positioned themselves in roles within UNB that allowed them to align institutional growth with the cultural outcomes they sought, thus modelling a use of the modern university that had rare precedent outside of Canada's largest post-secondary institutions. In fact, the nineteenth-century UNB of James Robb, Marshall d'Avray, Thomas Harrison, George E. Foster, and William F.P. Stockley that Bailey knew from his ancestry was the closest example at hand, an example that illustrated the complementarity of universities and cultural vibrancy.[39] The work of the Fiddlehead modernists must thus be conceived of broadly: it was directed not only at reanimating a literary New Brunswick but also at positioning key institutions in the province – from universities and museums to government departments – to undertake the leadership that a marginalized New Brunswick needed. Bailey and his lieutenants showed that organizing for culture in the modern university harnessed resources and energies not easily found in non-urban locales, enabling places like New Brunswick to partake of some of the dynamism of cosmopolitan centres. Pacey's overtures toward regional university cooperation, distance learning, and curriculum development, all of which continue to be concentrated in universities today, speak to the efficacy of using universities as incubators for social change.

Cogswell's emergence as the most visible of the Fiddlehead modernists was paradigmatic of that effort, for he was quite literally a product of UNB and the Fiddlehead school. Mentored by Bailey and Pacey inside their project, he was the subject that a decentralized, democratized modernism was designed to animate. And he did, indeed, become animated, finding ample room in the repurposed modernism of his teachers to express the independence that a radical Baptist upbringing had instilled. The combination of his being rooted in parish narrowness and desirous of that which lay beyond made him an embodiment of the hybrid modernism theorized by his mentors. His training at UNB after his service in Europe accelerated that desire to assist a New Brunswick that was yearning, as he was, to grow beyond its parochialisms – not to become something else, but to become a more enlightened and therefore freer version of itself. That freedom became liturgy for Cogswell, an aspect of democratized modernism that he shaped toward an acceptance of difference that was expressed as a doctrine of the eclectic. In opposites he found compatibility, in strife the motive energy that impelled art. Even in the crudest novices he saw the potential to create something of lasting worth. The principles he inherited from his mentors, then, furthered an intelligence that was predisposed to using art as a means of finding voice, much as New Brunswick had been voiced in the literature of the Confederation poets.

Cogswell came to his work with a disposition toward the personal that was stronger than that of his mentors. His interest in realism as literary expression is a case in point. Unlike Pacey, he had little interest in realism as functional textuality – as a means, that is, to locating and advancing national maturity – but was drawn to realism for how it complemented the spiritual dramas in which all Canadians, in their different inflections, were engaged. For him, the *performance* of realism that a human-centric modernism allowed freed individuals from "the half-light of provincialism" that Arthur Lower had assigned to out-of-the-way, rather conservative places like New Brunswick.[40] Cogswell was the Fiddlehead group member who pushed most vigorously against that sort of condescension by encouraging a catholicity of performance across multiple locales, believing that it was in immediate circumstance that individuals discovered themselves. To do otherwise was to censor speech, and thus to denigrate individuals by the same operation as others had denigrated New Brunswick. His, then, was a self-described "humbler kind of pilgrimage" that advanced individuals, wherever they were and however peculiar or unrefined their voices.[41]

Cogswell's dispositions must be underscored because they were so integral to how Fiddlehead modernism advanced and what it achieved. The most potent symbol of that modernism – the literary magazine – reflected those dispositions. The *Fiddlehead* may have been Bailey's creation but it was Cogswell's child. His inheritance of the magazine in 1952 is thus more accurately described as an adoption. And so, at mid-century, there were really two magazines, pre- and post-1952. The first editorial change that Cogswell oversaw illustrates that: he applied to his mentor's fledgling instrument one of that mentor's core principles by taking down the "Chinese wall" that sheltered it. Writers from outside the Bliss Carman Society would be welcomed, standards of assessment and quality enhanced, and alliances made with distant editors to internationalize the magazine's reach. As soon as he began, Cogswell set out to test the conceptual apparatus (the democratized modernism) on which the magazine was premised. He would change its features – in some ways radically – but not its values. It would follow a middle path, striving to be progressive without being combative or dogmatic. Likewise, it would blend high standards with an encouraging editorial modesty that challenged authors to become better, more informed students of craft, but not at the expense of jettisoning particularities of reference. Cogswell's writers could thus develop the technical proficiency of avant-garde modernists without having to adopt their subject matter. In those ways did the *Fiddlehead* both retain and refine its mission as a teaching journal. The key difference from the days of private circulation was that Cogswell tested the concept of a teaching journal by throwing open the classroom "to all the winds that blow." By combining high-quality creative work and dispassionate, sometimes searing reviews, his mag-

azine incubated talent in a high-stakes exchange of authors and critics. If New Brunswick was to produce good writers, as it produced
good hockey players, such seriousness was necessary. The "expansive
puppets" that became easy targets for F.R. Scott and his cohort were
no longer admitted.[42] This was not an editor being exclusive but
exacting. This was an editor saying that literary artists must be personal and professional at the same time. Again, a denuded New
Brunswick could accept nothing less than narrating excellence in all
that it did.

The confusion this editorial stance caused among Canadian nationalists was palpable. Not only did there seem to be a disconnect
between Cogswell's editorial modesty and exacting standards, but
there was also incongruity in his efforts to raise the standard of poetry in Canada (and New Brunswick) while accepting the work of non-
Canadian authors. Even in New Brunswick there was confusion. How
could the *Fiddlehead* claim to support provincial authors when it published so many authors from away? Poet emerita Dorothy Livesay
expressed the same concern at a national level, expressing bafflement
and anger. "[A] Canadian magazine [must] be Canadian," she plead-
ed.[43] The stakes, then, were as high for artists as for Fiddlehead
modernists, and this at a time when the recommendations from the
Massey-Lévesque Commission were beginning to change the Canadian cultural landscape. Cogswell, though, ever the student of Pacey,
would not bow to arguments that put politics (i.e., loyalty to tribe)
above art. For him, art had an integrity that politics did not, and so the
only way to serve province and tribe in cultivating art was to showcase
the best that was being written in the hope that locals were paying
attention. To do otherwise was to peddle a callow favouritism that
confirmed the "half-light-of-provincialism" assumptions routinely
being made about the province. What did that say about the post-
1952 Fiddlehead project as it was steered by Cogswell? That its aims
aligned with Bailey's most fervent hope of a revival of excellence in
New Brunswick literature; that its methods paralleled Pacey's insistence that social improvement is advanced by artistic mastery; and
that New Brunswick, the subject (direct and indirect) of all these
attentions, was worthy of participation in the larger Canadian federation but had to be prodded and coached to do so. Cogswell was the
most representative of the Fiddlehead modernists because his fierce
loyalty to New Brunswick was always accompanied by fury with its
parochialisms. His cultural work was thus never theoretical but

undertaken (and often endured) with a full knowledge of the provincial reflex. That he persisted, as Bailey and Pacey did, is all the evidence one needs of their devotion.

WAVES AND REPERCUSSIONS

It is difficult to measure the trajectory of an idea, let alone follow how emphases mutate and advance. After all, how does one track the consequence of mentorship or the influence of an editorial disposition? To be definitive in doing so is to invite dismissal. Yet critics speculate about such diffusions in order to challenge the simple causality that some people want and propose. As Bailey's socio-historical studies revealed, however, the context that envelopes all social exchange, including artistic endeavour, is wide, deep, and complex – so much so that questions and probes instead of answers and maps seem the best way to approach conclusions and invite further inquiries. With that in mind, it seems fitting to suggest a few implications and extensions of Fiddlehead modernism that bear more scrutiny. The first is to think more broadly about how Bailey's modernists modelled a way to consolidate intellectual and cultural energies in mid-century New Brunswick. A comparative study of the work of the Fugitive Poets of the American South – the link has not yet been made – would be useful for understanding, generally and comparatively, how such consolidation of interests is achieved, sustained, and mutates into other intellectual forms and expressions.[44] Do all such movements have a central visionary like Bailey and John Crowe Ransom? Do they all begin in quarrel, split from earlier traditions, find direction in internal dialogue and experiment, and work to develop a poetics that is unique to place? Understanding such modelling in parallel would be an important spatial referent because, just as surely as "Mr. Ransom's poems are composed of Tennessee,"[45] so are Bailey's and Cogswell's poems composed of and therefore illuminate New Brunswick. But that is not all, for just as the work of the Southern Fugitives ignited proximate energies, so did the work of the mid-century Fiddlehead modernists extend outward in many directions. How, then, did the work of the latter make possible what developed in cognate cultural nodes, namely the Ice House Gang, the Maritime Writers' Workshop, the Acadian Renaissance, and even the establishment of universities in Moncton and Saint John?

By shaping UNB's mandate at senior administrative levels, especially with regard to community outreach and development, Bailey, Pacey, and their colleagues (presidents and patrons) showed how an institution could be mobilized for provincial work, an important lesson for today. When New Brunswick's first elected Acadian premier, Louis J. Robichaud, took office in 1960, he "had already made up his mind about [the creation of a French-language university]," later declaring that l'Université de Moncton was "his proudest accomplishment."[46] Robichaud had learned his lessons well. King's College, UNB's first iteration, had been founded to advance the interests of the English Loyalists shortly after they arrived in New Brunswick from New York in 1783, that action, said Bailey, guaranteeing durability of "those principles of religion and morality for which so many [Loyalists] fought throughout the War of Independence."[47] Why could a French-language university not advance the interests of Acadians similarly? Robichaud asked the question because he saw the effects of institutional stewardship first-hand – and how those effects had served English New Brunswickers almost exclusively. If that seems tenuous, then UNB's central role in post-war New Brunswick is being underestimated. Not only did the university work in consort with the J.B. McNair and Hugh John Flemming provincial governments (1940–52; 1952–60), but those governments thought of UNB as *New Brunswick's* university, covering its annual deficits, appointing senior members to its board, and using it to implement social, scientific, and educational policy in communities across the province.[48] Successive governments even toyed with the idea of mandating bilingualism at UNB to serve the Acadian population, especially in the area of teacher training.[49] Rather than fight against an anglophone institutional hegemony, Robichaud chose to emulate the model that Fiddlehead modernists had been a part of constructing. Only by mirroring that solidarity of educational purpose, wrote Robichaud biographer Della Stanley, "could the Acadians achieve prominence within New Brunswick."[50] Robichaud was lyrical about that outcome: "pour nous connaître, il faut nous réunir et nous réunir, c'est nous unir" (to know ourselves, we must meet, and meeting unites us).[51] The further inquiries these institutional investments beg should consider New Brunswick's major infrastructures as tools of provincial remediation. Were universities in Fredericton and Moncton influential to the extent they were because of the small size of New Brunswick and its cities, and was there comparable co-option of universities by first- and second-generation reformers in Quebec and Ontario? Did universities in those provinces have a similar effect in moving larger provinces to progressive ends? If remediation and improvement were goals, then whose vision and what policy efforts inside government sustained those? Perhaps New Brunswick's example provides evidence to increasingly tight-fisted governments that a concentration of resources in key institutions can effect comprehensive social change. Perhaps arm's-length investments in intellectual and cultural capital are not as risky or frivolous as today's neo-liberal political elite suspects. Regardless of the conclusion, the reciprocal relationship of New Brunswick's intellectual and political classes between the 1940s and 1960s seems an important aspect of provincial history that is worth investigating.

More direct, perhaps, is pursuing the reach of Fiddlehead modernism into the province's and region's other writing and creative communities. Whether the Ice House Gang of writers, active in Fredericton from 1967 to 1983, or the coeval Windsor Castle group (Alden Nowlan's coterie of young poets and fiction writers), the mid-century modernist connection was close at hand. The Ice House leaders, all people that Bailey and Pacey either hired or taught, provided a forum to a many-voiced choir that became the who's-who of the next generation's literary talent in New Brunswick. So was the case in Alden Nowlan's circle. And, while some of those writers who apprenticed in the spaces made available at UNB will vigorously deny help or influence, there is no denying that they accepted publication in the *Fiddlehead* or Fiddlehead Poetry Books, sought mentorship in the Fiddlehead circle, and benefited from the rising cultural tide for which mid-century Fiddlehead modernists had been responsible. In entering the creative commons that had been built for them, and achieving success therein, they proved one of Bailey's operative theses: that, contrary to the "great man" thinking of Whistler and Alfred Weber, imaginative expression is not unpredictable or sporadic but rather nurtured in environments that accommodate art.[52] What also cannot be denied is that the most successful of the two groups, those who became national figures, took the imprint of Fiddlehead modernism and shaped it to their own ends. Clearly detectable in their work, then, are realism, technical experiment, ironic detachment, unadorned speech, honesty of vision, and a sophisticated aesthetics of empathy that follow exactly what Pacey and John Zanes observed in Bailey's modernism and Cogswell's editorial disposition.[53] Because Fiddlehead modernism had found its own traction in hybridized form, so did it encourage hybrid versions of itself; however, many of its core characteristics remain alive in New Brunswick and Maritime writing today. Broader study of that extension is certainly warranted in the generation of writers that the Fiddlehead modernists both accommodated and mentored.

One attribute in particular bears examining: the carefully worked-out aesthetic of empathy that is evident in the confessional voices of Alden Nowlan, Elizabeth Brewster, Al Pittman, and other peers and students of the Fiddlehead modernists, including the Saint John visual artists whose influence Bailey absorbed when he worked at the New Brunswick Museum.[54] While post-Darwinian humanism abounded in Marxist and Social Gospel sympathies in the first half of the twentieth century, humanism as aesthetic practice (critical and creative) is especially prominent in Bailey's ethnomethodology, Pacey's social Christianity, Cogswell's Taoism, and Elizabeth Brewster's refinement of a provincially nuanced moral realism. The absence of the New Brunswick-born Brewster in this study of Fiddlehead modernism might be addressed here, for, though she did not participate fully in institutional, editorial, or publishing capacities, she certainly was at the scene of the burgeoning of mid-century modernism in Fredericton and was considered by her peers to be the most gifted of the early Fiddlehead poets. Bailey termed her poems "the finest flowers of this poetry movement"[55] and Pacey never tired of promoting her work to the country's most influential publishers.[56] She was also the first, and thus a precursor to Cogswell and Nowlan, to perfect a style of lamentation that evoked empathy without resorting to sentimentality, following the lead, she later told Bailey, of T.S. Eliot's admiration for George Crabbe.[57] Had she emerged at a time more accepting of women in the academy she would have taken a place at UNB next to the Fiddlehead male principals with and under whom she apprenticed. That said, Bailey and Pacey steered her path toward library science, a discipline, said UNB's chief librarian Gertrude Gunn, that was as valuable as teaching in higher education.[58] With the consistent support of Bailey and Pacey, Brewster eventually accepted an academic appointment in Saskatchewan in 1972. Further examination of her work and relationship to Fiddlehead modernism – particularly her modelling of the figure of the

independent artist – is needed, as is more in-depth study of the contributions made by the early women of the Fiddlehead school, namely Eleanor Belyea, Frances Firth, and Margaret Cunningham.

Further study in the same vein might open Bailey's ethnohistory to
wider disciplinary inquiry, considering how his social theories of cross-
cultural exchange – explored in his contact studies of European and
Eastern Algonkian cultures – prompted deeper sensitivity to social
harms.[59] Applying Bailey's pioneering work to today's decolonization
efforts would likely render that influence anachronistic, since his work
on Indigenous cultures, at least in his mind, was separate from his cultural stewardship. But there can be no doubt that his reading of history as a field of social excitation and disintegration shaped his activism
about Maritime and Indigenous rights alike. That activism found its
way into his own poetry, notably the poems "North West Passage,"
"Lament of the Montagnais," "Hochelaga," "The Blood of the Lamb,"
and "Miramichi Lightning." His attempt to work out an ecology of pro-
portionality in his art – that is, an ethics of what is appropriate and
"mete" to individuals and societies[60] – likely found expression in later
artists who were thinking about other zones of contact across species
and biome. Is it coincidental, we should ask, that the country's first
eco-poets of consequence apprenticed in the east where the influence
of "North America's first identifiable ethnohistorian"[61] held such powerful sway? More study is certainly needed to source, locate, and define
eco-poetics in a mid-century New Brunswick cultural activism that
conjoined the cosmopolitan and local in reciprocal fashion; that resuscitated the subalterns of progress (the "losers of history") from the status of the subordinate clause;[62] and that worked out an aesthetics of
openness to accommodate the eclectic, the plural, and the personal.
The ample instances in New Brunswick and Maritime literature of a
poetics of the underclass and of sustained reflections on the intertidal,[63] marginal, and other spaces of interspecies contact suggest that
region and environment are not just physical apparatus but moral
potencies that find their way into art. "Analysis of tides is philosophic,"
wrote Bailey,[64] the phrase suggesting that life on periphery and fringe
hastens the contemplative and kinetic. Such reflection and involvement invite a politics of the personal that renders the human horizontal, thus open to sodalities, rather than vertical, which repudiates
those for ego and autonomy. As Pacey observed in Cogswell's efforts to
stimulate an aesthetics of concern, the objective was to license a "poetry of our people by our people for our people."[65]

Attentiveness to that "peculiar typography" of the personal, as Al Purdy described it,[66] was not restricted to the creative, and so a similar study of the growth of a critical industry and style in the region also warrants attention. Such study might begin with considering the role that Bailey's "Creative Moments in the Culture of the Maritime Provinces," first published in the *Dalhousie Review* in 1949, played in restarting what had been a robust socio-cultural criticism in the region two decades before and after 1900. Such study might also consider the influence of Pacey's *Creative Writing in Canada* (1952) and *Ten Canadian Poets* (1958), not for a critical signature but for the fact that Pacey had the boldness to undertake a national criticism in New Brunswick. More significant was Pacey's mentorship of the graduate students who became the leading critical voices of the second half of the twentieth century. Yet another productive avenue of inquiry might connect the influence of the *Fiddlehead*'s vibrant and at times combative review section to the emergence of the self-assured, evaluative criticism of the 1980s. Crucial in that context is the appearance of the *Atlantic Provinces Book Review* in 1974, particularly during the editorship of Terry Whalen from 1982 to 1990. Under Whalen's leadership, the critical broadsheet expanded its reach into every corner of the region, striving to build a critical literacy in ways similar to how the Fiddlehead modernists cultivated creative capacities. Whalen achieved a success equal to that of the mid-century modernists by operationalizing a scholarly activism – he termed it "intelligent attention"[67] – that opened the critical field to local application of international ideas, thus shepherding the growth of a critical industry to respond to an increasingly assertive regional literature. Whalen's editing of *The Atlantic Anthology: Critical Essays* (1985) spun out of that, as did his own studies of Bliss Carman and Charles G.D. Roberts in 1985 and 1989. The pinnacle of that work was his annotated critical edition of Roberts's animal stories, which featured his reading, through Schopenhauer, of Roberts's own eco-poetics of animal agency.

Was it coincidence that Whalen embarked on that work when and how he did, or that waves of regionally focused, summative criticism hit Atlantic Canadian shores in quick succession, starting in 1979 with Patrick O'Flaherty's literary study *The Rock Observed: Studies in the Literature of Newfoundland* and Ernest Forbes's historical work *The Maritime Rights Movement, 1919–1927: A Study in Canadian Regionalism* (1979) and then continuing in subsequent years with Margaret Conrad's *Recording Angels: The Private Chronicles of Women from the*

Maritime Provinces of Canada, 1750–1950 (1982), David Alexander's *Atlantic Canada and Confederation* (1983), Janice Kulyk Keefer's *Under Eastern Eyes: A Critical Reading of Maritime Fiction* (1987), John Reid's *Six Crucial Decades: Times of Change in the History of the Maritimes* (1987), and Gwendolyn Davies's *Studies in Maritime Literary History* (1991)? What these works share is a solid and enabling foundation – scholarship of this frequency and concentration stems from what came immediately before – and a belief that the subject matter is sufficiently demarcated and accomplished to be worthy of advanced study. Further inquiry into this late-century critical renaissance is warranted, and would likely credit Fiddlehead modernism with generating some of the motive energies that followed.

Not the least of those energies can be attributable to Cogswell's commitment to French-language literature and translation, a commitment vigorously encouraged by the Quebec-born Bailey, whose interest in New France propelled his first contact studies of Europeans and Indigenous peoples. Coincident with New Brunswick enacting Bill 88 and Canada enshrining minority-language protections in the Charter of Rights and Freedoms, Cogswell's recognition of a francophone agency in national history and culture developed in parallel with Acadian cultural activism in New Brunswick. And, while critical consensus posits that Acadian activists looked to Quebec's Quiet Revolution for inspiration and direction, more work needs to be done to place Fiddlehead principals at the scene of that larger influence. Cogswell, for example, published *One Hundred Poems of Modern Quebec* as a Fiddlehead Poetry Book in 1970, adding his translations of Rina Lasnier and Gaston Miron to John Glassco's *Poetry of French Canada* that same year. He contributed directly, then, as a national pioneer to a bi-cultural momentum that Acadian New Brunswickers emulated for their own ends. More work needs to be done, too, on intra-provincial connections, that work examining the modelling of cultural consolidation that Fiddlehead modernism occasioned.[68] If Premier Louis Robichaud was aware of institutional stewardship at UNB, then it is likely that the cultural brokers of Acadian aspirations were also aware of what had been accomplished by Fredericton's cultural workers a generation earlier. Consider, for example, the echo of early Fiddlehead ambitions in Acadian Renaissance pioneer Calixte Duguay's "To Have a Homeland": "To call out ... / The words of an archaic speech / Brought up to date / For the staging of a new kind of play."[69] Though New Brunswick's English and

French programs of renewal were different – being contained in a minority setting, Acadian renewal was more ubiquitous, raucous, and politically consequential – their fashioning of strategic localisms to serve history and place was very similar, as was their adaptation of modernism to community need. More study, then, would shed light on New Brunswick settler histories that are as congruent and contiguous as they are distinct.

That modernism takes many forms is perhaps its best definition. And that the Fiddlehead modernists were at the forefront of adapting an inherited Anglo-American modernism to Canada's unique political topography is perhaps their most important legacy. For them, New Brunswick had a distinct history and culture that Canada, as principal actor in a large cast, could not accommodate. Canada, it seemed, had a structural bias that required that New Brunswick perform a certain role in an evolving drama of federation. That role was supplicant. Led and sustained by Bailey's historio-cultural theories of social ebb and flow, mid-century Fiddlehead modernists intervened in that evolving drama of nationhood not to disrupt but to adjust (and clarify) the terms of Confederation. Desiring a united Canada of distinct and equal regions and provinces, they resuscitated a New Brunswick that would rise above the narrative assigned to it. Their project thus began in a recognition of grievance, yes, but moved swiftly from there to a positive construction. Canada, they announced, must be hyphenated multiply across regions and provinces if it is to thrive. A mature Canada, they insisted, must be culturally syncretic, a chorus of many voices and expressions. By the late 1970s, a century after Confederation and a generation after they started their work, that view had become common, even a formerly stingy Northrop Frye conceding that all mature nations grew over time into composite regionalisms. That maturity, he said, allowed the "creative mind [to escape] from a centralizing uniformity."[70] New Brunswick's Fiddlehead modernists were at the forefront of that effort, nudging a still-nascent federation into the allowances and configurations that it had to adopt if it were to provide any durable unifying function. They forged an alternative way for the nation to speak – and for New Brunswickers and Atlantic Canadians to think of themselves. "We can now explore the variety of our culture – as we should – without feeling that we are out of step with the literature of the world," wrote Terry Whalen about an emancipated Atlantic Canadian imagination. "There is here."[71] Indeed, there is. There is here.

Notes

PREFACE

1 Quoted in Thompson, "College Life," 107.
2 Gammon, "Fiddlehead," 17.
3 Quoted in Chilibeck, "Province," B1.
4 MacLeod, *No Great Mischief*, 279.
5 Chong, "Julia Catherine Beckwith Hart."
6 Churchill, *My Early Life*, 42.
7 Quoted in Moritz, "From a Far Star," 6.
8 Flaherty, "No 'Corporate Welfare,'" A4.
9 Trueman, "Foreword," 2.
10 Cogswell to Livesay, 25 July 1957.

CHAPTER ONE

1 Brewster, "East Coast – Canada," 94.
2 Pacey, "Canadian Literature in the Fifties," 9.
3 Whalen, "Atlantic Possibilities," 2.
4 Trehearne, *Aestheticism*, 313–14.
5 Trehearne, *Montreal Forties*, 13.
6 Glenn Willmott repeats the assumption that "the rural regions of the Maritimes, like those of Quebec, modernized much later than those of Ontario or the Prairie provinces. The latter shifted from a colonial-based social-economy of subsistence to a postcolonial one of exchange in the early decades of this century – yielding the modern anti-pastorals of writers like Grove and

Ostenso in the West, and Duncan and Knister in Ontario" (*Unreal Country*, 153).

7 See, for example, Naves's *Robert Weaver: Godfather of Canadian Literature*; Fetherling's *The Gentle Anarchist: A Life of George Woodcock*; Davey's *Louis Dudek/Raymond Souster*; and Friskney's *New Canadian Library: The Ross-McClelland Years*.

8 *Canadian Forum*, 205–12.

9 Dudek to Cogswell, 4 June 1962.

10 In magnanimous fashion, Cogswell excused these oversights, welcoming the launch of Gnarowski's *Yes* magazine in a November 1956 supplement to the *Fiddlehead*, and attributing Dudek's outbursts to a "cantankerousness" that stems from "a genuine love of poetry" (Cogswell to Alan Reidpath, 26 July 1958). Not to be thought naive, however, he concluded three months later that Dudek is "attempt[ing] to gain more attention to *Delta* and to himself" (Cogswell to Helen Ball, 25 October 1958).

11 *Aesthetic Underground*, 94.

12 Keefer, *Under Eastern Eyes*; Creelman, *Setting in the East*; Fuller, *Writing the Everyday*; Wyile and Lynes, *Surf's Up!*

13 Patterson, "New Brunswick Renaissance," 40.

14 Brewster to A.G. Bailey, 26 September 1973.

15 Ross, "Fort, Fog and Fiddlehead," 119–20.

16 Wright, *Saint John River*, 151.

17 Saffell to Fred Cogswell, 18 May 1958.

18 Gibbs, "Three Decades," 233–5.

19 Marshall, *Harsh and Lovely Land*, 117. Marshall's reference was to a "realistic Maritime school," but he was at least close. On the other hand, John Marshall, associate director of New York's Rockefeller Foundation, was the first to describe the *Fiddlehead* poets as a distinct Canadian "literary school." In a letter to A.G. Bailey, he observed the likeness between the "school of younger poets ... growing up at Fredericton" and two schools he watched develop in the United States. "I refer first to the one at Harvard," he wrote, which "included among its members E.E. Cummings, John Dos Passos, Malcolm Cowley, Foster Damon, and Robert Hillyer. The second one was, of course, the so-called fugitive group at Nashville, including Robert Penn Warren, Allen Tate, John Crowe Ransom, Merrill Moore, and others" (J. Marshall to A.G. Bailey, 17 February 1947).

20 Pacey, "Contemporary Writing," 35.

21 Cogswell, "Literary Traditions in New Brunswick," 294.

22 Bennett and Brown.

23 Irvine, "'Little Magazines' in Canada."

24 Gibbs, "English Poetry," 126; Whiteman, "Introduction," x.
25 Irvine, "Little Magazines," 625.
26 Ibid., 620.
27 McKay, *Rebels, Reds;* Rifkind, *Comrades;* Jessup, *Antimodernism.*
28 Fuller, *Writing the Everyday.*
29 Wyile, *Anne of Tim Hortons.*
30 Godard, "Notes," 269.
31 Szeman, "Introduction," 6.
32 Banks et al., "Risk and Trust," 455.
33 Pound, "Provincialism the Enemy," 189–203.
34 Stegner, *Where the Bluebird Sings,* 59.
35 Friesen, "Defining the Prairies."
36 van Herk, *Mavericks; Unsettled Pasts.*
37 Thorburn, *Politics in New Brunswick,* 16.
38 Bailey, "Overture," 76–7.
39 Montgomery, *Anne of Green Gables,* 7.
40 Nowlan, *Wanton Troopers,* 66.
41 Quoted in Wilbur, *Rise of French New Brunswick,* 211.
42 Doyle, *Front Benches and Back Rooms,* 14.
43 Quoted in Raymond, *Winslow Papers,* 508; MacFarlane, *Fredericton History,* 21.
44 Wiseman, *In Search of Canadian Political Culture,* 152.
45 Wynn, "1800–1810," 225.
46 Maillet, *Pélagie,* 7.
47 Paratte, *Acadians,* 193.
48 Marston, *Diary,* 52.
49 MacNutt, *New Brunswick,* 90.
50 Bumstead, "Scottish Immigration," 65–7.
51 Quoted in Rawlyk, *Champions of Truth,* 16.
52 F. Sutherland, "Lot of There, There," 13.
53 Armstrong, *Charlotte Taylor,* 370.
54 Nowlan, "For Jean Vincent D'Abbadie," 162.
55 Tremblay, *David Adams Richards,* 9–11, 33.
56 See Tremblay, "Moving Beyond," 341–3.
57 Hounsell, "Divisive Bilingualism Debate."
58 Fitzpatrick, "New Brunswick," 116.
59 Ibid., 119.
60 Curtis, *Earthly and River Things,* 85–6.
61 Hunt and Campbell, *K.C. Irving,* 153.
62 "Forestry Plan."

63 "Irving Ltd. to Invest $513M."
64 "Forestry Plan."
65 "Irving Clout with Government."
66 Dauphin, "Foresterie." My translation.
67 The question of New Brunswick's fortunes under Confederation continues to be addressed. The latest contributor to the debate is Phillip Buckner in "Beware the Canadian Wolf."
68 F. Sutherland, "Lot of There, There," 12.
69 MacNutt, *New Brunswick*, 144.
70 Levy and Siracusa, *Essays*, 315.
71 MacNutt, *New Brunswick*, 150.
72 Crouzet, "Wars, Blockade."
73 MacNutt, *New Brunswick*, 151.
74 Wynn, "1800–1810," 221.
75 Wynn, *Timber Colony*.
76 Buckner, "The 1860s," 360.
77 Alexander, *Atlantic Canada*, 4.
78 Innis, *Cod Fisheries*, xii–xiii; "Decline," 16–22.
79 Morton, *Kingdom of Canada*, 356, 359.
80 Acheson, "National Policy," 1.
81 See Acheson, ibid., 2–10; Forbes, *Challenging*, 118.
82 Acheson, "National Policy," 5n.6.
83 Alexander, *Atlantic Canada*, 83.
84 Ibid., 46.
85 Savoie, *Visiting Grandchildren*, 31; see also Alexander, *Atlantic Canada*, 68–9.
86 Forbes, *Challenging*, 116.
87 Ibid., 117.
88 Acheson, "National Policy," 13.
89 Forbes, *Challenging*, 119, 120.
90 Ibid., 103.
91 Reid, *Six Crucial Decades*, 164–5.
92 Savoie, *Pulling against Gravity*, 25.
93 Acheson, "National Policy," 18.
94 Ross, "Fort, Fog and Fiddlehead," 119.
95 Frost, "Nationalization," 53.
96 Saunders, *Economic History*, 88.
97 Frank, "Cape Breton," 18–20.
98 Alexander, *Atlantic Canada*, 48.
99 Arseneau, Interview.

100 Lefebvre, *Production of Space*, 325. Italics in original.
101 Ibid., 323.
102 N. Smith, *Uneven Development*, 112.
103 Ibid., 69.
104 Ibid., 4.
105 Savoie, *Harrison McCain*, 271–2.
106 Saul, *Fair Country*, 27.
107 Quoted in Upton, *Micmacs and Colonists*, 165.
108 Francis, *National Dreams*, 9.
109 Quoted in MacFarlane, *Fredericton History*, 35.
110 McCulloch, "Letter IX," 71.
111 Haliburton, "Clockmaker," 10.
112 Haliburton, "Aiming High," 180.
113 Dionne and Cantin, *Bibliographie*, 209–10; C. Roy, "French-Canadian Literature," 467.
114 Bourque and Merkle, "De Evangeline," 129.
115 MacMillan, "Seaward Vision," 84.
116 Carman, "Ships of Saint John," 7, 9.
117 Roberts, "Tantramar Revisited," 58.
118 Montgomery, *Anne of Green Gables*, 29–30.
119 Creelman, *Setting in the East*, 216.
120 See Forbes, *Maritime Rights*, 158–81.
121 Constitution Act, 1867, s. 91.
122 Alexander, *Atlantic Canada*, 73.
123 Acheson, "Introduction," 8.
124 Grove, *Settlers*, 24.
125 Ibid., 27.
126 Grove, *Fruits of the Earth*, 257.
127 Quoted in Forbes, *Challenging*, 59.
128 Ibid., 51.
129 Underhill, *Image of Confederation*, 63.
130 Simpson, "Truth," A7.
131 Flaherty, "No 'Corporate Welfare,'" A4.
132 Barthes, *Mythologies*, 151.
133 Ibid., 148.
134 Ibid., 143.
135 Eagleton, *Marxism*, 6.
136 Barthes, *Mythologies*, 127.
137 Friesen, "Western Canadian Identity," 13–19.
138 Forbes, *Maritime Rights*, 149.

139 Quoted in Carpenter, *Serious Character*, 150.
140 Marquis, "English-Canadian Literature," 558.
141 Ibid., 572.
142 Ibid.
143 Cappon, *Influence*, 1.
144 Ibid., 22–3.
145 Cappon, *Charles G.D. Roberts*, 95.
146 Cappon, *Influence*, 50.
147 Stringer, "Canadians," 3.
148 Hathaway, "Bliss Carman," vii.
149 Bentley, *Confederation Group*, 293.
150 A.J.M. Smith, "Rejected Preface," 7.
151 Brown, *Canadian Poetry*, 53.
152 Ibid., 55, 56, 57.
153 Ibid., 58.
154 Barthes, *Mythologies*, 151.
155 Collin, *White Savannahs*, 3.
156 See Tony Tremblay, "Landscapes of Reception: Historicizing the Travails of the New Brunswick Literary Modernists," in Irvine, Lent, and Vautour, eds., *Making Canada New*, 307–26.
157 Collin, *White Savannahs*, 39.
158 Ibid., 14.
159 Kennedy, "Directions," 14; emphasis added.
160 J. Sutherland, *Essays*, 49.
161 A.J.M. Smith, "Introduction," 31.
162 Pacey, "Bliss Carman," 10.
163 Alexander, *Atlantic Canada*, 74.
164 Bailey, "Guide," 61.

CHAPTER TWO

1 A.G. Bailey, quoted in Toole, "Dr A.G. Bailey," Part I, 5.
2 Ross, "UNB's Bailey."
3 Bailey, "Verse," 55.
4 Ibid.
5 Ibid.
6 Ibid. Bailey's use of the term "eugenic" will undoubtedly raise concerns for contemporary readers. He was using the word, however, in 1927; using it to refer to "the tradition," as his later reading of T.S. Eliot would confirm; and using it long before the Nazis had turned Sir Francis Galton's work into a

doctrine of master and lesser races. Bailey's use of the term, and his later work to locate the place of genius in the rise and fall of historical periods and provincial societies, aligned with Galton's early attempts to think through questions of social and cultural inheritance. For further reading, see Sir Francis Galton, *Hereditary Genius* (London: Macmillan 1869). Also, for a sense of Bailey's turn from Galton, see his well-known essays "Creative Moments in the Culture of the Maritime Provinces" and "Literature and Nationalism after Confederation" in *Culture and Nationality*, 44–57, 58–74.

7 Chaney, *Birth of Missions*, 107–8.
8 Tyler, *History*, 859.
9 Quoted in ibid., 217.
10 Ibid.
11 *Stoddard's Encyclopedia*, 773.
12 Bailey, "Literary Memories," Part I, 2.
13 Ibid., 3; emphasis added.
14 Quoted in Lane, "Interview," 3, 2.
15 Bailey, "Literary Memories," Part II, 20.
16 MacDonald, *Learning to Be Modern*, 72.
17 L.W. Bailey, "Series."
18 C.M. Young, "Bailey," n.p.
19 Pound, ABC *of Reading*, 17–18.
20 Christian, *Parkin*, 10–12.
21 Bailey writes, in imperial fashion, of his great-grandfather: "Joseph Marshall de Brett, 2nd Baron d'Avray, Professor of Modern Languages and Literature in the University of New Brunswick, 1848–1871, son of the Physician Extraordinary to King Ferdinand and Queen Maria Carolina of Naples, and a participant in the events leading to the downfall of Napoleon and the Restoration of the Bourbons to the French Throne" ("Preface," 6n.7). See also Bailey's "Origins of the Study of History in the University of New Brunswick," 9–10.
22 Bailey, "Creative Moments," 55.
23 Quoted in Toole, "Dr A.G. Bailey," Part I, 7.
24 Bailey, "Creative Moments," 56.
25 Bailey, "Colour Chart," 10.
26 Only one of Loring Woart Bailey, Jr's novels is extant, the unpublished *Mixed Society* [c. 1920s]. See Bailey Family Fonds (MG H1. MS3.5.1–3), Archives and Special Collections, Harriet Irving Library, University of New Brunswick.
27 Pierce, "Francis Sherman," 4.
28 Toole, "Dr A.G. Bailey," Part I, 4; A.G. Bailey, "Origins," 14.

29 Bailey, "Literary Memories," Part I, 7; see also Toole, "Dr A.G. Bailey," Part I, 7.
30 MacFarlane, *Fredericton History*, 44.
31 This was the same secondary school that Canadian poet F.R. Scott attended. Though Scott was older than Bailey by six years – in senior form while Bailey was in prep – the families knew each other, as did young Frank and Alfred.
32 Djwa, *Politics of the Imagination*, 32.
33 Bailey, "Lord Beaverbrook," 59.
34 Quoted in Lane, "Interview," 40–1. The story of that trip abroad provides more evidence of a particular way of thinking that influenced Bailey's work and sense of vocation. In the summer of 1926, Bailey and his uncle Joseph Whitman Bailey (1865–1932) travelled to London and Paris to investigate the role that A.G.'s great-grandfather (Joseph Marshall, 1st Baron d'Avray) played in the events leading to Napoleon's downfall and the restoration of the Bourbons to the French throne. It was the kind of voyage that later-generation nobles take to investigate their birthright. Uncle Joseph W. had always been close to A.G. Bailey. The eldest of Laurestine and Loring Woart's children, Joseph was a Boston lawyer, a genealogist, and an author of family biographies and travel books about Europe and the St John River. See A.G. Bailey's "Lord Beaverbrook," 5n.2.
35 Bailey, "Literary Memories," Part I, 3.
36 Bailey, "Need to Hand On," 2.
37 Quoted in letter from Finch to Ian Pearson, 1 December 1933.
38 Bailey's most influential teacher was Claude Thompson, an Oxford graduate, who encouraged his best students to set their sights on a British education. He encouraged Bailey to pursue his literary ambitions.
39 Frank, "The 1920s," 234.
40 Bailey, "Literary Memories," Part I, 15; "Desmond Pacey," 3.
41 Toole, "Dr A.G. Bailey," Part I, 16.
42 Bailey, "Literary Memories," Part I, 15–16.
43 Bailey, ibid., 17–18.
44 Bailey, *Songs of the Saguenay*, 6.
45 Ibid., 21.
46 "Literary Memories," Part I, 15–16; emphasis added.
47 Bailey's hope of pursuing a PhD at Harvard, and thus following his ancestral tradition, was dashed when he was told during an interview that he wouldn't be able to study Canadian history or sociology there because of a lack of supervisory mentorship.
48 Bailey, "Origins," 29.

49 Ibid., 3, 18a.

50 Ibid., 14.

51 Showing Talman's influence, Bailey published a version of an MA paper from his University of Toronto Canadian History class in the *Brunswickan* in 1928 entitled "Early Manifestations of Culture in Upper Canada, 1791–1840." See "Literary Memories," Part I, n.19. Talman's influence is also evident in Bailey's later work, notably the essay "Literature and Nationalism in the Aftermath of Confederation" published in the *University of Toronto Quarterly* (July 1956).

52 Bailey, "Preface," 2.

53 Chester Bailey Martin was yet another in a long line of figures to whom A.G. Bailey felt a special affinity. A native of Saint John, Martin was a graduate of UNB and was North America's first Rhodes scholar. As A.G. Bailey would do at UNB in the late 1930s and 1940s, Martin built a history department from the ground up when he was appointed the first professor of history at the University of Manitoba in 1909. He became head of the History Department at the University of Toronto in 1920, the year before Bailey began his doctoral studies. It was Martin who suggested that Bailey work with Harold Adams Innis and Thomas F. McIlwraith on his study of New World first contact. For more on the University of Toronto and Chester Martin's influence, see Trigger's "Alfred G. Bailey – Ethnohistorian," 3–4.

54 Quoted in Bailey's "Retrospective Thoughts," 17.

55 Ibid., 16; see also Lane, "Interview," 37, and Bailey, "Saint John," 6.

56 McIlwraith (1899–1964) was part-time lecturer at the university as well as keeper of Indian collections at the ROM. He was later hired as the university's first professor of anthropology, teaching the first courses of that kind in Canada. See Bailey, "Retrospective," 14. See also Bruce G. Trigger's account of McIlwriath's study of the Bella Coola Indians of British Columbia, particularly how that study focused Bailey (Trigger, "Alfred G. Bailey – Ethnohistorian," 5).

57 Bailey, "Origins," 28.

58 Bailey, "Retrospective Thoughts," 17.

59 Ibid.

60 For more on Bailey's pioneering work in ethnomethodology, see Bruce G. Trigger's review of *Culture and Nationality* in *American Anthropologist* 77 (September 1975): 636–7, as well as his essay "Alfred G. Bailey – Ethnohistorian" in *Acadiensis*. For more on Bailey's and Innis's methodological influence on what McLuhan and Postman would contribute to media studies, see chapters 2, 3, 4, and 8 of Lance Strate's *Echoes and Reflections: On Media Ecology as a Field of Study* (Cresskill, NJ: Hampton Press 2006).

61   Saul, *A Fair Country*; and Harris, *Making Native Space*.

62   Bailey, "Literary Memories," Part I, 18.

63   Quoted in Toole, "Dr A.G. Bailey," Part I, 17.

64   Bailey met Pierce shortly after arriving in Toronto, their meeting suggested by Bailey's New England cousins who were assisting Pierce with his biographical study of Bliss Carman.

65   Bailey, *Tâo*, 1.

66   McInnis, "Minor Notes," 10.

67   Bailey, "Literary Memories," Part I, 20, 21.

68   Toole, "Dr A.G. Bailey," Part I, 24–5.

69   For a delightful account of how Bailey kept up with issues of the *Canadian Forum*, a journal thought dangerous in royalist Saint John in the 1930s, see Bailey's "Saint John," 28–9.

70   Lane, "Interview," 12–13.

71   Bailey to Malcolm Ross, 21 July 1980.

72   Bailey to Ross, 12 October 1984.

73   See Djwa, *Professing English*, 9. See also Malcolm Ross's "Alfred Goldsworthy Bailey" in the *Dictionary of Literary Biography*, 12.

74   Bailey, "Literary Memories," Part I, 23.

75   Ibid., 24.

76   Williamson, *Reader's Guide*, 59–60.

77   Bailey to Daniells, 1 January 1936.

78   Gibbs, "Portents and Promises," 16.

79   Bailey to Roy Daniells, 30 November 1934.

80   Eliot, *After Strange Gods*, 53.

81   Weber was a German geographer and sociologist who studied patterns of social change in the west. For an articulation of his thought, see Luc-Normand Tellier, "The Weber Problem: Solution and Interpretation," *Geographical Analysis* 4, no. 3 (1972): 215–33.

82   For Bailey's take on Lewis H. Morgan's work, see *The Conflict of European and Eastern Algonkian Cultures, 1504–1700*, 84–6.

83   Eliot, "Tradition," 49.

84   Ibid.

85   Ibid., 50; emphasis added.

86   Ibid.

87   Bailey, "Literary Memories," Part II, 20.

88   Cogswell, "Literary Traditions," 295.

89   Gibbs, "Portents and Promises," 16.

90   Eliot, "Tradition," 52–3.

91   Quoted in Toole, "Dr A.G. Bailey," Part II, 2.

92 Bailey, "Literary Memories," Part I, 26.

93 Bailey, ibid., 31.

94 Pugh, "Alfred Goldsworthy Bailey," 81.

95 Bailey, "Lord Beaverbrook," 6.

96 *Conflict*, xxii–xxiii, 46. For more on Bailey's Marxist experiences, see Lane, "Interview," 11–13; Bailey, "Literary Memories," Part I, 29–32nn.24, 25; and Bailey, "Saint John," 3, 28–9. For his opposition to Marxism as structural system, see "Retrospective Thoughts," 16–17.

97 Bailey to Daniells, 15 August 1934.

98 Bailey, "Preface," 4.

99 Bailey, "Origins," 28; Lane, "Interview," 4.

100 "Preface," 5. Bailey's fullest articulation of this idea is to be found in the essay "Creative Moments in the Culture of the Maritime Provinces," first delivered as a paper in 1949 at a Canadian Humanities Research Council meeting in Halifax. The paper soon after appeared in the *Dalhousie Review* (October 1949), where it received compliments from American historian J.B. Brebner, a professor at Columbia University who was born in Canada. It was later reprinted in Bailey's collection *Culture and Nationality*, 44–57.

101 Bailey, "Preface," 6.

102 Bailey, "Literary Memories," Part II, 21.

103 Bailey, "Origin," 35.

104 "Angel Gabriel," 27.

105 For a sense of the New Brunswick Museum's layout and holdings in the 1930s, see Bailey's "Saint John," 12.

106 Bailey, "Preface," 7.

107 Bailey, "Origins," 1–2; "Saint John," 1–3.

108 Bailey had a long history and fascination with Asia, as the title of his second collection, *Tâo*, indicates. For first-hand accounts of his early exposure to Asian culture, see "Origins," 30–1; "Literary Memories," Part II, 36; "Saint John," 8; and Lane, "Interview," 34. When he was a student at the University of Toronto, he had immersed himself in the Chinese collection at the Royal Ontario Museum. Most practically, he was pursuing his interest in Asian artifacts to prepare for a job at the New Brunswick Museum.

109 Much of my knowledge of Webster comes from George Stanley's essay "John Clarence Webster" in *Acadiensis*. See also A.G. Bailey's account of his "patron" in "Saint John," 10–11.

110 Quoted in Stanley, "John Clarence Webster," 57.

111 Ibid.

112 Bailey, "Saint John," 1–3.

113 Webster to W.F. Ganong, 10 March 1935.

114 Bailey, "Saint John," 3.

115 Harvey, "Intellectual Awakening," 1.

116 Quoted in Lane, "Interview," 17.

117 Slumkoski, "Fair Show," 126. For Bailey's account of Paterson's compact theory, see "Saint John," 20–5. For a discussion of the compact theory that was contemporaneous with Paterson and Bailey, see Roy's "The Compact Theory of the Canadian Constitution." In essence, the theory of a "compact" among signatories to the constitution of the Dominion of Canada moves beyond questions of unanimous consent to considerations of provincial autonomy. Compact theorists like Paterson believed that the provinces had far more power than the Dominion government and the British North American Act allowed, thus pushing against the subordinate status that Dominion legislation conferred.

118 E.R. Forbes suggests that Paterson used Bailey to advance his own reading of history: "Paterson proposed to establish Bailey in a chair of Maritime history directly responsible to the Minister of Education. From this position the incumbent might be expected to produce a suitable version of Canadian history which he would then disseminate at the University and in lectures and study groups throughout the province. As an independent scholar, Bailey was less than enthused" (Forbes, *Challenging*, 56).

119 Paterson to Bailey, 16 June 1936.

120 Quoted in Lane, "Interview," 19.

121 See Bailey's "Saint John," 21.

122 S.C. Scobell to Bailey, 26 February 1944.

123 Peacock, "Report," 9.

124 Ibid., 10.

125 For more information on Ted Campbell and the Saint John art community's influence on Bailey and the literary artists of the period (P.K. Page, John Sutherland, and Kay Smith), see my chapter "Mid-Century Emergent Modernism, 1935–1955" in *New Brunswick at the Crossroads*, 101–27.

126 Larocque, "Fine Intentions," 40.

127 Bailey, "Saint John," 17.

128 Bailey, "Literary Memories," Part II, 10.

129 Quoted in Toole, "Dr A.G. Bailey," Part II, 10.

130 Bailey, "Origins," 2; "Saint John," 8.

131 Bailey to G.A.B. Addy, 13 September 1937.

132 Bailey, "Origins," 3.

133 For an overview of the Webster/MacIntosh feud and its fallout for Bailey, see J.C. Webster's "Report on the Financial Arrangements" and MacIntosh's "Reply, June 21, 1937." See also Bailey's "Saint John," 3–5.

134 Bailey to C.C. Jones, 29 March 1937; Bailey, "Saint John," 25–6.

135 Bailey, "Origins," 5.

136 Bailey to Webster, 4 September 1937.

137 Quoted in D.A. Wright, *Professionalization*, 86.

138 UNB president Jones considered making Bailey's appointment a dual one across history and English, thus establishing a chair of Canadian history and literature. The idea coincided with the acquisition of the Rufus Hathaway Collection of Canadian Literature that had come to UNB in 1933; however, the dual appointment idea was eventually abandoned for more pressing political expediencies. See Bailey, "Origins," 6–8; "History," 3.

139 Quoted in Toole, "Dr A.G. Bailey," Part II, 5.

140 Bailey, "Preface," 4.

141 Quoted in Lane, "Interview," 3.

142 Quoted in ibid., 42.

143 Carman, "Spring Song," 47.

144 Bailey, "Retrospective," 19.

145 Hoyt, *A Brief History*, 55–7.

146 Toole, "Dr A.G. Bailey," Part II, 5.

147 Bailey, "Foreword."

148 Johnson, "Old Provinces," 36.

149 Quoted in Toole, "Dr. A.G. Bailey," Part II, 8.

150 Bailey, "North West Passage," 28.

151 Bailey, "Discourse on Method," 40.

152 Toole, "Dr A.G. Bailey," Part II, 6.

153 Cunningham, quoted in Bailey, "Transcript," 3.

154 Initiated by Fredericton radio station CFNB as part of a series of educational broadcasts given by UNB researchers, the Fiddlehead program was "devoted to the activities of the Poetry Club, as the Bliss Carman Society was often called" (Bailey, "Desmond Pacey," 4). Bailey wrote the script for the broadcast, which included a general statement of the group's aims, and four members, including Bailey, read representative samples of the group's verse. The broadcast was later transcribed as issue 7 of the *Fiddlehead* (December 1947), that release bridging the resignation of first editor Donald Gammon (issue 6) and the instalment of new co-editors Robert Rogers and Fred Cogswell.

155 Quoted in Bailey, "Transcript," 2.

156 Quoted in ibid.

157 Toole, "Dr A.G. Bailey," Part II, 6; Bailey, "Literary Memories," Part II, 5.

158 "In 1886," reports D.M.R. Bentley, "Matthew Arnold famously responded with condescending scorn to a recently published *Primer of American Litera-*

ture: 'Are we to have a *Primer of Canadian Literature* ... These things are not only absurd; they are also retarding'" (17). See Bentley, "Reflections," in Janice Fiamengo, ed., *Home Ground and Foreign Territory: Essays on Early Canadian Literature* (Ottawa: University of Ottawa Press 2014), 17–43.

159 Brown, *On Canadian Poetry*, 14.

160 Ibid., 17.

161 Ibid., 26–7.

162 Ibid., 17.

163 Scott, "Canadian Authors Meet," 70.

164 A.J.M. Smith, "Introduction," 23.

165 Ibid., 5.

166 Bailey was asked, and agreed, to arrange the state funeral for Roberts in New Brunswick.

167 Pomeroy, "Some Books," 12.

168 Ibid., 32.

169 Ibid., 13.

170 Though F.R. Scott published "The Canadian Authors Meet" in 1927 – the poem disparaging the effete and contrived Victorian "society" of letters in Canada, with which Roberts and Carman were closely associated – the aesthetic of the Confederation group lingered nationally and provincially until the early 1940s. In fact, Bailey wrote his first two volumes of poetry in tones and metres reminiscent of Carman.

171 Bailey, "Literary Memories," Part II, 9.

172 A.J.M. Smith, "Introduction," 15.

173 A.J.M. Smith to Bailey, 9 July 1942.

174 Willmott, *Unreal Country*, 153.

175 Son of UNB alumnus, First World War vet, Rhodes scholar, and Saint John lawyer Arthur Carter, Norwood Carter had enlisted in the Royal Navy as a wireless telegrapher and served aboard the frigate *Hallowell*. Like his father (New Brunswick Rhodes scholar for 1913) and older brother Erskine (New Brunswick Rhodes scholar for 1947), he too won a Rhodes scholarship to study at Oxford. Norwood had been one of the promising UNB students – a friend of Elizabeth Brewster – whom Bailey had identified early in his work. He studied English and philosophy at UNB and McGill ("Arthur Norwood Carter").

176 Brewster to Bailey, 26 September 1973.

177 Brewster, "Looking," 15; Bailey, "Desmond Pacey," 3.

178 Elizabeth Brewster wrote in her diary that night that Don Gammon thought Pacey was "radical" and "made rash statements," which she interpreted in a later letter to Bailey as a "youthful effervescence" that was

responding to the general climate of exuberance in the city (Brewster to A.G. Bailey, 13 September 1975).

179 Bailey, "Fiddlehead," 1.
180 Brewster, "Looking Both Ways," 15.
181 Johnson, "Old Provinces," 39–40.
182 Bailey, "Fiddlehead," 1.
183 Bailey to Birney, 22 February 1950.
184 Rogers to Gibbs, 18 December 1952.
185 Moore, "Fiddlehead."
186 Bailey, "Literary Memories," Part II, 21.
187 Ross, "Fort, Fog and Fiddlehead," 118.
188 Whalen, "Atlantic Possibilities," 33–4.
189 Ibid., 33.
190 Ibid., 58.
191 Wyile, *Anne of Tim Hortons*, 234–5.
192 Mill, *On Liberty*, 8.
193 Mullen, "University of New Brunswick," 27.
194 Wade and Lloyd, *Behind the Hill*, 80.
195 Quoted in Toole, "Dr A.G. Bailey," Part II, 25.
196 Bailey, "Faculty of Arts Report," 1.
197 Bailey to Brebner, 23 February 1944.
198 Bailey, "Origins," 23.
199 The Rockefeller Foundation came to Bailey's attention through UNB president Norman MacKenzie's association with members of the foundation's Humanities Division. See Bailey, "History," 8.
200 Bailey, "Origins," 24.
201 Rawlyk, "New Golden Age," 55.
202 Buckner, "Acadiensis," 8.
203 Ibid., 9.
204 Bailey, "History of the UNB Library" 1, 35.
205 Ibid., 11. For clarification of the 1959 end date – most earlier accounts say 1961 – see Bailey, "History," 11.
206 Bailey would eventually go back to Toronto in 1955–56 as Harold Adams Innis Visiting Lecturer. Fittingly, a Rockefeller Foundation grant funded that lectureship. See Bailey, "History of the UNB Library," 24.
207 Founded in 1921 and published continuously since that time, the *Dalhousie Review* is Canada's oldest.
208 Bailey, "Early Foundations," 16.
209 Bailey, "History," 2.
210 Ibid., 6.

211 Quoted in Lane, "Interview," 25; "Retrospective Thoughts," 19.

212 Quoted in Bailey, "Lord Beaverbrook," 50.

213 Bailey, "History," 6.

214 Much of my information on Beaverbrook comes from Bailey's "Lord Beaverbrook."

215 Quoted in Montague, *Pictorial History*, 89.

216 See Bailey, "History," 26–8, for an example of how Donald Gammon, a Beaverbrook scholar, ran afoul of Beaverbrook for not offering the requisite obeisance.

217 Bailey, "History," 12.

218 For more on Beaverbrook's generosity to UNB students, see Montague, *Pictorial History*, 101.

219 "Guide for Assessment."

220 Bailey to Lord Beaverbrook, 17 October 1946.

221 Bailey, "Lord Beaverbrook," 16.

222 Among Bailey's most active former students were Linden Peebles and Robert Rogers, who catalogued the R.B. Bennett Papers and Bailey's own collection of John Clarence Webster and William F. Ganong materials; Eleanor Belyea, who was Bailey's part-time library secretary; Frances Firth, who became manager of UNB's research archives; and Gertrude Gunn, a history student, who followed Bailey as chief librarian in 1959. It was Bailey who encouraged many of these students to enter programs of library science. See Bailey, "History," 24–7, 33–5.

223 Quoted in Lane, "Interview," 29.

224 Beaverbrook and Bailey agreed that the name of the new library should honour both New Brunswick-born prime ministers.

225 Rogers to Bailey, 21 December 1951.

226 Quoted in Bailey, "Lord Beaverbrook," 17.

227 Bailey, "Early Foundations," 15.

228 Quoted in Montague, *Pictorial History*, 112–13.

229 Kent, *Inventing Academic Freedom*, 32–3.

230 MacKenzie to Humphrey, 15 April 1942.

231 Murray, *Daffodils in Winter*, 145, 223, 235.

232 Bailey, "Lord Beaverbrook," 48.

233 Bailey to McNair, 5 June 1947.

234 Bailey to McNair, 19 October 1951.

235 Bailey, "Lord Beaverbrook," 52.

236 Ross, "Ross Notes."

237 "Introduction [MacNaughton]," 8.

238 Ibid.

239 To fund these fellowships, Beaverbrook called on former colleague Jesse Jones of Houston, Texas, a member of Roosevelt's cabinet during the Second World War (Bailey, "Origins," n.24). Beaverbrook and Jones sat next to each other in Roosevelt and Churchill's war room.
240 Bailey, "Verse," 55.
241 "Early Foundations," 15.
242 Bailey to Murray, 18 March 1948.
243 Milton, *Areopagitica*, 206; quoted in Bailey, "Fiddlehead," 1947, 72.
244 Watt, "Letters in Canada," 442.
245 Bailey, "Faculty of Arts Report," 5.
246 Bailey, "Need," 1.
247 Quoted in Beck, *Joseph Howe*, 25.
248 Alexander, *Atlantic Canada*, 74.
249 Anderson, *Imagined Communities*, 202.
250 Quoted in MacMechan, *Headwaters*, 46.
251 Bailey, "Saint John," 9–10.
252 Bailey, "Reflections," 186.

CHAPTER THREE

1 A.J.M. Smith, "Wanted: Canadian Criticism," 32–3.
2 Daniells to Pacey, 3 September 1958.
3 Pacey to Dudek, 9 November 1973.
4 Smith, "Introduction," 29.
5 "Style," 1.
6 Ibid., 3, 4.
7 Ibid., 2.
8 Ibid.
9 Ibid., 3.
10 Ibid., 4.
11 Ibid.
12 Pacey to Dudek, 9 November 1973.
13 For a consideration of this topocentrism, see Surette's "Here Is Us."
14 Cogswell, "Nineteenth Century Poetry," 16.
15 MacMechan, *Headwaters*, 103.
16 Ibid., 104.
17 Blodgett, *Five Part Invention*, 56.
18 Stevenson, *Appraisals*, 12.
19 Smith, *Book*, 436.
20 Brown, *On Canadian Poetry*, 53.

21 Ibid., 25.
22 Ibid., 58.
23 Smith, "Introduction," 31.
24 Bailey, "Foreword."
25 Bailey, "Tradition," 49.
26 Eliot, "Euripides," 74.
27 Bailey's discomfort with Smith's representation, and in some cases rejection, of nineteenth-century Canadian poets was an extension of tensions that had first surfaced publicly in the pages of the *Canadian Forum* in 1928. Smith's rejection of earlier poets in the article "Wanted: Canadian Criticism" (April 1928) was rebutted by F.R. Scott in the June 1928 number of the same magazine. The scenario was replayed, and the tensions kept alive, when Smith and Scott co-edited *New Provinces: Poems of Several Readers* (1936). The Toronto modernists E.J. Pratt and Robert Finch, both close friends of Bailey, objected to Smith's preface to that anthology, as did Scott, threatening to pull their work out if Smith's preface stood. Their objection centred again on Smith's dismissal of older Canadian poets and more specifically on his disdain for what he termed "the Georgian," by which he meant hyper-symmetry and ordered regularity of form, and a late-Romantic pastoral sensibility that looked backward instead of forward. In Canada, the Georgian style was associated most closely with the tastes and poetic manners of the Loyalists, among whose number were the Fredericton Confederation poets. When *New Provinces* was released in 1936, Smith's preface had been replaced by a shorter one written by Scott.
28 Bailey, "Address," 2.
29 Ibid., 3.
30 Ross's opposition to the war was perhaps perceived as a potential source of tension at UNB, where the decorated war veteran Milton F. Gregg, VC, was the new president.
31 MacKenzie to MacLennan, 1 April 1943.
32 MacLennan to McCourt, 26 July 1944.
33 Quoted in Cameron, *Hugh MacLennan*, 185.
34 Stirling, "Count Almaviva," 797.
35 When his mother's cancer took a particularly worrisome turn years later, Pacey wrote to her about his "faith in God's mercy and love" and sought to comfort her with memories of their bond. He said, "I remember those evenings in New Zealand when you read to me about David and Goliath, our bicycle rides together along the roads of Oxfordshire and Cambridgeshire, walks back to the bush in Glanford – and all these [memories] are

bathed in love and the sense of deep security which came from having you with me" (2 December 1958).

36 The little that is known about Desmond Pacey's ancestry is found in clippings and correspondence in the W.C.D. Pacey Fonds at the Harriet Irving Library, University of New Brunswick, from which some of the biographical content in this chapter comes (specifically, MG LI, Series 1 and 2). Unlike A.G. Bailey, Pacey expended very little energy exploring and recording his ancestry, or passing it along to his children.

37 Pacey, "On Becoming a Canadian," 3.

38 "Magnus Speech Day."

39 "On Becoming a Canadian," 1.

40 Ibid., 1–2.

41 Ibid., 2.

42 Ibid., 4.

43 Though the title is actually a fragment from a line of Arthur Hugh Clough's poem "Say Not the Struggle Nought Availeth" – "In front the sun climbs slow, how slowly / But westward, look, the land is bright" (206) – both Clough's poem and Pacey's title impart the same sense of forward optimism. Arthur Clough's work was important to Pacey's mother, for the English poet was an assistant to nurse Florence Nightingale and the brother of suffragist Anne Clough, who became principal of the women-only Newnham College, Cambridge, alma mater of a number of the leading feminists and intellectuals of the last two centuries. It is likely that Mary Pacey introduced Clough's work to her son.

44 Hicks, "General Letter of Reference," 23 January 1934.

45 Victoria College federated with the University of Toronto in 1890.

46 Pacey, "Field of Oats," 106.

47 Quoted in Slater, *Minerva's Aviary*, 262.

48 Ayre, *Northrop Frye*, 94.

49 In his senior year, Pacey spoofed Frye in the welcoming "Bob Party" for incoming freshman. The annual Victoria College ritual consisted of witty sketches and spoofs of Pratt, Edgar, Robins, and other popular figures.

50 Sissons, *Nil Alienum*, 45.

51 Ayre, *Northrop Frye*, 70.

52 Frye, "Editor's Introduction," x.

53 Edgar, "Literary Criticism," 118.

54 Ibid., 77.

55 Ibid., 127.

56 Ibid., 120.

57 Pacey to Daniells, 2 August 1944.
58 Djwa, *Politics of the Imagination*, 132–40.
59 Quoted in Friedland, *University of Toronto*, 335.
60 For a useful overview of "social Christianity" in a mid-century Canadian context, see Christie and Gauvreau, *Christian Churches*, 142–78.
61 Ibid., 153, 176.
62 Quoted in Friedland, *University of Toronto*, 336.
63 Allen, *Social Passion*, 302–5.
64 Christie and Gauvreau, *Christian Churches*, 74.
65 Arnold, *Culture and Anarchy*, 169.
66 Ibid., 172.
67 Ibid., 173.
68 Ibid., 175.
69 Ibid., 34.
70 Ibid., 176.
71 Daniells, quoted in Djwa, *Politics of the Imagination*, 136.
72 Arnold, *Culture and Anarchy*, 5.
73 Quoted in Ayre, *Northrop Frye*, 114.
74 Quoted in ibid., 77.
75 Pacey, "On Becoming a Canadian," 4.
76 Pacey, "At Last," 146.
77 Ibid., 146.
78 Ibid., 147.
79 Ibid.
80 Brown, *On Canadian Poetry*, 27. Pacey would eventually find the source of this idea in W.B. Yeats, his favourite modernist poet, using Yeats's lines as inscription for *Essays in Canadian Criticism, 1938–1968*: "Cosmopolitan literature is, at best, but a poor bubble, though a big one. Creative work has always a fatherland. There is no fine nationality without literature, and ... no fine literature without nationality" (n.p.). See Yeats, *Letters to the New Island*, ed. George Bornstein and Hugh Witemeyer (New York: Macmillan 1989), 12.
81 Pacey to A.J.M. Smith, 27 December 1943.
82 Desmond Pacey to Mary Pacey [mother], 2 February 1937.
83 Pacey held a Massey Overseas Fellowship in 1938–39 and 1940–41.
84 For more on Brown's primary interest in French culture, see Groening's *E.K. Brown*, 20–39.
85 Pacey to Daniells, 22 November [1938].
86 Edgar, "Literary Criticism," 123, 124–6.
87 Two months earlier, Pacey lost a close competition with Henry Noyes for an

assistant professor position at the University of Missouri. Both close to Roy Daniells, Noyes and Pacey knew each other at the University of Toronto, where Noyes graduated with an English degree in 1936. Then, during the latter part of his first year at Brandon, Pacey was offered a position at St John's College in Winnipeg. He turned the position down because St John's president, Canon Sidney Seeley, couldn't match his Brandon salary.

88 Pacey to Daniells, 20 May 1940.

89 Pacey's poem in the first number of the *Fiddlehead* articulates an essential link between himself and Grove that was likely an early point of interest for Pacey. That link was an existential loneliness that both experienced in Canada. Pacey's poem opens with an image of a forlorn soul, perhaps Grove himself, lost in the vastness of Prairie space:

> North, south, east, west the prairies stretch and fade
> Under the web of twilight.
> Across the waste of stubble, alien, alone,
> Moves the stooped figure of a man.
> Far is the homeland, near the night,
> And all around him in a narrowing ring
> Slink the white wolves of silence and fear.
> (Pacey, "Prairie Episode," 3)

90 After the radio broadcast, Pacey continued his work on Grove. He initially expanded his radio talk into an article for the *Manitoba Arts Review* in 1943, then got to work in earnest on a Grove book, which was published as *Frederick Philip Grove: A Biographical and Critical Study* in 1945. Encyclopedia entries on Grove for *Encyclopedia Canadiana* (1956) and *Encyclopedia Britannica* (1961) followed, as did the consensus that Pacey was the authority on the accomplished prairie author. Pacey's authority and confidence were severely shaken, however, with the publication of Douglas O. Spettigue's *Frederick Philip Grove* in 1969 and *FPG: The European Years* in 1973, as well as Margaret Stobie's *A Critical Study of Frederick Philip Grove* (1973). Undaunted, Pacey forged ahead with his response to Grove's "con job," continuing his work on Grove up to his death. His *Frederick Philip Grove: Critical Views of Canadian Writers* appeared in 1970, followed by editions of Grove's short stories (*Tales from the Margin*, 1971) and the posthumously published letters (*The Letters of Frederick Philip Grove*, 1976). A useful gloss to the problem that Grove's self-created identity posed for critics, especially Pacey, can be found in Paul Hjartarson's "Design and Truth in Grove's 'In Search of Myself,'" *Canadian Literature* 90 (autumn 1981): 73–90.

91 Woodcock, "Valedictions," 4.

92 For an assessment of Frye's time ministering in Saskatchewan, see Ayre's *Northrop Frye*, 95–104.

93 Grierson to Pacey, 10 December 1943.

94 Pacey, "Humanities in Canada," 356.

95 Ibid., 354.

96 See Christie and Gauvreau, *Christian Churches*, 175–7.

97 Pacey, "Humanities in Canada," 360.

98 The abbreviations stand for Social Sciences and Humanities Research Council of Canada, Association of Canadian University Teachers of English, Maritime Provinces Higher Education Commission, and Atlantic Canada Studies.

99 Pacey, "Humanities in Canada," 357.

100 Ibid.

101 Ibid., 358.

102 Pacey to Daniells, 7 August 1944.

103 Pacey, "Penetrating Analysis," 24.

104 Quoted in Wiens, "Horses of Realism," 187.

105 Pacey, "Literary Criticism," 117.

106 Pacey, *Frederick Philip Grove*, 139.

107 Quoted in Verduyn, *Dear Marian*, 42.

108 Cogswell, "Desmond Pacey," 8.

109 Pacey to Roy Daniells, 29 September 1944.

110 Desmond Pacey to Mary Pacey [spouse], 21 September 1944.

111 Ibid.

112 Pacey to Daniells, 29 September 1944.

113 Ibid.

114 Ibid.

115 Pacey to Mary Pacey, 21 September 1944.

116 Pacey to Mary Pacey, 30 October 1944. Pacey proposed a similar initiative fifteen years later when he sought support from Canadian writers for "The Sir Charles G.D. Roberts Prize" for the best short story written by a Canadian undergraduate student (Pacey to Ronald Everson, 25 May 1959).

117 A.G. Bailey had written and sung the official "UNB Anthem" around 1942. See Montague, *A Pictorial History*, 46, 159.

118 Pacey to Mary Pacey, 30 October 1944.

119 Pacey to Mary Pacey, 28 September 1944. Further evidence of Pacey's sense of belonging to UNB is found throughout the 1950s, first when Louis Dudek, ironically, invites him to apply for the position Hugh MacLennan receives at McGill in 1951, and also in 1953 when he is wooed by Memorial University to head its English Department. In 1957 he is again lobbied, this

time to replace Lorne Pierce at Ryerson Press. After many months of reflection, Pacey writes the following to his parents about replacing Pierce: "I feel that I should be much happier in a university than in a publishing house. I have come to identify myself with the ideals and purposes of the university, I feel I belong, and that sense of belonging to something in which you sincerely belong is worth more than money" (Pacey to Mary and Ben Bolton, 16 December 1957).

120 Pacey, "The Novel in Canada," 326.

121 Ibid., 323; emphasis added.

122 Ibid., 325.

123 Ibid.

124 Frye, "Preface," ii.

125 Pacey, "The Novel in Canada," 328.

126 Pacey, *Creative Writing*, 103.

127 Pacey, "Plea for the Study," 4.

128 Bailey, "Literary Memories," Part II, 21.

129 Pacey, "The Novel in Canada," 330.

130 Ibid., 329.

131 Pacey, "Penetrating Analysis," 25.

132 Brown, *On Canadian Poetry*, 17.

133 It would be as sorter and classifier that Pacey was remembered, even among those with whom he most frequently quarrelled. In a letter to Fred Cogswell, Louis Dudek praised Pacey "for his usefulness as a literary historian [and] surveyor" (4 June 1962).

134 With Raymond Knister's *Canadian Short Stories* (1928), Pacey's anthology was only the second such anthology of prose fiction in the country. Ralph Gustafson's *Canadian Accent* (1944) was a collection of stories and poems.

135 Pacey, *Book of Canadian Stories*, xi; emphasis added.

136 Pacey, "Plea for the Study," 3.

137 Pacey to Frye, 18 June 1947.

138 Pacey, *Book of Canadian Stories*, xviii.

139 Woodcock, "Great Impresario," 29. For more insight into the differences between Frye and Pacey, see Davey's "Desmond Pacey" and Kokotailo's "Manifold Division," especially 2–3.

140 Though he regretted that the anthology did not have the room, and English Canadians the capacity, to accommodate French content, he did write frequently of French Canadian authors in his articles. See, in particular, "Canada's Poets and Prose Writers" and "A Plea for the Study of Our Own Literature."

141 Gerson, "*Anne of Green Gables*," 20. A more generous assessment of Pacey would note that he also wrote favourable things about Montgomery, such as

the fact that "she created the famous Anne of Green Gables, a character like-ly to live much longer than the people in books far more pretentious" ("Canada's Poets and Prose Writers," 5110). It might also take note of the fact that, in consideration of his promotion of women's writing in Canada, Pacey was appointed chair of Status of Women Committee of the Associa-tion of Universities and Colleges of Canada in 1974. Terminal illness limit-ed his work on the committee.

142　Quoted in Ayre, *Northrop Frye*, 75.

143　Pacey, *Book of Canadian Stories*, xx.

144　Ibid., xxv.

145　Ibid., xxviii.

146　Ibid., xxxii.

147　Ibid., 25. Pacey was no less harsh in his assessment of R.E. Watters for induction into the Royal Society of Canada. "I regard him as a most useful and estimable person," wrote Pacey to Father Joseph Owens, RSC secretary, "but as one who lacks just that touch of distinction that a fellow of the Society should have" (2 December 1969).

148　In a letter to Pacey about his rejection of an article by Pacey for the *University of Toronto Quarterly* (on the contemporary Canadian novel), Philip Child, an editor and Canadian novelist, scolded Pacey for his harsh criticism, con-trasting "positive criticism" and "negative criticism," the former "vital if Canadian literature is to be helped" (15 August 1945).

149　Pacey to Pierce, 8 November 1954.

150　Pacey, *Book of Canadian Stories*, xxxvi.

151　Moore, "Theatre," 76.

152　Pacey, "Areas of Research" [1953], 58.

153　Bailey, "Here in the East," 28.

154　For more on Pacey's interest in the republicanism of early Maritime authors, see his essay "The Goldsmiths and Their Villages," especially his contrast of Haliburton and the younger Goldsmith (34).

155　Quoted in Wiens, "Horses of Realism," 186.

156　Purdy to Pacey, [1960?].

157　Pacey to Daniells, 5 June 1945.

158　Pacey to Dudek, 4 February 1953.

159　Pacey to Pierce, [8] May 1947.

160　Ibid.

161　English Department.

162　Pacey to A.W. Thomson, 30 December 1965. In his draft for "The Outlook for Canadian Literature" (1968), Pacey states that "there is dawning a recognition [in the United Kingdom] of the fact that if the Commonwealth is to survive at all it will be as a cultural and social entity rather than as a political and military one. The study of Commonwealth literature is an obviously important element in this *entente*" (5). Though he would modify that statement in the final submission to *Canadian Literature*, he did continue to stress the development of a "Commonwealth cultural entente" (19). Also important at the time of the article was that the Modern Language Association had formed a Commonwealth Literature group to reflect the growing popularity of the study of the Commonwealth at universities in the United States, and that a new Institute of Commonwealth Literature was established at Leeds University. Special issues of the *Times Literary Supplement* and other leading periodicals also focused on the Commonwealth.

163 Pacey's best students formed the nucleus of the English and other UNB departments in the 1950s, 1960s, and 1970s. Some of those students included Fred Cogswell, Robert Gibbs, Allan Donaldson, Robert Hawkes, and William Prouty. Because of Beaverbrook's closeness to UNB, many of Bailey's and Pacey's students received Beaverbrook Overseas Scholarships to fund their graduate work at British universities. Beaverbrook's money, then, was leveraged by Pacey in ways similar to how it was leveraged by Bailey. See Pacey's 3 March 1954 letter to UNB president Colin B. Mackay for concrete evidence of this practice. Also significant was that Pacey's appointed colleagues (former students) were, like him, creative writers as well as critics. One of his governing beliefs was that literary criticism benefited directly from creative practice.

164 Pacey to Daniells, 4 December 1957.

165 The exchange between Pacey and Daniells about their department's PhD plans reveals an interesting side to Pacey, who was critical of the American system of PhD coursework: "Don't you think that all this coursework smothers the creative imagination, and that there is much to be said for the British system whereby the emphasis is placed on the thesis as a piece of truly original research or criticism?" (Pacey to Daniells, 13 December 1957).

166 Pacey, "Humanist Tradition," 67.

167 Pacey, "Literary Criticism," 119.

168 Ibid., 115.

169 A rare display of Pacey's self-censoring reductionism (even when he tries, his attempts to reduce Canada meet his own unconscious opposition) can be found in the second part of his essay "Two Accents, One Voice." In that essay he writes that Canada is British in loyalty, northern in sensibility, and American in optimism for the future, a rather safe and general reduction but as far as he would go in declaring distinctiveness.

170 Pacey, *Creative Writing in Canada*, 7.
171 Pacey, "Two Accents," 51.
172 Pacey to A.J.M. Smith, 17 March 1955.
173 Pacey to Lower, 2 April 1962.
174 Pacey's repurposed article "A Garland for Bliss Carman" (1961) was another effort at reputational remediation. It was deliberately published in the *Atlantic Advocate* so that it would reach a regional audience.
175 Pacey, "Introduction" [1955], xix.
176 Pacey to Rhodenizer, 11 February 1954.
177 Ibid.
178 Pacey, "Contemporary Writing in New Brunswick," 6.
179 Pacey, "Penetrating Analysis," 25.
180 Pacey, "English-Canadian Poetry," 65.
181 Pacey, *Creative Writing*, 236.
182 Bailey to Pacey, 11 December 1955.
183 At the same time as he was dressing down Dudek, however, Pacey was also promoting his importance to Canadian literature, submitting a formal application to elect Dudek to membership in the Royal Society of Canada in 1969. The apparent contradiction is informative. Pacey sometimes quarrelled publicly with his peers, but he also promoted their interests, more often than not displaying much private affection for them. His countless letters of reference for colleagues whom he opposed publicly point to this fact. When it came to matters of professional discernment, he was unrelenting, taking aim at colleagues, friends, and even mentors. While that sharpness rarely influenced how he felt about people, it did affect how others saw him.
184 Pacey, Review of *The Making of Modern Poetry*, 91, 92.
185 Bennett, "Conflicted Vision," 142.
186 Kokotailo, "Manifold Division," 5–6.
187 Pacey, *Creative Writing*, 3. Emphasis in original.
188 Pacey, Review of *The Making of Modern Poetry*, 94.
189 Tippett, "Writing of English-Canadian Cultural History," 558.
190 Davey, "Desmond Pacey," 229.
191 Pacey to Mackay, 22 November 1955.
192 Minutes [of the First Meeting].
193 Atlantic Canada English Language Arts Curriculum, 166.
194 Patterson, "New Brunswick Renaissance," 40.
195 Report on Visits.
196 Daniells to Pacey, 26 December 1962.
197 Pacey to Mackay, 5 April 1965.

198 Pacey's correspondence is rife with letters inviting Canadian writers to apply for the position of writer-in-residence at UNB. To replace Norman Levine for the 1966/67 year, for example, Pacey invited Brian Moore, Raymond Souster, Earle Birney, Gabrielle Roy, Dorothy Livesay, Ernest Buckler, Yves Thériault, and Miriam Waddington. Livesay was selected.

199 Pacey to Mackay, 23 September 1964.

200 Pacey, "Young Writer," 1.

201 Ibid., 11.

202 Ibid., 7.

203 Pacey to Reaney, 10 March 1960.

204 Pacey, "Outlook for Canadian Literature," 24.

205 Ibid., 15.

206 Pacey to Mary and Ben Bolton, 16 December 1957.

207 Pacey to Daniells, 13 December 1973.

208 Bailey to Frye, 28 July 1965.

209 Pacey to Daniells, 19 November 1969.

210 Klinck, *Giving Canada a Literary History*, 131.

211 Frye, "Desmond Pacey," 1.

212 Ibid., 3.

213 Bailey, "Desmond Pacey," 4.

CHAPTER FOUR

1 Cogswell, "On Canadian Poets," 11.

2 Nowlan, "First Impressions [of Fred Cogswell]," 16.

3 Cogswell, "Literary Traditions," 287.

4 Ibid., 296.

5 Bailey, "Foreword."

6 For a more comprehensive and detailed biography, see my *Cogswell*. Much of the information in this section of the chapter on Fred Cogswell is derived from my personal interviews with him (March, April, May 2002, Fredericton), with his daughter Kathleen Forsythe (June 2010, January 2015, Vancouver), and with Cogswell's first cousin Geneva King (August 2015, Alberton, PEI).

7 A. Roy, *Bulletin*, 300.

8 Andrew, "Development of Elites," 277.

9 Bourque and Richard, *Conventions Nationales*, 334.

10 Jameson, *Cogswells in America*, xvi, xxi.

11 Bushman, "Cultural Orientations," 7, 11.

12 Cogswell, "New Brunswick," 16.

13 Cogswell, "Valley-Folk," 1.
14 Quoted in Bauer, "Fred Cogswell," 35.
15 Hartland *Observer*, 19 June 1952, 6.
16 Nowlan to Cogswell, 22 March 1963.
17 "Smallpox Warning," 1.
18 Camp, *Gentlemen, Players and Politicians*, 32.
19 "Local News," 5.
20 Griffiths, "Acadians," 132; Frank, "1920s," 268.
21 Surette, "Les Acadiens et la campagne," 203–5.
22 Aunger, *In Search*, 72–3; Knights of the Ku Klux Klan, Circular.
23 Cogswell, "Moses Hardy Nickerson," 474.
24 Ibid.
25 Ibid.
26 The brand of Baptist orthodoxy that Cogswell inherited still saw itself as a radical departure from establishment Catholicism and Protestantism.
27 Cogswell, "Valley-Folk," 1.
28 Cogswell, "The Double-Headed Child," 12. An early conceptualization of this poem was published in the *Fiddlehead* under the title "Lyric." Cogswell wrote it as follows:

> I could not tear down the walls that hemmed me in.
> For every stone I dropped a hundred hands
> Sprang up to put it back in place again.
>
> At last I asked those willing workers:
> "Know you not that when these walls are razed
> You will be free?" "This place is safe," they said,
> "Against the rocs and unicorns outside." (119)

29 Cogswell, "Singing Fool," 92.
30 William Langland's *Piers Plowman* stayed with Cogswell for the remainder of his life. In 1969 Cogswell published *Immortal Plowman* as a testament to Langland's sustaining vision.
31 Bailey, quoted in Toole, "Dr A.G. Bailey," Part II, 2.
32 Galloway, "scl Interviews," 209.
33 Cogswell, "Canadian Novel," 216.
34 Quoted in Montague, *Pictorial History*, 56.
35 Koo's 1912 dissertation at Columbia was appropriately titled "The Status of Aliens in China."
36 Burt, Powell, and Crow, "V.K. Wellington Koo," 53.
37 Cogswell, "It Began in 1935," 42.
38 Ibid.

39 Ibid., 41.

40 Ibid., 42.

41 Ibid.

42 The parallel of Cogswell's experience to Northrop Frye's, and at almost the same age, is uncanny. Frye recalls: "Suddenly that whole shitty and smelly garment [of fundamentalist teaching I had all my life] just dropped off into the sewers and stayed there. It was like the Bunyan feeling, about the burden of sin falling off his back only with me it was a burden of anxiety ... I just remember that suddenly that that was no longer a part of me and would never be again" (quoted in Ayre, *Northrop Frye*, 44). The parallel of this experience in two leading New Brunswick authors warrants further study of the saturation of evangelical Christianity in New Brunswick, particularly among its precocious youth. Rawlyk's *Champions of Truth* is a useful place to begin that study.

43 Quoted in Hatt, "Fred Cogswell," 39.

44 Tweedie, *On with the Dance*, 11.

45 Quoted in Folster, "Seeds Planted," 4.

46 Cogswell, "Little Magazines," 162–3.

47 "Origins and Evolution," 14.

48 Gregg, "Confidential Memo."

49 Camp, "Alexander College," 183.

50 Macquarrie, *Red Tory Blues*, 72.

51 Montague, *Pictorial History*, 112.

52 Camp, "Alexander College," 183.

53 Innis, "A Plea."

54 Dalton Camp and Fred Cogswell were well acquainted with one another, having attended UNB at the same time, having taught together, and having received attention as two of the university's most promising students. Also, both were from the upper St John River valley, Camp having grown up in Woodstock. Visible on campus because of his editorials in the *Brunswickan* and his support of UNB president Milton F. Gregg as Liberal candidate in the 1947 York-Sunbury by-election, Camp was decidedly Liberal in his politics at the time, a leaning that was noted by Premier John B. McNair's chief of staff, Robert Tweedie, in 1946 (Stevens, *The Player*, 64–5; Tweedie, *On with the Dance*, 79). Both affable and intelligent, Camp became Cogswell's fast friend at Alexander College, at least until they found themselves working for different candidates in the 1947 by-election (Camp for the Liberal Gregg and Cogswell for the CCFer Murray Young). When Camp learned that Cogswell had joined Young's election team, he walked up to Cogswell in the dining hall of the Lady Beaverbrook residence and exclaimed, "I can

no longer have the luxury to call you a friend" (Cogswell to Tony Tremblay, 3 October 2003). Camp's later swerve to the right to support Hugh John Flemming for Conservative premier of New Brunswick in the 1952 provincial election further alienated Cogswell, who had already vowed to avoid politics. For more on Camp's time at UNB, and as a Liberal, see Camp's *Gentlemen, Players and Politicians*, Tweedie's *On with the Dance*, and Stevens's *The Player*.

55 Camp, "Alexander College," 184.

56 Quoted in G. Stevens, *The Player*, 51.

57 Quoted in Mullen, "University of New Brunswick," 34–5.

58 Cogswell, "Ode to Fredericton," 35.

59 Mullen, "University of New Brunswick," 27.

60 Ibid., 28.

61 MacKay, *Rebels*, 45.

62 Galloway, "SCL Interviews," 210.

63 Tweedie, *On with the Dance*, 79.

64 Cogswell to Tremblay, 3 October 2003.

65 Quoted in Macquarrie, *Red Tory Blues*, 71.

66 "Outlines By-Election Issues," 7.

67 Flemming, "Reviews Political Situation," 11.

68 Cogswell, "How Can I Say ...?" 43.

69 For A.G. Bailey's account of this, see his poem "Angel Gabriel" and the notes accompanying that poem in *Thanks for a Drowned Island* (26–7, 94). The poem is essential for understanding Bailey's ideas of ancestry. It was published in *Wascana Review* in 1969.

70 Bailey, "Angel Gabriel," 26.

71 Lane, "Muskrat in His Brook," 97.

72 Bailey, "Angel Gabriel," 27.

73 "Lt.-Gen. Sansom," 10.

74 Cogswell to Tremblay, 3 October 2003. When fellow UNB student Gérard La Forest won the Rhodes that year, Cogswell called to congratulate him. La Forest was also an Upper St John River valley boy – from Grand Falls. La Forest explained on the phone that his Liberalism had been the focus of genial discussion during the interview, the dynastic Liberalism that felt so threatened by Cogswell's CCF leanings (interview with author, April 2002).

75 Cogswell to Pacey, 5 January 1950.

76 Cogswell to Bailey, 14 November 1950.

77 Cogswell to Bailey, 20 September 1951.

78 Cogswell to Bailey, 2 June 1950.

79 Cogswell's interest in French literature was sparked by a course from David

Galloway that surveyed French poetry from André Chénier to Arthur Rimbaud. See Cogswell's letter to Phyllis Webb, 19 October 1955.

80 Cogswell to Tremblay, [23] September 2003.

81 Bailey, "Desmond Pacey," 4.

82 Quoted in Galloway, "SCL Interviews," 211.

83 Quoted in Zanes, "Where the Fiddleheads Grow," 71.

84 Ibid., 72–4. Bailey's influence would stay with Cogswell right up to the point when he took on the permanent editorship of the *Fiddlehead* in 1953. In an editorial response to a poem that Blanche Muirhead Howard sent to the *Fiddlehead*, Cogswell wrote: short poems should carry their meaning "by the choice and arrangement of concrete evocative images or by traditional denotative statement so exact and neat as to be epigrammatic" (Cogswell to B.M. Howard, [November 1952]).

85 Cogswell, "Prisms," 37.

86 Smith, "Introduction," 29.

87 Emerson, "Nature," 13.

88 Cogswell, "Prisms," 37.

89 Cogswell, "The Man Who Climbed," 39.

90 Buckler, *Mountain and the Valley*, 294.

91 Ibid., 7.

92 Quoted in Hatt, "Fred Cogswell," 40. Cogswell further qualified this notion of upbringing in his article on Moses Hardy Nickerson, writing that "Nickerson found his philosophy ["Christian ethics," "good health," and "optimism"] in Darwin and in other writers because it was in himself first. Not realizing this, he believed that it had been determined from his reading and thinking" ("Moses Hardy Nickerson," 480). Cogswell would come to accept, though at first reluctantly, the same imprinting from his Baptist upbringing, believing that it, and not reading, had given him his advantages.

93 Cogswell, "The Mill," 39.

94 Cogswell, "Conclusion," 50.

95 Cogswell, "Acceptance," 52.

96 Cogswell, "For an Artist," 217.

97 In style, statement, and execution, Cogswell's survey of the Canadian novel from Confederation to the First World War also anticipates and models the sweep of Pacey's essays of the 1950s, especially "Literary Criticism in Canada" (1950), "Areas of Research in Canadian Literature" (1953), "English-Canadian Poetry, 1944–54" (1954), and "The Canadian Writer and His Public, 1882–1952" (1956). Cogswell was later annoyed that Pacey borrowed liberally from his work, despite the fact that he had invited it. In a letter to Pacey on 5 January 1950, Cogswell wrote: "Anything you may find in my

thesis that is of any help to you, you are welcome to use. That is what theses are for." The mature scholar would come to regret what the novice allowed.

98 Cogswell, Introduction, 1.

99 Ibid.

100 Cogswell was one of the first critics in Canada to note the importance of Sara Jeannette Duncan. He introduced her in his thesis as employing "a good prose style, a sense of form acquired through the study of the best American and British models ... acute moral perception, freedom from sentiment and a cosmopolitan outlook" ("The Canadian Novel," 6).

101 Cogswell, Introduction, 3.

102 Cogswell, "The Canadian Novel," 218.

103 Pacey, *Book of Canadian Stories*, xi.

104 Cogswell, "Way of the Sea," 375.

105 Ibid., 379.

106 Ibid.

107 Ibid., 374.

108 Cogswell, "The Canadian Novel," 216.

109 More on Cogswell's views of puritanism can be found in his 1961 article "Nineteenth Century Poetry in the Maritimes and Problems of Research" and in his chapter "The Development of Writing" (25).

110 Cogswell, "Nineteenth Century Poetry," 17, 18.

111 Ibid., 18.

112 Cogswell, "Development of Writing," 25. A few years before that important 1961 article came out, Cogswell wrote to Robert McDougall that "the greatest creative moment in Nova Scotia in the nineteenth century was not politics, as many suppose, but religion" (Cogswell to McDougall, 16 June 1958).

113 Cogswell, "Statement of Position," 96.

114 Cogswell to Pacey, 5 January 1950. That view of catholicity, ironically, challenged the secular bias of the *Fiddlehead*'s editorial board, which was initially wary of Cogswell's poem "The Cross of Conformity." In Cogswell's view, a healthy catholicity should be as open to religious expression as to secular expression. Cogswell's poem eventually appeared in issue sixteen of the *Fiddlehead* (November 1952).

115 Cogswell, "On Canadian Poets," 11.

116 Cogswell to Gammon, 26 July 1950.

117 Though he didn't win a Rhodes scholarship, Cogswell was accepted at Oxford just the same. He also was accepted at the universities of Leeds, London, and Edinburgh (Cogswell to Bailey, 25 May 1950).

118 Cogswell to Bailey, 16 August 1951.

119 Quoted in letter from Cogswell to Bailey, 18 February 1951.

120 Cogswell to Pacey, 5 January 1950.

121 Grader, *Life of Sir Walter Scott*, 136-40.

122 Bailey to Malcolm Ross, 12 March 1977.

123 To that end, Cogswell was able to write: "The British government provided the Loyalist colony [in New Brunswick] with a more generous supply of capital than that received by any previous British colony. This aid distributed among 12,000 people – and augmented by what remained of the private fortunes of some Loyalists and by the pensions of discharged soldiers – was sufficient to enable a differentiated culture to survive its transplanting" ("Development of Writing," 22).

124 Cogswell, however, also thought that Grove's *Fruits of the Earth* and *Search for America* were better novels than *Master of the Mill*. See his article "New Canadian Library" in *Edge* 2 (spring 1964): 125.

125 Galt, *Annals of the Parish*, 66.

126 In *Fred Cogswell*, I explain how Walter Cogswell's anachronistic approach to farming contrasted with the technological fetishism of the McCain brothers: "[Walter Cogswell] refused to own a tractor, preferring to work his farm with his beloved horses long after his potato-exporting neighbour, the now-famous A.D. McCain, had made the switch. His decline began with just that kind of stubbornness: another recalcitrant refusal to put up an electric fence to separate his livestock from the sprawling potato fields of the McCain brothers. One day his prized herd of Holstein cattle broke through his flimsy wire barrier and wandered into the nearby McCain field, where potato shoots had just been sprayed with insecticide. After gorging on the new potato leaves, the entire herd died, a loss that Walter would never make up. His son Fred would have lifetime memories of his father and local farmers trying to revive the slowly dying cows" (Tremblay, *Fred Cogswell*, "Biography/Ancestry," n.p.). For Alden Nowlan's take on this event, see his poem "The Fynch Cows," 73-4.

127 Interview with author, April 2002.

128 Cogswell to Bailey, 20 September 1951.

129 Bailey, "Literary Memories," Part II, 21.

130 Gibbs to Rogers, 30 December 1952.

131 Cogswell to Rogers, 22 December 1951.

132 Cogswell to Pacey, 23 October 1951.

133 J. Sutherland, "Past Decade," 72.

134 MacSkimming, *Perilous Trade*, 24. The dearth of publishing in the Maritimes was just as marked, Cogswell commenting that in the mid-nineteenth century "Halifax published 60 book titles of verse over a period of 50 years; Saint John had 23. In all, 140 titles by 91 different Maritime poets

were published during the period under survey" ("Nineteenth Century Poetry," 5).

135 *Report of the Royal Commission*, 222–7.

136 Ibid., 105–7, 119–22.

137 Ibid., 65.

138 Rogers to Cogswell, 22 December 1951.

139 A.J.M. Smith, "Wanted," 33.

140 Cogswell to Bailey, 14 November 1950.

141 A similar momentum was gathering in French New Brunswick, where planning had begun to commemorate the 200th anniversary of the Acadian deportation. At the forefront of those efforts were professors at the Université Saint-Joseph and editors at *L'Évangéline*. Father Clément Cormier, president of Université Saint-Joseph, had also begun lobbying the federal government for public-broadcasting infrastructure, an effort that resulted in CBC French-language outlets in the province for radio (1954) and television (1959). For more on these 1953–54 activities and campaigns, see Wilbur's *The Rise of French New Brunswick* (182–7); Belliveau's "Acadian New Brunswick's Ambivalent Leap" (63–8); and Pichette's "'Longtemps l'Acadie a attendu un chef'" (242–3).

142 "Notes," 162.

143 Gibbs to Rogers, 27 March 1953.

144 Rogers to Dudek, 21 February 1953.

145 Cogswell to Gibbs, 18 December 1952.

146 Cogswell to May, 4 December 1953. As difficult as it must have been to reject poems from senior Canadian figures, some of whom were pioneers in modern Canadian poetry, Cogswell stuck by his principles. To Louis Dudek he wrote: "I am returning your three poems from 'Europe ...' The general consensus of opinion was that although they may be, as you suggest, better in context, appearing in *The Fiddlehead* they would not be in context. We also feel that we have seen better poems of yours elsewhere and would like to have a whack at publishing some of the best." Cogswell next shrewdly observes Dudek's transition to the longer poem of ideas: "I detect, I think, a change in these poems from your usual attitude. Most of your earlier poems ... owed much of their charm to your ability to look at things, even the simplest of things, with a sense of wonder, something of the freshness of the child's vision. [In your new poetry] there is, I feel, an attempt at a greater depth, an attempt to evaluate as well as to see, which I am very pleased to see in your work" (Cogswell to Dudek, 6 November 1953). In similar fashion, Cogswell wrote to Dorothy Livesay, the important wider context being that her poem "Lament" in an earlier issue (nineteen) was the most prize-

winning poem the *Fiddlehead* had ever published: "I am returning 'Camp,'" wrote Cogswell, "not because we don't like it, but because we think it can be made better" (Cogswell to Livesay, 31 January 1954).

147 Cogswell to Floris McLaren, 7 December 1953.

148 J. Sutherland to Cogswell, 1 December 1953.

149 May's comment was not hyperbole. The former associate editor of *Poetry* (Chicago), Nicholas Joost, had written to Cogswell to tell him "how very much I like your magazine, as I have a little more knowledge of what it takes to produce one. It is both literate and interesting – really, I did like your selection of poetry and the way you placed the various pieces ... Knowing Canada from three stays in various parts, I am astonished at your courage and persistence in continuing to publish the *Fiddlehead* in so sparsely populated a land. I do hope this remark doesn't sound condescending, as I mean it admiringly" (quoted in Cogswell to Livesay, 25 July 1957).

150 Cogswell, "Choosing a Printer," 35; Cogswell to Marleen Hayes, 23 February 1958.

151 Purdy to Cogswell, 8 December 1953.

152 Trueman, "Foreword," 2.

153 Rogers to Trueman, 21 April 1953.

154 Cogswell to Alan Crawley, 7 February 1954.

155 With Crawley, the left-leaning editorial board principals of *Contemporary Verse* included Dorothy Livesay, Doris Ferne, and Anne Marriott.

156 Crawley, "Editor's Note," 3.

157 Dudek, "Role of Little Magazines," 208.

158 Cogswell to editor of the *Canadian Forum*, 14 November 1953. Cogswell's letter continues, "When we heard that *Contemporary Verse* was being discontinued, we decided to take its place as far as our ability warranted."

159 Rogers to Smith, 9 March 1953.

160 McLaren to Cogswell, 30 April 1953.

161 Waddington to Cogswell, 4 February 1954.

162 Gibbs to Pacey, 14 May 1953.

163 Ibid.

164 Purdy to Cogswell, 23 November 1953.

165 Cogswell to Bourinot, 14 December 1953.

166 Cogswell to the *Observer*, 29 January 1954.

167 Cogswell, "Choosing a Printer," 35.

168 Ibid.

169 Cogswell to the editor [*Canadian Forum*], 7 January 1954.

170 Souster to Louis Dudek, 23 June 1951; quoted in Gnarowski, *Contact*, 3.

171 Cogswell, "Editorial," 1.

172 Ibid.

173 Livesay to Cogswell, 18 July 1957.

174 Cogswell to Livesay, 25 July 1957.

175 Pacey, Draft Review.

176 Cogswell to Bourinot, 6 January 1955.

177 Acorn to Cogswell, 16 July 1970.

178 Cogswell to McLaren, 7 December 1953.

179 Pacey, Draft Review.

180 Purdy to Cogswell, 1 January [1954].

181 Ives, "Alden Nowlan's Poetry," 61.

182 Quoted in Metcalf, "Alden Nowlan," 16.

183 Pacey, Draft Review.

184 Gustafson, Review of *The Stunted Strong*, 21.

185 Cogswell to Holmes, 10 December 1955.

186 "Editorial," 3.

187 In the summer of 1959, with the financial support of UNB and a Nuffield Travelling Fellowship, Cogswell took a twelve-month sabbatical in Scotland and England to expand his knowledge of the novelist John Galt. When he returned in September 1960, UNB had shut down Fiddlehead Poetry Books and reallocated its resources. Faced with the prospect of losing the press, Cogswell assumed ownership. Cogswell ran the press and the *Fiddlehead* out of his own office, the magazine until 1967 and the press until 1981. In 1981 he sold Fiddlehead Poetry Books to his English Department colleague Peter Thomas for one dollar. Thomas was the more discriminating publisher, accepting substantially fewer manuscripts and taking works other than poetry. In 1988 Thomas's press was sold as Goose Lane Editions.

188 By "constructive" I do not mean that Cogswell was uncritically laudatory. He was direct and honest about a poem's shortcomings, but always encouraging, believing that criticism is most useful when it is frank. In writing about E.J. Pratt's literary reputation, for example, he took a page from Pacey in pointing out that "Canadian literary criticism is the kindest in the world" because it is written by people who do not wish to "cause pain" to those they admire (Cogswell, "E.J. Pratt's Literary Reputation," 7). Illustrating the problems with that approach, Cogswell proceeded to identify Pratt's strengths and weaknesses, concluding that Pratt's work will soon be "consigned to the stony limbo of that which was not for all time but for an age" (8). Though generous with his encouragement, then, Cogswell's criticism was often harsh, its edge issuing partly from the radical Baptist tradition of his youth.

189 See Pacey's review of Birney's anthology in the *Fiddlehead* 20 (February) 1954: 17–19.

190 Frye, "Letters in Canada," 447.
191 Livesay to Cogswell, 18 July 1957.
192 Cogswell, "Restatement of Policy," 1.
193 Moore, "The Fiddlehead."
194 Macpherson to Cogswell, 9 March [1961].
195 Nowlan to Cogswell, 10 January 1961.
196 Cogswell to Orlovitz, 23 February 1959.
197 Cogswell to Pacey, 9 June 1960.
198 Bailey, "Literary Memories," Part II, 6.
199 F. Sutherland, "A Lot of There, There," 13.
200 Cogswell, "Editorial" (1965), 76.
201 Cogswell, "Mystery of Synthesis," 27.
202 Galloway, "SCL Interviews," 212.
203 Quoted in Hatt, "Fred Cogswell," 39.
204 McKay, "Sporangia Eclectica," 5.
205 Quoted in D. McKay, "Common Sense and Magic," 237.
206 Woodcock, "Poetry," 293.
207 See Galloway's interview with Cogswell in *Studies in Canadian Literature/Études en littérature canadienne* (208) and also Zanes's "Where the Fiddleheads Grow" (107–8).
208 Lee to Cogswell, 17 July 1973.
209 Quoted in Zanes, "Where the Fiddleheads Grow," 108.
210 *Five New Brunswick Poets* was the sixth of the Fiddlehead Poetry Books. The first four – by Cogswell, Gladys V. Downes, Al Purdy, and Alden Nowlan – had been subsidized and published by UNB; the fifth, Cogswell's *Descent from Eden* (1959), by the *Fiddlehead*; and the sixth, *Five New Brunswick Poets*, by Cogswell. Cogswell would publish the rest under his own direction.
211 Nowlan to Cogswell, 16 April 1962.
212 Bowering, "Poetry as Recreation," 237.
213 Mandel, "Five New Brunswick Poets," 67.
214 Ibid., 68.
215 McRobbie, "Canadian Chronicle," 269; Wilson, "Letters in Canada," 384.
216 Flint, "Imagisme," 129.
217 Bowering, "Poetry as Recreation," 237.
218 Brown, *On Canadian Poetry*, 53.
219 Cogswell, "Nineteenth Century Poetry," 5.
220 Ibid.
221 "Development of Writing," 25.
222 Lucas, Review, 11.
223 Cogswell, Review, 11.

224 Cogswell goes on to be critical of A.G. Bailey in the 1961 article "Nine-
    teenth Century Poetry in the Maritimes and the Problems of Research."
    Aimed at challenging the authority of Bailey's influential "Creative
    Moments in the Culture of the Maritime Provinces," Cogswell's article con-
    cludes that "Bailey's thesis ignores the moral and religious ferment of the
    Maritime provinces" as well as the fact that Nova Scotia's two principal lit-
    erary figures of the nineteenth century (Joseph Howe and T.C. Haliburton)
    "were atypical Nova Scotians" in their religious attitudes (18). Cogswell is
    likewise critical of Pacey in the 1964 article "E.J. Pratt's Literary Reputation,"
    stating that Pacey has "shown not so much insight as [a] desire to supply in
    Pratt's poetry what currently seems necessary to be found in great poetry"
    (8). Thus, he accuses Pacey, as he accuses Dudek, John Sutherland, and Frye
    in the same article, of literary boosterism, one of the sins of the culturally
    effete.
225 Dudek to Cogswell, 4 June 1962.
226 Pound, *ABC of Reading*, 17.
227 Along with *The Arts in New Brunswick*, Cogswell's other significant editorial
    achievement in his post-*Fiddlehead* years was the compilation of two major
    anthologies of Atlantic Canadian writing, *The Atlantic Anthology, Volume 1:
    Prose* (Ragweed 1984) and *The Atlantic Anthology, Volume 2: Poetry* (Ragweed
    1985).
228 In explaining why he wrote *Descent from Eden* (1959), Cogswell says on the
    dust jacket that his intention was "partly to record the struggle in my own
    mind between an environmentally acquired Puritanism and an outgoing
    nature which collided with it."
229 Pacey, *Creative Writing*, 250.
230 Cogswell, "Nineteenth Century Poetry," 14.
231 Cogswell to Jean Boucher, 3 October 1966.
232 Nowlan, "Something to Write About," 9–10.
233 Ibid., 10.
234 Cogswell to Hatfield, 30 December 1970.
235 Draft of Proposal for a Permanent Appointment, 2.
236 Cogswell to Hatfield, 30 December 1970.
237 Cogswell to Jean Boucher, 3 October 1966.
238 In April 1969 the Official Languages Act specified that English and French
    were the province's "official" languages, thus ensuring that New Brunswick-
    ers could receive government services in either language. On 17 July 1981
    the province of New Brunswick enacted Bill 88, further guaranteeing the
    equal rights of both language populations and dividing key services along
    language lines. A year later, in 1982, New Brunswick had its unique lan-

guage provisions entrenched in the Canadian Charter of Rights and Freedoms. In 1982 and 1986 the Poirier-Bastarache Report and the Report of the Guérette-Smith Advisory Committee on Official Languages in New Brunswick provided detailed data on demography, attitudes, and other aspects of bilingualism in the province.

239 Wilbur, *Rise of French New Brunswick*, 215.

240 Cogswell, "Development of Writing," 21.

241 John Glassco's edition of *The Poetry of French Canada in Translation* was released the same year (Oxford, 1970). Cogswell was one of a number of translators featured in Glassco's collection.

242 See *Liberté* 11, no. 5 (fall 1969).

243 Cogswell, "Modern Acadian Poetry," 64.

244 Ibid.

245 Cogswell, "Poetry of Modern Quebec," 56.

246 Cogswell, "Modern Acadian Poetry," 65.

247 Ibid.

248 For more on Cogswell's role in translating Acadian literature and fostering a translating culture in New Brunswick, see my article "Strategy and Vision for an Intercultural New Brunswick." Cogswell's list of French texts translated into English include *One Hundred Poems of Modern Quebec* (1970); *A Second Hundred Poems of Modern Quebec* (Fredericton: Fiddlehead Poetry Books 1971); *Confrontation = Face à face* [by Gatien Lapointe] (Fredericton: Fiddlehead Poetry Books 1973); *The Poetry of Modern Quebec: An Anthology* (Montreal: Harvest House 1976); *The Complete Poems of Emile Nelligan* (Montreal: Harvest House 1983); *Unfinished Dreams: Contemporary Poetry of Acadie* [with Jo-Anne Elder] (Fredericton: Goose Lane 1990); *Climates* [by Hermé-négilde Chiasson, with Jo-Anne Elder] (Fredericton: Goose Lane 1999); *Conversations* [by Herménégilde Chiasson, with Jo-Anne Elder] (Fredericton: Goose Lane 2001); *The Sales of Honour I: The Overseer of the Poor* [by Anna Girouard] (Sainte-Marie-de-Kent, NB: Balises Editions 2001); and *Lumberjack's Yoga* (Sainte-Marie-de-Kent, NB: Balises Editions 2002).

249 Cogswell and Elder translated and co-edited Chiasson's *Climates* (1999) and *Conversations* (2001).

250 Cogswell, "Modern Acadian Poetry," 65.

251 Galloway, "SCL Interviews," 219.

252 Cogswell to Ashman, 30 September 1957.

253 Gibbs, "Fred's Overcoat," 164.

254 Unpublished poem sent to author.

255 Cogswell, "Art," 40.

256 Gibbs, "Fred's Overcoat," 162, 164.

CHAPTER FIVE

1 Roberts, "Beginnings of a Canadian Literature," 258–9.
2 Robert Rogers to Louis Dudek, 21 February 1953.
3 Brewster to Bailey, 26 September 1973.
4 In a preface to the anthology *New Provinces* that was rejected by editor/contributor E.J. Pratt, A.J.M. Smith wrote that earlier poetry in Canada was overly "concerned with pine trees, the open road, God, snowshoes or Pan. The most popular experience is to be pained, hurt, stabbed or seared by Beauty – most preferably by the yellow flame of the crocus in the spring or the red flame of a maple leaf in autumn" (Smith, "Rejected Preface," 7). Smith's animus for Carman and Roberts is clearly evident in references to "the open road" (Carman's Vagabondia poems) and "Pan" (Roberts's mystical *Orion* and Carman's *Pipes of Pan*).
5 Norris, *Little Magazine*, 5.
6 Alexander, *Atlantic Canada*, 74.
7 Kennedy, "Directions," 14.
8 Said, *Orientalism*, 12.
9 Brewster to Bailey, 26 September 1973.
10 Dudek, "Patterns," 276.
11 Howe, "Address," 298.
12 Gibbons, *Edmund Burke and Ireland*, 68.
13 Ibid., 39.
14 Frank, "The 1920s," 234.
15 Miller, "The 1940s," 345.
16 Derrida, *Of Grammatology*, 24.
17 Underhill, *Image of Confederation*, 63.
18 Barthes, *Pleasure of the Text*, 49.
19 Ibid.; emphasis in original.
20 Gellner, *Nations and Nationalism*, 56.
21 Bhabha, "Dissemination," 177.
22 Rushdie, "Imaginary Homelands," 14.
23 Ibid.
24 Bailey, "Literary Memories," Part II, 21.
25 Ibid.
26 Cogswell, "New Brunswick," 16.
27 Bailey, "Literary Memories," Part II, 21.
28 The only other North American schools with similar aims were the Fugitives of the American South and the Harlem Renaissance writers of New York, both of which appeared in 1920s. Bailey and Cogswell were keen read-

ers of the former, Cogswell modelling parts of *The Stunted Strong* (1954) on the work of Donald Davidson. For earlier incubators of literary culture in Canada that paralleled the social conditions of the Fiddlehead group, see the *Literary Garland* in Montreal (Eggleston, *Frontier*, 83–7) and the activity around Octave Crémazie's bookshop in Quebec (MacMechan, *Headwaters*, 59–75).

29 Bailey, "Confederation Debate," 137.
30 Bailey, "Literature and Nationalism," 72, 73.
31 Quoted in Hotchner, *Papa Hemingway*, 57.
32 Bailey, "Literary Memories," Part II, 21.
33 Pacey, *Book of Canadian Stories*, xxxvi.
34 Whalen, "Atlantic Possibilities," 33.
35 Ibid., 34.
36 Anderson, *Imagined Communities*, 202.
37 Quoted in Eggleston, *Frontier*, 111–12.
38 Pacey, Review, 94.
39 Bailey, "Creative Moments," 54–6.
40 Lower, *Colony to Nation*, 414.
41 Cogswell, "Statement of Position," 96.
42 Scott, "Canadian Authors Meet," 70.
43 Livesay to Cogswell, 18 July 1957.
44 For a New Brunswick-specific examination of socio-cultural commonalities across historical periods, see my edited collection *New Brunswick at the Crossroads*, as well as Johnson's "Old Provinces, New Modernisms," which examines small modernist magazines in New Brunswick, Nova Scotia, and Prince Edward Island.
45 W. Stevens, "John Crowe Ransom," 368.
46 Cormier, "Robichaud Legacy," 192, 191.
47 Bailey, "Early Foundations," 15.
48 Godin, "Education Reforms," 181.
49 LeBlanc, Godin, and Renaud, "French Education," 546–7.
50 Stanley, *Louis Robichaud*, 98.
51 Quoted in ibid., 13.
52 Bailey, "Literature and Nationalism," 60.
53 Pacey, Draft Review; Zanes, "Where the Fiddleheads Grow," 71–4.
54 For more on the humanism of the Saint John artists, see my essay "Mid-Century Emergent Modernism" in *New Brunswick at the Crossroads*, 110–12.
55 Bailey, "Literary Memories," Part II, 7.
56 Pacey to Lorne Pierce, 7 October 1946.
57 Brewster to Bailey, 23 September 1968.

58 Montague, *Pictorial History*, 174.
59 See, for example, Bailey's understanding of harm in his assessment of social change (*Conflict of European and Eastern Algonkian Cultures*, 95, 96–116).
60 Bailey, "The Muskrat," 48.
61 Trigger, "Alfred G. Bailey – Ethnohistorian," 21.
62 Overdue here is an examination of Bailey's studies of the effects of first contact on the country's First Nations – extending the inquiry into Bailey's influence that Bruce Trigger began in "Alfred G. Bailey – Ethnohistorian." Bailey was as early as Marius Barbeau, W.N. Fenton, T.F. McIlwraith, and George F. Clarke in applying serious study to the character and decline of Indigenous populations under European occupation. His 1933 "The Significance of the Identity and Disappearance of the Laurentian Iroquois," for example, was both groundbreaking and influential. His work was at the forefront of what now is a booming critical industry. Saul's *A Fair Country* borrows from his ideas.
63 For an explanation of the intertidal, see Campbell's essay "'Every Sea-Surrounded Hour.'"
64 Bailey, "The Human Form," 181.
65 Pacey, Draft Review.
66 Purdy to Cogswell, 1 January [1954].
67 Whalen, "Introduction" [to *Atlantic Anthology*], 1.
68 For a start on that work, see my articles "Strategy and Vision for an Intercultural New Brunswick" and "Antonine Maillet, Marshall Button, and Literary Humor."
69 Duguay, "To Have a Homeland," 83.
70 Frye, "From Nationalism to Regionalism," 11.
71 Whalen, "Introduction" [to *Atlantic Anthology*], 3.

Bibliography

ARCHIVES

Archives and Special Collections, Harriet Irving Library, University of New Brunswick (Fredericton) (ASC, HIL, UNB)
Bailey Family Collection
Dr Alfred Goldsworthy Bailey Fonds
Fiddlehead/Cogswell Fonds
[UNB] Presidents' Papers
Rufus Hathaway Collection of Canadian Literature
W.C.D. Pacey Fonds
Winslow Papers

Library and Archives Canada (Ottawa) (LAC)
Desmond Pacey Fonds
Elizabeth Brewster Fonds
Louis Dudek Fonds

McGill University Library, Rare Books and Special Collections (Montreal)
Hugh MacLennan Papers

New Brunswick Museum (Saint John)
John Clarence Webster Collection

Provincial Archives of New Brunswick (Fredericton)
Ku Klux Klan Fonds

Thomas Fisher Rare Book Library, University of Toronto
A.J.M. Smith Papers
Malcolm Ross Papers
Robert Finch Papers

University of British Columbia Archives (Vancouver) (UBCA)
Roy Daniells Fonds

University of Calgary Archives and Special Collections
Alden Nowlan Fonds

Victoria University Library, University of Toronto
Northrop Frye Fonds

NEWSPAPERS/MEDIA

L'Acadie Nouvelle
Carleton Observer
Carleton Sentinel
CBC News Online, New Brunswick
Country Life
Globe and Mail
[Hartland] *Observer*
McGill Daily
[Moncton] *Times & Transcript*
Newark *Herald*
[New Brunswick] *Telegraph-Journal*

BOOKS, ARTICLES, LETTERS*

Acheson, T.W, ed. *The Economic History of the Maritime Provinces*, by S.A. Saunders. Fredericton: Acadiensis 1984. Introduction. 5–14.

---

* All citations of letters from the Dr Alfred Goldsworthy Bailey Fonds and the Fiddlehead/Cogswell Fonds held at ASC, HIL, and UNB are used with the permission of Francesca Holyoke, archivist, and the literary executors G.S. d'A. Bailey (for A.G. Bailey) and Kathleen Forsythe (for Fred Cogswell). Similarly, all citations of letters from the Desmond Pacey Fonds at LAC and the W.C.D. Pacey Fonds at ASC, HIL, and UNB are used with the permission of executor Peter Pacey.

- "The National Policy and the Industrialization of the Maritimes, 1880–1910." In T.W. Acheson, David Frank, and James D. Frost, eds., *Industrialization and Underdevelopment in the Maritimes, 1880–1930*. Toronto: Garamond 1985. 1–26.

Acorn, Milton. Letter to Fred Cogswell. 16 July 1970. Fiddlehead/Cogswell Fonds, UA RG83, box 18, MS2.698, ASC, HIL, UNB.

Adams, John Coldwell. *Sir Charles God Damn: The Life of Sir Charles G.D. Roberts.* Toronto: University of Toronto Press 1986.

Alexander, David G. *Atlantic Canada and Confederation: Essays in Canadian Political Economy*, compiled by Eric W. Sager, Lewis R. Fischer, and Stuart O. Pierson. Toronto: University of Toronto Press 1983.

Allen, Richard. *The Social Passion: Religion and Social Reform in Canada, 1914–28*. Toronto: University of Toronto Press 1971.

Anderson, Benedict. *Imagined Communities*. 1983. Rev. ed. London: Verso 2006.

Andrew, Sheila M. "The Development of Elites in Acadian New Brunswick, 1861–881." PhD diss., University of New Brunswick, 1992.

Appiah, Kwame Anthony. *The Ethics of Identity*. Princeton, NJ, and Oxford: Princeton University Press 2004.

Armstrong, Sally. *The Nine Lives of Charlotte Taylor*. 2007. Toronto: Vintage 2008.

Arnold, Matthew. *Culture and Anarchy: An Essay in Political and Social Criticism*. 1869. Edited and introduced by Ian Gregor. Indianapolis, IN: Bobbs-Merrill 1971.

Arseneau, Bernard. Interview with author, 11 August 2014. Fredericton.

"Arthur Norwood Carter." *McGill Daily*, 6 October 1948, http://archive.org/stream/McGillLibrary-mcgill-daily-v38-n004-october-06-1948-5386/mcgill-daily-v38-n004-october-06-1948_djvu.txt.

Atlantic Canada English Language Arts Curriculum: High School. Fredericton: New Brunswick Department of Education Curriculum Development Branch 1998.

Aunger, Edmund A. *In Search of Political Stability: A Comparative Study of New Brunswick and Northern Ireland*. Montreal and Kingston: McGill-Queen's University Press 1981.

Ayre, John. *Northrop Frye: A Biography*. Toronto: Random House 1989.

Bailey, Alfred Goldsworthy. "Address." N.d. Transcript. Dr Alfred Goldsworthy Bailey Fonds, UA RG80, case 89, file 1, ASC, HIL, UNB.

- "Angel Gabriel." *Wascana Review* 4 (1969): 47–9. [Reprinted in *Thanks for a Drowned Island*, 26–7. Toronto: McClelland and Stewart 1973.]

- "Colour Chart." In *Thanks for a Drowned Island*. Toronto: McClelland and Stewart 1973. 10.

- "Confederation Debate." In *Miramichi Lightning: The Collected Poems of Alfred Bailey*. Fredericton: Fiddlehead Poetry Books 1981. 136–7.
- *The Conflict of European and Eastern Algonkian Cultures, 1504–1700: A Study in Canadian Civilization*. Saint John: New Brunswick Museum 1937. [Reprint: Toronto: University of Toronto Press 1969.]
- "Creative Moments in the Culture of the Maritime Provinces." In *Culture and Nationality: Essays by A.G. Bailey*. Carleton Library no. 58. Toronto: McClelland and Stewart 1972. 44–57.
- "Desmond Pacey, The Bliss Carman Society, and the Fiddlehead." *Fiddlehead* 107 (fall 1975): 3–5.
- "Discourse on Method." In *Border River*. Toronto: McClelland and Stewart 1952. 40.
- "Dramatic Incidents in New Brunswick's History and the Historical Solution of Our Problems." Transcript. Address to Saint John Vocational School [1937]. Dr Alfred Goldsworthy Bailey Fonds, UA, RG80, Series 3, case 89, file 1, ASC, HIL, UNB.
- "Early Foundations: 1783–1829." In A.G. Bailey, ed., *The University of New Brunswick Memorial Volume*. Fredericton: University of New Brunswick 1950. 15–21.
- "Early Manifestations of Culture in Upper Canada, 1791–1840." *Brunswickan* (April 1928): 16–19.
- "Faculty of Arts Report." Dr Alfred Goldsworthy Bailey Fonds, UA RG80, case 11, file 4, ASC, HIL, UNB.
- "The Fiddlehead." *Fiddlehead* 1 (February 1945): 1.
- "The Fiddlehead." *Fiddlehead* 7 (December 1947): 65–72. [Written by Bailey; read on CFNB radio (Fredericton) in December 1946 by Bailey, Robert Lawrence, Dorothy Johns, and Margaret Cunningham.]
- Foreword. "Minutes of the Bliss Carman Society of Fredericton, founded December 1940." Ms. PS 8455.A72 Z512 1940, ASC, HIL, UNB.
- "Guide." In *Border River*. Toronto: McClelland and Stewart 1952.
- "Here in the East." In *Thanks for a Drowned Island*. Toronto: McClelland and Stewart 1973. 28.
- "History of the UNB Library to 1959." N.d. [1981]. Transcript. Bailey Family Collection, MG H1, MS4.7.1.7, ASC, HIL, UNB.
- "The Human Form Is Practically Resilient." In *Miramichi Lightning: The Collected Poems of Alfred Bailey*. Fredericton: Fiddlehead Poetry Books 1981. 181.
- Introduction to *The Development of the Theory and Practice of Education in New Brunswick, 1784–1900: A Study in Historical Background*, by Katherine

MacNaughton. Edited by Alfred G. Bailey. Fredericton: University of New Brunswick Historical Studies 1947. 7–8.

– *The John Clarence Webster Collection*. New Brunswick Museum Collections no. 1. Saint John: New Brunswick Museum 1936.

– Letter to George A.B. Addy. 13 September 1937. Dr Alfred Goldsworthy Bailey Fonds, UA RG80, box 32, file 4, ASC, HIL, UNB.

– Letter to Lord Beaverbrook. 17 October 1946. Dr Alfred Goldsworthy Bailey Fonds, UA RG80, box 45, file 6, ASC, HIL, UNB.

– Letter to Earle Birney. 22 February 1950. Dr Alfred Goldsworthy Bailey Fonds, UA RG80, box 39, file 4, ASC, HIL, UNB.

– Letter to J.B. Brebner. 23 February 1944. Dr Alfred Goldsworthy Bailey Fonds, UA RG80, box 34, file 10, ASC, HIL, UNB.

– Letter to Roy Daniells. [15 August 1934]. Roy Daniells Fonds, Correspondence Series, 1908–80, box 2, file 2 (1934), UBCA. Used with permission of G.S. d'A. Bailey, literary executor, and Erwin Wodarczak, archivist.

– Letter to Roy Daniells. 30 November 1934. Roy Daniells Fonds, Correspondence Series, 1908–80, box 2, file 3 (1934), UBCA. Used with permission of G.S. d'A. Bailey, literary executor, and Erwin Wodarczak, archivist.

– Letter to Roy Daniells. 1 January 1936. Roy Daniells Fonds, Correspondence Series, 1908–80, box 2, file 11 (1936), UBCA. Used with permission of G.S. d'A. Bailey, literary executor, and Erwin Wodarczak, archivist.

– Letter to Northrop Frye. 28 July 1965. Northrop Frye Fonds, 1988 Accession, box 35, file 11, Victoria University Library [University of Toronto]. Used with permission of G.S. d'A. Bailey, literary executor, and Lisa J. Sherlock, chief librarian.

– Letter to C.C. Jones. 29 March 1937. Dr Alfred Goldsworthy Bailey Fonds, UA RG136, box 13, file 1, ASC, HIL, UNB.

– Letter to J.B. McNair. 5 June 1947. Dr Alfred Goldsworthy Bailey Fonds, UA RG80, box 36, file 5, ASC, HIL, UNB.

– Letter to J.B. McNair. 19 October 1951. Dr Alfred Goldsworthy Bailey Fonds, UA, RG80, box 45, file 4, ASC, HIL, UNB.

– Letter to Jack Murray. 18 March 1948. Dr Alfred Goldsworthy Bailey Fonds, UA RG80, box 48, file 4, ASC, HIL, UNB.

– Letter to Desmond Pacey. 11 December 1955. Desmond Pacey Fonds, MG30, D339, vol. 1, "Bailey, Alfred G. – Correspondence," LAC.

– Letter to Malcolm Ross. 12 March 1977. Malcolm Ross Papers, 277, box 2, Thomas Fisher Rare Book Library, University of Toronto.

– Letter to Malcolm Ross. 21 July 1980. Malcolm Ross Papers, 277, box 2,

Correspondence, 1983–85, Thomas Fisher Rare Book Library, University of Toronto.

– Letter to Malcolm Ross. 12 October 1984. Malcolm Ross Papers, 277, box 2, Correspondence, 1980–82, Thomas Fisher Rare Book Library, University of Toronto.

– Letter to John C. Webster. 4 September 1937. Dr Alfred Goldsworthy Bailey Fonds, UA RG80, box 32, file 4, ASC, HIL, UNB.

– "Literature and Nationalism after Confederation." In *Culture and Nationality: Essays by A.G. Bailey*. Carleton Library no. 58. Toronto: McClelland and Stewart 1972. 58–74.

– "Literary Memories of Alfred Goldsworthy Bailey, Part I." N.d. Transcript. Dr Alfred Goldsworthy Bailey Fonds, UA RG80, box 108, file 3, ASC, HIL, UNB.

– "Literary Memories of Alfred Goldsworthy Bailey, Part II." 1974. Transcript. Dr Alfred Goldsworthy Bailey Fonds, UA RG80, box 108, file 3, ASC, HIL, UNB.

– "Lord Beaverbrook in New Brunswick: Reminiscences of Alfred Goldsworthy Bailey." 1975. Transcript. Dr Alfred Goldsworthy Bailey Fonds, UA RG80, 95:3, file 6, ASC, HIL, UNB.

– "The Muskrat and the Whale." In *Miramichi Lightning: The Collected Poems of Alfred Bailey*. Fredericton: Fiddlehead Poetry Books 1981. 47–8.

– "The Need to Hand On." *Fiddlehead* 125 (spring 1980): 1–2.

– "North West Passage." In *Border River*. Toronto: McClelland and Stewart 1952. 27–8.

– "Origins of the Study of History in the University of New Brunswick." N.d. Transcript. Dr Alfred Goldsworthy Bailey Fonds, UA RG80, 3:100, file 9, ASC, HIL, UNB.

– "Overture to Nationhood." In *Literary History of Canada: Canadian Literature in English*. 2nd ed., vol. 1. General Editor Carl F. Klinck. Toronto: University of Toronto Press 1976. 69–81.

– Preface. *Culture and Nationality: Essays by A.G. Bailey*. Carleton Library no. 58. Toronto: McClelland and Stewart 1972. 1–9.

– "Reflections on a Hill Behind a Town." In *Miramichi Lightning: The Collected Poems of Alfred Bailey*. Fredericton: Fiddlehead Poetry Books 1981. 185–6.

– "Retrospective Thoughts of an Ethnohistorian." *Historical Papers/Communications historiques* 12, no. 1 (1977): 14–29.

– "Saint John and the New Brunswick Museum in the Hungry Thirties, 1935–1938." Rev. ed. 1982. Transcript. Bailey Family Collection, MG H1, MS4.7.1.6, ASC, HIL, UNB.

- "The Significance of the Identity and Disappearance of the Laurentian Iroquois." *Transactions of the Royal Society of Canada*, Series 3, vol. 27, sect. 2 (1933): 97–108.
- "Social Revolution in Early Eastern Canada." *Canadian Historical Review* 19 (1938): 264–76.
- *Songs of the Saguenay and Other Poems.* Quebec: Chronicle-Telegraph Publishing Company 1927.
- "Style of the Canadian Culture." N.d. Transcript. Dr Alfred Goldsworthy Bailey Fonds, UA RG80, case 89, file 1, ASC, HIL, UNB.
- *Tâo.* Toronto: Ryerson Poetry Chapbooks 1930.
- "Transcript of December 1946 [CFNB] Radio Broadcast." Reprint, *Fiddlehead* 7 (December 1947): 2–8.
- "Verse." *Brunswickan* 46, no. 7 (Graduation Number 1927): 54–5.
Bailey, Loring Woart. "A Series of Letters and Events in the Life of Professor Jacob Whitman Bailey." Unpublished draft, 1858. Bailey Family Collection Fonds, MG H1, Genealogy, MS1.3.4.1, ASC, HIL, UNB. Used with permission of Francesca Holyoke, archivist, and G.S. d'A. Bailey, literary executor.
Bailey, Loring Woart, Jr. Bailey Family Collection Fonds, MG H1, MS2.3.782–8, ASC, HIL, UNB. Used with permission of Francesca Holyoke, archivist, and G.S. d'A. Bailey, literary executor.
Baker, Ray Palmer. *A History of English-Canadian Literature to the Confederation.* Cambridge, MA: Harvard University Press 1920.
Banks, M., A. Lovatt, J. O'Connor, and C. Raffo, "Risk and Trust in the Cultural Industries." *Geoforum* 31 (2000): 453–64.
Barthes, Roland. *Mythologies.* 1957. Trans. Annette Lavers. London: Paladin Grafton Bourque 1988.
- *The Pleasure of the Text.* 1973. Trans. Richard Miller. New York: Hill and Wang 1975.
Bauer, Nancy. "Fred Cogswell: Creating Space and Time." *Arts Atlantic* 3, no. 4 (1981): 34–5.
Bayley, Robin. "Spring's Coronation." *Fiddlehead* 1 (1945): 6.
Beck, J. Murray, ed. *Joseph Howe: Voice of Nova Scotia.* Carleton Library no. 20. Toronto: McClelland and Stewart 1964.
Belliveau, Joel. "Acadian New Brunswick's Ambivalent Leap into the Canadian Liberal Order." In Magda Fahrni and Robert Rutherdale, eds., *Creating Postwar Canada: Community, Diversity, and Dissent, 1945–75.* Vancouver: University of British Columbia Press 2008. 61–88.
Bennett, Donna. "Conflicted Vision: A Consideration of Canon and Genre in English-Canadian Literature." In Robert Lecker, ed., *Canadian Canons:*

Essays in Literary Value. Toronto: University of Toronto Press 1991.
131–49.

Benstock, Shari. *Women of the Left Bank: Paris, 1900–1940.* Austin: University
of Texas Press 1986.

Bentley, David M.R. *The Confederation Group of Canadian Poets, 1880–1897.*
Toronto: University of Toronto Press 2004.

– "Reflections on the Situation and Study of Early Canadian Literature in
the Long Confederation Period." In Janice Fiamengo, ed., *Home Ground
and Foreign Territory: Essays on Early Canadian Literature.* Ottawa: University
of Ottawa Press 2014. 17–43.

Bhabha, Homi K. "Dissemination: Time, Narrative, and the Margins of the
Modern Nation." In Bill Ashcroft, Gareth Griffiths, and Helen Tifflin,
eds., *The Post-Colonial Studies Reader.* London and New York: Routledge
1995. 176–7.

– *The Location of Culture.* New York: Routledge 1994.

Blodgett, E.D. *Five Part Invention: A History of Literary History in Canada.*
Toronto: University of Toronto Press 2003.

Bourque, Denis, and Denise Merkle. "De Evangeline à l'américaine à
Évangéline à l'acadienne: une transformation idéologique?" In D. Merkle
et al., ed., *Traduire depuis les marges/Translating from the Margins.* Quebec:
Éditions Nota bene 2008. 121–45.

Bourque, Denis, and Chantal Richard. *Les Conventions Nationales Acadiennes. Tome 1, 1881–1890.* Moncton, NB: Institut d'études acadiennes
2013.

Bowering, George. "Poetry as Recreation." Review of *Five New Brunswick
Poets*, ed. Fred Cogswell. *Canadian Forum* 42 (January 1963): 237–8.

Brewster, Elizabeth. "East Coast–Canada." *Fiddlehead* 10 (fall 1948): 94. Used
with permission of Paul Denham, literary executor of the estate of Elizabeth Brewster.

– Letter to Alfred G. Bailey. 23 September 1968. Elizabeth Brewster Fonds,
MG30 D370, Correspondence: Personal and Literary, box 15, file 4, LAC.
Used with permission of Paul Denham, literary executor.

– Letter to Alfred G. Bailey. 26 September 1973. Alfred Goldsworthy Bailey
Fonds, UA RG80, case 95, file 3, ASC, HIL, UNB.

– Letter to Alfred G. Bailey. 13 September 1975. Alfred Goldsworthy Bailey
Fonds, UA RG80, case 95, file 3, ASC, HIL, UNB.

– "Looking Both Ways." *Fiddlehead* 125 (spring 1980): 15–16.

– "Only the Subtle Things." *Fiddlehead* 1 (1945): 5.

Brown, Edward Killoran. *On Canadian Poetry.* 1943. Ottawa: Tecumseh Press
1973.

– "Memoir of Duncan Campbell Scott." In E.K. Brown, ed., *Selected Poems of Duncan Campbell Scott.* Toronto: Ryerson 1951. xi–xlii.

Buckler, Ernest. *The Mountain and the Valley.* 1952. Toronto: McClelland and Stewart 1989.

Buckner, Phillip A. "The 1860s: An End and a Beginning." In Phillip A. Buckner and John G. Reid, eds., *The Atlantic Region to Confederation: A History.* Toronto: University of Toronto Press 1994. 360–86.

– "Acadiensis II." *Acadiensis* 1, no. 1 (autumn 1971): 3–9.

– "Beware the Canadian Wolf: The Maritimes and Confederation." *Acadiensis* 46, no. 2 (summer/autumn 2017): 177–95.

Bumstead, J.M. "Scottish Immigration to the Maritimes 1770–1815: A New Look at an Old Theme." *Acadiensis* 10, no. 2 (spring 1981): 65–85.

Burt, A.R., J.B. Powell, and Carl Crow, eds. "V.K. Wellington Koo (Gu Weijun) 顧維鈞. " [Translation of the China Story Project]. *Biographies of Prominent Chinese*, 53. Shanghai: Biographical Publishing Company 1925.

Bushman, Richard L. "Cultural Orientations: Migrations West, Migrations North." In Margaret Conrad and Barry Moody, eds., *Planter Links: Community and Culture in Colonial Nova Scotia.* Fredericton: Acadiensis 2001. 1–11.

Cameron, Elspeth. *Hugh MacLennan: A Writer's Life.* Toronto: University of Toronto Press 1981.

Camp, Dalton. "Alexander College." In Scott Wade and Hugh Lloyd, eds., *Behind the Hill.* Fredericton: UNB 1967. 182–4.

– *Gentlemen, Players and Politicians.* Toronto: McClelland and Stewart 1970.

Campbell, Wanda. "'Every Sea-Surrounded Hour': The Margin in Maritime Poetry." *Studies in Canadian Literature/Études en littérature canadienne* 33, no. 2 (2008): 151–70.

Cappon, James. *Charles G.D. Roberts.* Toronto: Ryerson [1923].

– *Charles G.D. Roberts and the Influence of His Times.* 1905. Ottawa: Tecumseh 1975.

Carman, Bliss. "The Ships of Saint John." In *Later Poems by Bliss Carman.* Introduction by R.H. Hathaway, 7, 9. Illustrated by J.E.H. MacDonald. Toronto: McClelland and Stewart 1926.

– "Spring Song." In *The Selected Poems of Bliss Carman.* 1954. Edited and introduced by Lorne Pierce. Toronto: McClelland and Stewart 1960. 47–8.

Carpenter, Humphrey. *A Serious Character: The Life of Ezra Pound.* New York: Delta 1988.

Carvell, Pamela. "Donald B. Gammon." In Tony Tremblay, ed., *The New Brunswick Literary Encyclopedia.* Fredericton: New Brunswick Studies Centre 2010. http://stu-sites.ca/nble/g/gammon_donald.html.

Chaney, Charles L. *The Birth of Missions in America*. South Pasadena, CA:
   William Carey Library 1976.

Child, Philip. Letter to Desmond Pacey. 15 August 1945. Desmond Pacey
   Fonds, MG30, D339, vol. 6, file 9, Correspondence, 1945, LAC.

Chilibeck, John. "Province in a 'Death Spiral,' Warns McKenna," [Moncton]
   Times & Transcript, 25 October 2014, B1, 2.

Chong, Corinna. "Julia Catherine Beckwith Hart." In Tony Tremblay, ed.,
   The New Brunswick Literary Encyclopedia. Fredericton: New Brunswick
   Studies Centre 2011. http://stu-sites.ca/nble/h/hart_julia_catherine
   _beckwith.html.

Christian, William. *Parkin: Canada's Most Famous Forgotten Man*. Toronto:
   Blue Butterfly 2008.

Christie, Nancy, and Michael Gauvreau. *Christian Churches and Their Peoples,
   1840–1965: A Social History of Religion in Canada*. Toronto: University of
   Toronto Press 2010.

Churchill, Winston. *My Early Life: 1874–1904*. 1930. Intro. William Man-
   chester. New York: Touchstone 1996.

Clough, Arthur Hugh. "Say Not the Struggle Nought Availeth." In F.L. Mul-
   hauser, ed., *The Poems of Arthur Hugh Clough*. 2nd ed. Oxford: Clarendon
   Press 1974. 206.

Cogswell, Fred. "Acceptance." *Fiddlehead* 6 (February 1947): 52. Used with
   permission of Kathleen Forsythe, literary executor of the estate of Fred
   Cogswell.

– "Art" [after Theophile Gautier]. In *In My Own Growing*. Ottawa: Borealis
   1993. 38–40. Used with permission of Kathleen Forsythe, literary executor
   of the estate of Fred Cogswell.

– "For an Artist." In *A Long Apprenticeship: The Collected Poems of Fred
   Cogswell*. Fredericton: Fiddlehead Poetry Books 1980. 217.

– "The Canadian Novel from Confederation until World War One." MA thesis, University of New Brunswick, 1950.

– "On Canadian Poets." *Fiddlehead* 10 (March 1950): 11.

– "Choosing a Printer." *Fiddlehead* 185 (1995): 35–6.

– "Conclusion." *Fiddlehead* 5 (November 1946): 50.

– "Desmond Pacey." *Canadian Literature* 66 (autumn 1975): 7–13.

– "The Development of Writing [in New Brunswick]." In R.A. Tweedie,
   Fred Cogswell, and W. Stewart MacNutt, eds., *Arts in New Brunswick*.
   Fredericton: Brunswick Press 1967. 19–31.

– "The Double-Headed Child." In *Ghosts*. Ottawa: Borealis 2002. 12–13.

– "Editorial." *Fiddlehead* 23–4 (February 1955): 1.

– "Editorial." *Fiddlehead* 64 (spring 1965): 76.

- "E.J. Pratt's Literary Reputation." *Canadian Literature* 19 (winter 1964): 6–12.
- "How Can I Say ...?" In *Later in Chicago*. Nepean, ON: Borealis 2003. 43.
- Interview with author, March, April, May 2002. Fredericton.
- Introduction to "The Canadian Novel from Confederation until World War One." MA thesis, University of New Brunswick, 1950.
- "It Began in 1935." In *Ghosts*. Ottawa: Borealis 2002. 41–2.
- Letter to Richard Ashman. 30 September 1957. Fiddlehead/Cogswell Fonds, UA RG83, MS1, Correspondence # 1.2782, ASC, HIL, UNB.
- Letter to A.G. Bailey. 25 May 1950. Dr Alfred Goldsworthy Bailey Fonds, UA RG80, box 39, file 6, ASC, HIL, UNB.
- Letter to A.G. Bailey. 2 June 1950. Dr Alfred Goldsworthy Bailey Fonds, UA RG80, box 39, file 6. ASC, HIL, UNB.
- Letter to A.G. Bailey. 14 November 1950. Dr Alfred Goldsworthy Bailey Fonds, UA RG80, box 39, file 6, ASC, HIL, UNB.
- Letter to A.G. Bailey. 18 February 1951. Dr Alfred Goldsworthy Bailey Fonds, UA RG80, box 39, file 6, ASC, HIL, UNB.
- Letter to A.G. Bailey. 16 August 1951. Dr Alfred Goldsworthy Bailey Fonds, UA RG80, box 39, file 6, ASC, HIL, UNB.
- Letter to A.G. Bailey. 20 September 1951. Dr Alfred Goldsworthy Bailey Fonds, UA RG80, box 39, file 6, ASC, HIL, UNB.
- Letter to Helen Ball. 25 October 1958. Fiddlehead/Cogswell Fonds, UA RG83, MS1, Correspondence # 1.3969, University of New Brunswick Libraries Archives and Special Collections.
- Letter to Jean Boucher [director, Canada Council]. 3 October 1966. Desmond Pacey Fonds, MG30, D339, vol. 4, Library and Archives Canada.
- Letter to Arthur Bourinot. 14 December 1953. Fiddlehead/Cogswell Fonds, UA RG83, MS1.108–1.244. ASC. HIL, UNB.
- Letter to Arthur Bourinot. 6 January 1955. Fiddlehead/Cogswell Fonds, UA RG83, MS1.1.740(b), ASC, HIL, UNB.
- Letter to Alan Crawley. 7 February 1954. Fiddlehead/Cogswell Fonds, UA RG83, box 1, file 4, ASC, HIL, UNB.
- Letter to Louis Dudek. 6 November 1953. Fiddlehead/Cogswell Fonds, UA RG83, box 1, file 3, ASC, HIL, UNB.
- Letter to the Editor, *Canadian Forum*. 14 November 1953. Fiddlehead/Cogswell Fonds, UA RG83, MS1.108–1.244, ASC, HIL, UNB.
- Letter to the Editor, *Canadian Forum*. 7 January 1954. Fiddlehead/Cogswell Fonds, UA RG83, box 1, file 4, ASC, HIL, UNB.
- Letter to Donald Gammon. 26 July 1950. Fiddlehead/Cogswell Fonds, UA RG83, MS1.1–19 (1945–52), ASC, HIL, UNB.

- Letter to Robert Gibbs. 18 December 1952. Fiddlehead/Cogswell Fonds, UA RG83, MS1.1–19 (1945–52), ASC, HIL, UNB.
- Letter to Richard Hatfield. 30 December 1970. Fiddlehead/Cogswell Fonds, UA RG83, box 18, MS2.941, ASC, HIL, UNB.
- Letter to Marleen Hayes. 23 February 1958. Fiddlehead/Cogswell Fonds, UA RG83, MS1, Correspondence # 1.3241, ASC, HIL, UNB.
- Letter to Lawrence Holmes. 10 December 1955. Fiddlehead/Cogswell Fonds, UA RG83, MS1, Correspondence # 1.1600, ASC, HIL, UNB.
- Letter to Blanche Muirhead Howard. [November 1952]. Fiddlehead/Cogswell Fonds, UA RG83, MS1.1–19 (1945–52), ASC, HIL, UNB.
- Letter to Dorothy Livesay. 31 January 1954. Fiddlehead/Cogswell Fonds, UA RG83, box 1, file 3, ASC, HIL, UNB.
- Letter to Dorothy Livesay. 25 July 1957. Fiddlehead/Cogswell Fonds, UA RG83, MS1, Correspondence # 1.2431, ASC, HIL, UNB.
- Letter to James Boyer May. 4 December 1953. Fiddlehead/Cogswell Fonds, UA RG83, box 1, file 3, ASC, HIL, UNB.
- Letter to Robert L. McDougall. 16 June 1958. Fiddlehead/Cogswell Fonds, UA RG83, MS1.3532(b), ASC, HIL, UNB.
- Letter to Floris McLaren. 7 December 1953. Fiddlehead/Cogswell Fonds, UA RG83, MS 1.108–1.244, ASC, HIL, UNB.
- Letter to Alden Nowlan. 8 January 1958. Fiddlehead/Cogswell Fonds, UA RG83, box 28, MS6 (1955–60), ASC, HIL, UNB.
- Letter to the *Observer*, c/o the *Family Herald* & *Weekly Star*, 29 January 1954. Fiddlehead/Cogswell Fonds, UA RG83, box 1, file 4, ASC, HIL, UNB.
- Letter to Gil Orlovitz. 23 February 1959. Fiddlehead/Cogswell Fonds, UA RG83, MS1, Correspondence # 1.4384, ASC, HIL, UNB.
- Letter to Desmond Pacey. 5 January 1950. Desmond Pacey Fonds, MS30, D339, vol. 17, file 29, LAC.
- Letter to Desmond Pacey. 23 October 1951. Desmond Pacey Fonds, MG30, D339, vol. 17, file 29, LAC.
- Letter to Desmond Pacey. 9 June 1960. Desmond Pacey Fonds, MG30, D339, vol. 17, file 30, LAC.
- Letter to Al Purdy. 1 January [1954?]. Fiddlehead/Cogswell Fonds, UA RG83, MS1.245–356, ASC, HIL, UNB.
- Letter to Alan Reidpath. 15 October 1958. Fiddlehead/Cogswell Fonds, UA RG83, MS1, Correspondence # 1.2431, University of New Brunswick Libraries, Archives and Special Collections.
- Letter to Robert Rogers. 22 December 1951. Fiddlehead/Cogswell Fonds, UA RG83, MS1.1–19 (1945–52), ASC, HIL, UNB.
- Letter to Tony Tremblay. [23] September 2003.

- Letter to Tony Tremblay. 3 October 2003.
- Letter to Phyllis Webb. 19 October 1955. Fiddlehead/Cogswell Fonds, UA RG83, MS1.1473, ASC, HIL, UNB.
- "Literary Traditions in New Brunswick." *Transactions of the Royal Society of Canada* Series 4, vol. 15 (1977): 287–99.
- "Little Magazines and Small Presses in Canada." In Diane Bessai and David Jackel, eds., *Figures in a Ground: Canadian Essays on Modern Literature.* Saskatoon: Western Producer Prairie Books 1978. 162–73.
- "Lyric." *Fiddlehead* 12 (March 1951): 119.
- "The Man Who Climbed and Came Back." *Fiddlehead* 4 (February 1946): 39. Used with permission of Kathleen Forsythe, literary executor of the estate of Fred Cogswell.
- "The Mill." In *The Best Notes Merge.* Ottawa: Borealis 1988. 38–9.
- "Modern Acadian Poetry." *Canadian Literature* 68–9 (spring-summer 1976): 62–75.
- "Moses Hardy Nickerson: A Study." *Dalhousie Review* 38 (winter 1959): 472–85.
- "The Mystery of Synthesis." *Fiddlehead* 125 (spring 1980): 27[–36].
- "New Brunswick." In *The Stunted Strong.* Fredericton: Fiddlehead Poetry Books 1954. 16.
- "New Canadian Library." *Edge* 2 (spring 1964): 124–6.
- "Nineteenth Century Poetry in the Maritimes and the Problem of Research." *Newsletter: The Bibliographical Society of Canada* 5, no. 1 (September 1961): 5–19.
- "Ode to Fredericton." In *A Long Apprenticeship: The Collected Poems of Fred Cogswell.* Fredericton: Fiddlehead Poetry Books 1980. 35. [First published in the *Brunswickan*, January 1948.] Used with permission of Kathleen Forsythe, literary executor of the estate of Fred Cogswell.
- "On Canadian Poets." *Fiddlehead* 10 (March 1950): 11. Used with permission of Kathleen Forsythe, literary executor of the estate of Fred Cogswell.
- "The Poetry of Modern Quebec." In Norman Penlington, ed., *On Canada: Essays in Honour of Frank H. Underhill.* Toronto: University of Toronto Press 1971. 54–70.
- "Prisms." *Fiddlehead* 4 (February 1946): 37. Used with permission of Kathleen Forsythe, literary executor of the estate of Fred Cogswell.
- "Restatement of Policy." *Fiddlehead* 38 (autumn 1958): 1–2.
- Review of *Creative Writing in Canada*, by Desmond Pacey. *Fiddlehead* 19 (November 1953): 11, 13.
- "The Singing Fool." In *Deeper Than Mind.* Ottawa: Borealis 2001. 92.

- "Statement of Position." *Fiddlehead* 10 (fall 1948): 96. Used with permission of Kathleen Forsythe, literary executor of the estate of Fred Cogswell.
- "The Way of the Sea: A Symbolic Epic." *Dalhousie Review* 35 (1955): 374–81.
- "Valley-Folk." In *The Stunted Strong*. Fredericton: Fiddlehead Poetry Books 1954. 1. Used with permission of Kathleen Forsythe, literary executor of the estate of Fred Cogswell.
Cogswell, Fred, ed. *The Atlantic Anthology, Volume 1: Prose*. Charlottetown, PEI: Ragweed 1984.
- *The Atlantic Anthology, Volume 2: Poetry*. Charlottetown, PEI: Ragweed 1985.
Collin, W.E. *The White Savannahs*. 1936. Toronto: University of Toronto Press 1975.
Cormier, Michel. "The Robichaud Legacy: What Remains?" In *The Robichaud Era, 1960–70*. N.p.: ICRDR 2001. 187–98.
Crawley, Alan. "Editor's Note." *Contemporary Verse* 1, no. 4 (June 1942): 3.
Creelman, David. *Setting in the East: Maritime Realist Fiction*. Montreal and Kingston: McGill-Queen's University Press 2003.
Crouzet, François. "Wars, Blockade, and Economic Change in Europe, 1792–1815." *Journal of Economic History* 24, no. 4 (December 1964): 56–88.
Curtis, Wayne. *Of Earthly and River Things: An Angler's Memoir*. Fredericton: Goose Lane 2012.
Daniells, Roy. Letter to Desmond Pacey. 3 September 1958. Desmond Pacey Fonds, MG30, D339, "Daniells, Roy – Correspondence 1956–61," file 14, LAC.
- Letter to Desmond Pacey. 26 December 1962. Desmond Pacey Fonds, MG30, D339, "Daniells, Roy – Correspondence," file 15, LAC.
Dauphin, Damien. "Foresterie: un cinéaste livre une charge contre la compagnie Irving." *L'Acadie Nouvelle*, 30 March 2014, http://www.acadien ouvelle.com/actualites/2014/03/30/foresterie-cineaste-livre-charge-contre-compagnie-irving-2/.
Davey, Frank. "Desmond Pacey." In *From There to Here: A Guide to English-Canadian Literature since 1960*. Our Nature – Our Voices II. Erin, ON: Press Porcepic 1974. 228–9.
- *Louis Dudek & Raymond Souster*. Vancouver: Douglas & McIntyre 1980.
Derrida, Jacques. *Of Grammatology*. 1974. Trans. Gayatri C. Spivak. Baltimore, MD: Johns Hopkins University Press 1998.
Dionne, René, and Pierre Cantin. *Bibliographie de la critique de la littérature québécoise et canadienne-française dans les revues canadiennes (1760–1899)*. Ottawa: University of Ottawa Press 1992. 209–10.

Djwa, Sandra. *The Politics of the Imagination: A Life of F.R. Scott*. Toronto: McClelland and Stewart 1987.

– *Professing English: A Life of Roy Daniells*. Toronto: University of Toronto Press 2002.

Doyle, Arthur T. *Front Benches and Back Rooms: A Story of Corruption, Muckraking, Raw Partisanship and Intrigue in New Brunswick*. Toronto: Green Tree Publishing 1976.

Draft of Proposal for a Permanent Appointment for Alden Nowlan. [1972]. Desmond Pacey Fonds, MG30, D339, vol. 4, LAC.

Dudek, Louis. Letter to Fred Cogswell. 4 June 1962. Fiddlehead/Cogswell Fonds, UA RG83, MS1, Correspondence 1.6157, ASC, HIL, UNB.

– "Patterns of Recent Canadian Poetry." *Culture* 19, no. 4 (December 1958). Reprinted in Louis Dudek and Michael Gnarowski, eds., *The Making of Modern Poetry in Canada*. Toronto: Ryerson 1970. 270–85.

– "The Role of Little Magazines in Canada." In Louis Dudek and Michael Gnarowski, eds., *The Making of Modern Poetry in Canada*. Toronto: Ryerson 1970. 205–12.

Duguay, Calixte. "To Have a Homeland." In Fred Cogswell, ed., and Jo-Anne Elder, trans., *Unfinished Dreams: Contemporary Poetry of Acadie*. Fredericton: Goose Lane 1990. 82–3.

Eagleton, Terry. *Marxism and Literary Criticism*. Berkeley: University of California Press 1976.

Edgar, Pelham. "Literary Criticism in Canada." In Northrop Frye, ed., *Across My Path*. Toronto: Ryerson 1952. 118–28.

"Editorial." *Tamarack Review* 9 (autumn 1958): 3–4.

Eggleston, Wilfrid. *The Frontier and Canadian Letters*. 1957. Carleton Library no. 102. Toronto: McClelland and Stewart 1977.

Eliot, Thomas Stearns. *After Strange Gods: A Primer of Modern Heresy*. London: Faber and Faber 1934.

– "Euripides and Professor Murray." In *The Sacred Wood: Essays on Poetry and Criticism*. 1920. London: Methuen 1964. 71–7.

– "Tradition and the Individual Talent." In *The Sacred Wood: Essays on Poetry and Criticism*. 1920. London: Methuen 1964. 47–59.

Emerson, Ralph Waldo. "Nature." In *Nature*. Boston: James Munroe and Company 1836. 9–14.

English Department, UNB. Desmond Pacey Fonds, MG30, D339, vol. 20–3, "Klinck, Carl Professor 1945–1975," LAC.

Fetherling, Douglas. *The Gentle Anarchist: A Life of George Woodcock*. Vancouver: Douglas & McIntyre 1998.

Finch, Robert. Letter to Ian Pearson. 1 December 1933. Robert Finch

Papers, MS Coll. 324, box 14, file 15, Thomas Fisher Rare Book Library, University of Toronto.

Fitzpatrick, P.J. "New Brunswick: The Politics of Pragmatism." In Martin Robin, ed., *Canadian Provincial Politics: The Party Systems of the Ten Provinces.* Scarborough, ON: Prentice-Hall 1972. 116–33.

Flaherty, Jim. "No 'Corporate Welfare' for Closing Mills: Flaherty." [New Brunswick] *Telegraph-Journal,* 13 December 2007, A4.

Flemming, Hugh John. "Reviews Political Situation in Radio Address Friday." *Observer,* 4 December 1947, 11.

Flint, F.S. "Imagisme." [March 1913.] In Peter Jones, ed., *Imagist Poetry.* New York: Penguin 1972. 129–30.

Folster, David. "Seeds Planted in Native Soil." *UNB Perspectives* (August 1982): 4.

Forbes, Ernest R. *Challenging the Regional Stereotype: Essays on the 20th Century Maritimes.* Fredericton: Acadiensis 1989.

– "In Search of a Post-Confederation Maritime Historiography, 1900–1967." In *Challenging the Regional Stereotype: Essays on the 20th Century Maritimes.* Fredericton: Acadiensis 1989. 48–66.

– *The Maritime Rights Movement, 1919–1927: A Study in Canadian Regionalism.* Montreal and Kingston: McGill-Queen's University Press 1979.

"Forestry Plan to Be Unveiled Today." CBC News Online, New Brunswick, 12 March 2014, http://www.cbc.ca/news/canada/new-brunswick/forestry-plan-to-be-unveiled-today-1.2568734.

Francis, Daniel. *National Dreams: Myth, Memory, and Canadian History.* Vancouver: Arsenal Pulp Press 1997.

Frank, David. "The 1920s: Class and Region, Resistance and Accommodation." In E.R. Forbes and D.A. Muise, eds., *The Atlantic Provinces in Confederation.* Toronto and Fredericton: University of Toronto Press and Acadiensis 1993. 233–71.

– "The Cape Breton Coal Industry and the Rise and Fall of the British Empire Steel Corporation." *Acadiensis* 7, no. 1 (autumn 1977): 3–34.

Friedland, Martin L. *The University of Toronto: A History.* Toronto: University of Toronto Press 2002.

Friesen, Gerald. "Defining the Prairies: Or, Why the Prairies Don't Exist." In Robert Wardhaugh, ed., *Toward Defining the Prairies: Region, Culture, and History.* Winnipeg: University of Manitoba Press 2001. 13–28.

– "The Western Canadian Identity." *Canadian Historical Association Historical Papers* (1973): 13–19.

Friskney, Janet B. *New Canadian Library: The Ross-McClelland Years, 1952–1978.* Toronto: University of Toronto Press 2007.

Frost, James D. "The 'Nationalization' of the Bank of Nova Scotia, 1880–1910." In T.W. Acheson, David Frank, and James D. Frost, eds., *Industrialization and Underdevelopment in the Maritimes, 1880–1930*. Toronto: Garamond 1985. 27–54.

Frye, Northrop. "Desmond Pacey (1917–1975)." Northrop Frye Fonds, 1988 Accession, box 60, file 5, Victoria University Library [University of Toronto]. Used with permission of Lisa J. Sherlock, chief librarian.

– Editor's Introduction. *Across My Path*, by Pelham Edgar. Toronto: Ryerson 1952. vii–xi.

– "From Nationalism to Regionalism: The Maturing of Canadian Culture [Robert Fulford Talks with Northrop Frye]." In Morris Wolfe, ed., *Aurora: New Canadian Writing 1980*. Toronto: Doubleday 1980. 5–15.

– "Letters in Canada 1957: Poetry." *University of Toronto Quarterly* 27, no. 4 (July 1958): 434–50.

– Preface. *The Bush Garden: Essays on the Canadian Imagination*. Toronto: Anansi 1971. i–ix.

Fuller, Danielle. *Writing the Everyday: Women's Textual Communities in Atlantic Canada*. Montreal and Kingston: McGill-Queen's University Press 2004.

Gair, R., et al., eds. *A Literary and Linguistic History of New Brunswick*. Fredericton: Fiddlehead and Goose Lane, 1985.

Galloway, David. "SCL Interviews: Fred Cogswell." *Studies in Canadian Literature/Études en littérature canadienne* 10, nos. 1–2 (1985): 208–25.

Galt, John. *Annals of the Parish and the Ayrshire Legatees*. 1821. Edinburgh: John Grant 1936.

Gammon, Donald B. "The Fiddlehead." *Fiddlehead* 2 (April 1945): 17. Used with permission of Carolyn Gammon, literary executor of the estate of Donald Gammon.

Gellner, Ernest. *Nations and Nationalism*. Oxford: Basil Blackwell 1983.

Gerson, Carole. "*Anne of Green Gables* Goes to University: L.M. Montgomery and Academic Culture." In Irene Gammel, ed., *Making of Avonlea: L.M. Montgomery and Popular Culture*. Toronto: University of Toronto Press 2002. 17–31.

Gibbons, Luke. *Edmund Burke and Ireland: Aesthetics, Politics, and the Colonial Sublime*. Cambridge: Cambridge University Press 2003.

Gibbs, Robert. "English Poetry in New Brunswick, 1940–1982." In R. Gair et al., eds., *A Literary and Linguistic History of New Brunswick*. Fredericton: Fiddlehead and Goose Lane 1985. 125–44.

– "Fred's Overcoat." *Ellipse* [Fred Cogswell Special Issue, edited by Jo-Anne Elder] 68 (autumn 2002): 162, 164.

- Letter to Desmond Pacey. 14 May 1953. Desmond Pacey Fonds, MG30,
  D339, vol. 2, LAC.
- Letter to Robert Rogers. 30 December 1952. Fiddlehead/Cogswell Fonds,
  UA RG 83, MSI.1–19 (1945–52), ASC, HIL, UNB.
- Letter to Robert Rogers. 27 March 1953. Fiddlehead/Cogswell Fonds, UA
  RG83, MSI.1–19, ASC, HIL, UNB.
- "Portents and Promises." In Special Issue of the *Fiddlehead* [Fiddlehead
  Gold: 50 Years of the Fiddlehead Magazine, edited by S. Campbell et al.]
  185 (1995): 11–16.
- "Three Decades and a Bit under the Elms: A Fragmentary Memoir." In
  Terry Whalen, ed., *The Atlantic Anthology. Vol. 3: Critical Essays.* Toronto:
  ECW Press 1985. 231–9.
Gnarowski, Michael. *Contact 1952–1954: Notes on the History and Back-
  ground of the Periodical and an Index.* Montreal: Delta Canada 1966.
Godard, Barbara. "Notes from the Cultural Field: Canadian Literature from
  Identity to Commodity." In Smaro Kamboureli, ed., *Canadian Literature
  at the Crossroads of Language and Culture: Selected Essays by Barbara
  Godard, 1987–2005.* Edmonton: NeWest Press 2008. 235–71.
Godin, Alcide. "Education Reforms in New Brunswick, 1960–70." In *The
  Robichaud Era, 1960–70.* N.p.: ICRDR 2001. 173–86.
Grader, Daniel, ed. *The Life of Sir Walter Scott by John Macrone.* Edinburgh:
  Edinburgh University Press 2013
Gregg, Milton F. "Confidential Memo to All Faculty Departments." 13 Octo-
  ber 1944. W.C.D. Pacey Fonds, MG HI, Series 1, case 2, file 5, ASC, HIL, UNB.
Grierson, John. Letter to Desmond Pacey. 10 December 1943. W.C.D. Pacey
  Fonds, MG LI, Series 1, case 2, file 3, ASC, HIL, UNB.
Griffiths, Naomi. "Acadians." In Paul Robert Magocsi, ed., *Encyclopedia of
  Canada's Peoples.* Toronto: University of Toronto Press 1999. 114–36.
Groening, Laura S. *E.K. Brown: A Study in Conflict.* Toronto: University of
  Toronto Press 1993.
Grove, Frederick Philip. *Fruits of the Earth.* 1933. Toronto: McClelland and
  Stewart (NCL) 1965.
- *Settlers of the Marsh.* 1925. Toronto: McClelland and Stewart (NCL) 1965.
"Guide for Assessment of Applicants" [Beaverbrook Overseas Scholarships].
  Dr Alfred Goldsworthy Bailey Fonds, UA RG80, box 48, file 4, ASC, HIL, UNB.
Gustafson, Ralph. Review of *The Stunted Strong,* by Fred Cogswell. *Fiddle-
  head* 23–4 (February 1955): 21–2.
Haliburton, Thomas Chandler. "Aiming High." *The Attache or, Sam Slick in
  England.* 2nd vol. Chapter X. http://www.gutenberg.org/files/7823/7823-
  h/7823-h.htm#link2HCH0025.

– "The Clockmaker." *The Clockmaker, or The Sayings and Doings of Samuel Slick of Slickville*. New York: Leviathan Press 1927. 9–15.

Harris, Cole. *Making Native Space: Colonialism, Resistance, and Reserves in British Columbia*. Vancouver: UBC Press 2003.

Harvey, D.C. "The Importance of Local History in the Writing of General History." *Canadian Historical Review* 13, no. 3 (September 1932): 244–51.

– "The Intellectual Awakening of Nova Scotia." *Dalhousie Review* 13, no. 1 (April 1933): 1–21.

Hathaway, Rufus H. "Bliss Carman: An Appreciation." [Introduction to] *Later Poems by Bliss Carman*. Illustrated by J.E.H. MacDonald. Toronto: McClelland and Stewart 1926. vii–xxii.

Hatt, Blaine E. "Fred Cogswell: A Well-Placed Candle." *Atlantic Advocate* 81, no. 4 (December 1990): 38–40.

Hicks, T.J. General Letter of Reference for Desmond Pacey. 23 January 1934. W.C.D. Pacey Fonds, MG LI, Series 1, case 2, file 2, ASC, HIL, UNB.

Hotchner, A.E. *Papa Hemingway: A Personal Memoir*. New York: Random House 1966.

Hounsell, Kayla. "Divisive Bilingualism Debate Rears Its Head in N.B. Election Campaign," CBC News Online, New Brunswick, 13 September 2018, http://www.cbc.ca/news/canada/new-brunswick-election-language-bilingualism-french-1.4822491.

Howe, Joseph. "Address at the Howe Family Gathering" [1871]. In *Joseph Howe: Poems and Essays*. Edited and introduced by M.G. Parks. Toronto: University of Toronto Press 1973. 276–98.

Hoyt, Don. *A Brief History of the Liberal Party of New Brunswick*. Saint John: N.p., n.d.

Hunt, Russell, and Robert Campbell. *K.C. Irving: The Art of the Industrialist*. Toronto: McClelland and Stewart 1973.

Innis, Harold Adams. *The Cod Fisheries: The History of an International Economy*. 1940. Toronto: University of Toronto Press 1978.

– "The Decline in the Efficiency of Instruments Essential in Equilibrium." *American Economic Review* 43, no. 1 (March 1953): 16–22.

– "A Plea for the University Tradition." *Dalhousie Review* 24 (1944): 298–305. [Commencement address, UNB, May 1944.]

Irvine, Dean. "'Little Magazines' in English Canada." In Peter Brooker and Andrew Thacker, eds., *The Oxford Critical and Cultural History of Modernist Magazines*. Vol. 2, North America, 1894–1960. Oxford: Oxford University Press 2012. 602–28.

Irvine, Dean, Vanessa Lent, and Bart Vautour, eds., *Making Canada New:*

Editing, Modernism, and New Media. Toronto: University of Toronto Press 2017.

"Irving Clout with Government Challenged in Wake of Forest Deal." CBC News Online, New Brunswick, 14 March 2014, http://www.cbc.ca/news/canada/new-brunswick/irving-clout-with-government-challenged-in-wake-of-forest-deal-1.2572410.

"[J.D.] Irving Ltd. to Invest $513M in Its Mills." CBC News Online, New Brunswick, 13 March 2014, http://www.cbc.ca/news/canada/new-brunswick/j-d-irving-ltd-to-invest-513m-in-its-mills-1.2570971.

Ives, Edward. "Alden Nowlan's Poetry: A Personal Chronicle." *Fiddlehead* [Alden Nowlan Special Issue] 81 (August, September, October 1969): 61–6.

Jameson, E.O. *The Cogswells in America*. Boston: A. Mudge and Son 1884.

Jessup, Lynda, ed. *Antimodernism and Artistic Experience: Policing the Boundaries of Modernity*. Toronto: University of Toronto Press 2015.

Johnson, James W. "Old Provinces, New Modernisms: Toward the Editorial Poetics of the Maritime Little Magazine." MA thesis, University of New Brunswick, 2015.

Keefer, Janice Kulyk. *Under Eastern Eyes: A Critical Reading of Maritime Fiction*. Toronto: University of Toronto Press 1987.

Kennedy, Leo. "Directions for Canadian Poets." In Peter Stevens, ed., *The McGill Movement: A.J.M. Smith, F.R. Scott and Leo Kennedy*. Toronto: Ryerson 1969. 11–19.

Kent, Peter. *Inventing Academic Freedom: The 1968 Strax Affair at the University of New Brunswick*. Halifax: Formac 2012.

Klinck, Carl F. *Giving Canada a Literary History: A Memoir by Carl F. Klinck*. Edited and introduced by Sandra Djwa. Montreal and Kingston: McGill-Queen's University Press 1991.

Knights of the Ku Klux Klan. Circular No. 888 [1935]. Ku Klux Klan Fonds, MC1950, Provincial Archives of New Brunswick.

Kokotailo, Philip. "Manifold Division: Desmond Pacey's History of English-Canadian Poetry." *Studies in Canadian Literature/Études en littérature canadienne* 22, no. 2 (1997): 1–27.

Kymlicka, Will, and Kathryn Walker, eds. *Rooted Cosmopolitanism: Canada and the World*. Vancouver: University of British Columbia Press 2012.

Lane, M. Travis. "Interview with Alfred Goldsworthy Bailey, September 1985." Transcript. Dr Alfred Goldsworthy Bailey Fonds, MS4, 7.4.3, ASC, HIL, UNB.

– "The Muskrat in His Brook." *Fiddlehead* 100 (1974): 95–101.

- "A Sense of the Medium: The Poetry of A.G. Bailey." *Canadian Poetry* 19 (1986): 1–10.

Larocque, Peter J. "Fine Intentions: An Account of the Owens Art Institution in Saint John, New Brunswick, 1884–1893." MA thesis, University of New Brunswick, 1996.

Lawner, Lynne, ed. *Letters from Prison by Antonio Gramsci.* Trans. Lynne Lawner. New York: Harper and Row 1973.

Lawrence, Robert. "Transcript of December 1946 Radio Broadcast." *Fiddlehead* 7 (December 1947): 2–8.

LeBlanc, Gilberte Couturier, Alcide Godin, and Aldéo Renaud. "French Education in the Maritimes, 1604–1992." Trans. Faith J. Cormier. In Jean Diagle, ed., *Acadia of the Maritimes.* Moncton: Chaire d'études adaciennes 1995. 523–62.

Lee, Dennis. Letter to Fred Cogswell. 17 July 1973. Fiddlehead/Cogswell Fonds, UA RG83, box 19, MS2.1892, ASC, HIL, UNB.

Lefebvre, Henri. *The Production of Space.* Trans. Donald Nicholson-Smith. Oxford: Blackwell 1991.

Levy, Leonard W., and Carl Siracusa, eds. *Essays on the Early Republic, 1789–1815.* Hinsdale, IL: Dryden Press 1974.

Livesay, Dorothy. Letter to Fred Cogswell. 18 July 1957. Fiddlehead/Cogswell Fonds, UA RG83, MS1.2431, ASC, HIL, UNB.

"Local News." *Carleton Observer,* 15 November 1916, 5.

Lower, Arthur R.M. *Colony to Nation: A History of Canada.* Toronto: Longmans, Green 1946.

"Lt.-Gen. Sansom to Contest York-Sunbury for the P.-C.s." *Observer,* 18 September 1947, 10.

Lucas, Alec. Review of *Border River,* by A.G. Bailey. *Fiddlehead* 18 (summer 1953): 11.

MacDonald, Gail. *Learning to be Modern: Pound, Eliot, and the American University.* Oxford: Clarendon 1993.

MacFarlane, W.G. *Fredericton History: Two Centuries of Romance, War, Privation and Struggle.* 1893. Woodstock, NB: Non-Entity Press 1981.

MacIntosh, William. "WILLIAM MACINTOSH's Reply to Dr Webster's Report, June 21, 1937." Transcript. Dr Alfred Goldsworthy Bailey Fonds, UA RG80, box 32, file 4, ASC, HIL, UNB.

MacKenzie, Norman. Letter to Jack Humphrey. 15 April 1942. Presidents' Papers, 1909–1945, UA RG136, Series 4, box 5, file 4 (1942, E-H), ASC, HIL, UNB. Used with permission of Francesca Holyoke, archivist.

- Letter to Hugh MacLennan. 1 April 1943. Hugh MacLennan Papers, MS

466, CI, file 10, Rare Books and Special Collections, McGill University
Library. Used with permission of Richard Virr, head and curator of
manuscripts, rare books and special collections, McGill University
Library.

MacLennan, Hugh. Letter to E.A. McCourt. 26 July 1944. Desmond Pacey
Fonds, MG 30, D339, vol. 7 (Hugh MacLennan), LAC.

MacLeod, Alistair. *No Great Mischief*. Toronto: McClelland and Stewart
1999.

MacMechan, Archibald. *Headwaters of Canadian Literature*. 1924. New Canadian Library no. 107. Toronto: McClelland and Stewart 1974.

MacMillan, Carrie. "Seaward Vision and Sense of Place: The Maritime
Novel, 1880–1920." In Larry McCann, ed., *People and Place: Studies of
Small Town Life in the Maritimes*. Fredericton: Acadiensis 1987. 79–97.

MacNutt, W.S. *New Brunswick, A History: 1784–1867*. Toronto: Macmillan
1984.

Macpherson, Jay. Letter to Fred Cogswell. 9 March [1961], Fiddlehead/
Cogswell Fonds, UA RG83, MS1, Correspondence # 1.6034, ASC, HIL, UNB.

Macquarrie, Heath. *Red Tory Blues: A Political Memoir*. Toronto: University of
Toronto Press 1992.

MacSkimming, Roy. *The Perilous Trade: Book Publishing in Canada,
1946–2006*. 2003. Toronto: McClelland and Stewart 2007.

"Magnus Speech Day." Newark *Herald*, 22 December 1934, 10.

Maillet, Antonine. *Pélagie, The Return to Acadie*. 1979. Trans. Philip Stratford.
Fredericton: Goose Lane 2004.

Mandel, Eli. "Five New Brunswick Poets." Review of *Five New Brunswick
Poets*, edited by Fred Cogswell. *Fiddlehead* 56 (spring 1963): 65, 67–8.

Marquis, Thomas Guthrie. "English-Canadian Literature." 1913. In Douglas
Lochhead, ed., *Literature of Canada: Poetry and Prose in Reprint*. Introduction by Clara Thomas. Toronto: University of Toronto Press 1973.
493–589.

Marshall, John. Letter to Alfred G. Bailey. 17 February 1947. Fiddle-
head/Cogswell Fonds, UA RG83, MS1.1–19, ASC, HIL, UNB.

Marshall, Tom. *Harsh and Lovely Land: The Major Canadian Poets and the
Making of a Canadian Tradition*. Vancouver: University of British Columbia Press 1979.

Marston, Benjamin. *Diary of Benjamin Marston*. 24 July 1785. In Winslow
Papers, MG H2, vols. 20, 21, 22 (1776–1787), ASC, HIL, UNB. Used with permission of Francesca Holyoke, archivist.

McCulloch, Thomas. "Letter IX." In Malcolm Ross, ed., *The Stepsure Letters*.
Toronto: McClelland and Stewart [NCL] 1960. 67–75.

McInnis, Edgar. "Minor Notes." Review of *Tâo*, by A.G. Bailey. *Saturday Night*, 4 April 1931, 10.

McKay, Don. "Common Sense and Magic." *Fiddlehead* 185 (1995): 233–8.

– "Sporangia Eclectica." *Fiddlehead* 183 (1995): 5–6.

McKay, Ian. *Rebels, Reds, Radicals: Rethinking Canada's Left History*. Toronto: Between the Lines 2005.

McLaren, Floris. Letter to Fred Cogswell. 30 April 1953. Fiddle-head/Cogswell Fonds, UA RG83, MS1.02–107, ASC, HIL, UNB.

McRobbie, Kenneth. "Canadian Chronicle." Review of *Five New Brunswick Poets*, ed. Fred Cogswell. *Poetry* 103 (January 1964): 266–70.

Metcalf, John. *An Aesthetic Underground: A Literary Memoir*. Toronto: Thomas Allen Publishers 2003.

– "Alden Nowlan." [Interview] *Canadian Literature* 63 (winter 1975): 8–17.

– *Kicking against the Pricks*. 1982. Guelph, ON: Red Kite 1986.

Mill, John Stuart. *On Liberty*. 1859. Kitchener: Batoche Books 2001.

Miller, Carman. "The 1940s: War and Rehabilitation." In E.R. Forbes and D.A. Muise, eds., *The Atlantic Provinces in Confederation*. Toronto and Fredericton: University of Toronto Press and Acadiensis 1993. 306–45.

Milton, John. *Areopagitica*. 1644. Paris: Aubier 1956.

Minutes [of the First Meeting of the English Subcommittee of the New Brunswick Department of Education]. W.C.D. Pacey Fonds, MG LI, Series 4, case 33, file 4, ASC, HIL, UNB.

Montague, Susan. *A Pictorial History of the University of New Brunswick*. Fredericton: University of New Brunswick 1992.

Montgomery, L.M. *Anne of Green Gables*. 1908. Toronto: Ryerson 1965.

Moore, Andrew. "The Fiddlehead." In Tony Tremblay, ed., *The New Brunswick Literary Encyclopedia*. Fredericton: New Brunswick Studies Centre 2010. http://stu-sites.ca/nble/f/fiddlehead.html.

Moore, Mavor. "Theatre in English-Speaking Canada." In Malcolm Ross, ed., *The Arts in Canada*. Toronto: Macmillan 1958. 68–76.

Moritz, Albert. "From a Far Star." *Books in Canada* 11, no. 5 (May 1982): 5–8.

Morton, W.L. *The Kingdom of Canada*. 1963. Toronto: McClelland and Stewart 1969.

Mullen, Vernon. "University of New Brunswick." In *Them Lions Will Eat Them Up*. Richmond, ON: Voyager Publishing 1999. 27–42.

Murray, Joan, ed. *Daffodils in Winter: The Life and Letters of Pegi Nicol MacLeod, 1904–1949*. Moonbeam, ON: Penumbra 1984.

Naves, Elaine K. *Robert Weaver: Godfather of Canadian Literature*. Montreal: Véhicule 2007.

Norris, Ken. *The Little Magazine in Canada, 1926–80: Its Role in the Development of Modernism and Post-Modernism in Canadian Poetry.* Toronto: ECW Press 1984.

"Notes." *Fiddlehead* 16 (November 1952): 162.

Nowlan, Alden. "First Impressions." *Bread, Wine and Salt.* 1967. Toronto: Clarke, Irwin and Company 1973. 16.

– "The Fynch Cows." In Brian Bartlett, ed., *Alden Nowlan: Collected Poems.* Fredericton: Goose Lane 2017. 73–4.

– "For Jean Vincent D'Abbadie, Baron St.-Castin." In Brian Bartlett, ed., *Alden Nowlan: Collected Poems.* Fredericton: Goose Lane 2017. 162.

– Letter to Fred Cogswell. 10 January 1961. Fiddlehead/Cogswell Fonds, UA RG83, box 20, MS6 (1961–72), ASC, HIL, UNB.

– Letter to Fred Cogswell. 16 April 1962. Fiddlehead/Cogswell Fonds, UA RG83, box 20, MS6 (1961–72), ASC, HIL, UNB.

– Letter to Fred Cogswell. 22 March 1963. Fiddlehead/Cogswell Fonds, UA RG83, box 20, MS6 (1961–72), ASC, HIL, UNB.

– "Something to Write About." *Canadian Literature* 68–9 (spring-summer 1976): 7–12.

– *The Wanton Troopers.* Fredericton: Goose Lane 1988.

"The Origins and Evolution of Veterans Benefits in Canada, 1914–2004." Reference Paper. Veterans Affairs Canada – Canadian Forces Advisory Council. March 2004. 9 March 2017. http://www.veterans.gc.ca/public/pages/forces/nvc/reference.pdf.

"Outlines By-Election Issues." *Observer,* 25 September 1947, 7.

Pacey, Desmond. "Areas of Research in Canadian Literature." *University of Toronto Quarterly* 23, no. 1 (October 1953): 58–63.

– "Areas of Research in Canadian Literature: A Reconsideration." *Queen's Quarterly* 81 (spring 1974): 62–9.

– "At Last – A Canadian Literature." *Cambridge Review* 60 (2 December 1938): 146–7.

– "On Becoming a Canadian." Desmond Pacey Fonds, MG30, D339, vol. 27, LAC.

– "Bliss Carman: A Reappraisal." *Northern Review* 3, no. 3 (February/March 1950): 2–10.

– "Canada's Poets and Prose Writers." In Ellen McLoughlin, ed., *The Book of Knowledge,* vol. 14. New York: Grolier Society 1948. 5101–18.

– "Canadian Literature in the Fifties." Desmond Pacey Fonds, MG30, D339, vol. 27, file 18, LAC.

– "The Canadian Writer and His Public, 1882–1953." In E.D.G. Murray, ed., *Studia Varia: Royal Society of Canada Literary and Scientific Papers.* Toronto: University of Toronto Press 1957. 11–20.

- "Contemporary Writing in New Brunswick." Desmond Pacey Fonds, MG30, D339, vol. 51, file 13, LAC. [Reprinted in R.A. Tweedie, Fred Cogswell, and W. Stewart MacNutt, eds., *Arts in New Brunswick*. Fredericton: Brunswick Press 1967. 33–40.]
- *Creative Writing in Canada: A Short History of English-Canadian Literature.* 1952. Toronto: Ryerson 1961.
- Draft Review. *The Stunted Strong*, by Fred Cogswell. Desmond Pacey Fonds, MG30, D339, vol. 2, file 9, LAC.
- "English-Canadian Poetry, 1944–1954." *Culture* 15 (1954): 255–65.
- "The Field of Oats." In *The Picnic and Other Stories*. Toronto: Ryerson 1958. 97–106.
- *Frederick Philip Grove*. Toronto: Ryerson 1945.
- "A Garland for Bliss Carman." *Atlantic Advocate* 51, no. 8 (April 1961): 18–20, 23–4.
- "The Goldsmiths and Their Villages." *University of Toronto Quarterly* 21, no. 1 (October 1951): 27–38.
- "A Group of Seven Poets." [*Queen's Quarterly*, autumn 1956.] Reprinted in *Essays in Canadian Criticism, 1938–1968*. Toronto: Ryerson 1969. 112–21.
- "The Humanist Tradition." In Alfred G. Bailey, ed., *The University of New Brunswick Memorial Volume*. Fredericton: University of New Brunswick 1950. 57–68.
- "The Humanities in Canada." *Queen's Quarterly* 50 (1943–44): 354–60.
- Introduction. *A Book of Canadian Stories*. Edited by Desmond Pacey. Toronto: Ryerson 1947. xi–xxxvii.
- Introduction. *The Selected Poems of Sir Charles G.D. Roberts*. Edited by Desmond Pacey. Toronto: McGraw-Hill Ryerson 1955. xi–xxv.
- Letter to Mary Bolton [mother]. 2 February 1937. W.C.D. Pacey Fonds, MG LI, Series 1, case 2, file 1, ASC, HIL, UNB.
- Letter to Mary Bolton. 2 December 1958. W.C.D. Pacey Fonds, MG LI, Series 1, case 3, file 4, ASC, HIL, UNB.
- Letter to Mary and Ben Bolton [parents]. 16 December 1957. W.C.D. Pacey Fonds, MG LI, Series 1, case 3, file 4, ASC, HIL, UNB.
- Letter to Roy Daniells. 22 November 1938. Roy Daniells Fonds, Correspondence Series, 1908–80, box 3, file 8, UBCA. Used with permission of Erwin Wodarczak, archivist, and Peter Pacey, literary executor.
- Letter to Roy Daniells. 20 May 1940. Roy Daniells Fonds, Correspondence Series, 1908–80, box 3, file 16, UBCA. Used with permission of Erwin Wodarczak, archivist, and Peter Pacey, literary executor.
- Letter to Roy Daniells. 2 August 1944. Roy Daniells Fonds, Correspon-

dence Series, 1908–80, box 4, file 14, UBCA. Used with permission of
Erwin Wodarczak, archivist, and Peter Pacey, literary executor.

- Letter to Roy Daniells. 7 August 1944. Roy Daniells Fonds, Correspondence Series, 1908–80, box 4, file 14, UBCA. Used with permission of
Erwin Wodarczak, archivist, and Peter Pacey, literary executor.

- Letter to Roy Daniells. 29 September 1944. Roy Daniells Fonds, Correspondence Series, 1908–80, box 4, file 14, UBCA. Used with permission of
Erwin Wodarczak, archivist, and Peter Pacey, literary executor.

- Letter to Roy Daniells. 5 June 1945. Roy Daniells Fonds, Correspondence
Series, 1908–80, box 4, file 17, UBCA. Used with permission of Erwin
Wodarczak, archivist, and Peter Pacey, literary executor.

- Letter to Roy Daniells. 4 December 1957. Roy Daniells Fonds, Correspondence Series, 1908–80, box 7, file 13, UBCA. Used with permission of
Erwin Wodarczak, archivist, and Peter Pacey, literary executor.

- Letter to Roy Daniells. 13 December 1957. Desmond Pacey Fonds, MG30,
D339, vol. 2, file 14, "Daniells, Roy – Correspondence," LAC. Used with
permission of Peter Pacey.

- Letter to Roy Daniells. 19 November 1969. Desmond Pacey Fonds, MG30,
D339, vol. 2, "Daniells, Roy – Correspondence," LAC. Used with permission of Peter Pacey.

- Letter to Roy Daniells. 13 December 1973. Roy Daniells Fonds, Correspondence Series, 1908–80, box 8, file 10, UBCA. Used with permission of
Erwin Wodarczak, archivist, and Peter Pacey, literary executor.

- Letter to Louis Dudek. 4 February 1953. Desmond Pacey Fonds, MG30,
D339, vol. 2, "Dudek, Louis – Correspondence 1952–1962," LAC.

- Letter to Louis Dudek. 9 November 1973. Desmond Pacey Fonds, MG30,
D339, vol. 2, "Dudek, Louis – Correspondence 1964–1974," LAC.

- Letter to Ronald Everson. 25 May 1959. Desmond Pacey Fonds, MG30,
D339, "Everson, Ronald – Correspondence," LAC.

- Letter to Northrop Frye. 18 June 1947. Northrop Frye Fonds, Series 1,
Correspondence Files, 1991 Accession, box 9, file 5. Victoria University
Library [University of Toronto]. Used with permission of Lisa J. Sherlock,
chief librarian.

- Letter to A.R.M. Lower. 2 April 1962. Desmond Pacey Fonds, MG30, D339,
box 16, file 3, LAC.

- Letter to Colin B. Mackay. 3 March 1954. Desmond Pacey Fonds, MG30,
D339, vol. 21, file 5, LAC.

- Letter to Colin B. Mackay. 22 November 1955. Desmond Pacey Fonds,
MG30, D339, vol. 21, file 5, LAC.

- Letter to Colin B. Mackay. 23 September 1964. Desmond Pacey Fonds, MG30, D339, vol. 21, file 1, LAC.
- Letter to Colin B. Mackay. 5 April 1965. Desmond Pacey Fonds, MG30, D339, vol. 21, file 2, LAC.
- Letter to Joseph Owens, SJ. 2 December 1969. Desmond Pacey Fonds, MG30, D339, box 16, file 3, LAC.
- Letter to Mary Pacey. [21 September 1944.] W.C.D. Pacey Fonds, MG LI, Series 1, case 2, file 4, ASC, HIL, UNB.
- Letter to Mary Pacey. 28 September 1944. W.C.D. Pacey Fonds, MG LI, Series 1, case 2, file 4, ASC, HIL, UNB.
- Letter to Mary Pacey. 30 October 1944. W.C.D. Pacey Fonds, MG LI, Series 1, case 3, file 1, ASC, HIL, UNB.
- Letter to Lorne Pierce. 7 October 1946. Desmond Pacey Fonds, MG30, D339, vol. 9, file 36, LAC.
- Letter to Lorne Pierce. [8] May 1947. Desmond Pacey Fonds, MG30, D339, vol. 9, file 36, LAC.
- Letter to Lorne Pierce. 8 November 1954. Desmond Pacey Fonds, MG30, D339, vol. 9, file 43, LAC.
- Letter to James Reaney. 10 March 1960. Desmond Pacey Fonds, MG30, D339, box 4, file 42, LAC.
- Letter to V.B. Rhodenizer. 11 February 1954. Desmond Pacey Fonds, MG30, D339, vol. 23, file 17, LAC.
- Letter to A.J.M. Smith. 27 December 1943. A.J.M. Smith Papers, MS15, box 2, Correspondence A-Z, Thomas Fisher Rare Book Library, University of Toronto. Used with permission of Peter Pacey.
- Letter to A.J.M. Smith. 17 March 1955. Desmond Pacey Fonds, MG30, D339, "Smith, A.J.M. Correspondence, 1946, 1955, 1964, 1966, 1973," LAC.
- Letter to A.W. Thomson. 30 December 1965. Desmond Pacey Fonds, MG30, D339, vol. 17, file 4, LAC.
- "Literary Criticism in Canada." *University of Toronto Quarterly* 19, no. 2 (January 1950): 113–19.
- "The Novel in Canada." *Queen's Quarterly* 52, no. 3 (autumn 1945): 322–31.
- "The Outlook for Canadian Literature." Desmond Pacey Fonds, MG30, D339, vol. 27, file 56, LAC. [Reprinted in *Canadian Literature* 36 (spring 1968): 14–25.]
- "A Penetrating Analysis of the Role of the Critic." *Canadian Author and Bookman* 32 (summer 1956): 24–6.
- "A Plea for the Study of Our Own Literature." *Curriculum Bulletin* [Manitoba] 3 (May 1969): 3–4.

- "Prairie Episode." *Fiddlehead* 1 (February 1945): 3.
- Review of *The Making of Modern Poetry in Canada*, edited by Louis Dudek and Michael Gnarowski. *Wascana Review* 3 (1968): 90–4.
- "Two Accents, One Voice," *Saturday Review* [of Literature], 7 June 1952, 15–16, 50–1.
- "The Young Writer and the Canadian Cultural Milieu." Transcript. Student Conference on Creative Writing in Canada, Hart House, Toronto. 25 February 1962. Desmond Pacey Fonds, MG30, D339, vol. 28, file 19, LAC.
Pacey, Desmond, ed. *A Book of Canadian Stories*. Toronto: Ryerson 1947.
Paratte, Henri-Dominique. *Acadians: Peoples of the Maritimes*. 1991. Rev. ed. Halifax: Nimbus 1998.
Paterson, A.P. Letter to A.G. Bailey. 16 June 1936. Dr Alfred Goldsworthy Bailey Fonds, UA RG80, box 56, file "P," ASC, HIL, UNB.
Patterson, William D. "New Brunswick Renaissance," *Saturday Review* [of Literature], 17 May 1958, 40.
Peacock, Fletcher. "Report of the Director of Educational Services." In A.P. Paterson, ed., *Annual Report of the Department of Education of the Province of New Brunswick for the School Year Ended June 30th, 1938*. Fredericton: Province of New Brunswick 1939. 6–27.
Peebles, Linden. "Day and Night at Wegesegum." *Fiddlehead* 1 (1945): 7.
Perloff, Marjorie. *The Futurist Moment: Avant-Garde, Avant-Guerre, and the Language of Rupture*. Chicago: University of Chicago Press 2004.
Pichette, Robert. "'Longtemps l'Acadie a attendu un chef': Clément Cormier, CSC (1910–1987)." *Les Cahiers de la Société historique acadienne* 30, no. 4 (1999): 235–56.
Pierce, Lorne. "Francis Sherman: A Memoir." In *The Complete Poems of Francis Sherman*. Toronto: Ryerson 1935. 1–18.
Pomeroy, Elsie M. "Some Books of Canadian Poetry Published in 1943." *Maritime Advocate and Busy East* (April 1944): 10–13, 31–2.
Pound, Ezra. *ABC of Reading*. 1934. New York: New Directions 1987.
- "Provincialism the Enemy." In William Cookson, ed., *Selected Prose: 1909–1965*. New York: New Directions 1973. 189–203.
- "A Retrospect." In T.S. Eliot, ed., *Literary Essays of Ezra Pound*. 1918. New York: New Directions 1968. 3–14.
Pugh, Anthony. "Alfred Goldsworthy Bailey." *Proceedings of the Royal Society of Canada: Biographical Sketches of Deceased Fellows* 12 (2001): 81–4.
Purdy, Alfred W. Letter to Fred Cogswell. 23 November 1953. Fiddlehead/Cogswell Fonds, UA RG83, box 1, file 3, ASC, HIL, UNB.
- Letter to Fred Cogswell. 8 December 1953. Fiddlehead/Cogswell Fonds, UA RG83, MS1.108–1.244, ASC, HIL, UNB.

- Letter to Desmond Pacey. N.d. [1960]. Desmond Pacey Fonds, MG30, D339, box 4, file 38, LAC.

Rawlyk, George A. *Champions of Truth: Fundamentalism, Modernism, and the Maritime Baptists.* Montreal and Kingston: McGill-Queen's University Press and Centre for Canadian Studies, Mount Allison University, 1990.
- "A New Golden Age of Maritime Historiography?" *Queen's Quarterly* 76 (1969): 55–65.

Raymond, W.O., ed. *Winslow Papers, A.D. 1776–1826.* Saint John: Sun Printing Company 1901.

Reid, John. *Six Crucial Decades: Times of Change in the History of the Maritimes.* Halifax: Nimbus 1987.

Report of the Royal Commission on National Development in the Arts, Letters and Sciences 1949–1951. Ottawa: Edmond Cloutier 1951.

Report on Visits to High School English Teachers in the Province. [David Yarrow, lecturer, Department of English, UNB, 24 December 1968.] W.C.D. Pacey Fonds, MG LI, Series 4, case 33, file 2, ASC, HIL, UNB.

Rifkind, Candida. *Comrades and Critics: Women, Literature, and the Left in 1930s Canada.* Toronto: University of Toronto Press 2009.

Roberts, Charles G.D. "The Beginnings of a Canadian Literature." In W.J. Keith, ed., *Selected Poetry and Critical Prose* [of Charles G.D. Roberts]. Toronto: University of Toronto Press 1974. 243–59.
- "The Tantramar Revisited." In *In Divers Tones.* Boston: D. Lothrop 1886. 53–8.

Rogers, Robert. Letter to A.G. Bailey. 21 December 1951. Dr Alfred Goldsworthy Bailey Fonds, UA RG80, box 56, file "R," ASC, HIL, UNB.
- Letter to Louis Dudek. 21 February 1953. Fiddlehead/Cogswell Fonds, UA RG83, MSI.02–107, ASC, HIL, UNB.
- Letter to Bob Gibbs. 18 December 1952. Fiddlehead/Cogswell Fonds, UA RG83, MSI.1–19 (1945–52), ASC, HIL, UNB.
- Letter to Kay Smith. 9 March 1953. Fiddlehead/Cogswell Fonds, UA RG83, MSI.02–107, ASC, HIL, UNB.
- Letter to A.W. Trueman. 21 April 1953. Fiddlehead/Cogswell Fonds, UA RG83, MSI.02–107, ASC, HIL, UNB.

Ross, Malcolm. "Alfred Goldsworthy Bailey." In *Dictionary of Literary Biography, 1920–1959.* Vol. 68: Canadian Writers, edited by W.H. New. Detroit: Gale 1990. 11–14.
- "Fort, Fog and Fiddlehead: Some New Atlantic Writing." *Acadiensis* 3, no. 2 (spring 1974): 116–21.
- "Ross Notes." Malcolm Ross Papers, 277, box 55, Thomas Fisher Rare Book Library, University of Toronto.

- "UNB's Bailey." Malcolm Ross Papers, 277, box 64, Thomas Fisher Rare Book Library, University of Toronto.

Roy, A. *Bulletin des recherches historiques*. Vols. 7–9. Quebec: Société des études historiques 1901.

Roy, Camille. "French-Canadian Literature." 1913. *Bourinot, Marquis, Roy*. Reprinted in Clara Thomas, ed., *Literature in Canada: Poetry and Prose*. Toronto: University of Toronto Press 1973. 435–89.

Roy, Naresh C. "The Compact Theory of the Canadian Constitution." *Indian Journal of Political Science* 3, no. 1 (July-September 1941): 41–55.

Rushdie, Salman. "Imaginary Homelands." In *Imaginary Homelands: Essays and Criticism 1981–1991*. London: Granta 1991. 9–21.

Saffell, Hilmur. Letter to Fred Cogswell. 18 May 1958. Fiddlehead/Cogswell Fonds, UA RG83, Correspondence 5/58, MS1.3509, ASC, HIL, UNB.

Said, Edward. *Orientalism: Western Conceptions of the Orient*. 1978. London: Penguin 1991.

Saul, John Ralston. *A Fair Country: Telling Truths about Canada*. Toronto: Viking 2008.

Saunders, Stanley A. *The Economic History of the Maritime Provinces*. 1939, edited by T.W. Acheson. Fredericton: Acadiensis 1984.

Savoie, Donald J. *Harrison McCain: Single-Minded Purpose*. Montreal and Kingston: McGill-Queen's University Press 2013.

- *Pulling against Gravity: Economic Development in New Brunswick during the McKenna Years*. Montreal: Institute for Research on Public Policy 2001.

- *Visiting Grandchildren: Economic Development in the Maritimes*. Toronto: University of Toronto Press 2006.

Scobell, S.C. Letter to A.G. Bailey. 26 February 1944. Dr Alfred Goldsworthy Bailey Fonds, UA RG80, box 43, file 6, ASC, HIL, UNB.

Scott, Frank R. "The Canadian Authors Meet." In *Selected Poems*. Toronto: Oxford University Press 1966. 70.

Simpson, Jeffrey. "The Truth about Atlantic Canada's Economy." *Globe and Mail*, 20 June 2001, A7.

Sissons, C.B. *Nil Alienum: The Memoirs of C.B. Sissons*. Toronto: University of Toronto Press 1964.

Slater, John G. *Minerva's Aviary: Philosophy at Toronto, 1843–2003*. Toronto: University of Toronto Press 2005.

Slumkoski, Corey. "'... A Fair Show and a Square Deal': New Brunswick and the Renegotiation of Canadian Federalism, 1938–1951." *Journal of New Brunswick Studies* 1 (2010): 124–42.

"Smallpox Warning." *Carleton Sentinel*, 9 November 1917, 1.

Smith, A.J.M., ed. Introduction. *The Book of Canadian Poetry: A Critical and Historical Anthology.* Chicago: University of Chicago Press 1943. 3–31.
- Letter to A.G. Bailey. 9 July 1942. Bailey Family Fonds, MG HI, MS2.3.890, ASC, HIL, UNB.
- "A Rejected Preface." *Canadian Literature* 24 (spring 1965): 69.
- "Wanted: Canadian Criticism." [*Canadian Forum*, April 1928]. In Louis Dudek and Michael Gnarowski, eds., *The Making of Modern Poetry in Canada.* Toronto: Ryerson 1970. 31–3.
Smith, Neil. *Uneven Development: Nature, Capital, and the Production of Space.* 1984. Athens: University of Georgia Press 2008.
Stanley, Della M.M. *Louis Robichaud: A Decade of Power.* Halifax: Nimbus 1984.
Stanley, George F.G. "John Clarence Webster: The Laird of Shediac." *Acadiensis* 3, no. 1 (autumn 1973): 51–71.
Stegner, Wallace. *Where the Bluebird Sings to the Lemonade Springs: Living and Writing in the West.* New York: Penguin 1992.
Stevens, Geoffrey. *The Player: The Life & Times of Dalton Camp.* Toronto: Key Porter 2003.
Stevens, Wallace. "John Crowe Ransom: Tennessean." *Sewanee Review* 56, no. 3 (August-September 1948): 367–9.
Stevenson, Lionel. "A Manifesto for a National Literature." In *Appraisals of Canadian Literature.* Toronto: Macmillan 1926. 3–25.
Stirling, Gertrude. "Count Almaviva at the Rectory." *Country Life*, 16 March 1951, 797–9.
Stoddard's Encyclopedia Americana ([American] *Supplement to Encyclopedia Britannica).* 9th ed. vol. 2. New York: J.M. Stoddard 1884. 770–8.
Stringer, Arthur. "Canadians in New York – America's Foremost Lyricist." *National Monthly of Canada* 4, no. 1 (January 1904): 3–5.
Surette, Leon. "Here Is Us: The Topocentrism of Canadian Literary History." *Canadian Poetry* 10 (spring 1982): 44–57.
Surette, Paul. "Les Acadiens et la campagne électorale provinciale de 1935 au Nouveau-Brunswick." *Cahier* [Société historique acadienne] 45 (1974): 200–4.
Sutherland, Fraser. "A Lot of There, There." *Books in Canada* 21, no. 2 (March 1992): 11–13.
Sutherland, John. *Essays, Controversies and Poems*, edited by Miriam Waddington. Toronto: McClelland and Stewart 1972.
- Letter to Fred Cogswell. 1 December 1953. Fiddlehead/Cogswell Fonds, UA RG83, MS1.108–1.244, ASC, HIL, UNB.
- "The Past Decade in Canadian Poetry" [*Northern Review* December 1950–

January 1951]. In Miriam Waddington, ed., *John Sutherland: Essays, Controversies and Poems.* Toronto: McClelland and Stewart 1972. 70–6.

Szeman, Imre. "Introduction: A Manifesto for Materialism." *Essays on Canadian Writing* 68 (1999): 1–18.

Thomas, Peter. "Editorial." *Fiddlehead* 130 (summer 1981): 3.

Thompson, Marjorie J. "College Life." In Alfred G. Bailey, ed., *The University of New Brunswick Memorial Volume.* Fredericton: UNB 1950. 102–12.

Thorburn, Hugh G. *Politics in New Brunswick.* Toronto: University of Toronto Press 1961.

Tippett, Maria. "The Writing of English-Canadian Cultural History, 1970–85." *Canadian Historical Review* 67, no. 4 (March 1986): 548–61.

Toole, Janet. "Dr A.G. Bailey – The Literary Tradition – Part I." March 1974. Transcript. Dr Alfred Goldsworthy Bailey Fonds, MS4, 7.4.1, ASC, HIL, UNB.

– "Dr A.G. Bailey – The Literary Tradition – Part II." April 1974. Transcript. Dr Alfred Goldsworthy Bailey Fonds, MS4 7.4.1, ASC, HIL, UNB.

Trehearne, Brian. *Aestheticism and the Canadian Modernists: Aspects of a Poetic Influence.* Montreal and Kingston: McGill-Queen's University Press 1989.

– *The Montreal Forties: Modernist Poetry in Transition.* Toronto: University of Toronto Press 1999.

Tremblay, Tony. "Antonine Maillet, Marshall Button, and Literary Humor in New Brunswick: Towards a New Hybrid that Can Subsume Ethnolinguistic Division." In Marie-Linda Lord, ed., *Lire Antonine Maillet à travers le temps et l'espace.* Moncton: Institut d'études acadiennes 2010. 91–108.

– *David Adams Richards of the Miramichi: A Biographical Introduction.* Toronto: University of Toronto Press 2010.

– "Landscapes of Reception: Historicizing the Travails of the New Brunswick Literary Modernists." In Dean Irvine, Vanessa Lent, and Bart Vautour, eds., *Making Canada New: Editing, Modernism, and New Media.* Toronto: University of Toronto Press 2017. 307–26.

– "Moving Beyond the Urban/Rural Divide in New Brunswick and Atlantic Canada." In John G. Reid and Donald J. Savoie, eds., *Shaping an Agenda for Atlantic Canada.* Halifax: Fernwood 2011. 338–46.

– "Strategy and Vision for an Intercultural New Brunswick in the Recent Poetry of Herménégilde Chiasson and the Translation of Jo-Anne Elder." *Quebec Studies: Special Issue on Literary Translation* 50 (fall 2010/winter 2011): 97–111.

Tremblay, Tony, ed. *Fred Cogswell: The Many-Dimensioned Self.* Fredericton: New Brunswick Studies Centre (STU) and Electronic Text Centre (UNB) 2012. http://cogswell.lib.unb.ca/.

– *New Brunswick at the Crossroads: Literary Ferment and Social Change in the East*. Waterloo, ON: Wilfrid Laurier University Press 2017.

Trigger, Bruce G. "Alfred G. Bailey – Ethnohistorian." *Acadiensis* 18, no. 2 (spring 1989): 3–21.

Trueman, Albert W. Foreword. *Fiddlehead* 18 (summer 1953): 2.

Tweedie, R.A., Fred Cogswell, and W. Stewart MacNutt, eds. *Arts in New Brunswick*. Fredericton: Brunswick Press 1967.

Tweedie, Robert A. *On with the Dance: A New Brunswick Memoir, 1935–1960*. Fredericton: New Ireland Press 1986.

Tyler, Moses Coit. *A History of American Literature I (1607–1676) and II (1676–1765)*. New York: G.P. Putnam 1883.

Underhill, Frank. *The Image of Confederation*. Toronto: Canadian Broadcasting Corporation (Massey Lectures) 1964.

Upton, Leslie F.S. *Micmacs and Colonists: Indian-White Relations in the Maritimes, 1713–1867*. Vancouver: University of British Columbia Press 1979.

van Herk, Aritha. *Mavericks: An Incorrigible History of Alberta*. Toronto: Penguin 2001.

– "Washtub Westerns." In Sarah Carter et al., eds., *Unsettled Pasts: Reconceiving the West through Women's History*. Calgary: University of Calgary Press 2005. 251–66.

Verduyn, Christl, ed. *Dear Marian, Dear Hugh: The MacLennan-Engel Correspondence*. Ottawa: University of Ottawa Press 1995.

Waddington, Miriam. Letter to Fred Cogswell. 4 February 1954. Fiddlehead/Cogswell Fonds, UA RG83, box 1, file 4, ASC, HIL, UNB.

Wade, Scott, and Hugh Lloyd, eds. *Behind the Hill*. Fredericton: UNB 1967.

Watt. Frank W. "Letters in Canada: Humanities." *University of Toronto Quarterly* 42 (1973): 440–4.

Webster, John Clarence. *The Distressed Maritimes*. Toronto: Webster 1926.

– Letter to W.F. Ganong. 10 March 1935. Bailey Family Fonds, MG HI, MS2.3.883, ASC, HIL, UNB.

– "Report on the Financial Arrangements and General Management of the New Brunswick Museum." [Spring] 1937. Transcript. Dr Alfred Goldsworthy Bailey Fonds, UA RG80, box 32, file 4, ASC, HIL, UNB.

Whalen, Terry. "Atlantic Possibilities." *Essays on Canadian Writing* 20 (winter 1980/81): 32–60.

– Introduction. *The Atlantic Anthology: Critical Essays*. Charlottetown/Toronto: ECW/Ragweed 1985. 1–4. [Rpt. Whalen, Terry, ed. *Selected Animal Stories: A Critical Edition* [of Charles G.D. Roberts]. Ottawa: Tecumseh 2005.

310

Bibliography

Whiteman, Bruce, ed. Introduction. *The Letters of John Sutherland, 1942–1956*. Toronto: ECW Press 1980. ix–xxxv.

Wiens, Erwin. "The Horses of Realism: The Layton-Pacey Correspondence." *Studies in Canadian Literature/Études en littérature canadienne* 10, nos .1–2 (1985): 183–207.

Wilbur, Richard. *The Rise of French New Brunswick*. Halifax: Formac 1989.

Williams, Raymond. *Marxism and Literature*. Oxford: Oxford University Press 1977.

Williamson, George. *A Reader's Guide to T.S. Eliot*. 1953. New York: Noonday 1960.

Willmott, Glenn. *Unreal Country: Modernity in the Canadian Novel in English*. Montreal and Kingston: McGill-Queen's University Press 2002.

Wilson, Milton. "Letters in Canada: 1962." Review of *Five New Brunswick Poets*, ed. Fred Cogswell. *University of Toronto Quarterly* 32 (July 1963): 384–5.

Wiseman, Nelson. *In Search of Canadian Political Culture*. Vancouver: University of British Columbia Press 2007.

Woodcock, George. "A Great Impresario: A Subterranean Influence," *Globe and Mail*, 26 July 1975, Books 29.

– "Poetry." *Literary History of Canada: Canadian Literature in English*. 2nd ed., vol. 3. General Editor Carl F. Klinck. Toronto: University of Toronto Press 1976. 284–317.

– "Valedictions: Pacey and Crawley." *Canadian Literature* 66 (autumn 1975): 3–6.

Wright, Donald A. *The Professionalization of History in English Canada*. Toronto: University of Toronto Press, 2005.

Wright, Esther Clarke. *The Saint John River*. Toronto: McClelland and Stewart 1949.

Wyile, Herb. *Anne of Tim Hortons: Globalization and the Reshaping of Atlantic-Canadian Literature*. Waterloo, ON: Wilfrid Laurier University Press 2011.

Wyile, Herb, and Jeanette Lynes, eds. *Surf's Up! The Rising Tide of Atlantic-Canadian Literature*. Special Issue (Atlantic Canada), *Studies in Canadian Literature/Études en littérature canadienne* 33, no. 2 (2008).

Wynn, Graeme. "1800–1810: Turning the Century." In Phillip A. Buckner and John G. Reid, eds., *The Atlantic Region to Confederation: A History*. Toronto: University of Toronto Press 1994. 210–33.

– *Timber Colony: A Historical Geography of Early Nineteenth Century New Brunswick*. Toronto: University of Toronto Press 1981.

Young, C. Mary. "Bailey, Loring Woart." *Dictionary of Canadian Biography* online. Toronto: University of Toronto Press 2004.

Zanes, John P. "Where the Fiddleheads Grow and the Wind Blows Blue: A Consideration of a Canadian Literary Tradition." PhD diss., University of Texas at Austin, 1979.

Index

Aberhart, William "Bible Bill," 64

Acadian/Acadie: *Evangeline* myth, 29–31, 205; history/Expulsion, 8–10, 12–14, 18–19, 151, 268n141; language/language legislation, 9, 143, 203, 227, 272n238; literary/cultural renaissance, xvii, 91, 203–6, 232–3, 268n141; subordinate status, 9, 154

Acadiensis, 68, 84

Acheson, T.W., 21, 32, 193

Acorn, Milton, 188–9

Acta Victoriana (university journal), 111, 113, 116–17

Agassiz, Louis, 46, 200

Alexander, David, 20, 25, 39, 232

Alexander College. *See* University of New Brunswick

Allen, Richard, 114

Anderson, Benedict, 96, 220

Anderson, Patrick, 75, 77

Armstrong, Sally, 12

Arnold, Matthew, 75, 99, 111–12, 115–16, 122, 124, 247n158

Atlantic Publishers' Association, 206

Atwood, Margaret, xii, 95

Babbitt, Irving K., 45

Bailey, Alfred G.: ancestry/upbringing, 41, 44–50, 87, 165, 200, 222, 242n34; apprenticeship, 64–71, 97, 244n69, 246n125; creative work (early), 51–3, 56; creative work (mature), 47, 63, 96, 199, 219, 230; critical work/theorizing (early), 41–3, 97–9, 102–3, 240n6, 243n51, 245n100, 246n117; critical work/theorizing (mature), 55–6, 74, 80, 230–1, 243n60, 276n62; Daoism (spelled Taoism by Bailey and Cogswell), 64, 164–5, 245n108; education (in Canada), 36, 39–40, 49–51, 53; education (graduate), 54–5, 57–63, 215–16, 242n38, 242n47; institutional roles, 72–3, 80–1, 82–92, 94–6, 103–5, 161–2, 222–3, 227, 250n222; reception, 5–6, 56–7, 77, 80. *See also* Beaverbrook, Lord; Bliss Carman Society; modernism

Bailey, Ernestine Valiant Gale, 49

Bailey, Isaac, 44

Peacock, Fletcher, 67, 83
Peebles, Linden, 73, 74, 78, 250n222
Pickthall, Marjorie, 133
Pierce, Lorne, 48, 101, 115, 126, 134,
  136, 145, 244n64, 257n119
Poets' Corner of Canada, 50, 93–4,
  149, 183
Pomeroy, Elsie M., 76–7, 80
Postman, Neil, 55, 243n60
Pound, Ezra: as author/critic, 36, 46;
  contra provincialism, 7, 185; as
  modernist/mentor, 4, 38, 46, 69,
  73, 132, 199–200
Pratt, E.J.: as author/critic/editor, 58,
  112, 116, 118, 123, 128, 129,
  252n27, 270n188, 272n224; as
  modernist, 75, 130; as teacher/
  mentor, 57, 105, 110, 111, 119
Preview (magazine), 4, 75, 78, 185,
  210
Prouty, William, 259n163
Provincial Normal School [of New
  Brunswick], 67, 73, 157–8, 202
Pugh, Anthony, 62
Purdy, Al: as author, 181, 189, 190,
  231, 271n210; as supporter of Fiddlehead school, xvii, 136, 182, 186
puritanism. See evangelicals/
  evangelism

Quebec City, 47–50, 52, 54–5

Radcliffe-Brown, Alfred, 55
Raddall, Thomas, xvi, 131
Rawlyk, George A., 83–4, 263n42
Raymond, William O., 68, 170
Reaney, James, 145, 181
regionalism. See localism/localist
Rehabilitation Training Program/
  Veterans Rehabilitation Act, 82,
  122, 161

Reichwein, Adolf, 63, 64
Reid, John, 23, 232
Renwick, William L., 176
Rhodenizer, V.B., 99, 101, 140
Richards, I.A., 123, 130, 135, 221
Richardson, Maj. John, 136
Rifkind, Candida, 6
Robb, James, 222
Roberts, Canon George, 46
Roberts, Charles G.D.: in Bailey's
  orbit, 44, 48–50, 126; as editor/
  critic, 36, 38; as mentor/model,
  xii, xiii, 30, 36, 42, 77, 93–4, 127,
  136, 217; as poet, 31, 33, 36–7,
  112, 201, 213; and Elsie Pomeroy,
  77; as subject of ridicule/study,
  37–9, 101–2, 133, 137, 139, 142,
  197, 200, 213, 222, 231, 274n4
Roberts, Dorothy Gostwick, 51,
  181
Roberts, Theodore Goodridge, 47,
  51, 57, 182
Robichaud, Louis J., 15, 91, 205,
  227, 232; attacked by Irving press,
  204
Robins, J.D., 110, 111, 116, 119
Robinson, Edwin Arlington, 46
Roche, Mazo de la, 128, 131, 133
Rockefeller Foundation, 83, 85, 93,
  236n19, 249n199, 249n206
Rogers, Robert, 89, 178, 250n222;
  as Fiddlehead editor, 166,
  179–80, 181–5, 247n154; in
  Fiddlehead school, 74, 77, 79, 180,
  188
Ross, Malcolm, 104, 252n30; as
  critic/editor, 6, 24; as supporter
  of Fiddlehead school, 24, 80,
  92
Ross, Sinclair, 120, 131
Rowell-Sirois Commission.